The Western

Inside Film

Forthcoming Titles

Documentary	Dr Alan Marcus
The Horror Film	Dr Peter Hutchings
Shakespeare on Film	Dr Judith Buchanan
Women and Film	Pamela Church Gibson
French Cinema	Dr Lucy Mazdon
Italian Cinema	Dr Mary Wood

More information can be found at:
www.booksites.net/mclean

THE WESTERN

David Lusted

Harlow, England • London • New York • Boston • San Francisco • Toronto
Sydney • Tokyo • Singapore • Hong Kong • Seoul • Taipei • New Delhi
Cape Town • Madrid • Mexico City • Amsterdam • Munich • Paris • Milan

Pearson Education Limited
Edinburgh Gate
Harlow
Essex CM20 2JE
England

and Associated Companies throughout the world

Visit us on the World Wide Web at:
www.pearsoneduc.com

———————————

First published 2003

© Pearson Education Limited 2003

ISBN 0582 43736 9

British Library Cataloguing-in-Publication Data
A catalogue record for this book is available from the British Library

Library of Congress Cataloging-in-Publication Data
Lusted, David.
     The western / David Lusted.
          p. cm. — (Inside film)
     Includes bibliographical references and index.
     ISBN 0-582-43736-9 (alk. paper)
          1. Western films—United States—History and criticism.   2. Western films—
     History and criticism.   I. Title.   II. Series.

     PN1995.9.W4L87 2003
     791.43'6278—dc21   2003040452

10   9   8   7   6   5   4   3   2   1
05   04   03

Typeset in 10/13pt Giovanni Book by 35
Printed and bound in China
SWTC/01

DEDICATION

This book is dedicated to Henry Fonda's legs, James Coburn's fingers, Ernest Borgnine's stomach, Jeff Chandler's chest, Randolph Scott's neck, Dorothy Malone's cheekbones, Richard Boone's nose, Jack Elam's eyes and the bags under Robert Mitchum's, Clint Eastwood's squint, Robert Ryan's stare, Joan Crawford's eyebrows, John Carradine's moustache, Robert Wilke's stubble, Gary Cooper's lips, Burt Lancaster's teeth, Walter Brennan's gums, Lee Marvin's tongue, Burt Kennedy's dialogue, Alan Sharp's scripts, James Stewart's sneer, Kirk Douglas' cough, Steve McQueen's sweat, Karen Steele's silhouette, Harry Carey's stance, John Wayne's walk, Ben Johnson's ride, Woody Strode's hat, Barbara Stanwyck's whip, Russell Simpson's violin, Hank Worden's rocking chair, Budd Boetticher's cycle, Lucien Ballard's camera, Claire Trevor's Dallas, Sam Peckinpah's High Country, Anthony Mann's rivers, and John Ford's West. Some picture.

CONTENTS

ACKNOWLEDGEMENTS

My thanks go to everyone associated with lectures and courses on the Western down the years, especially in University of London extra-mural sessions, A Level Film Studies at Braintree College of Further Education, American Studies at the University of Reading and, currently, BA (Hons) Film Studies at Southampton Institute, among whose undergraduates I honour the elect who tested parts of this book; Jim Kitses for first making sense of the pleasure from watching Westerns; Jim Cook, Doug Pye, Martin Pumphrey and Brian Wooland for since disputing it; Peter Stanfield, for uncommon generosity of time, knowledge and films; Vanessa Shaw for lovingly explaining plots; Claire Shaw for letting me use the computer; Alexander Ballinger for unfailing patience; Phyllis Lusted for warm cinemas; and Alec Lusted, who's read and seen everything Western.

REFERENCING NOTES

There are a number of systems used by scholars to refer to the works, ideas and words of others. For many years, the most common was to number footnotes in the text and list them separately at the bottom of the page, at the end of chapters or together at the end. Increasingly, the system has fallen from favour, replaced by another which offers brief references bracketed in the text with the full reference in a bibliography. The advantage of this system is that all information is incorporated into the main body of writing, obviating the need for constant movement of eye or page. One disadvantage is that it can break up a rhythm in writing and may obstruct fluent reading. For the experienced scholar, this may prove less inhibiting, but for the reader new to academic writing, it can appear daunting and disrupt understanding.

I have therefore sought to simplify the system without threatening the demands of scholarship in the following way:

- Where reference is first made to an authority, it is followed in brackets with the writer's name, the date of the work cited and page number(s). This locates the full reference in the bibliography at the back of the book, where the reader can refer.
- In references to the same source immediately thereafter, I offer page numbers only.
- Since many original writings are in journals difficult to access beyond major national libraries, I have tried to reference those publications most likely to be available to the reader and not necessarily to the original publication date. Where the date of origin of the writing or some indication of the title of the work is important, I establish it in the very first reference in the text and again in the bibliography.
- With film titles, I offer generally accepted dates of production/registration in a final filmography. I date films when first mentioned in each chapter. Films known by alternative titles are listed by all alternatives first and then by the first, selected as the best known. An exception is non-English film titles, which are provided in the filmography only.

LIST OF PHOTOGRAPHS

We are grateful to the following for permission to reproduce the pictures which appear in this book:

PART ONE

THE BACKGROUND

CHAPTER ONE

The Western as an Imaginary Space

A CHILDHOOD GAME

When I was a child I played a game called Custer's Last Stand. It took its name from an event in American frontier history when Northern Plains Indians at the Little Big Horn River massacred a battalion of Seventh Cavalry troopers led by General George Armstrong Custer. Roberta Pearson has called it: 'an encounter of military insignificance but great symbolic resonance' (1998, p.199). In our game, though, just two roles mattered; all were soldiers with one exception who was an Indian. In the game, the soldiers took up a place and aimed pretend rifles and six-guns at the lone Indian. Contrary to appearances and despite the odds, history of a sort was re-enacted as the Indian would descend on his soldier victims and 'shoot' the lot of them. At this point, however, resemblance to the historical event and to life itself disappeared as the Indian chose his replacement from among the fallen, so that life and the game could revolve again.

My memory of this game demonstrates the power of the imagination to translate real events and fictions into everyday routines, practices and modes of living. Play is important for children as it provides opportunities to experiment with ways of relating to people in the social world around them. Good game-playing as children helps us to play at living with greater control and satisfaction as adults.

Fiction is another form of game-playing, and not just for children but for all of us, regardless of age. When we write and read novels, and make and watch fiction films, we enter into the imaginary, the cultural practice of imagining for pleasure and understanding. Fiction in films and other media offers popular cultures in which we can imagine our lives differently and learn ways of living better.

The fiction of the West as imagined in Western films is a good example. It offers a landscape of stories with a resonant vocabulary referencing a moment in American history and geography. Imagine a cattle drive on the Santa Fe trail, a gunfight in Abilene or carrying the mail for the Pony Express, and a cast of characters appears: outlaws like Billy the Kid, lawmen like Wyatt Earp and fictional pioneers like Chingachgook, the Last of the Mohicans. Hear the names of actors in Western films – like Broncho Billy Anderson, Randolph Scott, John Wayne and Clint Eastwood – in films directed by Raoul Walsh, John Ford, Budd Boetticher and Sam Peckinpah. Such textured language invokes imagery, in an associated iconography of visual décor (from open range to saloon bar), props (from bullwhips to Winchester rifles) and costumes (from spurs to Stetson hats). Such sounds and sights combine in dramas of conflict and resolution to inform and enrich our lives and the relationships we enter into. Such fiction is important, not just to escape out of ourselves, but to enter into ourselves more fully.

Playing 'Cowboys and Indians' was a regular feature of my childhood. The street was a prairie, sticks and fingers were guns and bows, appropriate props and dress were optional. The individual and collective imagination was fed by Westerns on the screens of cinemas and television sets, in the context of a wider culture which included novels, comic strips and advertising. In this, my childhood was little different from the childhood of twentieth-century generations around and before me. The idea of the West in Western fiction has been central to the global imaginary for over two hundred years.

THE WESTERN IMAGINARY TODAY

For generations today, games about the 'Cowboys and Indians' of Westerns may seem as remote as the geographical space and the historical period of the American West to which – however distantly – they refer. Certainly, Western fiction continues to be written and filmed but on far less a scale than at any time in the twentieth century.

There are obvious reasons for the decline, connected with the passing of history. The agrarian society of the Western disappeared as the twentieth century advanced. The ease with which Western actors and stunt men naturally and skilfully rode horses dwindled with the growth of a modern, urban America (Carey, 1995). Contrast Ben Johnson in *Wagonmaster* (1950) with Keifer Sutherland in *Young Guns* (1988) as they gallop and witness the difference in the saddle between Johnson's easy delight and Sutherland's mortal terror.

The loss of personal witness to the times in which Westerns are set is also a factor in the decline of the Western. Westerns were made by film-makers who knew the historical West at least through the personal experiences of older generations. Director John Ford claimed that his version of the Gunfight at the O.K. Corral that climaxes *My Darling Clementine* (1946) came from the very lips of its central character, frontier lawman, Wyatt Earp (Bogdanovich, 1967, p.85). Another director of Westerns, Delmer Daves, claimed his maternal grandfather took the trip West in a covered wagon and later rode as a Pony Express rider (Wicking, 1969, p.59). No one today can boast of such personal relationships, however fanciful.

The system of film production that supported prolific numbers of Western films made at this time also declined after the 1960s (Buscombe and Pearson, 1998, p.1). At the height of Western film production in the first half of the twentieth century, film studios had their own ranches and horse wranglers, their own standing sets of Western towns and interiors like saloons. Under pressure from the great structural changes that followed the Paramount decree of 1946, Hollywood studios gradually gave up this kind of ownership, making it more expensive to stage individual Westerns (Maltby, 1995, pp.71–3).

The decline of the Western is therefore due to changing conditions of cultural and film production. But the decline of the Western *imaginary* – the desire to make fictions about the West – is due more to matters of space as of time, in a number of senses. First, in the sense of physical space; as the motor car has taken over the streets, so streets have become a dangerous site for play. And alternative sites – like suburban gardens and homes – may make home-owning adults constrain children's game-playing for fear of property damage. Kids don't play Cowboys and Indians much anymore because the freedom of designated spaces for play have materially changed, and so have the games. Secondly, in one of those new domestic spaces, playing games takes as much virtual as material form; children's interactive game-playing increasingly happens in cyberspace with computer screens where many of the distinctions that former distribution media made between fantasy and reality are now scrambled.

The main reason kids don't play Cowboys and Indians as much concerns less physical or virtual spaces than the space in their heads; children today imagine other subjects for game-playing. Modern society and its toy consumer industry provide perhaps a far greater range of opportunities and tools for imaginative play. So, there is another, wider and arguably more important fictional space from which the Western has been displaced from the popular imaginary. This includes, as Richard Slotkin has suggested (1992, p.636), the disciplines of space fiction and science fiction, which are set in an imaginary future rather than in the imaginary past of the Western.

Like the Western, this outer space is centrally set on a frontier – 'the final frontier' as *Star Trek*'s Captain Kirk has it – and is far less known than the inner space of the Western. What might be going on beyond earthly dramas is a popular subject for contemporary fiction because there are stories yet to imagine about a physical space beyond it. Though Western fiction survives, its centrality has diminished because the fiction it imagines is predicated on a national frontier geography whose history is now largely settled. While America was still making itself, the Western had stories to tell, but when America emerged as a global force, matters of its own destiny diminished, and this was the destiny that many critics argue the Western centrally debates. Once America 'found' its modern identity, the Western became history.

Fictional forms are affected by changes in the cultures that produce them. As America's cities became gradually more dramatic spaces during the twentieth century, so the Western's rural landscape competed with the cityscape in new genres like the musical, the gangster and crime film. Later, the rise of suburbia would produce its own psychodramas in cycles such as the slasher and yuppie horror film. America's frontier also extended beyond its own territories with its participation in twentieth-century conflicts overseas (Europe in two 'World' Wars, the Cold War, combat in Korea and Vietnam, the Middle East and myriad elsewheres). Over time the idea of the American West as a dramatic space has been superseded by new generic spaces of war and conspiracy and in the displaced imaginary of new fictional genres like science fiction.

This movement from genres set in the past to contemporary and futuristic genres was encouraged by film industrial advances in special effects, computer-generated imagery and plastics technology. The ways in which alien lands and creatures could now be imagined and destroyed made the graphic possibilities of the West appear more limited. For a time in the 1960s and 1970s, the Western was a generic site of technology-led advances in film form. However, the slow-motion ballets of blood-splattered death in a Western such as Sam Peckinpah's *The Wild Bunch* (1969) gave way to further developments in the 1980s and 1990s, such as the body-morphing in science fiction films like *The Fly* (1986), *Terminator 2: Judgement Day* (1991) and *The Matrix* (1999). Developing sophistication in military technology also changed the iconography of action fiction in such a way that the potential armoury of science fiction made the six-gun, the Winchester repeating rifle and even the Gatling gun of the Western appear as primitive as the single-shot musket. For the Western, then, its historical frame lacks the modernity of more recent action genres, and its settled familiarity makes it now an historical form. An audience for the action film remains, but the Western has become more an American equivalent to the British empire or heritage film in the sense that its generic associations are with the past.

GENDER, RACE AND SOCIAL CLASS IN THE WESTERN

The story I told earlier of a childhood game makes it possible to see beyond an individual memory to significant political as well as cultural changes in the Western's meaning. As the use of the pronoun *he* suggests in assigning roles, my game was invariably played by boys. The girls available for play in our street were largely excluded from it and as commonly drew the line at joining in. There were no roles explicitly for females, clothes got dirty, and it was competitive and endlessly repetitive. And 'Who dies best?' is perhaps not a crucial feminine concern, though why it might be a male one is an intriguing question. Maybe these were qualities of boy-culture that implicitly sidelined girls. The game connects to the Western as a fictional genre more widely in that the Western has historically privileged stories centring on men, offering limited and exceptional roles for women. Women play roles which are conventionally secondary to male action such as 'saloon girls' and 'squaws', romantic foils for men, but only rarely heroes in their own right. The rise of feminism and its increased female self-consciousness in the second part of the twentieth century has provided fictional spaces for women to become central action protagonists, from the heroes of *Alien* (1979) and *Tomb Raider* (2001) to the villains of *Single White Female* (1992) and *The Hand that Rocks the Cradle* (1991) (Tasker, 1993). Such new female-centred action films appear to expose the Western as a more limited gendered space, a space of male action.

At the same time, this game was played not just by boys but by *white* boys. Although there was a role for an Indian, there were no Indians to join in. Real 'Indians' were to come later, though not from the Americas but from the Indian subcontinent, often as refugees from East Africa, to join racial 'others' of Afro-Caribbean descent in a racially diverse neighbourhood. But if any among these ethnic groups had been there, would they have seen a role for themselves any more than the white females?

What the game implies is not only the gender identity of the Western but also its racial and ethnic identity. Many Westerns invoke an imperialist history in which the westward movement of white travellers of European origin was made at the expense of a Native American population, reduced in numbers through successive military campaigns of genocide. The gradual acknowledgement during the twentieth century of America's foundation on the destruction of its indigenous peoples is emblematically measured in the way that the term 'Indian', which once described them, has been replaced by first 'American Indian' and secondly 'Native American'.

The problematic gender and ethnic relations in the idea of the foundation of the West make it no longer as culturally acceptable to make Westerns that ignore such transformations in the politics of gender and ethnicity. Such

7

changes make it more difficult to imagine Western scenarios for audiences in modern cultures.

Is the Western dead, then, a thing of the past, in more senses than one? Is it a sectarian white male genre whose concerns are politically unacceptable in a modern age? It may appear odd to start a book on the Western with this exploration of the declining interest in its imaginative world, but I do so in part as a corrective to a greater optimism among many Western comment- ators, especially those central critics whose ideas I explore later (Buscombe and Pearson, Kitses and Rickman). Yet it must equally be acknowledged that, despite an evident decline in the number of Westerns made over the past thirty years, they continue to be made and to surprise with their dramatic possibilities. Rather than searching for reasons for a notable decline, it may be that social, cultural and political changes such as these will challenge the Western imaginary to renewal. Recent films suggest such a possibility, including conventional titles such as *Tombstone* (1993) and *Geronimo: An American legend* (1994), and more unconventional titles produced on the fringes of the Hollywood system, such as *The Ballad of Little Jo* (1993) and *Dead Man* (1996). Perhaps a reason for a continuing faith in the vital possi- bilities of the Western imaginary lies in my childhood game or, rather more this time, in further reflection on my memory of it.

One feature of the game that resonates for me, with hindsight, is its implied award system. To be the Indian in the game was a reward, not a punishment. This was an odd ideological choice for white boys growing up in a country where the only racial divisions that 'Indians' represented were fictional ones in Westerns. Furthermore, the reward was predicated not on success in action so much as in spectacle, in the aesthetics of display. Power was conferred on the Indian, the power to judge and control the choice of a replacement in the game.

In addition to this, the grounds for choice lay in how the soldier boy died. In this simplest of narrative events, it was the manner and display of death that was rewarded. This could be a spectacular fall from a height, perhaps lying still as death, or the arrangement of the body in death. Where is the pleasure and meaning in this apparent racial confusion and macabre spectacle of masculine display? Maybe there was a meaning the game had only for boys, a thrill in playing out an aspirant masculine grace that enabled them to connect with realms of aesthetic feeling (more crudely, with ideas about what is beautiful) more associated with the other gender. Since the climactic reward of the game was to become the next killer of white men, there would be a certain play with ideas not only about gender identity but also about ethnic identity.

I attribute some biographical learning to Westerns. Westerns taught me that Indians could threaten white folk like me, but they also taught me that

Indians were victims of white racism. Something of both ideas redounds in the game. Despite its undoubted association with white supremacy, the Western imaginary is also sufficiently flexible to allow a more complicated and contradictory relation to ethnic identity than a simple division between racial categories. Westerns appear to provide a fictional space to consider one's own identity in terms of racial and ethnic difference.

Confounding the simple, negative divisions between gender and ethnicity made earlier, what the game suggests now is that complex dramas of identity played out through the spectacle of action are bound up in the Western imaginary. What enables the Western to construct such playful explorations of gender and ethnic identity is perhaps the overdetermination of social position. Although any children could play it, this was a game invented not only by white boys but by working-class white boys. They were on the street because the impoverished conditions of home offered few amenities, attractions and pleasures in Britain's post-war economic depression. They were together because the peer group is always as formative a social agency as the family. They were bound together in a game that rewarded the representation of an oppositional minority politics and the display of gender aesthetics. They invented the game because of the pleasure its display of repeated action offered to a group of white working-class boys in exploring their own social position, through a fictional scenario of gender and ethnic relations. They used the Western imaginary to play out in symbolic form matters impinging on their own individual and group identities in stratified positions of social conflict.

While we played, the images in our heads were drawn not from any *real* West – we had few history books and historical images, and The West was not a topic on the school curriculum – but from the fictional West of Western films, comics and television series. This popular representation of the West *is* The West to most people, even in the American West today, and it affords an otherworldly, imaginary space of dramatic excitement, film star glamour and pictorial splendour.

THE WESTERN IMAGINARY AND A CHILDHOOD GAME

The meaning of the game for me now is bound up in this more complex meaning of the Western film as a genre fiction. The Western has been a formative cultural experience for generations of audiences who have drawn on its evocative and affecting images, characters, narratives and spectacle to make life pleasurable, rich and meaningful. Yet, as my exploration of a childhood game demonstrates, the Western bears complex and contradictory pleasures and meanings. There are many interpretations of the Western and many problems of interpretation, emergent debates and disputes. Yet the bedrock of any first understanding must be that the Western is a fictional form, whose imaginary world provides pleasures, meanings and identities for those who choose to engage with it, because of the complex ways in which it speaks about who they are and aspire to be. Anyone willing can join in the game.

The Western is a film genre with a glorious and equally notorious past. However, a critical enquiry into that history is not just a thing of the past. It also has contemporary concerns. The purpose of studying the Western lies in coming to understand the complex popular memory of this resonant film history. Each new Western film produced adds to the layers of meanings around the Western from years of previous association. Each adds to a body of work of immense cultural substance and historical longevity. For these reasons, the Western deserves to be taken seriously.

To fans of the Western, this book provides an analysis of its pleasures and meanings. To the student of the Western, it surveys the ways in which it has been understood in critical writing and film theory, offering new ways of approaching that critical history. I hope it encourages those students and other readers who may not have considered themselves as fans to become fans. I hope also it encourages fans to reflect more on their own passion for the genre and to become students of the Western. Above all, I hope this book offers all readers pleasure in understanding the meaning of the Western for generations of ordinary people.

CHAPTER TWO

The Western in Film and Cultural Studies

THE WESTERN AND AMERICAN CINEMA

'The Western' is firstly a critical term adapted by film theorists and critics to understand a genre (a type) of film-making that began in the earliest days of American Cinema. As shall be explored in later chapters, the Western has antecedents, it extends beyond film to other fictional media and it was some time before films that we now call Westerns were known by that title. Nonetheless, the Western film was from the outset a creation of American Cinema. Even though Westerns have been made in other countries and by other national cinemas throughout its history, it is film production in America that determined how the Western was understood during its foundational period in the first half of the twentieth century.

American Cinema is extensive. Among its product, there have been centres of documentary, mainstream fiction and alternative fiction production. But American Cinema is best known for films made in and by the commercial production centre known as Hollywood. From its earliest days, Hollywood produced hundreds of Westerns. Until the early 1970s, the production of Westerns was central to the popularity and profitability of the Hollywood film industry. Since then, and although Westerns continue to be made, their mass production has declined. In the heyday of the Classical Hollywood Cinema, however, the Western outnumbered production of all other genres such as musicals, crime thrillers and horror films.

For over thirty years, most Westerns were series Westerns, made cheaply and aimed mainly at rural American audiences. However, production values increased from the 1940s and during that decade over four hundred Westerns were made. The genre became a staple A film production (first feature productions which were more expensive than second feature B films, and promoted as first features) from the 1950s on. The production of Westerns peaked in this decade, with over five hundred films and many more episodes of series Westerns produced for television. Although the 1960s saw a dramatic drop in production in America to just over two hundred titles, over five hundred were made in Europe, especially by the Italian film industry. The real fall in production began during the 1970s, reflecting a downturn in popular audience interest. It was a global decline and it continues today, with no promise of return to the previously high production figures. Westerns now are made occasionally and almost exclusively again in America.

WESTERN CRITICISM

The rise and fall of Western film production is in inverse proportion to the development of serious debate about the Western. Until the 1950s, the Western was the subject of very little serious critical enquiry. Perhaps the huge amount of Western film production at that time prompted more serious critical attention. Even if this was the case, it was not until the 1970s that sustained critical debate about the Western developed, and academic research came even later, in the 1990s. In the past five years, academic books and collections of scholarly essays on the Western have exceeded those Westerns produced. This topsy-turvy relation between Western film production and academic publications about the Western appears bizarre. This chapter explores the history of critical debate about the Western in ways that may help to account for it.

EARLY FEARS OF THE HOLLYWOOD WESTERN

Until the 1950s, Western films were scarcely distinguishable from any other types of fiction films in the wider output of Hollywood; all films were simply the product of American Cinema's commercial film industry. As a whole, the Hollywood film has always been immensely popular with its audiences, especially in the Americas, Western Europe, Australasia and not only in English-speaking nations elsewhere. The Western is particularly associated with the classical period of Hollywood – from the time of its foundation as a leading film industry in the 1910s until the emergence of television in the 1950s. However, during this time when cinema was the central mass entertainment medium, there was little critical respect for Hollywood and its films. Among opinion-leaders and élite groups, Hollywood was considered a centre of moral laxity and cultural decline. Its leading personnel – the tyrannical studio heads or 'moguls' (French, 1973) especially – were considered vulgar and exploitative and their films were regarded as purveyors of decadence, corruption and anti-social behaviour. Though traces of such attitudes to Hollywood remain, in this early period the antipathy of leading cultural critics and groups in authority was extreme.

The reasons for resistance to the popular appeal of Hollywood films are long-standing and complex. In the first half of the twentieth century, élite, professional and conservative interests largely despised the Hollywood film and its popular associations. The popular Hollywood genres such as the gangster film, the musical and the Western were considered on both sides of the Atlantic as 'only entertainment' (Dyer, 1992), unworthy of comparison to the art cinemas of Europe, especially France and Germany. What little respect Hollywood commanded was given despite its general product. Films of certain directors, like D.W. Griffith and Orson Welles, and certain performers like the clowns, Charlie Chaplin and Buster Keaton, may have been individually valued, as even were certain genres like social realism and the literary adaptation. Admiration was extended to such talents and genres precisely because they were claimed as untypical, as artists and minority art in Hollywood's majority entertainment industry.

Hollywood's centre of production was established on the west coast of America in California, far from the settled Anglo-Saxon white protestant (WASP) élites on the east coast who ruled the country and determined its official cultural traditions. The WASPs were initially dismissive of this new film industry, refused to invest in it and were suspicious of its leadership. The heads of the developing studios were sons of Jewish immigrants who had found advancement in the petit-bourgeois retail trade, which was the one area of the American economy open to them at the time. Moreover, from its turn of the nineteenth-century origins, film had been associated with showground entertainment. It was the show business trade of Hollywood that particularly repulsed the mores of the bourgeois power groups, whose own cultural choices were more rooted in the European high cultures of classical music, theatre and literature passed down from their antecedents. Furthermore, the Hollywood film audience was entirely different. Hollywood films were consumed by a different social class and were located in downtown city nickelodeons, catering mostly for the poor sections of the new immigrant, black and working classes. The majority of the actors those audiences watched on the screen were also invariably from their own social class and immigrant backgrounds. The lowly origins of film stars, for many of whom stardom brought unprecedented wealth and luxury life styles, were promoted by Hollywood as part of its unlikely promise that every shop-counter assistant and labourer in the audience could emulate their rise to fame. Certainly, audience identification with the images of its stars was an important part of Hollywood's commercial success. WASP disapproval of the new film industry was thus a product of class difference, cultural snobbery and anti-Semitic racism.

As the studio system developed from its early chaotic beginnings, Hollywood films attracted the animus of conservative religious and moralist lobbies, including the Catholic League of Decency. The League's nation-wide power was sufficient to force Hollywood's trade organisation, the Motion Picture Producers and Distributors Association (MPPDA), into a negotiated regulation of Hollywood films. Anxiety about the effects of the Hollywood film was bound up in wider fears about the new mass communications media. The well-financed Payne Fund Studies of 1933 were used to support calls for closer official regulation of Hollywood. By the early 1930s, during the transition from silent to sound cinema, a censorship code had been introduced in an effort to control the growing power of the film image (Mast, 1982).

Elite groups in Britain were similarly suspicious of the Hollywood film. Literary bodies and educational organisations in particular were disturbed by its power to fill cinemas, especially with the young. British censorship controls were established even earlier in Britain, with the British Board of Film Censors in the 1920s. As in America, concerns among British élites focused on liberal sexual mores, but there was also much less tolerance of America's gun culture and therefore greater hostility to film violence. The gangster film was a particular focus of anxiety in America because of its contemporary setting and reference; however, if any single genre generated more disapproval of the Hollywood film in Britain, it was the Western. Colloquially called 'shoot 'em ups' by its audiences and derisively described as 'horse operas' by its detractors, the Western was singled out because it was a favourite among child audiences in Britain. The state was concerned about Hollywood's effect on impressionable minds, especially among the socially disadvantaged and the young.

Beginning in the 1930s and for the next twenty years, state support for investigation into the effects of films prompted many research studies. Sociological and/or psychological studies attempted to reconstruct viewing experiences in laboratory conditions to test the potential effects on the child mind of watching films like Westerns. The Mass Observation movement in the 1930s, a state-run scheme to record social patterns of everyday life, took part in studies of child responses to films, in particular Westerns. Even the cinema chains invested in studies that involved recording children watching films in cinemas. The resulting photographs, taken by cameras hidden beneath the screen, were first published in a popular magazine, *Picture Post*, and thereafter more widely disseminated in the press, which led to a widespread moral panic about the hypothetical ill-effects of Westerns on the child mind (Staples, 1997, 157–73).

One of the founding figures of the British documentary film movement, the influential John Grierson, typified this British attitude to Hollywood film.

Grierson met and admired the films of Hollywood film-makers like Charles Chaplin and Joseph von Sternberg, but he saw the wider Hollywood system as 'a big racket' (Grierson in Hardy, 1946, p.106), the body of its films 'unreal' (ibid., p.126) and its commercial imperative destructive of the artistic sensibility. In a book of his essays collected by Forsyth Hardy, Grierson has little to say about the Western. The only positive reference is to an epic Western, *The Covered Wagon* (1923) and tellingly, Grierson condemned Hollywood for the treatment of its film artists with the words: 'when they go into the West, they seldom come back' (ibid., p.105). In combining the historical movement of European migrants westward to America with the slang metaphor of 'going West' to mean 'lose out' or 'go bust', Grierson knew he could count on the assumptions shared with his élite readership and thereby use the low status of the Western to attack Hollywood as a whole.

Bound up in a transatlantic antipathy to the Hollywood film in Britain was an added anti-Americanism in British élite culture. Even more than in America, British official culture rested on its history of literature, classical music, ballet and the legitimate stage. American culture was associated with mass culture, despised not for its democratic possibilities but for fear of its potential distraction from what was perceived as the educative potential of high culture. American cinema was dismissed along with American popular recorded music and dance such as jazz and tap-dancing, which were both significant new entertainment forms that were penetrating British popular culture through new gramophone records and live bands in dance halls. Elite British antipathy to Hollywood had an added national and even nationalist dimension, reflected in a resistance to its growing international power and the Americanisation of British popular culture. Britain had equivalent cultural forms to Hollywood's musicals, romances and crime films but, of all the Hollywood genres, the national specificity of the Western made it the major target of anti-American resistance.

Hollywood's attitude to its own product was little more encouraging. Hollywood depended on the production of a huge number of Westerns in the 1920s and 30s to fill its cinemas at a time of continuous programmes. The greatest proportion of these were produced quickly and cheaply as B films, second features in support of the A films the major studios invested in more extensively to attract a mass audience. Many of these B films were series Westerns, made in sufficient quantity to be programmed weekly and featuring the same actor in different stories. The huge commercial success of Westerns like *Stagecoach* in 1939, which featured a series Western star subsequently to become a major icon of the Western, John Wayne, began to change Hollywood's attitude to the profitability and therefore the status of the Western film. In a less obvious way, this change in its status also challenged criticism to take the Western more seriously.

THE CRITICAL PIONEERS

The audience for popular cinema until this time consisted largely of those who did not write for publication about their experiences and pleasures. Those who did write about popular cinema mostly did so in ignorance of it or, at least, in ignorance of the regular experience of it. It therefore required the developments in wider social class access to higher education, that occurred in the post-War period, to establish conditions in which fans of the Western might also become publishable critics of it.

As a direct result of this, it is in the period following the Second World War that serious critical studies of the Western begin to emerge and question this largely negative history. Essays by two critics, André Bazin and Robert Warshow, written in the early 1950s, were influential. It helps to place their new thinking in relation not only to the time but also to the places in which they were writing – Warshow in America and Bazin in France.

In his founding essay, *The Westerner* (1962), Warshow asks: 'Why does the Western . . . have such a hold over our imagination?' His answer, 'because it offers a serious orientation to the problem of violence' (1962, p.46), responds to moralist anxieties about the effects of action genres like the Western on impressionable audiences. Yet Warshow's essay has been most influential because it was the first to chart the nature of the Western's main protagonist, the hero who acts in order to remind us 'in the midst of our anxieties over the problem of violence . . . that even in killing or being killed we are not freed from the necessity of establishing satisfactory modes of behaviour' (ibid., p.47). At a time when the Western world was still dealing with the horrific war experience of destruction in Europe and the brutality of the Holocaust, it was extraordinarily daring for Warshow to offer the despised Western as a fictional form that could help in understanding violence.

Warshow views the landscape of the Western as inherently male, a dramatic space in which the Westerner, the man of the West, is the American ideal, representing an archetypal American national identity. Warshow's Westerner is a man complete and self-contained, at ease with himself in the knowledge of the complex world about him, a 'figure of repose' (ibid., p.36). His relaxed way of being embodies an idea of American civilisation based on honour, which he wears as a style. Despite this, he is an imperfect, even tragic and ultimately archaic figure, 'the last gentleman' (ibid., p.38). His life seems free but he is also a lonely individual. His violence sets him apart from a society that, paradoxically, requires his skills. Such 'pressures of obligation' renders the Western landscape not 'the arena of free movement' but 'a great empty waste, cutting down . . . the stature of the horseman who rides it' (ibid., p.41). This makes Warshow's Westerner a contradictory figure whose 'moral code is seen also to be imperfect', with 'a moral ambiguity which darkens his image' and which 'arises from the fact that, whatever his justification, he is a killer' (ibid., p.41).

Warshow's argument was contentious in its time. For most élite observers, the Western was a fictional form entirely dissociated from the historical period it was notionally set in. Its allegedly clichéd plots and predictable stereotypes made it unthinkable as a framework for serious investigation of history and society. Warshow powerfully established basic links between the Western hero, American history and an American national identity. His links between the Western landscape and ideas of masculinity were to be developed by subsequent critics.

FRENCH FILM CRITICISM AND THE WESTERN

Warshow's proximity to American culture enabled him to connect the hero of the Western to American cultural ideas about its national identity. However, André Bazin's greater geographical distance allowed him to distinguish pattern and shape among Western films which were less visible to indigenous critics.

Where Warshow focused on the hero of the Western film, Bazin made distinctions between forms of Western films. He regarded *Stagecoach* as the ultimate in the classical form of the traditional Western film, established by pre-War B films and characterised by an 'ideal balance between social myth, historical reconstruction, psychological truth and the traditional . . . Western mise-en-scène' (1971b, p.149). This mix of myth, history, drama and the visual image provides a framework for subsequent thinking about the Western film. Bazin distinguished the classical form of the Western from the post-War 'supra-Westerns' like *Shane* (1953) and *High Noon* (1952) which are formally more self-conscious, with subject matter more socially or morally aware. Bazin was among the first to argue that authorship was not only as possible in Hollywood's commercial cinema as in Europe's state-supported national and art cinemas, but also that the authors of films were their directors rather than their scriptwriters. Bazin established the names of directors whose Westerns he argued constituted the classical tradition, using this principle of authorship in the cinema. Foremost among these was an older generation of film-makers including John Ford, Howard Hawks and Raoul Walsh, together with a second generation of directors including Nicholas Ray and Anthony Mann. Bazin finds in such directors' Westerns an enviable lyrical and novel-istic tradition, emphasising the 'sincerity' of their individual approaches, which embrace the narrative drive and strong characterisation of the classical Western form. The importance of Bazin's argument is in discerning basic characteristics of difference in the Western film and in identifying directors who brought a thematic consistency and visual sensibility to its imaginary world.

It might strike one as odd that a French critic would be among the first to take such an American cultural form as the Western film seriously, especially against a background of universal critical hostility, but the French historical and cultural context was very different from that of the Anglophone nations. Of all the film-producing nations, France is among those mainly European countries which has historically considered film as a serious art form. France was one of the birthplaces of film, with the Lumière Brothers among the first film-makers. Its film culture has benefited from generous state support and France was the first country to establish a national archive and repertory cinema in the Cinémathèque Française. In a national cultural context sympathetic to the idea of film as art, Bazin conceived and edited one of the first serious journals of film criticism, *Cahiers du Cinéma*, among a new generation of film critics who embraced American popular cinema and many of whom would figure prominently as film-makers in the French New Wave of the 1960s. Bazin and his colleagues gloried in the post-War opportunity to view intensively the backlog of American films denied them during the wartime occupation of France. In such a sympathetic cultural context, Bazin could take the Western seriously in ways Anglophone criticism found difficult.

THE WESTERN AND AMERICAN STUDIES

The ideas of Warshow and Bazin were prompted by new thinking about society and culture in their respective nations. The experience of war in the two countries had been very different. America had entered the war late and its economic and military resources had been crucial in the winning of the war overseas. France had been an occupied nation, its armies humiliated and its economy destroyed. Intellectuals in the two countries emerged from the war with very a different confidence in their national cultures. Hollywood was taken for granted in America but in France the Hollywood film was associated among intellectuals with the New World, which was free from the constraints of traditional cultural assumptions. But if Bazin's appreciation of the Western was part of a wider national sympathy and regard for American popular culture, Warshow's analysis was informed by new understandings of American history wrought by the emerging global prominence of America in the post-War period.

In post-War America, universities began to develop the discipline of American Studies, a convergence of academic interest in American history and society prompted by new kinds of historiography – fresh ideas about how history was to be studied. Warshow was writing at a time when a new generation of historians was disputing a tradition of celebratory histories of America's westward development, foremost among them Francis Parkman's eight volumes, *France and England in North America* (1865–92) and politician Theodore Roosevelt's patriotic six volumes, *The Winning of the West* (1889–96). Central to this new enquiry was the idea of the West and westward expansion as a formative feature of American national identity.

Most importantly, Frederick Jackson Turner's 'frontier hypothesis' in *The Significance of the Frontier in American History* (1893) replaces conventional histories based on America's European origins and the sensitive issue of slavery with an account of exploits of the famous pioneers who became so central to the folklore of the Western's history. Instead of personalities, however, he analyses the socio-political forces that produced conditions in which pioneering could take place. For Turner, the frontier marked a mobile physical space but, more than this, it represented a political process that advanced ideas of individualism and democracy as exceptional characteristics of America's national identity. In addition to this, John Fiske's ideological theme of 'manifest destiny' (1885) in *American Political Ideas Viewed from the Standpoint of Universal History* argued for the divine right of white imperialism to claim land through conquest and thereby justified and encouraged the European advance across the Americas. As Charles Peterson has indicated in *The Oxford History of the American West* (1994), this influential work entered into political rhetoric and contemporary popular opinion, to become the definitive account of American history well into the 1960s.

This nineteenth-century history was invoked by a work of twentieth-century scholarship that transformed the idea of the West for later critics of the Western. As the title, *Virgin Land: The American West as Symbol and Myth* (1950), indicates, its author Henry Nash Smith is concerned with the meaning of the West to the pioneers of frontier days and to successive American generations. Smith's study is about how the history of westward expansion can be understood symbolically, how the meaning of the West since the time of its white settlement has less to do with a verifiable history than with the ideas people commonly have of it.

The attraction of Smith's thesis to film criticism of the Western lies in its concern not only with the *myth* of the West but also with its *signs*. Both connect to the visual imagining of the West, especially those visual imaginings in the temporal and spatial distance from the history and geography of the West of which the Western film is a formative part. Smith's work enabled film criticism to connect Western films to long-standing and deep-rooted understandings of American national identity.

Smith's book is a work of cultural history. He analyses not just earlier histories but also novels about the West, and not just respected literary novels but also the pulp literature of dime novels that popularised stories of Western pioneers, outlaws and lawmen, together with the narratives, themes and characters that became part of the Western film.

On the basis of his study, Smith argues that a collective American national identity grew from 'the yeoman ideal of an agricultural economy based on free labo(u)r' (1971, pp.viii–ix), which was itself inspired by the idealisation of the American landscape as a garden and the immigrant desire for a safe haven, a biblical promised land. The myth of the Garden of America authorised the imperial colonisation of a land already inhabited and adapted by peoples of a different race. A landscape that had been changed over generations by native clearing, farming and hunting was nonetheless conceptualised by the early pioneers and settlers as a natural wilderness, a tabla rasa. At the same time as conceiving of the West as a garden, it was also paradoxically imagined as a wild place, dangerous and desolate, whose landscape and inhabitants must be 'tamed' for settlement and agriculture. The problem with these antithetical conceptions of 'two distinct Wests' was that 'The agricultural West was tedious; its inhabitants belonged to a despised social class. The Wild West was by contrast an exhilarating region of adventure and comradeship in the open air. Its heroes . . . were . . . not members of society at all but . . . free denizens of a noble wilderness' (ibid., p.55). For Smith, the formation of American identity lies in a tension between these American landscape myths as both Garden and Desert, nature and culture, an ideological tension structuring fiction about the West, that is exposed by his analysis of the common concerns of Western literature.

FROM AMERICAN STUDIES TO FILM STUDIES

American Studies combined with the first serious critical attention to the Western film at a formative stage in the establishment of film studies in the 1960s and 1970s. The first books of criticism of the Western appear at this time. They are among the founding texts of Film Studies as an academic discipline and a subject of study in the education system. Books on the Western by Jean-Louis Rieupeyrout (*La Grande Adventure du Western*, 1964) and Henri Agel (*Le Western*, 1969) among other French critics (sadly, never translated into English) had as an immediate concern the validation of the Western film as a major area of popular film-making. Work like this inspired critics in Britain and America, notably Colin MacArthur, Alan Lovell, Jim Kitses, John Cawelti and Will Wright in the 1960s and 1970s to a progressively widening debate about the genre cinema of Hollywood and how important it is to understanding popular cinema and popular culture more generally.

In *Horizons West* (1969) Kitses develops from the critical pioneers the idea that 'the Western is American history', although he locates the historical period of most Westerns specifically 'from about 1865 to 1890 or so, a brief final instant in the process' of westward expansion (1969, p.8). Though eager to explore the complex of relations between American history and the Western, Kitses also makes it clear that even this most limited of frontier moments is a history refracted through the fiction of folklore and romance narratives. From Henry Nash Smith, Kitses extends the notion of an ideological tension between the myths of Garden and Desert to a wider frame of ideas rendered by the 'narrative and dramatic structure' of the Western film into a 'fabulous' world that makes fiction of history (ibid., p.25). Using a structuralist principle derived from Claude Lévi-Strauss, Kitses constructs what became an influential model of conflicts between opposing forces that Western narratives negotiate in individual ways. He reformulates the garden/ desert dichotomy as a main opposition between wilderness and civilisation, simultaneously turning Nash's terms of nature into implicitly political ideas. Within these main headings, Kitses offers three further sets of terms of opposition between individual/community, nature/culture and West/East. These terms are not to be viewed as fixedly positive or negative however, for each category can alter its value in 'an ambiguous cluster of meanings and attitudes that provide the traditional thematic structure' of the Western film. This cluster of meanings is organised into a pattern of changing binary oppositions that he calls 'shifting . . . antinomies' (ibid., p.11). The full model looks like this:

Table 2.1 Kitses' 'shifting antinomies' model

THE WILDERNESS	CIVILISATION
The Individual	*The Community*
freedom	restriction
honour	institutions
self-knowledge	illusion
integrity	compromise
self-interest	social responsibility
solipsism	democracy
Nature	*Culture*
purity	corruption
experience	knowledge
empiricism	legalism
pragmatism	idealism
brutalisation	refinement
savagery	humanity
The West	*The East*
America	Europe
the frontier	America
equality	class
agrarianism	industrialism
tradition	change
the past	the future

Kitses' model demonstrates that the values associated with any pair in the complex of binary oppositions are never fixed. The Western landscape, for instance, can be either barren and inhospitable or 'inspiring and civilising', the Western community either a 'positive force' for democracy (ibid., p.10) or 'a harbinger of corruption' (ibid., p.11), the Westerner an agent of civilisation or desperate to escape the advancing frontier. Importantly, conventional Western characters can embody specific functions among these conflicting values: 'If Eastern figures such as bankers, lawyers and journalists are often either drunkards or corrupt, their female counterparts generally carry virtues and graces which the West clearly lacks' (ibid., p.11). What Kitses demonstrates, then, is that the Western genre is a complex of deeply ambivalent attitudes to westward expansion, and thereby offers a framework for challenging and conflicting explorations of the meaning of American history and identity.

Kitses applies his model to the Westerns of three directors, Anthony Mann, Budd Boetticher and Sam Peckinpah. In each case, he finds a personal vision exploring American identity in individual ways, by placing the narrative and thematic structure together with the visual style of each director within his own model of the Western's 'shifting antinomies'. Kitses' book is a defiant assertion of the Western as a central American art form.

If Jim Kitses' book offers a subtle model of the thematic structure of the Western, Will Wright's *Sixguns and Society* (1975) offers a more detailed structuralist study of Western plots. Although Kitses is keen to establish the Western genre as a dynamic form 'saturated with conceptual significance' (ibid., p.21), Wright's book resists the implication that it is primarily fertile soil for the artistic sensibilities of talented individual directors exploring matters of American history and identity. Instead, Wright argues that the Western needs to be understood as a popular form that becomes 'part of the cultural language by which America understands itself' (Wright, 1975, p.10) at any one time. Critics following Kitses focus on a selected list of distinguished Westerns, but Wright analyses only highly financially successful Westerns since it is these that demonstrate what 'meanings viewers demand of the myth' (ibid., p.12). Drawing on the theory of character functions from the work of another structuralist critic, Vladimir Propp, Wright analyses the narrative organisation of the most popular Westerns. On the basis of findings from this exercise, he seeks to explain a correlation between the popularity of particular plot cycles of Westerns and what is happening in American society contemporaneously. As an example, he finds that 'the classical Western plot corresponds to the individualistic conception of society underlying a market economy' and 'the revenge plot reveals a new conception of society corresponding to the values and attitudes inherent in a planned, corporate economy' (ibid., p.15).

Wright's book establishes an important premise that films, even Westerns set many years in the past, connect to issues at the time of their production. Although he is not really concerned with the specific processes through which films relate to their contemporary issues, Wright established the principle that while the Western deals with American history and identity, albeit through fictional forms, it is not merely a matter of history. For Wright, Western films exercise certain combinations of ideas associated with frontier history and its fictional representation in order to explore crucially contemporary issues more fully.

Wright's implication is that the most popular Westerns are conservative interventions in contemporary cultures, unlike Kitses who argues that the best Westerns are sceptical explorations. This would suggest that what critics and audiences admire in Westerns tend to opposite political meanings. However, Philip French in *Westerns* (1972) neatly counters such a conclusion. Although he shares Wright's thesis that Westerns are more products of their time than their setting, French finds more contradictory relations between Westerns of the 1960s and 1970s and the fluctuating politics of the American President in office at the time of their production. For French, the Western is capable of a range of political meanings.

These first books of criticism on the Western opened up terms of debate about the meaning of the Western and its relations to both the period in which Westerns are set and the period of their production. Despite their conflicting political standpoints, Wright and French established a now firmly accepted principle that films can be seen in complex debate with their contemporary cultures. Among subsequent arguments powerfully deploying the principle, Brian Henderson in 1980/1, for instance, argues that the racial conflicts between white settlers and native Americans in *The Searchers* (1956) is an intervention in civil rights legislation at the time. Similarly, as recently as 2000, Stanley Corliss demonstrates 'how the Western was well suited to . . . rationales for (post-War) U.S. foreign policy . . . that guided the Truman administration's foreign policy' (2000, p.66).

THE WESTERN AS A GENRE

Film studies of Hollywood popular genres emerged during the same period of the 1960s and 1970s that saw these first books of criticism on the Western. Since Hollywood film production and, especially, marketing was organised in terms of film genres, developing a critical method to understand the subject of genre seemed an important task for film students. Studies of the Western film thus became important in early debates in genre criticism.

To call the Western a genre is to assume it is a definable type of fiction. Film Studies borrowed the concept from literary studies, where the term is used to describe forms of literature from lyric poetry to tragic drama. But film genre criticism deployed the concept to investigate the previously unexplored products of a commercial film industry such as Hollywood, rather than the legacy of valued literature. Kitses and Wright draw on the idea of myth from structural anthropology to justify selections of Westerns on the grounds that the themes and plots they respectively display reveal social and cultural meanings. Kitses' model of binary oppositions and Wright's taxonomy of plot structures contributed to debates about genre conventions, the characteristics that enable all genres to be recognised and interpreted by their audiences.

Foremost among genre critics who wrote about American popular genres is John Cawelti. His book on the Western, *The Six Gun Mystique* (1971), contributed to a wider genre criticism, including his own later *Adventure, Mystery, Romance* (1976). In these books, Cawelti offers a first attempt to elaborate inclusive conventions of what he termed the 'formula' narrative and drama of the Western as a popular genre of adventure, mystery and romance. Like Kitses, Cawelti notes that the Western is set on a frontier at a time when forces of law and criminality are in tension, 'a place where advancing civilisation met declining savagery' (1971, p.38). This situation provides a basic Western narrative of an adventure story with a hero who must mediate between opposing forces of good and evil in a 'narrative pattern [that] works out and resolves the tension between a strong need for aggression and a sense of ambiguity and guilt about violence' (ibid., p.14). Among the many attempts to catalogue the variety of plots available for narrative organisation, Cawelti cites Frank Gruber's seven plots and their implied character groups:

1. The Journey (railroad/stagecoach/wagon train versus raiders/indians).
2. The Ranch (ranchers vs. rustlers or cattlemen vs. settlers or sheepmen).
3. The Empire (an epic Ranch plot).
4. The Revenge (the wronged man vs. the truly guilty).
5. The Cavalry (cavalry vs. indians).
6. The Outlaw ((Southern) outlaws vs. (Northern) lawmen).
7. The Marshal (lawman vs. outlaws).

Such a list is as suggestive as any other, but also as reductive and arbitrary in its interchangeable mixture of settings, situations and implied narratives. Nonetheless, it suggests the potential variety of plot situations the Western makes available, and reinforces the explanatory strength of Kitses' model of 'shifting antinomies' between heroism and villainy (for instance, heroes and villains change places in the outlaw and marshal plots).

Cawelti also argues that the Western landscape is symbolic. The visual spectacle of an isolated town, ranch or fort, tenuously connected to a safer world across the openness, extremity and spectacle of the Great Plains, symbolises 'the thematic conflict between savagery and civilisation and its resolution' (ibid., p.40). The precision of Cawelti's detailed exploration of the plots, situations, settings and characters of Westerns contributes to the arguments set out by Kitses, Wright and others (Lovell, 1967; Buscombe, 1970; Ryall, 1970; Collins, 1970). It extends an understanding of the generic conventions of the Western and lays the groundwork for the more detailed film analyses that follow. This idea of convention – a much less negative term than Cawelti's 'formula' – inspired a body of critical work that turns attention to the significance of the film image and visual style.

GENRE AND ICONOGRAPHY

These first attempts to define genres like the Western study various constituents of a range of Western films. Kitses and Wright offer recurrent situations, character functions and narrative structures as generic conventions of the Western. What guides the first stage of genre criticism is the potential that conventions of setting, plot, situation, character etc., set boundaries and define a generic form. Yet the sense that the Western film *visualises* dramatic narratives prompted a second wave of genre criticism in Britain which advanced the proposition that genres are most distinguished by their iconography. Ed Buscombe, for instance, argues that 'Since we are dealing with a visual medium we ought surely to look for our defining criteria at what we actually see on the screen' (1970, p.36). Iconography refers to recurrent generic images, including characteristic settings, décor, props, costumes and actor types. Rather than listing elements in a catalogue, however, Buscombe demonstrates the dynamic significance of iconography in the production of meaning in the Western film. He instances how a choice of armaments and their use can betray character; how a Winchester rifle can connote the modernity of its owner or how a derringer up a sleeve implies deceit. But no example of the power of an iconographic analysis betters his graphic account of the opening of *Guns in the Afternoon/Ride the High Country* (1962):

Knowing the period and location, we expect to find a familiar Western town. In fact, the first few minutes of the film brilliantly disturb our expectations. As the camera moves around the town, we discover a policeman in uniform, a car, a camel and Randolph Scott dressed up as Buffalo Bill. Each of these images performs a function. The figure of the policeman conveys that the law has become institutionalised; the rough and ready frontier days are over. The car suggests, as in The Wild Bunch, *that the west is no longer isolated from modern technology and its implications. Significantly, the camel is racing against a horse; such a grotesque juxtaposition is painful. A horse in a Western is not just an animal but a symbol of dignity, grace and power. These qualities are mocked by it competing with a camel; and to add insult to injury, the camel wins.*

(Buscombe, 1970, p.44)

The quotation encourages us to see the deployment of Western iconography as meaningful because of the expectations aroused or confounded, expectations which can only exist on the basis of the foreknowledge an audience brings from previous experience of Westerns.

One useful further distinction arises between iconography which is cultural and that which is generic. If a Western hero appears on a street without his guns, an audience tutored in Western folklore knows its potential for comedy (the town marshal as figure of fun in *Destry Rides Again*, 1939) or drama (the hero confronted by the villain in *Winchester '73*, 1952). But when the Reno brothers in *Rage at Dawn* (1955) are shown eating with a knife and drinking from a saucer, a wider cultural knowledge about table manners informs judgement of their characters and their potential for villainy. In short, a genre like the Western combines generic and cultural sources to organise its meanings visually. The upshot is that, however discrete a genre, the boundaries of the Western are as flexible as the shifting antinomies of Kitses' model of Western thematic structures.

THE WESTERN AND GENRE CRITICISM

The work of these genre critics in America and Britain was important in three ways. First, it produced a dynamic framework of recurrent plots, characters and iconography in a system of thematic conflicts that collectively constitute the conventions of the Western film. Secondly, the debate over the Western offered a method for distinguishing the conventions of other popular film genres. Thirdly, it established an important principle that popular cultural forms like film genres interrelate with their cultural histories as well as contemporary cultures.

It is important to underline the dynamism of film genres like the Western. The Western form is not rigid and fixed but variant and changing. Rather than searching for a taxonomy or catalogue of definitions to establish generic boundaries, most critics would now agree with Tom Ryall's argument that genres are created through tacit yet common consent among the triangle of creators, the institutions they work in and their consumers (Ryall, 1978). Westerns can be comedies (like *The Paleface*, 1948 and *Blazing Saddles*, 1974), melodramas (like *Jubal*, 1956 and *The Last Sunset*, 1961), musicals (like *Calamity Jane*, 1953 and *Paint Your Wagon*, 1969), and even horror films (*Billy the Kid Versus Dracula*, 1965); they can be hybrids like *Westworld* (1973) and other science fiction films which, like *Star Wars* (1977), draw on such Western conventions as the stand-off, with laser swords replacing six-guns. Rather than regulating what is and is not a Western by attending to the films alone, Ryall argues that a definition must reside in the common agreement among film-makers, audiences and the institution of cinema that brings them together. This 'cinema institution' refers not only to the building in which films are seen but also to the system of production, distribution, exhibition (on a variety of screens, including television and computer), promotion and criticism. Christian Metz has argued that it is this mental machinery as much as the physical arrangements and personnel who work in and around this 'cinema machine' that encourage us in the assumptions and views we share about what constitutes a film.

One of the most prolific genre critics since this time, Steve Neale, has argued in *Genre* (1980) that this dynamism is crucial to the perpetuation of a genre cinema. Audiences return to their favourite genre films because they promise similar pleasures to those experienced before. But audiences also demand a new experience. If a Western is too similar to previous experiences it will be judged derivative; if too different it may deny generic pleasures and thus be judged 'not a Western'.

When expectations are not satisfied, audiences are disappointed, judging the film 'not a *good* Western'. Westerns therefore have to be similar to, but also different from, generic expectations. Successful popular genres are maintained over time by the emergence of renewable cycles of films that create new relationships between similarity and difference. The trick in perpetuating a genre comes from striking a balance between similarity and difference in a way that appeals to film-makers, the film industry and genre audiences.

THE WESTERN AND NEW THEORY

From the late 1970s onwards, as the popular appeal of the Western declined, genre studies turned attention away from male-centred action genres like the Western towards female-centred genres such as the woman's film (Haskell, 1977) and melodrama (Gledhill, 1987), and genres like film noir where the femme fatale offered more active heroines (Kaplan, 1998). Such genre studies were then caught up in wider debates in Film Studies about the production of meaning in films. Approaches to analysing films, to textual analysis, were subjected to major theoretical examination as the discipline of Film Studies interrogated its own knowledge and methods. New theory from a wide range of philosophical and inter-disciplinary sources was applied to the most extensive range of films and film-making practices from around the world. At the same time, Film Studies was attending to Hollywood's mainstream narrative film and its ideological role in the cultural reproduction of dominant ideas and attitudes. Just as in its early history, the Western film became part of this larger Hollywood category. Both the Western film and criticism of the Western was subsumed within this new development in Film Studies and targeted as reflecting aspects of a film history (and, indeed, Film Studies) thought to require substantial reinterpretation.

Common to much of this theoretical enquiry was a desire to deny the legacy of the celebratory genre and authorship studies in which studies of the Western had prospered. The reaction against the Western was now to do more with the bias of its gendered world than with moralist or sociological objections to its violent scenarios. This shift was impelled by several critical developments, foremost among them feminist film theory, new Marxist theories of ideology and adaptations of Freudian psychoanalytic theory to films known as cine-psychoanalysis. The key words in this period of new film theory are representation, form and spectatorship.

GENDER STUDIES AND THE WESTERN

Feminist film criticism developed from a desire to place the legacy of male-centred genres and genre criticism in wider contexts of film history and film criticism, in order to explore female genres and the place of women in cinema. Among early feminist critiques of the Western, Jacqueline Levitin in 'The Western: any good roles for feminists?' (1982) attacks the genre for the limited roles it offers women, finding women in Westerns functioning as deviations from or prizes for the hero's narrative quest. She sees frontier history as more amenable to a greater range of female roles and functions than can be imagined in the homosocial world of the Western.

Jane Tompkins in *West of Everything* (1992) denies this appeal to the history of the West and argues against earlier critical claims of connection between the Western and American history. According to Tompkins, the Western 'doesn't have anything to do with the West as such. It isn't about the encounter between civilisation and the frontier. It is about men's fears of losing their mastery, and hence their identity, both of which the Western tirelessly reinvents' (1992, p.45). Imposing a longer historical frame of reference on the Western, Tompkins sees its male-centred world as 'the antithesis of the cult of domesticity that dominated American Victorian culture' (ibid., p.39) and the popular female-centred domestic novel of the time. For her, 'the Western struggles and strains to cast out everything feminine' (ibid., p.127). By situating the Western in a longer history of cultural production, Tompkins perceives in the Western film a reaction against earlier female cultural traditions. Yet, in her account of the male-centred world of the Western which explores male fears as much as male mastery, she opens up new ways of thinking about the male drama of the Western, as one that is less secure in its masculine identity. As, more recently, Tassilo Schneider has put it in 'Finding a New Heimat in the Wild West' (1995), 'the wilderness/ civilisation dichotomy . . . can easily be read as a displacement of gender boundaries, the difficulty of delineating historical notions of masculinity, and the problems posed by sexual difference' (1995, p.55). Furthermore, for Janet Thumim, arguing in relation to the Western, *Unforgiven* (1992) in 'Maybe He's Tough But He Sure Aint No Carpenter' (1998), this can also explain the 'fascination for the female audience, because in deconstructing the myths of the west, the film is also obliged to deconstruct the myths of the masculine' (1998, p.351).

Such work at the time on the gendered world of the Western was part of a wider programme of work on film representation. The issue here was how films represented the sectional interests of wider cultural positions, especially across the social categories of gender, social class, race and generation. Feminist film criticism on the representation of women in male action genres like the Western developed new understandings of its masculine world.

THE LOOK IN THE WESTERN

Cine-psychoanalysis developed as an approach in order to move away from the structuralist task of reading popular films as cultural myths of society and history. In its place, studies began to explore the ideological function of films, the idea of film as cultural reproduction, reproducing dominant assumptions and ways of thinking. Rather than reading films thematically for their political meanings or analysing their representations, cine-psychoanalysis explored relationships buried in their *form* as opposed to in their content. The task of criticism became the work of connecting the form of films to the 'reading positions' they produced for their audiences. Now recast as a theoretical 'spectator', 'textual subjects' rather than social beings, these reading positions were seen as necessary to make sense and gain pleasure from the viewing experience. The aspects of film form that centrally position the spectator include the visual organisation of shots, composition within the frame (or mise-en-scène), editing procedures and the relationship between image and sound.

This new formal analysis shifted attention from generic conventions defined by setting, narrative, iconography etc. to the procedures of cinematography and editing. According to this approach, the form of a film organises the ways in which audiences are invited not merely to observe film conventions but to accept a particular point of view about them. This new understanding organised for the spectator by, especially, the dominant film form of popular cinema, amounted to a theoretical critique of earlier approaches to film criticism. The method suggested an unconscious manipulation of pleasure and meaning in the act of watching films.

The most influential cine-psychoanalytic essay is Laura Mulvey's 'Visual Pleasure and Narrative Cinema' (1975). In this essay, Mulvey introduces the concept of scopophilia which can be defined as the pleasure popular cinema conventionally provides through a structure of voyeuristic looks by the spectator via the on-screen male onto the sexualised body of a female character. Analysing moments in films by Alfred Hitchcock and Joseph von Sternberg, she demonstrates that a conventional editing system of shots and reverse shots requires the spectator, whether male or female, to take pleasure from a scopophilic system of looks which is actively male and sanctions heterosexual male desire and gender definitions. Mulvey thereby argued that 'the look' in popular cinema was inherently patriarchal since it made the male the active bearer of the look and the female the passive object. Women in cinema thereby became 'Other' to the norm of the male. Mulvey's task was political; to expose the ideological work of popular cinema as patriarchal. It was also polemical; to turn away from popular cinema and to build an alternative avant-garde cinema of formal disruption. Cine-psychoanalysis prompted a campaign for film practices to produce a cinema of formal disruption and to disturb the pleasures of conventional spectatorship.

LOOKING AT THE MALE BODY

It may appear from this account that cine-psychoanalysis would have little positive interest in popular cinema and the Western. However, Mulvey's 'theory of the look' has been applied extensively, substantially qualified in subsequent debate, not least by Mulvey herself, and developed along with changes in cinema over time. Although its application to the representation of women in cinema makes it revealing to feminist criticism, the idea of film spectatorship and the theory of the look has entered the critical fabric of film studies. It has inspired much work on the look of the Western hero. Paul Willemen has argued in 'Anthony Mann: Looking at the Male' (1981) that the heterosexual male look can equally be directed on the body of male characters, especially in Westerns directed by Anthony Mann. This prompts

Willemen to conclude that the structure of the look in Westerns is character-ised not by heterosexual desire but by 'a repressed homosexual look'. Steve Neale, however, denies that the only pleasure to be gained from Westerns is by adopting a homosexual spectator position. He suggests that the male look can be more narcissistic than voyeuristic when looking on idealised figures of masculinity. Rather than desiring other men, the male spectator derives pleasure from the 'auto-erotic' look of identification with fictional figures who, however problematically, he would ideally like to be.

Yvonne Tasker has further argued in *Spectacular Bodies* (1993) that the look directed on the body of the modern action hero bears many pleasures which are not just sexual, whether voyeuristic or narcissistic. Her references are to figures played by star actors like Arnold Schwarzenegger and Bruce Willis, whose body-built physiques are regularly exposed during the 'muscular cinema' (1993, p.5) of their action narratives. For Tasker, these heroes are too often placed as objects of the look to remain within conventional defin-itions of masculinity. Following Richard Dyer's work on the male pin-up in 'Don't Look Now' (1984), she sees them as ambivalently feminised by the cosmetic grotesquery of their exaggerated body appearance. This is a process heightened by the kinds of narrative tensions they find themselves in, caught between restraint and excess (ibid., p.9), and the ease with which they are offered as objects of the look.

The conventionalised body of the Western hero is rarely unclothed or observed in this way, so the same argument about the feminisation of the body of the action hero may not seem to apply to the Western hero. Martin Pumphrey, however, argues in 'Why Do Cowboys Wear Hats in the Bath?' (1989) that even when partially dressed, the display of the hero's body in Westerns is more coy than those of his counterparts in sword and sandal epics or modern action films. He suggests that the Western hero can rarely be seen out of Western uniform, separated from the conventional dress and armoury of the fictional cowboy and gunfighter, for fear of feminising his body and appearing to offer it for a sexualised look. The hero therefore takes a bath with hat firmly in place, perhaps additionally smoking a cigar, as in *Cowboy* (1958), and even using the murky bathwater to conceal a pistol, as in *High Plains Drifter* (1972), to deny any suspicion of homoeroticism and to confirm a conventional masculinity.

Pumphrey sees the clothes that the Western hero wears providing a further take on the look. They conventionally follow the contemporary fashions of the day of their design rather than those of the period in which they are set. The fashions of the day (indeed, in the case of the younger male hero, commonly the height of contemporary fashion) habitually adorn the body of the male hero in ways that Pumphrey suggests invite the eye of the spectator. Indeed, much of the physical prowess of the hero, including his display of handling guns and horses, invites sustained looks of admiration. Thus the Western hero too can be understood as both object and subject of the look, the focus of a series of complex acts of looking, with the result, as Pumphrey says, that 'the hero's masculine toughness must be partially feminised' (1989, p.52).

THE WESTERN AND CULTURAL STUDIES

Pumphrey's important essay recasts the cine-psychoanalytic project within the framework of British Cultural Studies, a burgeoning discipline of the 1980s concerned with the study of culture and society. Pumphrey incorporates theories of the look into cultural studies of youth sub-cultural styles, fashion and masculinity to explore the gendered regime of the Western. Kitses' model of shifting antinomies, he argues, is coded by gender, 'The town that stands for the social order the hero must save and then settle into or reject and leave is characterised . . . by the presence of women. The wilderness is a sphere for masculine action' (ibid., p.53).

Although the male sphere is always valued over the female sphere, the gender identity of the hero who moves between them becomes subject to change. As Douglas Pye has observed of Pumphrey's argument, the Western hero is 'faced with two frontiers, one separating civilisation and savagery and the other between masculinity and femininity' (1996a, p.12). For Pumphrey, Western narratives challenges assumptions that gender identity is fixed as either male or female. If Westerns are invitations to work through fantasies of 'what it means to be a man' (1989, p.52), they are also invitations to the gendered spectator to question easy definitions of masculinity and femininity. To adapt a term coined by Thomas Schatz, the Western thereby becomes 'a genre of gender-contested space' (Schatz, 1981).

MASCULINITY AND THE WESTERN

The work on the representation of women, the male look, the male body and gendered identity in Westerns gradually combines in ways that recast earlier arguments in Western criticism. The issue of to whom Westerns give pleasure and the meaning of that pleasure has recently produced significant new understandings. As early as 1971, John Cawelti argues that the Western appeals most to working-class adolescent males, rehearsing generational struggles and rites of passage, particularly between authority figures and rebellious opposition. Critics confront the new theory elicited from the pleasures that Westerns offer not just to marginal male groups like youth and the working class, but to all groups on the margins of social power. These are groups who, in the cine-psychoanalytic terms of Ina Rae Hark, 'symbolically if not biologically lack the signifying phallus' (1993, p.151).

Does this mean that despite the evident male landscape of the Western, it can speak to women about their social position too? One source of potential pleasures in the Western for women is offered by Raymond Bellour's argument that the Western cannot do without the figure of the woman from 'Alternation, segmentation, hynopsis' (1979). She initiates the Western narrative and is the source of subsequent narrative disruption. Bellour sees the Western as a romance genre where, like much popular cinema, the narrative drive is not so much towards the hero's quest as to a resolution in heterosexual partnership. In Mulvey's second take on her theory of the look ('Afterthoughts on Visual Pleasure and Narrative Cinema', 1981), she suggests that women deal with the male system of spectatorship by taking up a transsexual spectator position. Countering Bellour's understanding of the Western's narrative resolution, Mulvey argues that the implied resolution of the Western involves the com-mon choice forced on the male hero between heterosexual partnership and a fantasy of self-sufficiency. Mulvey argues that this is a transsexual fantasy not only for men but also for women who are equally attracted to the possibilities of independence and personal control.

One of the major British writers on the Western, Douglas Pye, expresses these choices for the Western's male protagonist's choices in the idea of 'the divided hero'. In his introduction to *The Movie Book of The Western* (1996), Pye sets out four conventional narrative closures in the Western which express the possibilities available to the Western hero; the hero rides off, dies or forms a couple who then either ride off together or remain in the community (1996a, p.14). In relation to Bellour and Mulvey's argument about the gendered spectator, this implies that partnership and independence are not absolute, but only potential choices in Westerns. Others are a radical integration of male and female independence that can also combine in partnership.

THE NEW HISTORY

Gender studies and cultural studies have been central influences on film studies of the Western in recent years. During the 1980s, however, a new historiography of the West developed in American universities to effectively undermine some of the central connections established by criticism of the Western between the Western film and history. New Western History emerges during 'the fifteen years between *The Outlaw Josey Wales* (1976) and *Dances*

With Wolves (1990)' (Worland and Countryman, 1998, p.184), to question the frontier thesis, the governing concept of much former history of the West. The work of historians like Patricia Nelson Limerick, Richard White and William Cronon *et al.* undermines the prominence given to earlier writers such as Frederick Jackson Turner. For them, Turner's frontier hypothesis does not represent the historiography of the period of nineteenth century westward expansion. These new historians attach more importance to the work of Paul Wallace Gates and other historians contemporary to Turner who explore questions of land acquisition and its disposition and for whom the concept of the frontier in American history has no meaning.

For the new historians, the 'frontier hypothesis' is a romantic conception, politically conservative, patriarchal and ethnocentric, precluding 'any understanding of the West's role in the contemporary world' (quoted by Stanfield, 2001, p.10). Eliot West summarises the impact on the Western and Western criticism in this way:

> *Under the old frontier interpretation, the story shimmered with a romantic, heroic glow. Suffering and tragedy were redeemed by the glorious results presumed to have followed – the nurturing of American individualism and the coming of a civilized order into a wilderness. The new themes, by contrast, emphasise a continuing cultural dislocation, environmental calamity, economic exploitation, and individuals who either fail outright or run themselves crazy chasing unattainable goals.*

> *(West 1994, p.105)*

New History unearths a far more complex and diverse history of America's origins, one in which issues of land ownership are complicated by earlier occupations by generations of Native Americans and Hispanics. Revisionist history renders racial conflicts more complex, with intersecting and co-existing European colonies and Indian republics, which contrasts with the frontier history claimed by earlier Western criticism to inform Western films. For Richard White, the West was not the violent setting assumed by Westerns although Native Americans were the victims of white genocide. Nor was the 'triumphal progress of white American civilisation' (Buscombe and Pearson, 1998, p.3) without other calamities, not least environmental destruction. Such new histories have proved highly contentious, with disputes over the political intentions and effects of such revisionism, and confusions about relations between cultural myth and verifiable history. The New History has reinvigorated debate about history and its representation in media such as films and genres like the Western, and placed issues of race, social class, gender and sexuality at the centre of discussion.

RACE AND THE WESTERN

The apparent contradictions here are played out in conflicting arguments about America's racial political history and the treatment of race in the Western. For a generation of ethnic minorities entering higher education and élite professions in America for the first time, the representation of Native America in films ranges merely from savagely white racist stereotypes of Indians in *The Battle of Elderbush Gulch* (1913) to a patronising liberalism in *Dances with Wolves* (Prats, 1998). Among this new generation of scholars, Ward Churchill sees the Western film as a major cultural purveyor of white America's rationalisation of nineteenth-century oppression. His indegist film analysis finds a persistent structure of racial supremacist assumptions with material consequences reflected in the marginal position of Native American communities and their exclusion from the American mainstream.

Vine Deloria, another critic working within the same intellectual framework, argues that racial stereotypes emerge from a white acknowledgement of the history, but an inability to accept responsibility for its consequences. Deloria terms this 'white trauma': 'Underneath all the conflicting images of the Indian one fundamental truth emerges – the white man knows that he is alien and he knows that North America is Indian' (1980, p.xxvi). This detection of racism in a racial psychosis is part of a new opposition external to the Western critical tradition for, as Andrew Sarris in *The John Ford Movie Mystery* (1976) has acknowledged, 'racism can never be dissociated from the romance' of the genre. These arguments return us to cine-psychoanalytic ideas about gendered dominance in the Western film, in the construction, now, not only of woman but also of the native American/Indian as 'Other'. At the same time, and paradoxically, it opens up possibilities that white/Indian conflicts can also be dramatised in terms of fantasies of male – but also of white – power and fears.

EMPIRICAL STUDIES

Since the 1990s, the production of Western films has declined to a few titles each year. Nonetheless, films like the female-centred *The Ballad of Little Jo* (1993), the epic *Ride with the Devil* (1993) and the independent film *Dead Man* (1996) draw on ideas and themes from these most recent Western debates. In the same period, there has been a movement in Film Studies away from the high theory of the preceding generation to apply inherited ideas and strategies to empirical research studies of historical moments, conditions of production and the audience reception of individual films and film genres. In relation to the Western genre, foremost among these is Peter Stanfield's analysis of series Westerns, *Hollywood, Westerns and the 1930s: The Lost Trail* (2001), a form so important to Hollywood during the 1930s, yet so little regarded in film criticism of the Western. Stanfield argues that the Western has less to do with frontier history than with land disputes, in a displaced engagement with issues central to the concerns of the series Westerns' rural audience. In suggesting that Westerns are best understood in 'their historical context' (2001, p.6), he joins other critics arguing against evolutionary theories of genre development and for models concerned more with the industrial, cultural and social determinants at the time Westerns are made (Gallagher, 1986b; Leutrat, 1986; Neale, 1990).

This concern to understand cycles of Westerns in their immediate context rather than in earlier American history takes the indegist debate over the racial politics of the Western a stage further. For instance, Richard Maltby and Steve Neale respond in conflicting ways to the indegist debate with careful textual and contextual analyses of 'the Indian question' in Westerns. Maltby (in Cameron and Pye, 1996), considers the generic demise of the Western properly corresponds to the emergence of new forces and minority voices in the academic community and in the wider popular culture. In these spheres of influence, both feminism and indigenous cultures have 'succeeded in establishing autonomous identities for themselves outside the constraints of Otherness' so that 'the classical imperial narrative of heroic repression . . . can no longer be told' (ibid., p.49). On the other hand, Neale sees the Western constantly adapting to each new contemporary moment, dealing with race conflicts according to shifts in race relations over time. In an essay of quite extraordinarily detailed scholarship (in Buscombe and Pearson, 1998), he charts a changing twentieth-century history of white/Indian relations in Westerns. Arguing against those who see Indian/white conflicts in Westerns as allegories of other racial conflicts, such as black civil rights, Neale demonstrates how cycles of indian Westerns correspond precisely to historical shifts in race debates about white/Indian relations. These would include Native American assimilation, separate development, white ethnocentrism and white racism. His concluding argument is that the Indian is more complex a figure in the Western than film studies allows, suggesting that there is still a great deal to learn about a subject 'relentlessly vanishing before our eyes' in film production, among film audiences and, crucially, among 'film commentators, critics and historians' (ibid., p.21).

RETURN OF THE WESTERN

Given the scarcity of recent Western film production, an unexpected number of critical books and essays have returned to the genre over the past few years. Lavishly illustrated coffee table books offer critical histories of the Western film (Hardy, 1991), together with cultural studies of frontier history (Buscombe, 1988). *The Western Reader* (Kitses and Rickman, 1998) reprints some of the major criticism of the Western film long out of print or otherwise difficult to obtain, together with *The Movie Book of the Western* (Cameron and Pye, 1996) and new work on the central director in the genre, John Ford (Studlar and Bernstein, 2001). There is a new book of cultural studies, considering the Western as a key twentieth-century signifier in popular culture, advertising, fashion and the tourist industry (Buscombe and Pearson, 1998). Essays on the Western appear again in issues of academic journals (*Cineaste* and *The Journal of Film and Video*). Major new research comes from Richard Slotkin (*Gunfighter Nation*, 1992), completing his trilogy on the Western and American history, and Peter Stanfield on the neglected field of series westerns.

If all this activity suggests more than simply nostalgia for a now marginalised genre, we can expect new generations of film-makers and critics to debate the Western for future audiences. There is still a sympathy among them all; even the pull-string toy cowboy, Woody, tragically displaced from the life of his child-owner by the modern space-age toy, Buzz Lightyear, gets to ride on into the sunset alongside his new sidekick at the end of the popular *Toy Story* (1995). If the genre also borrows from other genres and national cinemas, it also continues to influence; *The Magnificent Seven* (1960) reworked the earlier Japanese film, *The Seven Samurai* (1954), and returns in the animated form of *A Bug's Life* (1998). If the history of Western film production teaches us anything, it is that new cycles of Westerns and influential individual films repeatedly appear to re-energize the genre. As Kitses writes in the introduction to one of the most significant of recent readers, 'If no longer dominant, the genre remains a strong competitor in the semiotic marketplace, de-centred but nevertheless accessible as a style and form' (Kitses and Rickman, 1998, p.17) in cinema, fiction and the wider culture.

PART TWO

THE FILMS

CHAPTER THREE

Where the Western Came From: Antecedents of the Western Film

The Western film rides the range of the twentieth century. To mix the metaphors, there was a rich seam of antecedents for cinema to mine from nineteenth-century Western fiction, drama, imagery and spectacle (Rieupeyrout, 1964). The West was represented in many cultural forms after the frontier was officially closed and also during the long process of colonisation that advanced its territories. In the historical period in which Westerns are set, all types of writing about the West was available for reading, both in the West itself and beyond it. So many cultural representations of the West interacted with American history that it could be understood in some ways to have influenced its direction.

Where Part One explored the historiography and film studies that shape ideas about the West and the Western film, Part Two offers more detailed histories and studies in the development of Western films. This opening chapter begins the exploration of the Western film by locating its antecedents in Western fiction, pictorialisation and drama.

IMAGINING THE WEST BEFORE FILM

The Western genre is populated with a host of conventional character types. Imagine the Western and think of cowboy, Indian, saloon woman, ranch owner, gunfighter, sheriff, marshal, wagon master, cavalryman, scout, settlers, townsfolk, railroad builders . . . and writers.

Writers may not be the most conventional of characters but they do appear in Westerns. In *Unforgiven* (1992), we encounter the more conventional figure of a gunfighter, English Bob (Richard Harris), accompanied by his 'biographer', Mr Beauchamp (Saul Rubinek), who 'faithfully records' what is evidently Bob's pack of lies about his own reputation as a gunfighter. In

The Left Handed Gun (1958), a constant observer, Moultrie (Hurd Hatfield), chronicles the story of Billy the Kid (Paul Newman) in exaggerated tales published in the East. Contrast these writers who peddle fiction with the treatment of newspaper editors and journalists in Westerns. In *The Man Who Shot Liberty Valance* (1962), newspaper editor Dutton Peabody (Edmund O'Brien) is brutally killed by villains when he dares to broadcast their villainy in print. In *Posse* (1975), the editor of the Tesota Sentinel (James Stacey) is the conscience of the Western town, the only resident to see through the cynical politicking of the marshal (Kirk Douglas).

As the examples indicate, writers in Westerns may be a select few and yet there is pattern to their appearances. First, though they are invariably male (one exception is the newspaperwoman played by Gene Tierney in *The Return of Frank James*, 1940), their masculinity contrasts with the Westerners around them. Beauchamp is short, round and sweats with fear and excitement; the finery of Moultrie's suit and ruffle-fronted shirt becomes increasingly stained by drink and despair. The newspapermen are respectively a whisky-soaked drunk and disabled. The actors who play such roles do not share the physique of a conventional Western masculinity, but are marked by their physical difference. In Westerns, then, writers are an Other masculinity, like women are the Other gender and Indians and ethnic minorities Other races.

The two kinds of writers differ from other Westerners and from each other. Whereas the novelist is associated with the construction of myth of the West, newspapermen are associated with defence of an abstract idea of Truth. This opposition between what might be called fiction and faction arises from the kinds of writers and writing that appear in Westerns. Writers of fiction like Beauchamp and Moultrie are particular kinds of novelists, writers of cheap fiction. Since this was how the Western film was considered for many years, it is at first odd to see the Western film treat an antecedent like the Western novel so negatively, while writers of 'fact' are usually treated with more respect. This may be in part because newspapermen tend to be local rather than national, the conscience of a community, intervening for good in local politics, rather than relating preposterous stories for audiences elsewhere. Western films are wary of writers of fiction associated with the East, whereas local journalists are integral to the new Western community (an honourable exception is Horace Grealy, the newspaperman of the national New York Times, whose founding plea to 'Go West, young man!' supports the imperial enterprise of the Western).

REPRESENTING THE WEST

The West was written about in various media, from government policy documents to sensational journalism and from literary novels to dime novels

– cheap, slim papers that are the forerunners of comics and magazines. It is for these dime novels that we infer Beauchamp and Moultrie write. Yet, crucial as stories created by words were and still are to the formation of the Western film, there had to be pictures too. Imaging the West was just as central as writing was to imagining the West. Imaging took many forms, from paintings in exhibitions to illustrations in publications, and from photographs to films. Dime novels invariably included illustrations made from woodcuts and engravings, especially on front pages, with gunfight, lynching or Indian attack. The Western film also inherited traditions of drama from the nineteenth-century theatre and a peculiarly American variant of circus that staged stories of action and spectacle in Wild West Shows (Brasmer, 1977). The nineteenth-century forebears of the Western film are to be found in these interweaving words, pictures and dramatisations, all of which offered fertile soil for the later Western film.

As is clear from the above examples from *Unforgiven* and *Posse*, not all historical modes of representation preceding the Western film have been equally respected. Some media are associated with history and others with myth (even in Westerns), some with literary and cultural value and others with popular entertainments. If the printing press can produce tall tales as well as strive for accuracy, novelists operate in a hierarchy of writing. Henry Longfellow's epic narrative poem, *Hiawatha* (1858), or Jack Schaeffer's classic novel, *Shane* (1949), for example, may be dignified by study on a school English curriculum, but most fictional writing about the West – like the Western film itself – has been assigned the lower cultural status of romance, melodrama and the pulp novel. While literary forms like the novel and the poem are part of an official culture, the majority of Western fiction is not. The balance needs redressing and the full history should be better acknowledged.

THE WESTERN NOVEL

Western fiction is an intimate part of the rise of the American novel (Bold, 1987). Many fictions set in the West were written in the nineteenth century but two novelists in particular played a major part in founding conventions of the Western film. They are James Fenimore Cooper and Owen Wister.

The Leatherstocking Tales

The earliest antecedent of the Western action hero features in James Fenimore Cooper's series of five novels about Nathaniel Bumppo, the Leatherstocking. In a series of stories beginning with *The Pioneers* (1823) and ending with *The Deerslayer* (1841), Natty is a pioneer hero of adventure stories, the frontiersman journeying ever westward, between frontier settlement and the surrounding wilderness.

For John Cawelti in 1976, this movement makes him a figure caught between the contrasting ways of nature and civilisation, between lawlessness and settlement. Though responsible for opening the West up to Eastern advance, he is an isolated figure, distant from the social groups of settlers and townspeople who compose it. Cawelti sees him modelled on frontiersman Daniel Boone, whose ambivalence to the mobile frontier is wittily demonstrated in his story of a tendency to burn down his log cabin and move further west at the first sign of new settlers following his trail. For Henry Nash Smith, Natty has an ambiguous relation to the progress associated with the new forces of civilisation, existing both inside and outside them. In this relation, he represents the nineteenth-century ideological conflict between America's desire to continue the European westward drive and also to build a new democracy within a distinctively American national identity.

This ideological conflict is played out in tensions within Natty's own identity as well as in his actions. He is known by different names, including Deerslayer, Pathfinder and Hawk-eye (or Hawkeye, the name by which he is best known in over 30 subsequent film and television adaptations of the novel). He is 'a man who turns his back on white society. A man who keeps his moral integrity hard and intact. An isolate, almost selfless, stoic, enduring man, who lives by death, by killing, but is pure white' (Lawrence, 1956, p.329). He seems most like those with whom he chooses to keep intimate company. His closest ally is not a white man but the Indian, Chingachgook, last of the Mohicans, whose assimilation within the new (white) America contrasts with the brutal opposition of another tribe, the Hurons. Like Natty, Chingachgook stands in a contradictory relation to the racial groups around him, his own identity made less secure by events that appear fatally to determine his actions.

In *The Pioneers*, Cooper views westward advance optimistically but his most famous novel, *The Last of the Mohicans* (1826), is an elegy on the loss of positive values associated with a pastoral way of life contrasted with the violence and mob rule in the pioneer settlements. During the course of the novels, Natty becomes part of a wilderness tragically destroyed by the troubling advances of settlement. For Cawelti:

> *Cooper's transformation of his Western narrative from a story of the re-establishment of the gentry in the new West, to a tale of the isolated hero whose very virtues make him flee the oncoming civilisation, summarises the evolution of the Western from the epic of the pioneers in the nineteenth century to the ambiguous myth of the gunfighter in the 1950s (Western film).*

> *(Cawelti, 1976, p.195)*

Cooper's Leatherstocking Tales connect a European literary tradition to a burgeoning new American fiction, making him as central to American literature as he is to the Western. In the words of Clive Bush, Cooper:

> established the Manichean (American) landscape of storm and calm, settlement and wilderness, with characters modified from (Sir Walter) Scott romance, and enough political and ecological issues developed in a . . . world of . . . power plays to provide any genre with immortal life.

> (Bush in Buscombe, 1998, p.169)

Cooper's work influenced generations of classic American adventure novelists like Herman Melville and Ernest Hemingway, and informed the homespun stories of Mark Twain's Huckleberry Finn and Tom Sawyer (even though Twain was more cynical of Cooper's achievements). These writers were drawn upon by generations of Western film-makers, especially John Huston and Budd Boetticher. Stories of tragedy and survival at sea in Melville's *Moby Dick* (1859) and Hemingway's *The Old Man and the Sea* (1952) are transposed to a Western landscape in films like Huston's modern Westerns *The Treasure of the Sierra Madre* (1947) and *The Misfits* (1961), and in Boetticher's more traditional Westerns in the Ranown cycle of films with Randolph Scott, such as *The Tall T* (1957) and *Comanche Station* (1960). The masculine identity of the Western hero connects to Hemingway's exploration of a male culture of machismo forged by stress and pressure, especially in the exploration of the bullfight. The aphorisms of cracker barrel philosophy and wit characteristic of Mark Twain's stories find their way into the clipped, colloquial language of Western film scripts.

The Virginian

A generation later, Owen Wister's *The Virginian* (1902) is among the first of the popular literary Westerns of the twentieth century, and the best-selling book of its year. The cowboy hero is identified by no other name than The Virginian. Like The Man with No Name played over sixty years later by Clint Eastwood in the series of Italian Westerns directed by Sergio Leone, lack of personal identity marks the eponymous cowboy hero as exceptional, a breed different from other kinds of men, and a man of mystery.

The Virginian is recognisably the central protagonist of the classical Western film, a polite man of honour, assured in manner, laconic in speech, morally correct but unafraid of confrontation. The figure draws on a code of chivalry like Europe's mediaeval knights. A closer reference, however, is to an American development of this tradition of romance fiction, specifically to the courtly manners of the archetypal Southern gentleman embodied in a tradition of plantation fiction starting with Harriet Beecher Stowe's *Uncle Tom's Cabin* (1852).

The Virginian is just such a Southerner, taking his good manners and moral rectitude West. His actions also advance the expansion of Eastern interests just as much as Cooper's hero, although he is no pioneer. He represents generations that follow Natty, for whom the West offers firmer potential for occupation and settlement. Unlike Natty, the labours of the Virginian can be rewarded with marriage. These new conditions make the Virginian a character of romance fiction, in a narrative within which the combination of marriage and entrepreneurship is resolved. For Cawelti, Westerns made from 1900 to 1930 'follow Wister's *The Virginian* in creating plots of romantic synthesis' (Cawelti, 1976, p.72).

Yet the Virginian is no bourgeois gentleman, Southern or otherwise, but a new Western protagonist – the cowboy. From his first appearance, the Virginian is marked as a special kind of man, made heroic by his environment. The novel is narrated by an Easterner who is met by the cowboy at a Western rail station. During the journey to the ranch, Wister uses a debate between them about the landscape to explore the particularity of the Western experience. Many of the oppositions between the West and the East are played out. The East is associated with the constrictions of regulation and tradition, while the West is connected to ideas of freedom, potential and the future. As Cawelti says: 'Despite the appearance of wildness or squalor, this landscape is a place where deep truths of human nature and life, hidden in the East by artifices and traditions of civilization, are being known again' (ibid., p.220). Through the cowboy hero, the Easterner learns the code of the West, including an important distinction between law and justice in which the latter must prevail, even where it conflicts with (Eastern) law. The distinction can be taken to extremes of 'rough justice', where the behaviour of vigilantes may be justified in lawless conditions and it expresses the will of direct community action rather than remote legal institutions.

Cooper's troubled opposition between the natural wilderness and a lawless settlement is resolved in Wister's reconstruction of a burgeoning civilisation as lawless yet just. The cowboy hero thereby changes too. He becomes a hero who is prepared for violence and skilled in dealing with it, but only within the strict boundaries of defence of self or community. This code of honour rationalises and defends violent behaviour. It provides a morality that enables Westerns to honour the gunfighter whose actions against villainy may be unlawful, but embody a more meaningful justice.

The Virginian combines action adventure with romance. The hero courts the Eastern teacher and, in the same way as he wins over the Eastern visitor to a vision of the West at the start of the novel, he eventually persuades her to his side. This is not achieved without the usual romantic travails of courtship and obstacles to union. The heroine's resistance is however broken when she discovers the hero left for dead after an Indian attack and nurses him back to health. Union between East and West requires the heroine to change her affiliations, but not her feminine identity. In the process of exercising conventional feminine traits of caring, even mothering, she renounces her Eastern independence to join her Westerner in what might be called 'Western union'.

Where Cooper's pioneer hero is a figure uncertainly moving between civilisation and wilderness, Wister's hero functions to redefine those terms by opposing ideas of East and West. Elements of the two types of hero can combine in Western films in complex ways. For Cawelti (1976, p.209), Natty Bumppo represents central ideological ambiguities in the American dream of success through self-determination. For Douglas Pye (1996a, p.14), Natty's social position prohibits Cooper from conceiving of his working class hero as a subject of marriage and settlement in the new, classless, American ideal community. Alternatively, the Virginian's bourgeois refinement represents the idealised qualities desired in the new American democracy, enabling the hero to be rewarded with marriage and settlement.

THE ARCHETYPAL WESTERN HERO

Combining the two figures of the pioneer action adventurer and the romantic cowboy enables the Western film hero to take on a wide range of potential identities. Following Kitses, the hero can represent at a general level an ambivalence to a series of opposing ideas such as wilderness and civilisation, East and West and justice and law. Within that model, the hero may be classed or classless, a representative of bourgeois refinement or working class aspiration, and even an impossible ideal of a classless American future.

These two major American novelists provide the framework of central themes, characters, narrative structures and situations in the Western film. They directly and indirectly influence generations of film-makers, with many film versions using their titles, though more rarely their plots (especially in the many film versions and the television series of *The Virginian*). They also found wider Western fiction, including popular twentieth-century paperback novelists like Zane Grey, Max Brand and the British-based Louis L'Amour, whose extraordinarily prolific output constitute important contributions to the Western film as it developed.

Zane Grey is particularly influential. Between 1910 and 1930, Grey's novels had a huge influence on Hollywood Westerns, even on the use of the Western landscape. *Wildfire* (1915) is set in Monument Valley, a favoured venue for Westerns directed by John Ford. Five of Grey's novels were filmed in 1918 alone (Buscombe, 200, p.16). By the time of more recent writers like Cormac McCarthy, Thomas McGuane and Larry McMurtry, cinema and the novel become interconnected. However, whether this work should be seen in the tradition of the literary novel of Cooper, Wister and their contemporaries or in another tradition of pulp fiction is a moot point. It seems more likely that their novels are twentieth-century manifestations of the nineteenth-century dime novel.

THE DIME NOVEL

Between the publication dates of the major Western novels of Cooper and Wister lies the period in which most Western films are set. Concurrently, another Western hero develops in a shift away from Cooper's pastoral hero towards Wister's romantic ideal masculinity. This new Western hero appears in the mass publication pages of cheap fiction, such as dime novels. Although the Western novel has been treated with some respect as American literature, this is not the case for the dime novel. Western critics like Cawelti see the dime novel gradually simplifying Cooper's complex hero. However, cultural critics like Michael Denning understand this pulp fiction more positively.

American dime novels were cheap sensation fiction, pamphlets of no more than a hundred pages in length. They had European equivalents. In Britain, they were *penny dreadfuls*; 'dreadful' on account of both a sensational content to inspire dread and an indicator of the negative value placed upon them by consumers of the higher form of literary fiction. Their subjects were commonly crime, often violent crime. Elite attitudes to the nineteenth-century dime novel ape attitudes to the Western film in the first half of the twentieth century, which was one of despised popular entertainment. For Cawelti, the dime novel developed the Western 'as a form of adolescent escapism'. (1976, p.211). But for Denning, dime novels were a form of working-class recreation that offered a 'symbolic form of class conflict' (1987, p.66). Cawelti, like much Western film criticism, takes for granted the inferior literary status of the dime novel, yet cultural critics such as Denning argue that it was as meaningful to its largely working class readership as the literary novel was to its own, mainly bourgeois, readership.

According to Denning, the form of the dime novel inscribes the social class aspirations and interests of its working class readers. Though all social classes and genders read the dime novel, he associates its commercial rise with the newly politicised working classes of manual labourers, many of them immigrants, who were establishing themselves in American society in the latter part of the nineteenth century. Though dime novels were commercial enterprises, they were a central part of working class culture. Even labo(u)r newspapers –

newspapers read entirely by working class families – 'often carried serialised fiction that resembled dime novels in title and subject matter' (ibid., p.41). Denning's work helps to explain the powerful hold Western fiction has for a working class audience. His thesis is developed by Marcus Klein, who argues that it is the industrial class position of urban audiences whose response was most profound in contrast with the common assumption that the central appeal of the Western is to rural audiences.

Dime novels came in many genres, including detective stories, and romances aimed at a female readership (ibid., p.14). Even so, most critical attention has been paid to the Western dime novel and its male readership. Cawelti notes Robert Montgomery Bird's *Nick of the Woods* (1837) as a significant early transitional work, reducing Cooper's complex hero to a simpler avenging angel who rights wrongs, defending pioneers against savage Indians. Cawelti sees the dime novels continuing this process of simplification as the nineteenth century progresses. Increasingly, the West becomes a stage for male society, where camaraderie between men has little connection with their social institutions or regulations. The Western landscape also becomes less a stage for movement than for conflict. Villainy becomes as central as heroism, with villains as likely to be crooked Easterners as outlaw Westerners, though the worst villainy of all is overwhelmingly represented by savage Indians.

The emergence of the savage Indian as the central antagonist of Western dime novels has mainly been understood as a response to the frontier history of warfare between forces of colonising whites and Native Americans at the time of their writing. The dime novel was indeed responsible for new divisions, conflicts and evaluations entering Western fiction on racial lines. Richard Slotkin, however, argues in *The Fatal Environment* (1985) that this racial conflict should not be understood merely at face value, but needs to be placed in the context of industrial relations in an increasingly urbanised America. He notes how a new political rhetoric enters public debate in the late nineteenth century in response not so much to developments in the West as to increasing politicisation and labour conflicts in Eastern industrial and urban centres. The rhetoric concerns distinctions between the compliant worker and the self-interested labourer whose industrial action is constructed among élite circles in ways that favour the interests of capital and management. Slotkin's research into this period reveals that a politically-aware new industrial working class in America is constructed as 'savage' and hence allied to the 'savage Indian' as objects that the new America must overcome. For Slotkin, then, the emergence of the savage Indian in the dime novel is a fictional displacement of a newly class-conscious, activist and politically-oppositional American working class, whose new visibility is a shock to the body politic of an older WASP America. The importance of the revelation to subsequent generations is that it explores an interracial bond between white western consumers and Indians otherwise difficult to fathom (Pumphrey, 2001; Neale, 1998).

The interests of its working class readership can be seen in the narrative structures of dime novels. The new Western hero as a figure at the centre of a Manichean vision of good and evil is evident in Edward Ellis' *Seth Jones or The Captive of the Frontier* (1860). Here, however, the hero is an Easterner disguised as a backwoodsman, with both the native skills to track Indians and the courtly manners to win his sweetheart teacher. Nash Smith argues that Seth Jones is a 'neat manoeuvre for combining the picturesque appeal of the "low" hunter with the official status of the "straight" upper-class hero' (1971(50), p.25). In the figure of Seth Jones, the identity of Cooper's pioneer begins to be confused and looks forward to the courtly elements of Wister's hero.

In the Deadwood Dick stories of Edward L. Wheeler, character psychology and narrative development are less important than action and situation. *Deadwood Dick on Deck or Calamity Jane, The Heroine of Whoop-Up* (1878) – a shorter story than the length of its title might suggest – extends the disguise of Seth Jones to all its characters. The meaning of disguise is coded in a plot device in melodrama, where it features among a number of tropes to do with secrecy, surprise and revelation (Gledhill, 1987, pp.18–38). For Denning, disguise is a method by which working class readers and audiences can symbolically explore their class identity, by trying out other social class positions to contrast with their own (1987, pp.146–8).

Deadwood Dick also represents another feature of the Western dime novel, in the making of the outlaw hero. As Daryl Jones says: 'Never before had a Western hero openly defied the law. Never before had a Western hero reacted against social restraint so violently as to waylay stages and rob banks' (1978, p.81). For Nash Smith, Deadwood Dick loosens the ties to history so firmly represented by Natty Bumppo, reflecting instead the American ideal of the self-made man. Furthermore, Nash Smith sees the Deadwood Dick stories revealing 'a progressive deterioration in the Western story as a genre', losing 'whatever chance it might once have had to develop social significance' (1971(50), pp.100–2). Again, Denning's analysis is more positive. He claims Nash Smith overlooks Dick's outlawry and the social claims the novels make for his outlaw rebellion. Like the real life outlaws, the James Brothers (Settle, 1966) and the Dalton Gang, who are frequently fêted in fiction as Robin Hood figures rather than vicious thugs, Dick's outlawry is treated as a defensible response to Southern land dispossession and economic depression. Divorced from its Southern location, land dispossession becomes a defining feature of Westerns, particularly series Westerns (Stanfield, 1998).

For Denning, the Deadwood Dick novels reinterpret the myth of the frontier away from stories of westward expansion towards stories of social class conflict, making them easier to interpret for working class readers 'as an allegorical republic of outlaws, forming a cooperative commonwealth, threatened by the social structures of the East' (1987, p.165). Incredibly, the outlaw figure who emerges from the development of Western fiction in the dime novel is recognisably the gunfighter hero of the Western film (Rosa, 1969). Though an outlaw, possibly a mercenary or bounty hunter, who lives by the gun, Western fiction renders the figure a basically moral, democratic representative of a common man criminalized by Eastern law and values.

For Daryl Jones, among other critics of the dime novel, the ideological conflicts noted in Western literature are as evident in dime novels. However, the nature of the conflicts tends to change over time and with these come shifts in attitudes to the West. The pastoral vision of a wilderness waiting to be tamed by a Utopian eastern settlement is evident in mid-century dime novels like *Seth Jones*. Research into a collection of dime novels published by Beadle and Adams from the 1870s onwards suggests a 'Wild' West is more likely to be found as the century nears its end. The end-of-the-century dime novel offers a Badlands territory in which the isolated hero must brave perilous adventures in his quest for a missing partner or reward. As Stephen Tatum puts it in *The BFI Companion to the Western* (1988):

whereas early dime novels focussed on the settler's triumph over both nature and Indians, later ones emphasise both the social problems (gambling; political corruption; blackmail; theft; land hunger) besetting newly established frontier towns or mining camps and the actions taken to resolve them.

(Tatum in Buscombe, 1988, pp.109–10)

Such a shift is also evident in the history of the Western film, where romantic pastoral visions of the west are more likely in films before the Second World War, whereas quest narratives are a strong feature of post-War Westerns.

The cowboy hero of the dime novel evolves from the adventure figure of Cooper's frontier backwoodsman into the romantic hero of Wister's Virginian. The hero of the dime novel *Nick of the Woods* (1837) is a rough, violent Indian-hater but Harry Ringwood, turn of the century hero of *Old King Brady and Billy the Kid* (1890), is a more polished and youthful figure whose knowledge of the West is informed by his aged sidekick, Brady. The division of the earlier dime novel hero into this later partnership prefigures an important relationship between older and younger men in later Western films. The hero of many Westerns has a sidekick (Rothel, 1960), often a garrulous old-timer to the laconic, more youthful hero; for example, in series Westerns featuring George 'Gabby' Hayes as sidekick to – most famously – Hopalong

Cassidy (William Boyd), and in A features with actors like Walter Brennan, especially as Stumpy to John Wayne's Chance in *Rio Bravo* (1958).

Finally, the dime novel also demonstrates an evolution in the idea of westward expansion, from the idea of pioneer westward movement as a contradictory but inherently moral task towards the idea of a settled West as a stage for conflicts over more ambiguous treatments of law and order. This shift from the imperial narrative to the crime narrative is also evident in storytelling tendencies in later Western films. In the last days of the dime novel, the cowboy hero can represent community interests or, more problematically, moral authority over the community's unacceptable version of civilisation. Again, this prefigures a similar shift in the position of the Western film hero, from pre-War figures like Wyatt Earp (Henry Fonda) in *My Darling Clementine* (1946) as agents of pacification and settlement, to post-War figures like Patch Williams (Richard Widmark), whose rule of law is challenged by the town's elders in *Death of a Gunfighter* (1969).

During the lifetime of the dime novel, a major historical shift occurs. America experiences economic modernisation and develops from a centrally rural economy to an urban, industrial one. And since a comparable shift is evident in Western films before and after the Second World War, it would be valuable to investigate comparable wider correlations between these fictional changes and American society, perhaps drawing attention to the significance of America's changing global role in world affairs over the same period. That research, however, has yet to be done.

PICTURING THE WEST

Illustrations were essential to the popular success of dime novels. Front covers were dominated by a sensational image illustrating a story on the pages within. However, images of the West abounded elsewhere and long before. In the nineteenth-century, homes and public buildings displayed chromolithographs (colour prints made from tinted plates of paintings and drawings) and, later on, monochrome and colour-tinted photographs. Indeed, visual images were central to imagining the West from the very first days of the European colonisation of America.

And where pictures played a part, so too did drama. Fiction was not only illustrated but also dramatised and performed in a peculiarly American form of circus known as the Wild West Show. It was also adapted for the melodrama stage, as is suggested by the example mentioned earlier of the trope of disguise shared with the dime novel. This also points towards the important role that various forms of nineteenth-century dramatisation played in the narratives and situations of later Western films. But any dramatic form requires costume, setting, décor and props to visualise its drama. Visual sources for the Western film are as varied and complex as writing and drama.

PAINTING AND ILLUSTRATION

Chris Brookeman (in Buscombe, 1988, pp.60–3) offers a concise history of artists and illustrators of the West from the establishment of the first colonies on the eastern seaboard in the sixteenth-century. Later Western expeditions also charted a landscape through visual representations that contribute to the iconography of the West. Watercolour drawings and engravings were used to illustrate histories and fictions alike (Samuels, 1976).

From the outset, picturing the Americas was bound up in two conflicting European ideas of what North America was to mean. On one side were romantic images of the landscape and its native inhabitants, perhaps mingled with ethnographic studies attempting to record and preserve found nature and native culture. Later Western artists exemplify strains of this tradition, like the wild landscapes of the Rocky Mountain School, such as Albert Bierstadt's *The Oregon Trail* (1869) and Thomas Moran's paintings in Yellowstone Park. George Caleb Bingham's pictures of pioneer trappers and riverboat men on the Missouri River, begun in 1845, exemplify a clear ethnographic strain. Very different, however, is the tradition of sensationalised scenes of native torture and brutality illustrated by Seth Eastman's infamous picture of an Indian scalping in *The Death Whoop*. Eastman's additional paintings of Indians were more ethnographic and illustrated geographies of the Americas, yet, like many of his contemporaries, he was not averse to producing the occasional exaggeration for fictional publications.

These traditions of image-making served different interests. The land and its people might be idealised for the purpose of encouraging investment in exploration and land appropriation. Its peoples might be depicted as savages for quite another purpose, which was to fuel religious missions and/or to justify land appropriation through military conquest. These two conflicting themes of alternative representations of the idealised and barbarous West relate to Henry Nash Smith's idea of the contradictory relation between the West as Garden and Wilderness. Yet there is another way of thinking about how this binary theme can be located in images of the West. Landscape imagery may offer diverse natural scenery but it is invariably visual spectacle of great natural beauty, usually on a grand scale and observed by the artist from afar. Action imagery, alternatively, offers scenes of events and situations dramatised in still life, often on a more intimate scale and observed from close to or within the action itself. Both tendencies may be spectacular, but one tends towards the aesthetic and the other towards the dramatic. The tension in the Western between epic grandeur and sensational event, still life and dynamic action, is also evident in these two alternative traditions of image-making.

These themes and traditions of image-making were used in a wide range of publications and for many purposes, but with determinate effects. For instance, Seth Eastman's *Death Whoop* illustrates lurid dime novel tales, but his ethnographic drawings illustrate a serious government publication about the Indian. Bingham's popular engravings of frontiersmen were serious attempts at ethnographic record, but his epic painting of Daniel Boone fed ideologies of imperial advance. Often the same Western artists and illustrators worked in conflicting traditions and across many media.

The work of Western artists and illustrators had material and ideological effects. From the 1870s onwards, Thomas Moran's idealised paintings of Yellowstone Park contributed to the decision to designate it a national park. More dramatically, the landscapes and early ethnographies of native Americans painted by artists like Karl Bodmer and George Catlin contributed in different ways to understandings of Native American culture. During the 1830s, Bodmer painted exotic scenes of a range of tribes, including Mandan, Blackfoot and Cree Indians. As many of these tribes were exterminated by smallpox shortly after contact with whites, these images are all that remain of them and thus have become important historical documents. In contrast, from 1832, Catlin painted over five hundred portraits of Indian chiefs and their tribal cultures. Catlin's intention was to inform public awareness and government policy at the time to protect traditional ways of native life. The effect, however, was to stereotype Native Americans in the romantic image of the Plains Indian (Webb, 1931), in a process that ultimately led to policies of forced migrations and extermination. Catlin's images of the Plains Indian became the undifferentiated 'Indian' of the popular imagination, from the spectacle of the Indian village complete with tepees to the spectacle of male action in the buffalo hunt.

Perhaps more influentially, various vast canvasses on the theme of westward expansion exhibited in the East inspired a generation of settlers to make the dangerous trek westward and prompted capitalist investment in land acquisition that led to the almost total destruction of Native America. Among such imperialist imagery is Emanuel Leutz' romantic *Westward the Course of Empire Takes its Way* (1859) and Currier and Ives' primitive *Across the Continent* (1868), still on prominent display in the Museum of the City of New York. This tradition of landscape painting bolstered the frontier thesis and its association with the idea of a specifically American cultural identity (Teague, 1997, p.3).

Artists such as Charles Marion Russell and Frederic Remington have been seen as very influential in creating images and situations that inspired Western fiction. Russell's first paintings are of cowboys in action, roping and riding horses and, later, in scenes suggesting narrative dramas such as *In Without Knocking* (1909), where cowboys ride their horses raucously into a saloon, guns blazing. Prompted by Catlin's images of the Plains Indian, Remington's dynamic movement across the canvas and close to the action contributed to the iconography, framing and composition of typical Western scenarios. In *Downing the Nigh Leader* (1903), the Indian action of Catlin's buffalo hunt is copied with the added sensation of a stagecoach as the target. The self-explanatory *Cavalry Charge on the Southern Plain* (1907) provides a visual reference to similar scenes in many cavalry Westerns, in particular those directed by John Ford. While Russell and Remington pictorialised Western situations from the gunfight to the saloon brawl, the colour scheme and lighting style of John Ford's *She Wore a Yellow Ribbon* (1949) explicitly recall Remington's paintings.

Elsewhere, few films directly invoke Western painting, though Remington and Russell's paintings are reproduced in the credit sequences of *The Last Hunt* (1956) and *Monte Walsh* (1970). Perhaps the most significant use of a painting in a Western is in another of Ford's cavalry films, *Fort Apache* (1948). Ford climaxes the action of the film with Custer's Last Stand in all but name (Neale, 1995), as an equally vainglorious officer (Colonel Thursday played by Henry Fonda) brazenly ignores experienced advice and leads his men into an Indian ambush. Although Ford shows us the reality of unnecessary death, we witness the army sanction the myth of glorious defeat in a famous coda to the film. We have seen Major York (John Wayne) witness the true conditions of their defeat, but after acquiring Thursday's title and authority, he attests before journalists to the veracity of the overblown epic painting of the event displayed in Washington, the centre of American politics. Standing in front of a portrait of Thursday, superimposed images of the dead ride past before him as he delivers a eulogy to the memory of their bravery and sacrifice. In this moment, Ford shows an awareness of the myth-making function of much Western painting and of its power to serve the interests of westward expansion. Ford ensures that the audience is made absolutely aware that his characters are agents of both myth and history which demonstrates his own desire to expose the myth even as he honours it, in an ambivalent attitude to westward expansion found elsewhere in his films (French, 1998, pp.12–14).

A necessary caution must be exercised over attributing too much of the formation of the Western imaginary to these particular artists. Much of their work was done at the turn and in the first part of the twentieth century and was popularised through mass-produced magazine publications like *Harper's Weekly*, by which time many of the Western themes and situations had been established in earlier fiction and imagery. Indeed, by this time films had already begun to tell stories about the West, albeit in short and reductive form. Much of the influence of Russell and Remington should be seen as concurrent with rather than preceding the development of Western film iconography. Their influence on the Western film might be better considered as similar to twentieth-century Western novelists like Zane Grey and Louis L'Amour.

PHOTOGRAPHY OF THE WEST

The American novel, illustration and painting had long European traditions to draw upon and to adapt to American themes. The new technological media of photography and film emerged virtually simultaneously in Europe and America and crossed nineteenth-century national cultures, making it a more international medium. At this time it was also a bourgeois medium. The prohibitive costs of the technology and raw materials necessary to produce images on light-sensitive paper meant that only the moneyed and dedicated specialist could afford investment. It was not until the twentieth century, with the development of the domestic box camera, that home photography became affordable and widely available. This ensured that photography's earliest uses were bound up in the interests of a particular social class culture. Recognisable photographic conventions today such as snapshots of the family, holiday and special occasions are rooted in the domestic and tourist photography of the nineteenth-century bourgeoisie.

The impulse to record places and scenes to mark the passage of the European bourgeois traveller is just as evident in American Western photography (Goetzmann and Goetzmann, 1986). Yet few people experienced photographs of the West directly as photographs. Like paintings of the West they were more commonly accessible as reproductions in the form of illustrations in dime novels and publications like *Harper's Weekly*. This means that, on first publication, most images of the West could not be distinguished either as paintings or photographs. It is only twentieth-century viewers who are able to make such distinctions. Nonetheless, photography made its own individual contribution to the visual representation of the West.

Painting could construct the grandeur of landscape and freeze moments in a spectacle of action better than the monochrome prints and slow film speeds of nineteenth-century camera technology. But if photography was not up to some tasks, it was better at others. Photography would merely supplement earlier modes of representation were it not for the authority of the photographic image as record. In the reproduction of the likeness of living scenes and peoples, the photographic camera recorded the West with new ways of seeing. Most importantly perhaps, were photographic close-ups offered in portraiture. Indian chiefs are magnificently dignified in photographs of cragged faces by A.C. Vroman. Edward S. Curtis 'thought of himself as documenting [in artificially staged scenes] the last images of a vanishing race' (Jay, 2000, p.7). The wonderfully-named Camillus S. Fly photographed mug shots of captured outlaws and the bodies of dead captives on public display. Notorious lawmen and criminals alike volunteered to freeze their images for posterity by visiting any one of numerous photography studios in frontier towns and travelling wagons. The status of such photographs as evidence rather than representation accords with the use of historic photographs in Western films. The credit sequences of *Butch Cassidy and the Sundance Kid* (1969), *The Culpepper Cattle Company* (1972) and *Posse* (1993) use sepia-tinted authentic photographs to verify the films' fictionalised tales of their outlaws and cowboys.

Photographers are even more rare than wordsmiths in Western films, though there is one happy to record 'the only photographs of hostile Indians' in *Geronimo: An American Legend* (1994); another records for posterity the image of a woman who passed as a man at the end of *The Ballad of Little Jo* (1993); and *The Grey Fox* (1982) has the only female photographer in a Western. She appears as an independent free spirit, whereas frontier photography was more often bound up in the service of government agencies and commercial enterprises. These organisations required the same images and themes established by the painterly traditions of Western landscapes and ethnographic portraiture, with the added authentic recording properties of the photograph. Indeed, photographers and painters were often employed side by side to capture the grandeur and scale of the landscape in monochrome photography and its chromatic hues in paint (Taft, 1964). Photographer William Henry Jackson, for instance, accompanied painter Thomas Moran in the task of immortalising Yellowstone Park. Painters even worked from photographs rather than the original scene, including painters as famous as Frederic Remington.

From the manufacturers of wagon trains to the cattle ranchers who settled vast tracts of land, all agencies of westward expansion employed photographers to record their progress (Gidley in Buscombe 1988, p.199). Alexander Forbes recorded the race for land claims at the Cherokee Strip in 1889 in images of wagons lined up and then racing to stake claims. These have fed directly into film representations of any land rush, including *Tumbleweeds* (1925) and the various versions of *Cimarron* (1931, 1960). Andrew J. Russell photographed the progress of the Union Pacific Railroad and was present to record the symbolic joining of East and West coasts when the transcontinental track met at Promontory Point, Utah in 1869 (the photograph is brought to life in a scene from *The Iron Horse*, 1924). The photograph gave added authority to such historical events, validating ideological expressions of manifest destiny.

The climactic scene of *The Iron Horse* (1924) reproduces the photographing of the transcontinental track meeting at Promontory Point, Utah in 1869, symbolically joining America's East and West coasts.

As film references to photographs indicate, photography provided an important source of situations and compositions for the Western film. Photography 'established a very recognisable iconography of river bend, cattle on sandbars, mid-day meals, the corral, high noon, captured thieves, Deadwood and so on' (Bush in Buscombe 1988, p.169). Mick Gidley writes of how the lone figure in the landscape of William Henry Jackson's photograph, *North from Berthoud Pass*, 'is a definitive romantic evocation of the westering experience' (Gidley in Buscombe 1988, p.200). Photography's contribution to the imagining of the West was as varied, complex and ideological as the painterly tradition; what it added was a more pressing authority to the idea of the West as a material, physical space.

DRAMATISING THE WEST

The written word and the still image provide antecedents for the narratives, characters, themes, situations and iconography of the Western film. The final pieces of the jigsaw of antecedents can be found in those cultural forms that dramatise written stories and images in movement, sound and performance.

The facilitating term here is staging; how these writings and images were combined in the staging of the West through public entertainments. Western images and fictions were staged in various ways in the latter part of the nineteenth century, even as the frontier was still advancing. In a similar way to the simultaneous interaction of the history and the representation of the West, what was staged was closely allied to and yet significantly changing the real events and personalities they referred to. Staging the West through modes of performance was the crucial final element among the range of antecedents of the Western film.

Rodeo

Rodeo offers the closest connection between public entertainments and Western life. It is a wholly American cultural form. The dangers posed to participants by events centring on the control of wild animals allies the rodeo ring closer to the rituals of the Spanish bullring than the theatre of America's wrestling ring. In twentieth-century America, it evolved into a hugely popular spectator sport. Professionals competed for prize money in designated arenas in a network of staged events regulated by official bodies. But in the nineteenth century, rodeo was a loose and occasional federation of events, which exhibited a relaxed and informal exhibition of cowboy skills.

The word 'rodeo' is Spanish and refers to the 'round-up' of cattle on ranches for transportation to slaughter. The round-up was a significant climax to the seasons of annual activity on a cattle ranch. Although the precise origins of rodeo are unclear, it is likely they lie in the annual display of cowboy skills that formed a part of the celebrations after successful round-ups and market sales to the beef industry. The first rodeos probably offered displays of broncho-busting, in which captured wild horses are ridden to an exhausted standstill – with or without saddles – but not until many riders are thrown from their bucking mounts. Roping skills would probably be showcased since cowboys used ropes in their working lives to tether cattle for branding. Other rodeo events are less connected to a cowboy's daily routine and more to display related skills in imagined activities. Bull-dogging, which was jumping from a fast-moving horse onto the back of a running steer and pulling it to the ground and riding the Brahma bulls used in modern rodeos are unlikely events in the lives of working cowboys. That such additional events are features of rodeo in recent times is more likely due to the opportunities they offer for romantic extension of daily cowboy skills. Rodeo as it was then and is now suggests that nineteenth-century cowboys were as likely to contribute to myth-making about themselves as any others.

Rodeo's influence is everywhere evident in Western films. Riding, roping, broncho-busting and bull-dogging are common features of Westerns, especially those that stage the routines of cattle-ranch life. *Cowboy* (1958) integrates both rodeo's likely and less likely everyday cattle-ranch activities into its depiction of round-up and cattle trail, using the events to make a cowboy's life appear hard yet romantic. Such events also contribute significant conventions to Westerns. In *Cowboy*, again, the greenhorn Easterner, Frank Harris (Jack Lemmon) learns that life on the trail will be exhausting from the moment he is required by his trail boss (Glenn Ford) to bust a broncho. Rites of passage into manhood for young cowboys may be affirmed by the first branding (*Man Without a Star*, 1955) and the first roping (*Red River*, 1948) of steers. When the hero in *The Tall T* (1957) loses a bet to ride a bull in exchange for his horse, it demonstrates his risk-taking character and the sacrifice he is prepared to make to build his stock and his future life. The display of rodeo skills in a Western generally underlines the rugged masculinity and charismatic dynamism of the Western hero. Yet, when prepared to face challenges even without these skills, it may serve to demonstrate the hero's psychological maturity and moral strength. The Eastern hero of *The Big Country* (1958) will refuse to ride a difficult horse in front of a group of cynical cowboys yet test himself against the animal in the privacy of night.

Rodeo has also been the subject of a small number of films in a sub-genre of Westerns in modern settings. Indeed, the rodeo Western is an important component of the elegiac Western that develops from the 1950s onwards.

The Wild West Show

Rodeo was also a part of and a major influence on the first Wild West Shows that began to appear from around 1880. These were even more spectacular events, featuring displays of cowboy skills together with more traditional circus skills, but in the context of reconstructions of events in frontier history. The Wild West Show was thus a type of circus adapted from the older European tradition to service its own American cultural spectacle. Many Wild West Shows appeared in the late nineteenth century (Bush in Buscombe 1988, pp.238–40). The full title of '*Gordon W. Lillie/Pawnee Bill's Historical Wild West Exhibition and Indian Encampment*' (1888) suggests the content and its admixture of (historical and ethnographic) education and (sensational and voyeuristic) entertainment. Another touring Show, *The Miller Brothers 101 Ranch Wild West Show*, also provided personnel and props for many early films (Wallis, 2000). But William F. Cody's 'Wild West' was easily the best known and most influential Show in its time (Blackstone, 1986).

Better known by his stage-name, 'Buffalo Bill', Cody is a key figure in the transition between frontier history and the Western film (Buscombe, 1988, pp.91–2). He was a prominent celebrity in the frontier West, renowned as an army scout and buffalo hunter, whose fame exceeded his localised celebrity when he became the subject of *Buffalo Bill, the King of the Border Men*, a serial published in the New York Weekly in 1869 (Rainey, 1996, p.2) and subsequently the first of four dime novels about him written by Ned Buntline in the 1870s. In that decade, the huge popularity of these fictions enabled Cody to travel. In winter, he was in the East, playing himself in theatrical versions of his life in the West. In summer, he was back in the West, where he continued as a scout and also as an escort to Easterners touring the West. Cody's biography exemplifies the increasing interaction of Western history and its cultural representation as the nineteenth century wore on. His claim to killing and scalping the Indian chief, Yellow Hand, during Custer's campaign against the Sioux at the Battle of War Bonnet Creek, is just one of many that made Cody's fame widespread. Much of the purpose behind Cody's clothing was show business; familiar from photographs of him in light buckskin and long hair flowing behind him as he walked, he consciously dressed for the battle in a Mexican stage costume, so that he could boast it was the same he wore when he took 'the first scalp for Custer'. Cody capitalised on his fame by setting up 'Buffalo Bill's Wild West and Congress of Rough Riders of the World' in 1883, a Show that toured America and Europe for thirty years, dramatising the idea of the frontier West as a place of spectacle and drama (Slotkin, 1992, pp.66–9).

Buffalo Bill's Wild West set the pattern for all Wild West Shows. It had native Americans (including for a time, chiefs like Sitting Bull and Geronimo), playing out scenes from village life but in dramas about rescuing captive white women. Cowboys like Buck Taylor and Johnny Baker, 'The Cowboy Kid', reproduced skills of riding and roping. There were rodeo events like bull-dogging, provided for spectacle rather than prizes, and European circus-style acts featuring trained horses and trick riders. Set pieces were reconstructions of famous Western events that both borrowed from earlier representations and also contributed to new ones. An Indian attack on the Deadwood Stage, for instance, was probably modelled on Frederic Remington's painting, *Downing the Nigh Leader*. The massacre at the Little Big Horn was also reconstructed, with the final iconic (if highly unlikely) image of the heroic Custer as the last man standing. At the time, there were chromolithographs of Custer's Last Stand, all constructing the defeat as heroic, but later paintings famously fixed the final moment as Cody had staged it, especially in the most familiar version, by Cassily Adams (*Custer's Last Stand*, 1896). The spectacular climax, though, was invariably 'A Grand Hunt on the Plains' (Bush in Buscombe 1988, pp.238–9), where the full cast stampeded a bizarre mixture of deer, elk, mountain sheep, wild horses and cattle (some disguised as buffalo) around the circus ring, firing blank shots into the air. The Wild West Show incorporated a disparate array of Western, Eastern and European personnel, props and events into making the West spectacular.

Although the composition of Cody's variety programme changed over time, 'the bullet, not the plough' (Worland and Countryman, p.183) of Turner's 'frontier hypothesis' was central to his and all other Wild West Shows. Perhaps even more than Western characters, rodeo skills and frontier reconstructions, the stars of Cody's Wild West were sharpshooters like Lillian Smith and – for seventeen years – Annie Oakley (nicknamed 'Little Sure Shot', but born Phoebe Moses and raised in Ohio), whose skill with the rifle was unmatched. This much but little else is true of *Annie Oakley* (1935), in which Barbara Stanwyck plays her as a feisty romantic heroine, and the musical biopic, *Annie Get Your Gun* (1950), but both exhibit something of the variety and spectacle of the Show in the surrounding backdrops. Tricks and play with guns were the basic stock in trade of the Wild West Show and gave the word 'gunplay' to gunfights in Western films. The West became the Wild West when it was turned into a spectacle of action and costume, and a shrine to the power of the gun as entertainment.

William Goetzmann in *Exploration and Empire* (1966) suggests that the origins of the Wild West Show even precede the days of Western frontier expansion, seeing artist George Catlin as a precursor with his Indian Gallery of 1837 where he exhibited paintings of Indian tribes together with costumes and artefacts from 1839. But most critics accept Henry Nash Smith's suggestion that the precedent is Cody's orchestration of an 1882 Fourth of July celebration in Nebraska. Certainly, a range of cultural events in the East throughout the century offered the West as forms of staged spectacle, but it was Cody who brought theatre to what was essentially a new and specifically American circus experience. The Wild West Show dramatised and performed Western fiction. In staging the Wild West, this entertainment form provided the most direct antecedent to the spectacle of action in the Western film.

Theatre

'Buffalo Bill' Cody is a key figure among the antecedents of the Western film. As a Westerner, he contributed to the history of the West, to its fictionalisation and to its theatrical staging. He is the clearest individual demonstration of how nineteenth-century history interacted with its representation in fiction, pictorialisation and show business in the formation of the Western film (his image is interrogated in the revisionist Western, *Buffalo Bill and the Indians, or Sitting Bull's History Lesson*, 1976). Yet these are just the most recognised of the antecedents, as is revealed in one further role played by the ubiquitous Cody. He was also an occasional actor, playing his alter ego, Buffalo Bill, at first on the Chicago stage in *The Scouts of the Prairie* (1872), a fitting demonstration of theatre's importance in the origins of the Western film. If Cody's

Wild West established the spectacle of Western action, nineteenth-century theatre – specifically, melodrama theatre – merged all other antecedents in the spectacle of Western narrative.

Recognition of the role of nineteenth-century theatre is more common in Western films than in Western criticism. Theatres are common in Westerns though they tend to be disguised as or in saloons. The Western saloon invariably stages a sideshow to the main entertainment of drinking. This can take the humble form of a honky-tonk piano in the corner of a small town bar or perhaps a guitarist in a Mexican cantina. More likely, there will be a stage on which 'saloon girls' will form a chorus line to sing a song and down from which the leading chanteuse will tour the bar-room, tousling men's hair and flirting with them. The stage is especially important to musical Westerns like *Calamity Jane* (1953) where the numbers are choreographed on and around the stage, and include the more musical genre convention of backstage scenes. All this underlines the important contribution of theatrical forms of music, song and dance to the Western genre. It also acknowledges the importance of American vaudeville and the European music hall traditions, from whence the Western drew its catalogue of popular song and 'call and response' between performer and audience.

Dramatic theatre is less a feature of Westerns but it is very suggestive of antecedents when it appears. Although the Western town rarely has its own theatre as it does in *Calamity Jane*, any public space can be adapted into a theatre for touring players. Alan Mowbray features in theatrical roles in *My Darling Clementine* and in *Wagonmaster* (1950). In both, he is a comic figure and in the first, he hams his way through scenes from Shakespeare, even taken seriously for a brief moment before forgetting the words to Hamlet's soliloquy. But classics of another kind of theatre are the usual Western fare. In *Heller in Pink Tights* (1960), the cross-dressing heroine plays a classical Polish prince, Mazeppa, from the melodrama repertoire, tied naked to a horse and whipped through the wilderness. The scene is recreated with the aid of a body stocking on Sophia Loren, cross-dressing as the prince, while a screen revolves around a mechanical travelator on which a horse pounds away without leaving the stage. Meanwhile, an offstage wind machine and sound effects create the impression of a storm. The film points to a more general link between the construction of performance on stage and screen through the conventions of theatrical melodrama.

As the scene in *Heller in Pink Tights* suggests, nineteenth-century melodrama was sensational in its staging. Plays were 'theatrical spectacles with elaborate special effects and mechanisms – trains, fires and live animals on stage – while prefiguring the close relation between popular fiction and the modern cinema' (Denning, 1987, p.25). Melodrama theatres were a feature of all major American towns, especially in Eastern cities where they were the most popular of popular entertainments, especially for working class and immigrant audiences. There were also travelling theatre troupes, who toured frontier towns; *Heller in Pink Tights* is 'loosely based on the career of Adah Isaac Menken who brought culture and the footlights to the frontier in the 1860s' (Hardy, 1991, p.276).

Melodrama theatre drew on popular plays from Europe and America. There were many genres of melodrama, including domestic melodramas about innocent women seduced by immoral men, crime melodramas about moral men tricked into crime, and the frontier (or wilderness) melodrama, a wholly American form of melodrama and forerunner of the twentieth-century Western. Melodramatists regularly looked to sensational and scandalous events of their day to turn into stories to perform on the stage. Accordingly, some frontier melodramas featured famous Western characters, mainly those imagined in dime novels. William Cody was not the only Westerner to appear as himself; another Westerner starred as himself in Frank H. Murdoch's play *Davy Crockett* (1872).

This interaction of life and art is a common theme in Westerns featuring historical characters. In *The Return of Frank James* (1940), for example, the eponymous outlaw (Henry Fonda) witnesses just such a retelling of his own story and the creaky melodrama suddenly springs to life when Bob Ford (John Carradine) arrives to reproduce his dastardly shooting of Frank's brother, Jesse James. The film goes one stage further, reproducing the scene of the assassination of Lincoln as Frank leaps onto the stage from his theatre box to give chase to the actor/murderer.

Many films are also based on popular melodramas, among them *The Great Train Robbery*, made into a film in 1903. Actors in silent Western films were often stage actors before taking to the screen. Of the three notable Western film stars of the silent period, two were stage actors before performing on film; the film character of Broncho Billy was developed by G.M. Anderson and William S. Hart appeared in a stage version of Owen Wister's novel, *The Virginian* (1907), and also in *The Squaw Man* (1905), before this play was filmed as one of the first feature-length Westerns in 1914.

Melodrama

As the name suggests, melodrama is drama with music. America inherited this dramatic form from Europe where it originated when popular and low theatre forms were strictly controlled. Forbidden by law from using the spoken word, music was used instead to cue meaning and create empathy. Without speech, an elaborated performance style based on a language of gesture developed. By the late nineteenth century, the original prohibitions on the spoken word had died away, leaving behind a characteristically florid, declamatory and emotional language in dialogue, joining with excess in music and perform-ance to express an intensity of feelings.

Stories of innocent victims, unable to defend themselves against unspeak-able acts of villainy, are central to the Manichean (polarised moral) world of melodrama. Importantly, these stories are explored from the point of view of individuals who represent oppressed social groups. An innocent worker, youth and/or, especially, woman, is ranged against the villainy of exploitative landed gentry, bourgeoisie and/or corrupt élites, all invariably played by older men. There is an evident political project in melodrama's concern to side with the underdog or, as Michael Walker puts it: '. . . littleness, inadequacy, deprivation, grievance . . . the spirit of blame and indignation, the finding of scapegoats and the punishing of the guilty: in sum, a concern with ordering the world' (1982, pp.2–3).

However, not all melodramas are resolved happily. The aesthetic is flexible enough to draw on a range of narrative possibilities with no certain moral outcome. The only certainty is that the world is a moral one. As Robert Lang puts it, 'the melodramatic imagination is profoundly moral . . . clear notions of good and evil prevail . . . melodrama seeks to reveal a moral universe in operation, even where it is unable to show good triumphing' (1989, p.18). Or, in the words of one of the major theorists of the melodramatic imag-ination, Peter Brooks, melodrama turns 'less on the triumph of good over evil than on making the world morally legible' (1976, p.4).

The reason for this diversity and variability lies in the history of melodrama as a suppressed cultural form. Borrowing from more respectable forms around it made melodrama a cultural magpie. From tragedy, it takes a dystopian view of human society and human weakness, but melodrama changes its protagonist from one with social power to one with none, the lowliest of lowly subjects. From comedy, it takes the idea that the tragedy of life is indeed inherently comic but, unlike comedy, refuses to accept the social conditions it finds itself in. As Robert Heilman puts it: '. . . the melodramatic mode is one of protest, resistance, challenge, opposition, combat, war' (1968, p.94). From romance, it takes the idea of desire as its narrative drive and courtship as the ultimate celebration of human relationships. From realism, it insists on the material nature of conflict in the social world but makes it less of a cerebral than an emotional experience. Emphatic, sensational and spectacular staging provide the context for the emotional extremes and formal disparity of melodrama's aesthetic; what Christine Gledhill in *Home is Where the Heart is* (1987) poignantly calls melodrama's 'way of imagining' its contemporary social world.

The nineteenth-century melodrama stage was to provide a general dramatic framework of narrative, mood and point-of-view for all of Hollywood's pop-ular cinema, including the Western. Whether gunfighter or outlaw criminal, cowboy or sheriff, the Western hero is invariably a romantic hero of melo-drama. Though just as invariably a loner, he represents a certain social position and masculinity in moral terms, in conflict variously within himself or with others around him invested with greater social power. The moral world of the Western is also the moral world of melodrama and the demands of romance can align or conflict with the narrative task set before the central protagonist. As much as the Western genre owes to melodrama, so the binary models developed in Western criticism owe something to the polarised moral universe of melodrama.

Finally, a specifically American idiom of music and speech was developed in the frontier melodrama. The characteristic rhythms and melodies of Western film music draw on the various national folk music cultures of immigrants in the Western settler communities, whether this was Native American tribal dance rhythms or orchestral and contemporary popular music structures. Similarly, characteristic speech patterns and expressions in Westerns draw on Western, mid-Western and Southern speech patterns and idioms. The Westerner of fiction turns this legacy into a recognisable genre language of familiar greeting and wry observation. All this was available in the dialogue of the Western novel. But silent film – or at least, film without synchronised sound – required brief phrases in speech to translate into dialogue cards on the screen. As the hero had to say just enough to fit the con-fined space of the dialogue card, a pointedly witty, philosophical vernacular developed. Long after the arrival of the sound film, laconic speech rhythms remained a characteristic of the Western hero. For instance, when the hero comes across corpses swinging from a tree at the start of *The Tall Men* (1955), his phlegmatic yet moral character and his attitude to lynching and the forces that produce it, are all wittily expressed in the irony of his curt opening lines: 'Must be nearing civilisation.'

Melodrama theatre, then, brings together the nineteenth-century legacy of fiction, pictorialisation and Show to the antecedents of the Western, especially evident in the form of early film. Termed 'silent film', the next chapter seeks to free its modes of speech.

CHAPTER FOUR

The Silent Western

There are no more 'silent' Westerns than there are 'silent' films. The term is inaccurate, for 'silent' films were never silent, but invariably accompanied in public performances from the earliest days by music and/or a narrator standing to one side of the screen. The sound that 'silent films' lack is synchronised sound recorded on the film itself, a development established by the film industry only in the late 1920s. Nonetheless, the term survives to distinguish early films from later sound films. With this caveat, and begrudgingly, I use it here, but with implied inverted commas throughout.

For modern audiences, there are few opportunities to watch silent films. Indeed, the contents of an ancient pharaoh's tomb and salvage from a sunken transatlantic liner are more accessible today than prints of silent films. Museums and touring exhibitions display the most unlikely bounty from even the most remote past and the most inaccessible places. Yet the small proportion of films to have survived the early period are buried away in the vaults of national film archives. Apart from a handful of classic film titles available on video, it takes a cinephile to discover rare screenings at the National Film Theatre in London.

Reconstructed prints of silent films appeared on terrestrial television's Channel 4 (UK) during the 1980s though they have been more rarely seen since then, and satellite channels like TNT screen seasons of films featuring famous film stars that could include the occasional silent feature film. But for the most part, only older generations will remember silent films and even then probably from worn prints of Charlie Chaplin and the Keystone Cops screened at school, before the advent of video technology. And a generation of young people may not even be aware of this much of silent cinema. Modern society is almost entirely unaware of nearly the first third of cinema history.

This state of affairs is a tragedy, for silent cinema has its own aesthetic pleasures for the inquisitive viewer. This is certainly the case for students and fans of the Western, for whom the silent period conceals buried treasures. Westerns were ubiquitous in the silent era. This chapter opens the treasure chest.

THE WEST AND EARLY WESTERNS

The West was a subject for film-makers from the beginning of film history. Although Frederick Jackson Turner declared the frontier 'officially closed' in 1893, just before the advent of technology for recording moving images on film, the West as a space of 'free' land for settlement existed until after the turn of the twentieth century. So it is no surprise that film of the West had already been seen in and beyond its territories before then. Filming the West became part of the history of the West. As Kevin Brownlow says: 'The motion picture not only reconstructed Western history – it became part of Western history' (1979, p.327).

The Western as a genre of fiction rapidly grew into a major popular film genre. It was central to the early development of film, interacting more generally with the way narrative film developed into the dominant film form – the dominant language of film – by the time film-making was organised into an industry (Anderson, 1979). This chapter charts some of the earliest films of the West and some of the earliest Westerns. It also explores the central influence of the Western on the development of a wide variety of early films and film practices from around 1894 to the time that narrative sound film came to dominate film production in the late 1920s.

THE FIRST FILM OF THE WEST

It was to their immediate environments that the earliest film-makers first turned – quite literally – for film was hand-cranked through a camera before electricity was commonly available as a means to generate energy. But film-makers soon explored a variety of more remote locations. From 1893, Thomas Edison, founder of the first American films, produced film of cowboys and Indians at work and leisure rather than in conflict, in ethnographic scenes of daily life in the open vistas of the West. His single tableau shot of Native American tribesmen in the *Hopi Snake Dance* (1893) is among the earliest films made (Rollins and O'Connor, 1998, p.12).

In the first experimental days of film-making in America, the cumbersome technology made it more convenient to bring subjects to the camera, and most cameras were in New York. In Edison's primitive studio, the Black Maria, Edward S. Porter recorded sportspeople and entertainers in tableaux films, composed of a single shot lasting the length of the film in the camera. Many contemporaneous show-business stars were filmed in this way, among them circus acts and performers from Buffalo Bill's Wild West, including sharp-shooter Annie Oakley. A few fragments of the show also survive, providing evidence of the spectacle of action and costume in an open-air arena and in a promotional street parade.

Film-making developed from scientific and technical experiments to record movement on light-sensitive materials, rapidly extending beyond professional and domestic use into commercial entertainments. At first, individuals peeped into Edison's kinetoscopes at movement simulated by flipping individual photographic paper plates at speed. Subsequently, audiences watched films projected on screens by means of a more flexible and sturdier material, celluloid. The novelty of the peepshow was international but short-lived, as film-makers discovered that, despite technical limitations, public demand for this early cinema experience exceeded the peepshow's more private and individual mode of exhibition. Film and 'the film' had arrived.

EARLY CINEMA

By 1909, urban street buildings throughout Europe and America were converted into auditoria designed for the sole purpose of showing programmes of films continuously throughout the day. In America, these buildings were called nickelodeons, combining the promise of exotic entertainment for a cheap price of admission. In Britain and elsewhere in Europe, they were initially called a variant of 'kinemas' (shortened from kinematograph, the name the Lumière Brothers gave their film technology), gradually modernising into what is now known as 'cinema'. Film industries developed throughout the industrialised world to guarantee regular supplies of film product to cinemas. An international film trade was eased by the lack of synchronised sound, enabling Europeans and Americans to watch films from other countries when explanatory title and dialogue cards were translated into their own language. Films at this time were therefore truly international and subjects like the West became universally popular. So much so that Westerns were made not only in America, but also in other nations, particularly France and Germany.

The lack of synchronised sound did not mean that films were silent. Narrators might be found standing to the side of the screen to provide commentary on the action. Films were invariably exhibited with musical accompaniment and sound effects from an orchestra large or small. Even the most run-down cinema in the poorest district would employ a pianist, percussion (invaluable for sound effects) and possibly even a violinist. In the grand picture palaces of the major cities a few years later, an orchestra of a hundred instruments or more would play from music scores specially created for the purpose. As dialogue could not be synchronised, music and sound effects became central to this early cinema experience. A visual genre like the Western offered strong possibilities to a new medium lacking the technology to synchronise dialogue and to a new film industry in Hollywood. The Western provided a visual spectacle of scenery and action, and aural possibilities for music motifs and sound effects like gunshots (a strong drumbeat) and pounding horses' hooves (the clichéd coconut shells).

Film developed into the major new medium of the first half of the twentieth century in the cinema institution – producing, distributing and exhibiting films to the widest possible audience – rapidly becoming the most popular art and entertainment medium. By 1910, nineteenth-century popular entertainment forms like theatre and other antecedents of the Western film lost their popular audiences to cinema. Stage melodramas, for instance, decreased by half in the first ten years of the twentieth century, whilst in 1909 four million people visited over seven thousand cinemas a day in New York (Vardac, 1949, p.187).

By this time, cinema audiences were watching short narrative films of one and two reels in length and ten or twenty minutes of screen time, rather than the single-shot ethnographic or documentary films of the earliest days. The Western was central to the development of popular narrative film during this transitional stage around 1910, as these short narrative films evolved into the feature-length form that is now considered a 'film'. This was more than central as the Western was the most popular form of screen entertainment during this transitional period. 'By 1909, and during the next six years, there were probably more Westerns released each month than during the entire (peak) decade (of Western feature films) of the 1930s' (Gallagher, 1986b, p.204). 'In a typical week in 1908, a large distributor handled only eighteen pictures which were not Westerns' (Hampton 1931, p.41). The popularity of the Western was surely not unrelated to a visual, literary and theatrical legacy that provided conventions of setting, character, narrative and action for the early Western film to draw upon.

EARLY WESTERN SCENES

The Western film did not arrive fully formed. Film-makers experimented with representations of the West in a variety of ways. Among Edison's many early actualité films for the peepshow, two 1898 tableaux films could be taken for Western scenes (Buscombe, 1988, p.23). *Poker at Dawson City* shows a fight breaking out in a poker game and *Cripple Creek Bar-room* finds a barmaid ejecting drunks from a bar. Both films offer recognisable Western situations of gambling, drinking and violence, though setting and costume are less conventional. However, cinema looked to the melodrama stage for a more significant move from single scenes to the first Western narratives.

FROM MELODRAMA STAGE TO FILM SCREEN

The decline in theatrical melodrama and the rise of narrative film are intimately connected. Transferring allegiances from stage to screen was easy for contemporary audiences due to the close similarity between the experience of theatre and cinema. By 1920, cinemas resembled theatres in outward and interior appearance; the length of the theatre performance and the cinema programme was similar; even the presentation was alike – a darkening auditorium signalled the lifting of curtains, with light falling on both stage and screen. Film exhibitors did everything to make cinema echo the experience of theatre, even selling confectionery in intermissions. The purpose was not only to offer a new technological experience in a familiar cultural milieu, but also to attract a bourgeois audience to what had rapidly developed at first as a popular cultural form for and among lower economic and social classes. In America, this also meant the extensive, culturally and linguistically diverse, immigrant communities. Thus from the first, the cinema experience combined the familiar and the modern, offering universal entertainment to audiences, regardless of their location and social position.

Further to these commercial connections between stage and screen, film overlapped and directly developed from certain tendencies in late melodrama theatre. Raymond Williams shows in *Drama from Ibsen to Brecht* (1952) how a desire for greater realism and spectacle in nineteenth-century theatre in general was part of a wider cultural aspiration realised in the technological development of cinema. The theatre stage had moved from a reliance on painted scenery and single sets to three-dimensional staging and multiple sets. Theatre developed spectacular stage illusions of increased realism; waterfalls cascaded down stages, actors perilously scaled vertical, moving cliff-faces, the Valkyries appeared to ride across a cyclorama sky and, in London's Drury Lane, travelators enabled teams of horses to race chariots across the stage.

Film extended such spectacle into a new order of realism by setting its audience before remote, exotic locations on which to stage real train crashes and close in on the most intimate of embraces. Moreover, editing strategies and trick photography could convince audiences that the heroine's life was in peril when tied to the track in front of an oncoming train. Scene changes could be effected immediately by cross-cutting from one space to another, developing a continuous narrative. The editing technique of cross-cutting collapsed time and space across a series of shots, hastening the pace of narrative development by avoiding the time delays of theatrical scene changes. Parallel editing – showing two events as if occurring simultaneously – created suspense. All these filmic devices were developments of theatrical strategies constructed on the melodrama stage.

Theatrical melodrama offered cinema the raw material of pictorialism and narrative. It 'flourished on the screen because one of its chief characteristics was a dependence on variety of background, quick shifting from one place to another, water and land effects, three dimensional situations which called into play all the athletic powers of the players. These demands could be met and even amplified on the screen' (Moses, quoted in Vardac, 1949, p.187). Cinema inherited and developed theatre's drive towards greater spectacle and realism. And no genre was ready to respond to the challenge more effectively than the Western.

Why is the Western so central to the rise of American film? Certainly, the spectacle of melodrama set in the West and the narrative possibilities of the Western form made the genre attractive to early film-makers. The Western offers multiple scene-changes, from wilderness to township locations, and conventional rituals in multiple situations, from a saloon bar fist-fight to a street gunfight. The dramatic stand-off of a gunfight could be constructed by cross-cutting from one gunfighter to another. Alterity constructs action in chase scenes, with riders on horseback galloping across the scrublands adjacent to the base of the new film industry in California's Hollywood Hills. Parallel editing creates suspense, as the cavalry arrives just in time to rescue the encircled wagon train from Indian attack. The Western, indeed, is central to such developments in early film form because its genre conventions positively encourage those techniques. In turn, early cinema found a film language of evolving sophistication as the genre itself developed.

THE FIRST WESTERN?

But the Western did not arrive fully formed on the screen. It took a decade for a narrative film language to develop that did not require either an audience's previous familiarity with the story or an attendant narrator to make sense of the images on the screen. The earliest direct contributions to shaping this development depended on the melodrama stage for their sources. The frontier was an increasingly popular setting on the melodrama stage towards the end of the late nineteenth century. Among the most successful was *The Great Train Robbery*, written by Scott Marble and first produced at New York's Bowery Theatre in October 1896. Though there is evidence of other film titles with Western connotations made around the same time (for instance, *Kit Carson* in

A frame of the extra-scenic shot from *The Great Train Robbery* (1903) in which the outlaw leader fires his pistol at the camera.

1903), *The Great Train Robbery* (1903) is widely accepted as the first Western narrative film and foundational for the Western film genre.

It is likely that film-maker Edwin S. Porter at least knew of the stage production of *The Great Train Robbery*, even if he had not seen it, since his film reproduces scenes as described in contemporary reviews of the play (Vardac, 1949, pp.63–4 and pp.182–3). The film exists in several prints, though scenes in some are fragmented or transposed. It is celebrated not least for a close-up of the character of an outlaw firing his gun directly at the camera and, hence, at the audience. It is an extra-scenic shot (that is, a shot with no background or compositional reference to any other shot in the film, so existing outside the film's fictional world or diegesis). Since it is extra-scenic, the shot could be used at the beginning, the end or, notionally, at any point in the film. At the time of its making, film-makers either exhibited their own films or sold prints for others to exhibit. Exhibitors bought films by the length from catalogues, often in single tableau shots. It is therefore possible that some surviving prints were structured by exhibitors rather than in a sequence suggested by Porter.

The Great Train Robbery is composed of about fourteen tableau shots. A shot breakdown demonstrates both an early formation of the Western film and how the genre contributed to developments in the formal language of narrative film;

1. The film opens with two robbers entering a telegraph office. This is the third scene of the play, so it is likely that the film neglects preceding scenes of explication – possibly preparation for the robbery – with which it might be assumed audiences of the day would be familiar. Unlike the play, the film starts with the action and does not attempt to reproduce the stage set. Instead, it builds up a temporal sequence of contiguous but not continuous spaces from one shot to the next. It is not easy to work out what the robbers are up to in this shot, since the camera is set apart from the action, as if placed in the middle of theatre stalls, facing the stage. One robber wears a white hat, the other black, but they are otherwise indistinguishable in the knee-length boots and dark clothing of stage melodrama villainy. They appear to instruct the telegraphist (Vardac suggests they are 'forcing the operator to signal the engineer to stop his train for water' (1949, p.183)) and they hide when a face (probably the engine driver) appears at the ticket-office window. But the purpose of the scene seems simply to establish the modern communications technology of railroad and telegraph in a Western setting (though the film was actually shot in the East, in New Jersey!).

2. After knocking out and tying up the telegraphist, the robbers are seen sidling from left to right across the base of a water tower and on to the engine. The train departs.

3. The wagon guard hears the robbers off-screen left and locks his safe. The space of the carriage door shows a trick shot of an exterior, emphasising the passing movement of the train. It occupies the same space in the frame as a window in the first shot, also a trick shot of an exterior scene, and therefore offers a graphic match across shots. The robbers break through the door and exchange gunshots with the guard before shooting him. They blow the safe and escape with the money in sacks.

4. In a shot missing from some prints, there follows a struggle on top of the engine, shown from a camera position on the coal truck behind the moving train. A jump cut enables a robber to throw the body (but now an obvious dummy) from the train, further emphasising their ruthlessness. The action of this shot logically comes after shot 2 but is positioned here perhaps because it does not make for continuous action and would therefore appear as a jump cut.

5. A shot from the tracks, behind the halting engine, reveals the robbers alighting with the brakeman, who uncouples the engine. The camera is placed closer to the action and at an angle, adding extra dynamism to a scene of simple explanatory action.

6. Passengers alight from the centre of two carriages. The robbers move along the line of passengers from the extreme right, taking possessions, and are interrupted by a man who attempts to escape. He is shot in the back and falls melodramatically in the foreground. When the robbers leave, the passengers crowd round the fallen man.

7. From shot 5's camera position, the robbers run into the frame and board the train. As in all shots of the train moving in the frame, it moves off diagonally to the right. Though there are no precise match cuts across the transitions between these shots, the movement does offer directional action and therefore a greater sense of continuity than is evident in cuts between tableaux shots elsewhere in the film.

8. The train emerges into frame further up the tracks and stops. The camera pans left to follow the robbers as they run down an embankment.

9. The robbers run into a forest at the top of the frame, cross diagonally right and then left across a stream in the foreground, the camera panning left to reveal them riding their horses away.

10. Meanwhile, back in the office, the revived telegraphist attempts to send a message but falls back in a stupor. A child enters in a Little Red Riding Hood outfit and releases him, though not without first throwing a cup of water on him and praying to heaven.

11. A barn dance, where Westerners force a greenhorn Easterner to join in by shooting round his feet. They are interrupted by a messenger – presumably with news of the robbery, since they rush from the room.

12. On a forest path, men on horseback ride towards the camera. These are presumably the robbers, though much time has been lost between this and the preceding shot. The riders that follow them must then be a posse formed from the dancers. A robber is shot and falls from his horse.

13. In a third forest space, the robbers are dividing their spoils. The posse walks into the background, at the top rear of the frame and all the robbers are shot in the ensuing gunfight.

14. The close-up of the gun shot at the camera and audience goes here in most prints.

The Great Train Robbery exemplifies in primitive form some generic staples of the Western. Despite its lack of individual characterisation and character development, its narrative structure is classical – crime, chase, retribution. Within that simple structure, there are familiar situations; effectively two hold-ups, two gunfights, a fist-fight, and a dance that includes a ritual humiliation of an Easterner by Westerners. Not bad for ten minutes. Western types are also familiar, including criminal gunmen, lawmen, railroad workers, train passengers and townspeople. Perhaps most importantly, the gun and its uses (to threaten and harm) are central to the film's drama.

This film analysis contributes to an understanding of the role of the Western genre in the development of narrative film into dominant film form. In its first thirty years, film developed through four recognised stages. Early film is characterised by what Tom Gunning calls 'the cinema of attractions' (1990, p.63) which provides textual evidence of early film's showground and show business origins. Subjects in early films show awareness of the camera by 'playing up' for and to it. Regardless of whether they are in actuality or fiction films and whether they are acting or 'being themselves', they appear to be 'performing'. Notably, subjects in early films commonly look into the camera lens, thereby directly addressing the audience. This acknowledgement of the camera's presence is part of the novelty of early film as a new technology. But it is also a system of early film's aesthetic, as camera and audience share in the display and exhibitionism of its constructed world. Actors often demonstrate their awareness of the camera throughout *The Great Train Robbery* by acting towards and at times looking to the camera. But the shot of the robber firing directly at the audience is *prima facie* evidence that *The Great Train Robbery* is part of 'the cinema of attractions'.

The second stage of development towards narrative cinema is the moment of transition from early film to early cinema, as disparate film-making practices develop into a film industry. For a while, audiences rely on sound cues like music and, crucially, an attendant narrator to understand a story composed solely of a series of tableau shots. The narrator's function was to 'seal the joins' by making narrative connections between the separate spaces and the temporal gaps from shot to shot, in a sense *creating* a narrative from loosely connected scenes. As the above account of *The Great Train Robbery* may indicate, it is not easy to be certain what is occurring in some scenes. This is especially so in the opening scene, when the camera is some distance from the action and there is no dialogue or characterisation to anchor meaning. Neither is the drama centred – thereby failing to direct attention to a particular part of the frame. Nor are the scenes directly connected temporally or spatially. It may well be the case that contemporary audiences were familiar enough with the story to make sense of the first scene and the relations between those that follow. But it is also likely that an off-screen narrator's voice would be there to inform an audience anyway. Elsewhere, there is no dissection of a scene – no insert or close-up or cut on axis (along the line of a camera's view), etc. – to provide explanatory detail. During the robbery of the passengers, for instance, it takes time to appreciate that the centre of the action begins on the extreme right of the frame, as the robbers seem lost among the passengers busily alighting from the train and lining up for the camera. At this early stage of narrative film's development, there is evidence in the form of the film that an off-screen narrator's voice is needed for audiences of early cinema as much as audiences of today to follow the story.

In the third stage of film's development, as narrative films increase in length from short to feature-length form, the Victorian melodrama stage offered more to film than an aesthetic, a particular 'way of imagining' the world as a polarised moral system. Most obviously, it offered a developed acting style of heightened emotionality, expressed in exaggerated gesture and movement. Without dialogue and with the camera placed at a distance from the action, melodrama performance style enabled audiences to decode character and narrative action. Such an acting style is evident throughout *The Great Train Robbery*, but particularly in death scenes and emphatically in the child's performance. More complexly, early narrative cinema also inherited from theatre a system to organise a film's mise-en-scène and editing. This can be seen in *The Great Train Robbery* in its tendency to frontal staging, where the camera is placed directly before a backdrop fronted by actors performing on a single, central plane, as if on a stage. Exits and entrances are also arranged to left and right of the film frame, and doors are aligned with the edges of the frame, as if they mark the wings of a stage. In theatre, when actors disappear offstage, it is a convention that they re-enter from the same side in order to maintain continuity of action; the same rule applies to *The Great Train Robbery* even when the camera scene changes.

The final stage of development in narrative film is towards the system of continuous action that we recognise today. The continuity system organises mise-en-scène and editing according to the principle of matching on action. Bordwell, Thompson and Staiger in *The Classical Hollywood Cinema* (1985) claim that objects are centred according to their narrative importance and editing is organised to maintain spatial and temporal coherence between shots. Cuts from one shot to the next are therefore motivated by action across and beyond the frame. So, for instance, in contrast to theatrical principles, exits and entrances in film are matched directionally; a character exiting frame right for instance will reappear in the next shot from frame left. What is so extraordinary about *The Great Train Robbery* is that, though principles of theatrical staging appear to govern interior scenes, some evidence of the continuity principle is evident in exterior scenes. Despite some inconsistency, this is particularly noticeable in cuts on action between shots 5 – 8 which follow the direction of the moving train, and shots 9 – 10 which trace the downward movement of the robbers after the robbery. Where elsewhere the camera is static, it moves by panning on action. It is probably not coincidental that locations allow for much more dynamic movement across the depth of the screen, especially in shots 9, 12 and 13 with their diagonal movement across the frame from background to foreground. In contrast, interior scenes are constructed for the static camera more in line with the theatrical principles of staging.

The film form of *The Great Train Robbery* is in tension with all four stages of cinema's development towards the dominance of narrative film. There is formal evidence of 'the cinema of attractions', of theatrical staging, of primitive narration and of the later continuity system. The evidence of this singular film suggests how the Western was a genre amenable to combining related developments in film form with the commercial and institutional drives towards twentieth-century narrative cinema.

THE FIRST WESTERNS

The popular success of *The Great Train Robbery* quickly inspired imitations such as *The Bold Bank Robbery* (1904), *The Hold-up of the Rocky Mountain Express* (1906) (Buscombe, 1988, pp.23–4) and *The Little Train Robbery* (1905) (Flynn, undated). It also prompted Porter to make other Westerns, notably *The Life of an American Cowboy* (1906). A comparison with his earlier film is instructive.

The Life of an American Cowboy opens with a scene in a saloon, with 'Big Horn' painted in bold letters over the bar, probably a generic reference to the Battle. The action in this first scene is also not easy to follow and like *The Great Train Robbery* suffers from a lack of dramatic centring. Peter Stanfield's interpretation is that a cowboy intervenes when 'a Mexican is attempting to give an old Indian a drink against a young Indian woman's wishes' (1987, p.98). Then, in an incident looking forward to Frederic Remington's painting, *In Without Knocking* (1909), cowboys on horseback ride in, reproducing the humiliation of the tenderfoot in *The Great Train Robbery* by shooting close to the feet of two Easterners to make them dance. In the next scene, a stagecoach offloads the Easterners at a ranch, where the younger man's humiliation continues with a ritual and presumably good natured spanking by the cowboys. In the third of this series of tableaux shots, the cowboys display a range of riding and roping skills for the Easterners before, in a continuation of the second shot, bidding them farewell. As the ranch folk exit into the house, the skulking Mexican rides off. What follows is a classic chase and rescue narrative, initiated by Indians on horseback following the stagecoach and extended when the cowboys give chase to rescue a captured woman. In a closing scene missing from the British Film Institute print I have seen, Peter Stanfield recounts how, 'the cowboy and the heroine (sic) rest in a secluded spot, the Mexican creeps up on them, but, as he raises his gun, he is shot and killed by the Indian woman' (ibid., p.98).

Again, there is much incident but little character development. The conflicts are classic oppositions between East and West, and between white and ethnic Others. Nonetheless, the stereotypes are not simple. The cowboys display an easy-going masculine valour, combined with a knockabout violence; the ethnic

Other is not uniform but composed of Mexican villainy and Indian dependency; the Easterners are established as comically naive at first but, when they are later threatened, that naivety will inspire heroic rescue by the Westerners.

There is a formal similarity between the organisation of scene-shots in *The Life of an American Cowboy* and *The Great Train Robbery*, and a similar difficulty in reading scenes, especially opening scenes. However, the recurrent situations in specific settings of both films provide a recognisably generic foundation. Train station and saloon are sites of intrigue and deviancy, dance hall and ranch are sites of display and camaraderie, the open range of forests and plains are sites of male action. Much of Western convention is already in place in the situation and setting of these films. Furthermore, Stanfield argues that it *is* possible to construct a narrative from the series of contiguous scenes in *Life of an American Cowboy* since 'all of the main protagonists in this film have rigidly prescribed traits and functions' (ibid., p.98), deriving and familiar from Western antecedents. Certainly, the iconography of dress for each group is easily identifiable, even down to the bowler-hatted Easterner. Stanfield further argues that stock Western characters become so well-established that all Westerns made in the period 1909–14 can be read generically, despite their primitive form.

INDIAN DRAMAS

This is particularly true for Stanfield in relation to a group of films he calls Indian dramas, a group so distinct that Eileen Bowser in *The Transformation of Cinema 1907–1915* (1990, pp.173–7) considers them a genre separate from frontier melodramas. *The American Film Institute Catalogue* (1995) lists over one hundred and thirty films made between 1897 and 1910 with 'indian' in the title, compared to less than seventy with 'cowboy' in the name. Despite the surprising ubiquity of the Indian, however, Stanfield predictably finds conflict divided on racial lines in his survey of early Westerns. Villains are most often the racial Other to the white heroes, with treacherous Mexicans, savage Indians and a specially deviant role for half-breeds, whose racial mix make them doubly suspect. *The Life of an American Cowboy* is one of many films in the period that assume hostility between the races.

Native Americans have a prominent place in early film: 'hundreds of documentaries, shorts and features on Indian topics were produced from the turn of the century through 1920' (Jay, 2000, p.5). In many fictions, they merely embody a hostile Western environment that is dangerous to white incursion (Abel, 1998, pp.82–3). In some, their savagery is exceptional and explicitly identified as part of their racial identity. In *The Battle of Elderbush*

Gulch (1913), for instance, a tribe 'massacres helpless white women, scalps their victims, and beats a baby to death beside the body of its dead mother' (ibid., p.101), an act explicitly racialised in the language of its intertitles. This is one of a group of about thirty frontier melodramas directed by D.W. Griffith for Biograph, many of which feature vicious representations of the savage Indian, including *The Massacre* (1912), *The Last Drop of Water*, *Fighting Blood* (both in 1911) and the virulently racist *The Yacqui Cur* (1913). Gregory S. Jay finds two others, *The Call of the Wild* (1908) and *A Romance of the Western Hills* (1910), 'depict the Indian as incapable of "civilisation" and predisposed to savage regression' (Jay, 2000, p.4). Griffith was later to be celebrated as another kind of pioneer – this time, of early narrative film. But in these films, a legacy of Southern white racism is as evident as in Griffith's better-known feature film, *The Birth of a Nation* (1915) where white suprematism is celebrated in a climactic rescue, substituting the Ku Klux Klan for the cavalry and marauding blacks for the Indians.

Yet, in contrast, relations between whites and Indians elsewhere are more complex, even in other films directed by Griffith (Wagenknecht and Slide, 1975). In these films, it is surprising to find an ambivalent sympathy for Native Americans or, at least, to those who are 'Good Indians' to their white heroes. The eponymous *Apache Renegade* (1912), an outcast in *The Chief's Blanket* (1912) and drunken Indians in *Curse of the Red Man* (1911) are equally hostile to white colonisation and therefore feature as villains; whilst sympathetic squaws, tribal elders and sober Indians respectively support the whites against their deviant racial kin. The very conventionality of good and bad Indians can provide the means for dramatic ambiguity. In *A Romantic Tale of the West* (1911), the motives of the Indian who comes to the rescue of the white hero and heroine is initially uncertain, his potential threat to the young couple creating suspense, a dramatic device that fleetingly deceives them and the audience.

A group of films in which Indians take leading roles are even more surprising. These include films like *The Mended Lute* (1909) in which the central protagonist, a Sioux hero, is played by a Native American and a popular actor in the period, James Young Deer (Abel, 1998, p.85). Even in these, though, the dichotomy between good and bad Indian remains. In *Indian Justice* (1911), the names of the protagonists identify Agile Stag and White Dove as the romantic couple and Black Bison as the villain. In a further Griffith film, *Squaw's Love: An Indian Poem of Love in Pictures* (1911), Stanfield colourfully argues that 'the bad Indians are characterised as drunken buffoons, while the good Indians are shown to be resourceful and not lacking in animal courage . . . They are also physically handsome, whereas the bad Indians are downright plug ugly' (Stanfield, 1987, p.103).

In contrast with Griffith's representation of Indian savagery, *Squaw's Love* is one of several Indian melodramas (Jay, 2000, p.6) to display greater sympathy for the plight of the Indian. The titles of other Griffith films are suggestive: *The Indian Runner's Romance* (1909), *The Redman's View* (1909), *A Mohawk's Way* (1910), *The Chief's Daughter* (1911), *The Indian Brothers* (1911) and *A Pueblo Legend* (1912). These films are said to display a 'nostalgia for lost paradises: the antebellum South, the pastoral world of the Indians, the innocence of childhood, and the mother' (ibid., p.10). Thomas H. Ince also produced Indian dramas sympathetic to the plight of Native Americans. In *The Heart of an Indian* (1912), extraordinarily, settlers surround an Indian encampment and massacre its inhabitants. The plots of this and other Ince films like *The Invaders* (1912) concern the plight of Indian tribes marginalised by white incursion into their lands. They connect with the ethnographic tradition of the genre, exemplifying the more nostalgic strain of regret for the decline of what Leslie Fiedler has called the 'Vanishing American' (incidentally, also the title of a 1925 film for MGM). Gregory S. Jay argues that: 'most of these films are less reminiscent of later Westerns than . . . nineteenth-century sentimental fiction and drama' (ibid., p.6).

The Life of an American Cowboy is also the first example of a captivity narrative in film. When the Indians hold up the stagecoach, there is no explanation why or for what purpose the heroine alone is kidnapped. Yet Indian capture of whites, especially women, is a major theme of many great Westerns like *The Searchers* (1956) and *Major Dundee* (1964) as well as any number of lesser Westerns like *Unconquered* (1947), *Northwest Passage* (1940) and *Soldier Blue* (1970). In these films, the threat of captivity by Indians is also 'the fate worse than death' that implies the violation of white women, and the mutilation, torture and slow death of white men. The idea of the Indian as personification of barbarity emerges with the captivity theme early in the history of European colonisation. Richard Slotkin in *Regeneration Through Violence* (1973) argues that the captivity narrative is also the oldest of America's literary genres. In the first accounts of capture, such as in Mary Rowlandson's biography of 1682, it is more common to find a peaceful cultural transition from white to Indian ways. Sexual attack in particular only comes to dominate the theme in subsequent literary fiction and illustrations, starting with Fenimore Cooper. Clive Bush in *The Dream of Reason* (1977) argues that rape fantasy becomes central to captivity narratives during the nineteenth century, where it serves as ideological justification for white imperialism and the genocide of the Native American. Few Westerns emphasise peaceful assimilation, as happens for Stands With a Fist in *Dances With Wolves* (1990); in *Little Big Man* (1970), the Indian gets the worst of the deal when he captures the hero's shrewish Swedish wife.

Yet in early Westerns like *The Life of an American Cowboy*, there is no textual evidence of a motive for the kidnap. Elsewhere, in other Indian dramas, romance across the racial divide is a dominant theme. Indeed, many Indian dramas are romances, where courtship between heterosexual partners is a common narrative drive. Romance across the racial divide, however, is regularly doomed. In *Back to the Prairie* (1911), the white man rescued by Red Fox turns out to be the father of the white woman he loves. Although he saves the man's life, the father denies their partnership. In *Ramona* (1912), the fate of the Indian hero, Allessandro, is even more final, when he is shot and killed as punishment for his love of the Spanish heroine. Rarely can romance between races survive in the Western, though *Flaming Arrow* (1913) concludes with a rare shot of a white heroine in the arms of the mixed race hero, White Eagle.

Stanfield argues that in Indian dramas 'a positive portrayal of assimilation, though not of miscegenation, can be seen' (1987, p.104). Miscegenation is interracial sex and white racist fears of miscegenation account for the impossibility of interracial romance in Westerns. Though Westerns may mourn the tragedy of young love thwarted, it is rare that any allow interracial romance to survive its ending. In this they are no different from any of the later landmark Westerns, commonly considered to have broken through negative stereotyping of Native Americans. In the 1950s, for instance, the death of the white hero's Indian wife in *Broken Arrow* (1950) is narratively necessary to 'put a seal upon the peace', newly brokered to end the Indian wars. But it is also as ideologically necessary to its time as it is to the 1960s, where the white hero's identification with his Indian captors in *Little Big Man* is not enough for the survival of his wife from the cavalry massacre of her village. As a final example, the 1990s romance between the cavalry hero of *Dances With Wolves* and the Indian captive could be understood to survive the film (and, even then, presumably not for long), only because they are both white.

Though these Indian dramas of the silent period offer remarkable opportunities for narratives woven around Native Americans, they nonetheless sustain the abiding binary opposition of good and bad Indians and an inability to conceive of interracial romance surviving beyond a film's resolution.

THE WESTERN AND THE RISE OF THE FILM INDUSTRY

More generally, what the film trade press of the time calls these 'Indian and Western subjects' (Abel, 1998, p.84) establish the dramatic space of the West as a place of danger. Although *Rescued from an Eagle's Nest* (1907) has little Western iconography, it is set in a theatrical Western wilderness and tells the simple story of a pioneer rescuing his baby. The actor playing the pioneer is D.W. Griffith, making his first screen appearance. In his later films as director, Griffith widened the range of settings and situations in frontier melo-dramas, locating his films in Civil War battlefields, mining camps, frontier towns, Indian villages and both sides of the Mexican border (Stanfield in Buscombe 1988, p.348). Though he universally constructs the West of these settings as a hostile environment, villainy in his films takes many forms. His early Westerns seed a range of positive, negative and ambivalent representations of the Native American. He also finds greater narrative opportunity than other film-makers in the period for more developed characters and character relations, especially for women. In *The Goddess of Sagebrush Gulch* (1912), for instance, a woman residing in the East betrays her Western sister, the geographical divide deemed sufficient explanation for their contrasting moralities. Griffith's feature films are Victorian melodramas in which the young woman is a victim in a hostile male environment. The dramatic oppositions along gender lines from his more famous features like *Broken Blossoms* (1919) and *Way Down East* (1920) can be understood as developments from experimentation with genre conventions in his short Westerns.

The growth of the film industry from around 1907 impelled large-scale production of short narrative films, at the heart of which were Westerns. In that year *The Girl from Montana* and *Western Justice* were shot in Western landscapes, part of the increasing output of newly established production companies in the growing Californian film industry, based in Hollywood. Most previous Westerns were made on the eastern seaboard around New York, but serious production began in California from 1908.

California proved to be an ideal location for Westerns. Varied and spectacular scenery could be found within short travelling distances, including desert, scrubland, rocky terrain and distant mountaintops. By 1908/9, 'the Western had evolved into a standardised format with codified locales, actions and attitudes . . . the first fully articulated film genre' (Anderson 1979, p.31).

By 1910, '21 per cent of all American pictures made (213 out of 1001) were Westerns, a percentage which . . . was to remain remarkably consistent over the years' (Buscombe 1988, p.24). All the major film companies of the period made Westerns, including Selig, Biograph, Lubin, Vitagraph and Kalem. Selig and Biograph were particularly lauded by reviewers of the time for the vivid action and compelling narratives of their Westerns (Abel, 1998, p.80). Some film-makers were specifically associated with Westerns. Francis Boggs made several Westerns for Selig (Robinson, 1996, p.115), including *The Cattle Rustlers* (1908) (Abel, 1998, p.79) and *Boots and Saddles* (Rainey, 1996, p.7), both in 1909. In addition to Indian dramas, the wider range of Westerns made by Thomas H. Ince is indicated by the titles of *Custer's Last Fight* and *War of the Plains* (1912).

Frontier melodramas were diversely set; cattle country, cavalry stories and the Indian wars are all indicated in titles. *The Spoilers* starring William Farnum, was the first of many film versions of the novel of the same name and among the most popular films of 1914. Successful stage plays were adapted, including the first of several versions of *The Squaw Man* (1914) with Dustin Farnum. Traditional novels also offered ready-made Western plots; Vitagraph made the first screen adaptation of a Leatherstocking Tale in *The Deerslayer* (1911) with a popular star of the period, Wallace Reid, and Lasky made the first version of *The Virginian* (1914) with Dustin Farnum as the cowboy hero. The novels of more contemporary novelists were also adapted, including the ubiquitous Zane Grey, among whose most famous novels *Riders of the Purple Sage* was filmed many times, notably starring series cowboy-star, Tom Mix, in 1925.

Legendary Westerners are reputed to have been around Hollywood at this time. Director John Ford claimed that he based his staging of the gunfight at the O.K. Coral for the climax of *My Darling Clementine* (1946) on the personal account of its most famous participant, Wyatt Earp. Some Westerners appeared in films. Convicted felon, Al Jennings, recreated his own turn-of-the-century crime in *The Bank Robbery* in 1908 (Flynn, p.8). Even Buffalo Bill made films about his own exploits. In 1913, he founded the Colonel W.F. Cody Historical Pictures Company, but made just one film, *Buffalo Bill and the Indian Wars* (1914). Fragments still exist, showing reconstructions of events with some of the surviving participants, although the billed number of '11,000 troops' were played by lesser numbers of extras passing by the camera several times to make up the figures. Unfortunately, the film was neither financially nor formally successful. By the time of his death in 1917, cinema had adapted the spectacle of the Wild West Shows within fictional narratives. The variety structure of the Shows could not compete on film with the popularity of narrative form.

The passing of the Shows and audience resistance to semi-documentary and biographical fictions about real-life Westerners did not mean that Hollywood severed all connections with frontier days. What Western authenticity did survive was surely among the personnel and props of *The Miller Brothers 101 Ranch Wild West Show*. Located in Hollywood's Santa Ynez canyon, it supplied film studios with extras and props from its authentic cowboys, Indians, horses, livery, clothing, armoury and other incidental paraphernalia for the next fifty years. Many of its staff graduated into acting, writing and directing for film.

BRONCHO BILLY ANDERSON

The first most influential production companies were Bison and Essanay. Bison's *The Cowboy's Narrow Escape* (1908) appeared at a time when the company was making a Western a week (Abel, 1998, p.90). Even more prolific was Essanay, formed in 1907 by George K. Spoor and melodrama stage actor

Publicity portrait of Gilbert M. Anderson, dressed in a more flamboyant Show costume than the plain working clothes of the ordinary cowboy he plays in the Broncho Billy series. The Indian-head logo, bottom left, identifies Essanay, Anderson's film production company, formed in 1907 with George K. Spoor.

Gilbert M. Anderson from the initials of their surnames. The commitment of the company to Western production is evident even in its logo – the profile of an Indian in war bonnet. The company sought authentic locations for its Westerns and, after trying the southern border states of Colorado, Texas and Mexico, settled in Niles, California in 1910 (Robinson, 1996, p.116), on the fringes of Los Angeles.

Echoing William F. Cody's adoption of a Western-sounding soubriquet in 'Buffalo Bill', Anderson called himself 'Broncho Billy'. Under that name, he was to become the first actor whose career was centrally connected to a film genre and the first Western film star. Anderson acted in several films before 1910, including, reputedly, as a passenger in *The Great Train Robbery*. Following the huge success of *Broncho Billy's Redemption* in that year and until his career waned in 1915, Anderson made almost three hundred Westerns as Broncho Billy Anderson. In publicity stills, he can be found in something of the flamboyant dress of Wild West Shows, including a flowing kerchief around the neck, tasselled gloves and decorated holster. But in the films, Broncho Billy most often cuts the plainer figure of an ordinary cowboy whose stocky body and double chins epitomise premature aging through labour, so characteristic of the archetypal working man. Broncho Billy was a working class hero.

In a huge variety of roles and narratives during five years and three hundred films, the Broncho Billy film series set the mould for series Westerns over the next thirty years, a topic explored in the next chapter. Though Billy was always the central protagonist in his films, there is no consistency in character or story from one film to the next. He could be a law-abiding cowboy in one film and a villain in another, die at the film's climax, but reappear at the start of the next. Though the films were short (one reel films last approximately ten minutes and two reel films about twenty minutes), plots could be complicated and take place over a long period of time. They owe much to the intensity of action in the dime novel and to the narrative conventions of stage melodrama.

At their most simple, they are chase films, offering opportunities for spectacle of movement across landscape and frame. In *The Claim Jumpers* (1915), for instance, Billy outraces the villains to file a legitimate gold claim, in what is little more than a quest narrative organised by parallel editing. Other films are more clearly heroic narratives. One such is *The Outlaw and the Child* (1911) in which Billy is a fugitive from prison. Though he could escape, he sacrifices first his freedom, then his survival, to rescue a small child who has wandered into the desert. The rescue narrative is also strong in *Broncho Billy's Gratefulness* (1913), where the morality tale tells of hero Billy returning a favour, by saving the life of a husband attempting to defend his wife's honour.

In other films, however, Billy is less the hero of romance than the victim of melodrama. In *Broncho Billy* (1909), for instance, he falls for a woman from the city, only to realise too late his love for the woman of the West, when the Eastern femme fatale introduces him to her husband! In this instance Billy is no man of action, but the emotional victim of melodrama. *Broncho Billy* exemplifies a tendency in all these films to construct the West as a site for male action and the East as a site of emasculation, leaving the notional hero a passive innocent in a vindictive urban world. The binary opposition between the cruel East and constant West is represented by the two women; the Woman of the West is the heroine and the Woman of the East is the villain.

Other films in the series mix action romance with the emotional imaginary of melodrama. In these, Billy's role as hero becomes more marginal. Typical is *Broncho Billy's Love Affair* (1912), in which a husband admits to his wife and the broken-hearted Billy that – years before – he had deviously parted the loving couple. This is similar in plot to the structurally more complex *The Buried Letters* (1910), in which a jealous prospector pal divides Billy from his wife, by concealing letters from her until an Indian raid and imminent death prompts him to reveal his duplicity. The revelation enables the two to die with clear consciences and an abiding friendship. In both of these films, the emphasis is on a key feature of melodrama that connects personal sacrifice to moral reward, commonly (as here) in reunion. That the first reunion is between heterosexual partners and the second between homosocial friends suggests that the early Western incorporates a range of intimate gender relations. This variety is clearly connected to the varied aesthetic traditions the Western draws upon. The denial of Billy's heroism and his status as victim in these films demonstrates how the heroism of romance can be tempered by the victimhood of melodrama to produce a complex gendered figure.

The most complex of all Broncho Billy films interweave their romantic action and spectacle with the excessive narrative structure, performance and emotionality of family melodrama. To exemplify this, it is worth analysing *Naked Hands* (1909) in more depth. It opens with Edith, Billy's wife, looking out across a Western landscape. Intertitles tell us, however, that she is an Easterner and depressed by the isolation of life in the West. She abandons Billy for stockbroker Harry Stanton, just as the film's parallel editing informs us that Billy strikes gold. Summoning his saloon bar friends to transport a piano and other gifts of love for Edith back to his primitive ranch house, he arrives to find her note in which she explains her absence, delicately posed on a lamp. Billy refuses to take up the rifle offered by his friends to seek retribution. Instead, in an extraordinary frenzy of grief, he dowses the rooms with kerosene, before running wildly from the burning hut. Intercut with this scene, Billy's friends hunt down the errant couple and return them to face the now-exhausted Billy who simply sends them wearily on their way. Abandoning the mine (in what his sense of bitter betrayal causes him to name 'Faithless'), Billy moves into an eastern mansion fit for a millionaire, exchanging his cowboy duds for a very unlikely top hat and tails. In a revealing scene, he maintains cowboy ways, denied by a manservant, by insisting on his dog's right to sit on the dining room table rather than in an outside kennel and thus asserts the rights of Western informal democracy over the refined culture of the East. Billy seems at peace with himself and his dog until he coincidentally meets Harry at a party where he attempts to strangle him, much to the astonishment of the observing smart set and perhaps even the audience. Later, Billy fights bloodily and spectacularly in Harry's home until, on the point of finally strangling him, the sight of Harry's wife and child (as big a surprise to the audience as to Billy!) strikes Billy's conscience and he leaves. In a final coda, the abandoned Edith lies on her deathbed in hospital, but the Western couple are ultimately reunited as Billy reveals the photo he still keeps of his loved one in his fob watch. Edith dies in peace.

The characters in *Naked Hands* are morally ambiguous in ways that disrupt the conventional tensions between East and West that we might expect at this early stage of the Western genre's development. Although Harry remains a villain (luring Edith from her Western partnership and abandoning her in the city, presumably after he has 'had his way' with her), his familial situation exaggerates the terror of Billy's frenzied attacks. Though we may pity Billy when he is abandoned, sympathise with his grief and support his defence of a Western way of life over his manservant's promotion of eastern mores, his wild behaviour is a puzzling overreaction and makes it difficult for an audience to support him unequivocally. Though his heroism is assured at the end – when he withdraws from murder at the sight of family and returns to Edith in her dying moments – his behaviour in earlier scenes undermines our unqualified support. Edith is similarly ambiguous; she is first an Easterner left to a life of isolation by an otherwise loving Billy, then a Westerner abandoned in the ways of the East. Though she leaves Billy, she is abused by both men and the cultures they represent. Stanton abandons Edith through loss of desire; Billy also absents himself from her life through a self-centred, unremitting grief that threatens for a time to consume him. The film's central drive thus shifts between Billy's selfish, but finally heroic, romance narrative and Edith's melodrama. This makes for a surprisingly complex narrative for such a short and early narrative film, undermining any consistent audience sympathy and spectator position.

The dates of this sample of Broncho Billy films make clear that the generic evolution of the Western at this time was uneven. The complex *Naked Hands* is an early film, made before Broncho Billy the actor and character are combined, yet the structurally simpler *The Claim Jumpers* is made towards the end of his film career. In this uneven evolution, generic development would seem to echo developments in narrative film form more generally. *Naked Hands* features formal examples of both the early 'cinema of attractions' (especially in frontal staging inherited from theatrical conventions typical in other films of the time), as well as the match editing more typical of a later period of continuity film.

The performance style of Broncho Billy Anderson is, however, consistent. The only actor to be identified by name as well as character in the credits, Anderson was wholly the star of his films. Yet his performance style is otherwise theatrically melodramatic; even more than other actors, he consistently turns to the camera, rather than the action, to perform with gesture and facial tics. In addition to the number and regularity of his films (for periods, one a week), a performance style so connected to early film may well have been the reason for his decline in popularity by 1915. He made only eight more films until 1918, before a final appearance in *The Bounty Killer* (1965) nearly fifty years later.

ROMAINE FIELDING

New research into early film has unearthed remarkable Westerns made by and starring Romaine Fielding (Woal and Woal, 1995). Of Fielding's 107 films made between 1912 and 1917, only eight, some incomplete, survive (ibid., p.9). Made in Arizona, New Mexico, Colorado and Texas, on 'the former sites of forts, old mining camps, wagon train stops, and stagecoach junctions . . . Not merely set in the West, Fielding's films were *about* the West' (ibid., p.13). The films tend to be set contemporaneously, in desert locations of 'desolate, even lethal wasteland where men are stripped of their reason' (ibid., p.23). Their heroes are not 'the classic self-confidently masculine hero but . . . an outcast, one of society's victims' (ibid., p.19). In *The Toll of Fear* (1913), for instance, the hero tracks a band of outlaws, but is overcome with terror and kills himself. His brother in turn tracks him but he also succumbs to the desert. The film ends with the brother in a cave, crazily shooting until the walls collapse on him. The Woals attribute the neglect of Fielding's films to their dystopian mood, 'in an era before the formal conventions of "Hollywood-style" realism had been established' (ibid., p.23).

FROM BRONCHO BILLY TO WILLIAM S. HART

The last years of Broncho Billy Anderson's film career overlapped with the first of those of William S. Hart. In the silent period, what Anderson was to the Western short, Hart was to the Western feature-length film. A classical stage actor for twenty years, Hart starred in stage productions of *The Squaw Man*, *The Virginian* and *The Trail of the Lonesome Pine* before turning to films. He joined the Bison Company in 1914 after Thomas H. Ince acquired it from Native American owners, James Young Deer and Princess Red Wing, who were also actors and consultants on many films at the time. It was located in the Santa Ynez canyon, alongside *The Miller Brothers 101 Ranch Wild West Show*, from which it sourced authentic Western extras and props. In this context, Hart began to star in, sometimes write and most often also direct short Westerns, notably *The Taking of Jim McLane* and *Keno Bates, Liar* (both 1915), eventually developing the first Western feature films, starting with *Hell's Hinges* in 1916.

Most of Hart's subsequent feature films owe a visual debt to cinematographer Joseph H. August who rendered the various rocky locations into spectacular settings. Though shot on monochrome film, prints are invariably tinted, creating definitive Western 'moods' for conventional settings. In *Hell's Hinges*, for instance, saloon interiors are tinted yellow, other interiors filmed at dawn are pink, sunny exteriors are amber, night is blue-green and a fire scene is crimson.

Following Ince first to Triangle and then to Paramount in 1917, Hart was to become among the highest paid stars of the Hollywood of his day. By the time he made his last film, *Tumbleweeds* in 1925, (with the exception of a cameo appearance in *Show People* in 1928), he had made nearly eighty films.

Hart was already middle-aged before making his first film. Older than Anderson, he was well into his fifties at the height of his career. The maturity of Hart and Anderson define the first Western film hero as a knowing and pragmatic man of experience. Despite his maturity, Hart was an imposing figure, over six feet tall. In particular, his stone-faced, granite-jawed look of implacability and restrained acting style has characterised aging Western actors since this time, from Randolph Scott a generation later to, most recently, Clint Eastwood. Close-ups of Hart reveal weathered features through pale make-up (a legacy of stage melodrama), with versatile eyes that can stare down villains, yet glance coyly away from heroines. He moves with calm authority until danger threatens, when his body tenses, leans forward from the hips with legs bent and set on a diagonal, to outface villainy in a gunfight, often – and for the first time in film – with two pistols. Hart developed Anderson's functional costume – already in publicity shots a stage development from authentic cowboy gear – into one of greater flamboyance. Chaps on the legs have wide wings; a waistcoat and a huge knotted scarf overlay a checked rather than plain shirt; wrist cuffs are fringed and studded; two holster belts cross his waist; the showy costume is topped off with the deep-creased crown of a wide-brimmed Stetson hat. Though this Show costume distinguishes him from Anderson's more humble appearance, Hart's films seek a greater authenticity,

Stone-faced William S. Hart epitomises the imposing, mature Western hero, in a typically relaxed pose. A publicity portrait from *Wild Bill Hickock* (1923).

not least by being made amidst Westerners and in Western locales around Los Angeles. Although born an Easterner, he lived much of his life in the mid-West and, unlike Anderson, remained there after his active film career was over. His familiarity with rodeo and Show skills is evident at key moments in the films and especially at their climax, when Hart's character will invariably display a cowboy's riding or roping feat as part of the drama.

Hart played a number of different roles in his Westerns, including gamblers, policemen, preachers, soldiers and even an Indian chief, but his star persona was the cowboy. Like Anderson, Hart's cowboy hero could appear in his films either as law-abiding or outlaw, and frequently as a reformed outlaw, as in *The Return of Draw Egan* (1916). More often, however, like Broncho Billy in *Naked Hands*, he could turn bad during a film as a consequence of some evil deed done to him, only returning to lawful ways when wrong had been righted, often through the agency of a supportive heroine. This characterisation became so familiar that he is best known as the generic 'Good-Badman', rather than for any of the other characters he played (all of which typified the honest masculinity of the Westerner, including Blue Blazes Rawden, Silent Texas Smith, Draw Egan, Truthful Tulliver, Square Deal Sanderson and Hardwood Haynes).

The Silent Man (1917) is a good example of the dramatic, narrative and aesthetic complexity Hart brought to his Westerns. In this film, Hart's Westerner is both a romantic hero whose courtship suffers setbacks and a classic victim of melodrama who cannot defend himself because 'innocence cannot speak its name'. The melodrama drives narrative events tumbling one over another. Tricked out of his property rights by a most villainous villain, his attempts to seek justice only serve to criminalise him, until, in a triumphant *deus ex machina*, the villain is exposed and the hero's good name is restored. The romance punctuates the narrative in occasional sentimental and satiric scenes, and the coda resolves the romance in rare but satisfying marriage. Hart combines elements of romance and melodrama with spectacular locations, action and stunts to establish the first substantial narrative integration of generic conventions in Western feature films.

The Silent Man opens with Budd Marr (Hart) emerging from a sun-baked desert with packhorse and donkey. Intertitles echo the film title and call him 'The Silent One' (or, even better, in the Mexican print I have seen, 'El Silencioso'). Despite this soubriquet, he seems animated enough when talking to his animals. A rattlesnake, at first curled, then striking at an unseen target, signifies the danger of the desert. Our hero's response is equivocal, in part because the snake exists in shots separate from the hero, with no eye-line matches. Despite the obvious danger, perhaps our hero is as at home as his adversary in this natural landscape. For when he turns to the first township, he finds the human snake can be as venomous to the unwary traveller as the reptile.

The dangers of the desert will spill over into the mining town and is intimated first by its fitting name, Bakeoven. Marr enters a saloon, oddly crowded with mirrors high on walls and ceiling, together with the misleading friendly sign over the bar, 'Hello Thar'. Propping up the bar, Marr orders water to quake his raging thirst, much to the amusement of grizzled old-timer, Grubstake Higgins (J.P. Lockney). The owner, 'Handsome' Jack Pressley (Robert McKim), aroused by the lure of gold Marr draws from his gun belt to pay for his drink, mistakes the unmanly drinking of water rather than beer for naivety. He connives with the portly mine owner, Ames Mitchell (Milton L. Ross), to swindle Marr of his claim, though Marr is wise to the first attempt at a rigged gaming table. Marr is subsequently less perceptive when Pressley sets up a saloon woman, Topaz (Dorcus Matthews), to lure him to a card game. First seen primping at a dressing table mirror, Topaz changes into a more humble gingham outfit, in which disguise she persuades Marr that she is in Pressley's debt. However, Pressley's ruse is exposed in the ensuing card game. In an extraordinary close-up on the reflection of an oil lamp over the table, Marr spots Topaz behind him, revealing his hand to Pressley. In the following struggle, Marr is knocked out, the scene fading on Pressley viciously kicking him.

Thus begins Marr's victimisation. Released from prison, his gun returned surreptitiously by Grubstake, Marr returns to his claim, only to be confronted and denied by Ames Mitchell who has stolen deeds to the property. This scene is intercut with another, initiating the romance narrative as Pressley lures the innocent Vola Vale (Betty Bryce) from her home with false promises of affection. Marr's melodrama and the new romance meet when a masked Marr holds up a stagecoach carrying Pressley, Vola and her younger brother. Marr seeks retribution in the shape of Pressley and his gold, but Pressley escapes, shamelessly abandoning his young charges. Marr loses his quarry, but gets his gold – and the girl. In comic scenes involving attempted escape and inviting smells of prairie cooking, Marr keeps Vola captive. Through a series of flashbacks to key earlier moments in his story, Marr gradually persuades Vola of his worth, not least when it is vouched for by his aged backwoods' friends, Preachin' Bill Hardy (George Nichols) and his wife (Gertrude Claire).

The film then moves into a complicated series of action scenes. Pressley returns to town to persuade the law to form a posse. As individuals post wanted notices on him, Marr is gradually hunted down. Though he humbles Pressley and eludes the posse when cornered in a general store, he is powerless to stop the burning of the Hardy homestead. In a harrowing scene, Bill is bullied by the posse, but refuses to divulge Marr's whereabouts. The old man stoically stands to one side as his wife wildly seeks to save something of her life's possessions from the flames.

Meanwhile, Vola's brother, unaware of Marr's innocence, is injured in an attempted ambush, a misunderstanding which is soon settled as Marr attends to the wound. Together they connive a plot for the boy to return a trussed up Marr to town in exchange for the reward. In the heated atmosphere of a climactic courtroom trial, Pressley seeks to fuel hatred against Marr, who is only rescued from a threatened lynching by the sudden and unexpected intervention of Grubstake. Now dressed in smart suit and backed by armed soldiers, Grubstake reveals his true identity. No longer the penniless miner but an 'agent of the Governor General', Grubstake exposes the criminal Pressley and Ames. In the subsequent confusion, Pressley tries one last desperate act. Using Vola as a shield, he attempts an escape. With a dramatic and crowd pleasing leap from a high window, Marr lassos Pressley from his horse and the final melodrama scene fades on community congratulations. In contrast, the romance plot is resolved in a coda as Marr and Vola, witnessed by all the minor characters, make their vows in 'the silence of the mountains'.

William S. Hart's contribution to the Western lies in the way his films develop the conventions of the Western genre in the transitional period from shorts to feature length narratives. Hart extends the dramatic limitations of Western shorts into complicated plots around a central cowboy hero, developing psychological motivation and a wider range of character relationships. In films like *The Silent Man*, the narrative weaves together elements of romance and melodrama, providing an aesthetic framework from which later Westerns could extend the possibilities of the Western imaginary. The two central female characters, for instance, betray their origins in the opposing types of stage melodrama's Good Girl and Bad Girl. The good girl is associated with youthful innocence, the home and family, and the bad girl is associated with the vamp's sexuality, disguise and subterfuge. Yet the extended narrative space of the film's feature length allows Topaz to be cast first as a femme fatale and then as a victim of the villain's deception, and for ultimate redemption when the Bad Girl gives evidence against Pressley in the climactic courtroom scene. The heroine also has opportunity for psychological development as she moves from the victim of seduction through comic scenes with Marr and sympathetic scenes in the Hardy homestead. The two women finally join forces (though it must be acknowledged, this unmotivated connection is surprising), which also suggests a sorority that transcends their gender stereotypes, as well as satisfyingly merging the melodrama and romance narrative strands. Over and above devices such as these, however, stands Hart's cowboy hero of romance, melodrama and their combination in romantic Western melodrama. Hart's revenge drama is acutely felt, as he becomes the victim of deceit and is tossed about by the conspiracy to do him down. That he refuses to be defeated by such oppressive forces, that he struggles against his melodrama and pursues his courtship of the heroine, marks him as an action hero. And that he triumphs through recourse to the ways of the Westerner – deploying cowboy skills of riding and roping, survival skills in the wilderness and on the lonely trail – makes him the first fully developed star of the Western genre.

CHAPTER FIVE

The Series Western

Names can be generically evocative. Take these, for instance, listed alpha-betically: Art Acord, Gene Autry, Don 'Red Ryder' Barry, Rex Bell, William 'Hopalong Cassidy' Boyd, Johnny Mack Brown, Fred Burns, Rod Cameron, Yakima Canutt, Harry Carey, Sunset Carson, Lane Chandler, Ray 'Crash' Corrigan, Buster Crabbe, Bob Custer, William Desmond, William 'Wild Bill' Elliott, Hoot Gibson, Jack Holt, Al Hoxie, Fred Humes, Buck Jones, Allan 'Rocky' Lane, Ken Maynard, Tim McCoy, Tom Mix, Pete Morrison, Audie Murphy, George O'Brien, Bud Osborne, Bill Patton, Jack Perrin, Tex Ritter, Roy Rogers, Buddy Roosevelt, Reb Russell, Randolph Scott, Charles Starrett, Bob Steele, Roy Stewart, Fred Thomson, Tom Tyler, Wally Wales, John Wayne, Ted Wells.

Names like these evoke Westerns. They speak variations on a generic theme, mixing connotations of individualism, reliability and solid tradition (Harry, Fred, Jack, Tom and, especially, Bill), the informality of regular American 'guys' (Al, Art, Bud, Pete, Bob and Ray), the more exotic and glamorous Show names (Buck, Rocky, Tex, Lane, Red and perhaps even Sunset) with the historical and legendary (Carson, Cody, Wild Bill, Custer, Roosevelt, Reb). Apart from the occasional discrepancy of the less ruggedly masculine sounding Tim, Wally and Hopalong, the names also speak the gender and social class of the Western hero. In general, they are diminutives and nicknames that all-male groups typically apply among themselves. In particular, they express the easy-going, homosocial loyalties of working men rather more than, for instance, the schoolboy corruptions of élite groups (in Britain, these might be Freddie or Johnny, or focus more on surnames, like Smithy or Jonesy).

Some of these Western names may be familiar, recognisable film *stars* of Westerns, most famously John Wayne and Randolph Scott. George O'Brien is the leading man of a major silent melodrama, *Sunrise* (1927), as well as of the epic Western, *The Iron Horse* (1924). But the remaining names now ring with the quaintness of a bygone age. However, at times from the 1910s to the 1950s, these were all household names, akin to the status of stars of pop(ular) music and television soap opera today. Like soap actors, these are the names of film characters as much as film stars, though the two were more commonly the same. They are the names adopted by actors in Hollywood who were once identified as cowboy stars of a particular form of Western – the series Western. These names, the star personae and the films of the series Westerns provide much of the filmic soil in which the Western genre subsequently grew.

THE ORIGINS OF SERIES WESTERNS

Westerns were central to Hollywood's task of maintaining its audiences during its earliest days. There were many changes in short periods, especially the shift from short to feature-length films during the 1910s and from silent to sound cinema around the late 1920s. The expanding film industry required such novelties to keep its huge audiences, but it also needed to strike a balance and maintain continuity in the cinema experience. Continuity was centrally provided by genre production. The Western was a staple in the production schedules of the major and minor Hollywood studios, which were either vertically integrated (owning a chain of film production, distribution and exhibition sites, like MGM and Paramount), or 'independent' ('Poverty Row' production companies like Puritan and Victory). Some of the independents are particularly identified by their production of series Westerns; one of the largest, Republic, specialised in them from 1937.

All Hollywood studios made Westerns since they guaranteed a regular and predictable financial return. However small the return, this was crucial to the profitability and survival of the independents, for 'working under the shadow of (major studios) Universal, MGM and First National, shoestring budget studios such as Artclass, Anchor, Sierra and Sunset were surviving solely on the box-office draw of their westerns' (Flynn, p.7).

Hollywood maintained the loyalty of its audiences through periods of change not only by standardising regular genre production, but also through the evolution of its film form. In Bordwell, Staiger and Thompson's monumental work, *The Classical Hollywood Cinema: Film Style and Mode of Production to 1960* (1985), they chart the development of a film form associated with Hollywood's establishment of the continuity system of narrative construction, by the time of the advent of sound. The key to that development is the growing sophistication of its storytelling in images and sound, its power to create increasingly complex narrative structures, with shifting points-of-view, through multiple story lines.

Westerns play a revealing role in this formal history. However, while they constitute the numerically major genre, only a few Westerns in this period were A features (these were frequently the most expensive A features). The vast majority of Westerns were B film series Westerns; 'Of the 1,336 Westerns made . . . between 1930 and 1941, only 66, or a mere 5 per cent, could be classed as A features' (Buscombe, 1988, pp.38–9). The films of Broncho Billy Anderson and William S. Hart are series Westerns, though their huge popularity in their time distinguished them from their contemporaries, historically separating them from the series form and according them higher status.

SERIES AND SERIALS

There are also serial Westerns, though the genre was not as central to the serial form as other types of fiction. In the 1910s, while Anderson was king of the series Western, adventure 'serial queens' like Pearl White in Pathé's *The Perils of Pauline* (1914) ruled the serials. In the 1920s, the serial star equivalent to Hart was Elmo Lincoln, one of several muscular adventure heroes, best known for *Elmo The Mighty* (1919) and as the first screen Tarzan. During the 1930s, the genre focus shifted again as comic book superheroes and science fiction characters dominated serial form, including Batman, Superman and, most famously, swimming star Buster Crabbe as Flash Gordon (Singer, 1996). There are few enough Westerns among over 7,000 serials made until the early 1950s to suggest that it was not an ideal genre for the serial form. Buster Crabbe even appeared in a number of series Westerns, but, despite his serial fame, never in a Western serial. However, the Western has some claim to serial fame, for producing the first science-fiction Western hybrid (*The Phantom Empire*, 1935, featuring Gene Autry), the most expensive (*Riders of Death Valley*, 1941) and the last film serial, Columbia's *Perils of the Wilderness* (1956), starring Dennis Moore.

The Western was the major genre of the series form well into the days of television series in the 1950s. This chapter deals with the vast body of series Westerns in the period. It attempts to understand its relation to the Western genre as a whole and why it is the critically most neglected generic form of all Westerns.

SERIES WESTERNS AND FILM CRITICISM

Contemporary film reviewers were disparaging about the qualities of series Westerns, labelling them 'oaters' (after the predominance of horses and chases) and 'hayburners' (after the frequency with which barns were burned, usually in archive stock footage commonly incorporated for moments of spectacle). Studio managements and exhibitors could be equally dismissive of what they saw as mere programme fillers for the main A feature. It is certainly the case that series Westerns tend to be less aesthetically polished than Westerns in the critical canon; they can be conventionally repetitive in narrative structure and generically predictable. The low cultural value of the Western genre historically (which continues in some circles) stems from the reputation of the largely forgotten series Westerns of their time. They are the source of assumptions about the banality and predictability of the genre. An instance of this is perceived in the origin of the stereotyped colour coding of the Western hero and villain (though of all series stars, only Buck Jones is recurrently distinguished by white hat and horse, Silver, from the black hat and horse of regular villain Charlie King).

Against this background, it is not surprising to find very little serious study of the series Western. Most of the key critical writing about the Western tends to ignore this generic form. The writing that does attend to the series Western is less critical than celebratory, written by fans recalling their first cinema experiences of the genre in holiday and matinée performances. For these critics, series Westerns are nostalgic escapism into a past as much biographical as mythical. In the words of Buck Rainey, they are: 'fascinating historical examples of the romantic flavour of a haunting nostalgia for a more individualistic and flamboyant past' and 'part of the evasion of reality in a mundane world' (Rainey, 1996, p.6).

This mode of writing tends to centre on film star biographies and synopses of favourite films, listing and charting, reminiscing and reliving childhood (or, really, boyhood) fantasies. Rainey's overstated eulogy to series Westerns is typical: 'the most entertaining movies ever made and the finest aggregate of stars ever to inhabit Hollywood' (ibid., p.5). As a consequence of this, serious criticism of the Western seeks to distinguish itself largely by ignoring the place of series Westerns in the history of the genre, regarding it as marginal and juvenile. Yet there are notable films among series Westerns, despite their financial limitations and short production periods. More importantly, they collectively contribute significantly to developments in the Western genre. Some of the most recent critical attention in Western studies has deployed new approaches in film studies to the variety, role and cultural meaning of these films, among which are audience reception studies (Pumphrey, 2001) and cultural studies of how series Westerns can be understood to negotiate ideas about living in a modern world for their contemporary audiences (Stanfield, 2001). For these reasons, they are worth critical respect and consideration.

The film careers of the first cowboy stars were modelled on the pattern set by the first major Western film heroes, Broncho Billy Anderson and

William S. Hart. But these stars are the best known surviving names of an exhaustive number of other actors who adopted cowboy personae to front their own film series. Perhaps the reputations of Anderson and Hart have survived their periods best because they brought a contemporaneous realism – favoured by critics at the time – to the look of their films, highlighted in Anderson's ordinary working man's clothing and in Hart's dusty locations and mean buildings. In contrast, the films of other series stars were less concerned with expressions of authenticity and the aesthetics of the everyday. One of the ironies of this is that other, more flamboyant series Western stars were often genuine Westerners, unlike either Anderson or Hart. But this judgement only serves as a partial explanation, as shall become apparent when we consider the very different Tom Mix, the third major cowboy star of the silent period.

SERIES WESTERN FORM

The short Westerns of Anderson and Hart, and Hart's feature-length Westerns, set the pattern for series Westerns. They can be defined as films in which a cowboy star plays the hero in a series that can number hundreds, sometimes dozens in a year. The stars are known by their Western-sounding names and sometimes, like 'Broncho' Billy, with a nickname, such as 'Lash' LaRue or 'Colonel' Tim McCoy. Some, like McCoy, adopt different character names for each film; others, like Gene Autry, always play 'themselves', characters with their own star names.

The cowboy stars were actors contracted by a studio for six to eight films in a series, after which their contracts were reviewed. The actor would then negotiate pay for another series, or accept contracts better or worse with an alternative studio, the conditions of which would be wholly determined on the basis of audience response. Whilst some series stars worked all their active lives, the careers of others could be very short-lived (with a proportion meeting untimely deaths in accidents, most famously Tom Mix and Buck Jones). The production schedule for films in series Westerns was about ten days, less than half the time allocated to A features. Most were heavily reliant on stock footage, especially for action sequences often drawn from earlier Westerns. Many famous film directors began their careers working on series Westerns, among them William Wyler, Raoul Walsh and John Ford.

Each film in a series offers a discrete story, unlike serials which offer a continuing story in episodes. They are invariably shorter than features, sometimes less than an hour and rarely longer than eighty minutes (*Borderland* (1937) at 82 minutes, is the longest). Series Westerns develop from around 1911 and continue until the early 1950s. As a form, it no longer exists in cinema (although films such as the *Star Wars* and *Die Hard* series could be argued as titles in a short series form), but it is now a dominant form in contemporary television, especially in cop and crime drama. Series Westerns transformed from cinema to broadcasting during the 1950s, when seasons of Westerns became the most popular of weekly television series, with characters such as 'Cheyenne' Bodie (Clint Walker) and 'Bronco' Lane (Ty Hardin). The series form is particularly suitable to an entertainment medium of regular yet casual consumption, as popular cinema was in the first half of the twentieth century and as television has become over the last fifty years.

Beyond those defining similarities, there is diversity among series Westerns. Some contemporaries of Broncho Billy Anderson and William S. Hart, such as Francis Ford (elder brother of the celebrated director of Westerns John Ford), Harry Carey and Tim McCoy, are similarly modelled on their dramatic characters, yet others are less serious in tone. At one extreme are the comedy Westerns of Hoot Gibson, whose persona is that of a friendly, light-hearted cowboy. In *The Phantom Bullet* (1926), for instance, he plays the fool to ex-pose a murderer. Unlike most Western heroes, Gibson is often the comically clumsy butt of practical jokes. Different again are the Westerns of Gene Autry, which are more crime dramas in a contemporary Western setting. Yet, they are so often interrupted by Autry's songs that they look towards the sub-genre of musicals in a Western setting, like the later A features, *Calamity Jane* (1953) and *Paint Your Wagon* (1969). There is such diversity among series Westerners, that it makes sense to delineate them through representative sub-genres and their leading proponents.

Experienced Westerners

Harry Carey is perhaps best known in Western criticism for his character roles in classic Westerns such as *Red River* (1948) and *Duel in the Sun* (1946). Among Western film-makers and fans, however, he is remembered with much affection. Director John Ford dedicates *Three Godfathers* (1948) to his memory in an opening title card and John Wayne honours him when imitating his stance at the end of *The Searchers* (1956). What may be less known is the resonance of the stance and the reason for such affection in the earlier career of Harry Carey, star of silent series Westerns, most of which are lost (Buscombe, 2000, p.25). As the eponymous hero of *The Shepherd of the Hills* (1941), Carey is a man returning to his feuding mountain family after a forced separation of many years, faced with the difficult task of brokering a peace. His identity is concealed from his son (John Wayne) until the climactic revelation of his responsibility for the killing that prompted a feud he now aims to bring to an end. In this film, Carey demonstrates the qualities of the

A publicity portrait of Harry Carey, in the characteristic pose, with hand caressing arm, honoured by John Wayne as Ethan Edwards at the close of *The Searchers* (1956).

'lovable drifter' that Rainey claims defines Carey's star persona of earlier series Westerns (1996, p.15). More substantially, Carey confronts recalcitrants face to face with a typically stoic implacability, registering his complete assumption of responsibility and a refusal to be denied his task.

This easy-going resolution echoes the cowboy persona of William S. Hart, a contemporary Western series star. Carey's origins were in the East, but he moved to Hollywood with D.W. Griffith's stock company, later starring in the first Westerns directed by John Ford, often as 'Cheyenne Harry'. Critics also liken Carey to Hart in appearance, and Fenin and Everson compare his *Satan Town* (1926) (though less favourably) to Hart's *Hell's Hinges* (1916). But *The Prairie Pirate* (1925) suggests Carey's persona may be more haunted than Hart's and his films ultimately darker. *The Prairie Pirate* is a revenge narrative, predating the intensity of the search in later films like *The Bravados* (1958), *The Naked Spur* (1953) and, of course, *The Searchers*. The shocking opening scene charts the suicide of the hero's sister when threatened with rape by the villain. This triggers a relentless search in which the image of his sister impels Carey's hero through otherwise impassable terrain, only for him to break down in an unexpected depth of emotion when finally confronting the villain. The narrative similarity to John Ford's *The Searchers* indicates that the homage to Carey may extend beyond the impressionist stance of John Wayne's final performance gesture. Wayne plays the isolate, Ethan Edwards, whose narrative search to avenge the massacre of a female intimate in his family equally traumatises the hero and evokes the figure of Carey's original ghost-like character, a man driven by horrific personal experience to the edge of madness and therefore also to the edge of civilisation. In adopting Carey's pose, Wayne evokes the haunted Carey persona.

Carey was younger than Hart, but was still an older hero, in his mid 30s at the height of his popularity at the turn of the 1920s. The cowboy star of the successive period most like these two is Tim McCoy. McCoy worked on the epic *The Covered Wagon* (1923) before starting his first series for MGM in 1927. His most popular period, however, was when working for Poverty Row studios like Puritan and Victory, where he often took responsibility for his own projects, such as *End of the Trail* (1932), which was admired for its pro-Indian narrative. McCoy's military aloofness was the model for later series Westerners like the prematurely silver-haired William Boyd as Hopalong Cassidy (the nickname arising from a limp that appeared only in the first film titled by the character's name in 1935). Other notable experienced Westerners are Allan 'Rocky' Lane and Jack Holt.

Series Westerns are today far less available than feature Westerns. Christopher Wicking's teasing account of McCoy makes the study of his films, like the 'downbeat *Lightnin' Bill Carson* and sombre *Aces and Eights*', sound long overdue:

'On minute budgets and at a time when flamboyant singing cowboys were invading the range, these two films especially eschew virtually every marketable ingredient, concentrating instead on miniature tragedies with the McCoy character as helpless justicier (sic) whose "rightness" and control over his own life is of no value to the other people whose lives his intersects. So persuasive, intriguing and singular are his talent and manifest thematic concerns that one feels a complete archaeological dig is required before his true nature and value will be appreciated. He was one of a rare breed – just how rare awaits complete authentication.'

(*Wicking in Buscombe, 1988, p.363*)

Buck Jones is also a significant figure in this mould. Jones made about sixty series Westerns for Fox in the 1920s and his film roles continued into the 1930s, long after the end of Hart's career. In *Stone of Silver Creek* (1935), Buck Rainey finds a film that both exemplifies Jones' distinctive cowboy star qualities and yet can be distinguished from other B Westerns of the time. With minimal action until the climax, the film narrates an intricate plot in which Jones plays saloon owner, T. William Stone. In one strand, Stone inherits a part-share in a mine 'when he turns in two gamblers who cheated one of his customers in a card game' (Rainey, 1996, p.19). In the second strand, Stone and a local preacher vie for the attentions of the heroine, at one point joining the congregation and attracting greater church attendances by offering free alcohol. The two strands come together at the end, when the gamblers return for revenge; the preacher wins the heroine while 'Buck gets religion and one of his old girlfriends' (ibid., p.19).

Other cowboy stars in the Good-Badman framework that Rainey calls 'realists' (ibid., p.22) include Jack Holt (unusual for sporting a moustache, more usually a sign of villainy in the 1920s), Tom Tyler (star of a series from the 1920s to 1940s, but better known as villain Luke Plummer, killed off-screen in the climactic gunfight with the Ringo Kid (John Wayne) in *Stagecoach*, 1939), Roy Stewart, Art Acord, George O'Brien, Tom Keene and 'Wild Bill' (William) Elliott. Of Elliot, Everson states: 'When he played an outlaw, or a reformed outlaw, he was just that – not a lawman posing as a bad guy . . . he could also be ruthless, selfish, and even . . . not mind holding a gun on an unarmed opponent and beating the truth out of him if the circumstances warranted.' (quoted by Rainey, 1996, p.20). From accounts such as these, it is evident that series cowboy stars in the Hart tradition push at the conventions of the Hart legacy, appearing unafraid to take on a darker range of roles and narratives.

Many of the series Westerns featuring these more mature cowboy stars were produced by major studios on higher-than-average budgets. Although their audience appeal was wide and could vary during their careers, however short, most cowboy stars playing experienced Westerners tended to feature in dramas particularly popular with adult audiences. This may account for the greater risks the films and star personae take with unconventional stories, pushing at generic boundaries of the time. Though clearly indebted to Victorian melodrama, they explore darker emotional areas of the psyche, especially those associated in part with revenge narratives.

The Action Hero

A very different type of series Western cowboy star was more attractive to juvenile audiences, befitting a new age of significant political, economic and cultural change that emerged during the 1920s. This younger and more athletic cowboy hero features in less dramatic and motivated narratives than his older counterparts. These films mark a more general shift from Hollywood's aesthetic origins in Victorian theatrical melodrama and cultures associated with Europe to the faster pace of an expanding, urban, immigrant melting-pot culture of America's New World. This is the Jazz Age, a time when earlier social moralities are questioned in the more open life styles of younger generations who, emboldened by full employment, social mobility and a new affluence in a burgeoning economy, contribute to an increasingly confident national identity. In the classical period, Hollywood cinema in general was part of this condition of modernity (Charney and Schwartz, 1995). Hollywood was typical of new developments in industrialised entertainments, its cinema screens filled with images of the modern world's new prosperity and consumerism. The image of the new cowboy action hero, whilst remaining rooted in the open spaces of the Old West of the imagination, brokered a significant leap from the Hart tradition of ageing Westerners to embrace the modern world.

The series Western's action hero may owe debts to major studio stars of the late silent period like Douglas Fairbanks. Though best known for his later expensive costume spectacles of the 1920s, such as swashbucklers, *The Three Musketeers* (1921), *Robin Hood* (1922) and *The Thief of Bagdad* (1924), Fairbanks' career began more modestly, making shorts – including Westerns – for Triangle. Titles like *The Good Bad Man* (1916) indicate a degree of self-conscious awareness of series Westerns around him. Yet other titles suggest an entirely different kind of Western from those of Anderson and Hart; his debut film, *The Lamb* (1915), for instance, and *The Americano* (1916), *Wild and Woolly* (1917) and *The Mollycoddle* (1920). 'Usually playing an Eastern aristocrat youth seeking only excitement and romance, Fairbanks wove together madcap comedy and action using the West as a metaphor for freedom and adventure where all young men must go to prove their manhood and find true love.' (Flynn, p.6). These films introduce a faster pace and more knockabout comedy to Westerns films and action films more generally. They are full of Fairbanks' inventive acrobatic stunts and the physical exuberance of a 'body made for movement' (Studlar in Buscombe and Pearson, 1998, p.64). Their success signalled a new direction in the Western genre. Though Studlar argues that these films resist the trends of urban modernity, they can also be viewed as negotiating them, displacing the energy of the fast-living and energetic new urban male onto a new figure of the rural cowboy.

An example of this is *The Knickerbocker Buckaroo* (1919) in which Teddy Drake (Douglas Fairbanks) plays a selfish Eastern aristocrat who learns social responsibility in a series of adventures in the Great American Desert. Like the hero of *The Mollycoddle*, Teddy is so limited by Eastern ways of overprotective motherhood and absent fatherhood that only the wilderness of the West can provide the conditions for achieving proper manhood. For Gaylyn Studlar, Fairbanks' Westerns 'play with the contrast between masculinity East and West' (ibid., p.69), offering 'appealing fantasy versions of the transformative power of the West as the last romantic place in America' (ibid., p.72). Yet Studlar also argues that the films represent a negative WASP response to the threat of immigration, defining an ideal of American masculinity on traditional, Anglo-Saxon lines. Following this critic's arguments, these films are not displaced narratives of modernity, but anti-modern critiques of the new America. Whether the films of the new action hero are for or against modern America, they are certainly negotiating conflicts between the old and the new.

The influence of Fairbanks' action Westerns is evident in the range of new cowboy stars that follow, Tom Mix foremost among them. Mix was the third most popular cowboy star of the earliest period, though his career long exceeded those of Anderson and Hart. Mix's biographies detail a colourful personal history. Among the least likely claims are that he was a Texas Ranger and rodeo champion before entering films. More likely, he came to films through association with the Miller Brothers 101 Ranch and other Shows (DeMarco, 1980, p.12). Though raised in the East, in Pennsylvania, Mix typifies this new breed of Western action hero, a youthful Westerner greatly at ease as a cowboy. Like virtually all series cowboy stars, he is identified with a named horse, which he treats like a pal, even at times to rather one-sided conversation, where he confides feelings a masculine reserve otherwise represses in female company. Whilst Tex Ritter had the evocative White Flash and Ken Maynard had Tarzan (probably the most bizarre choice of name for a horse in a Western), Mix's groomed, chestnut horse had the simplest name, Tony.

Although cowboys such as Hart display skills in riding and roping at moments in their films, Mix and other action heroes promote their observably greater equestrian skills to the foreground of their plots, using them as a stage for elaborate stunts. Fenin and Everson in *The Western: From Silents to the Seventies* (1977) recount a series of complex predicaments in Mix's films, from which his cowboy hero must extricate himself with ingenious escapes based around his athleticism and acrobatic stunt work, assisted by a little trick photography (1977, p.116).

Although Rainey finds Mix's cowboy persona 'sexless', in keeping with the family orientation of his 'flirt and run' films (1996, p.23), Mix's performances echo those of Fairbanks in bringing a new kind of masculine display to the Western, which can be understood as sexualising the body of the cowboy hero. This is evident in Mix's attire, most flamboyant of Show costumes, finely and elaborately decorated, with short, hand-carved boots and light-reflecting giant spurs. Drawing more on circus tradition than authentic working clothes, Mix wears chaps with the widest wings, perhaps the largest ten-gallon hat outside of Western parodies like *Son of Paleface* (1952) and is the first cowboy star to sport gloves. Such extravagant design extended to Mix's horse, Tony, whose saddle and livery was as embellished as its rider.

Most importantly, however, Mix's clothing was tailored to shape his body and emphasise the sexuality of his physique. Mix posed for the camera, attracting the eye of the film spectator to the Western hero in ways denied to Hart and his generation of older cowboy stars. In *The Fighting Streak* (1922), for instance, Mix is Andy, typically introduced in intertitles as both 'best, rider, quickest on the draw, deadliest of shots' and yet 'a man of peace'. First seen in a blacksmith's forge, his behaviour exasperates his Uncle Jasper when he prefers playing with puppies to joining in the horseplay of his peers. This simple plot introduction is formally complicated by a series of images of the star filmed from the waist up, high-key lit against an out-of-focus background. Mix is offered as a glamorous pin-up, in a manner more commonly used in the classical period for female stars, and he clearly enjoys the lingering gaze of the camera. The blacksmith set motivates the choice of simple working clothes, rather than the more usual Show costume, but the style is a subtle mix of function and display, tailored and worn to emphasise the male body. The scene's impact derives from the formal invitation to look sexually on the body of the male figure. Seen today, the look is reminiscent of the sexualised appearance of one of the first of the new breed of Method actors, Marlon Brando in *A Streetcar Named Desire* (1951), which similarly startled its contemporary audiences.

The film form of *The Fighting Streak*'s opening scene sexualises the new cowboy star but, by showing him in a camera style normally reserved for the representation of heroines, it also feminises him. The style also serves the character's narrative function, for Andy exhibits a softer masculinity, unafraid of domestic pleasures like playing with puppies and yet strong enough to withstand the jeers of other men. Molly Haskell argues that Mix 'never enjoys

Tom Mix gets the drop on villains in a publicity still for one of his last films,
Terror Trail (1933).

violence nor deploys it to establish his manhood . . . enhanced by the admission of weakness' (1997, p.60). This analysis of the Mix persona suggests that
the action series Western of the 1920s dramatically shifts the conventional
cowboy hero's masculine image, which is a shift encouraged by the move
towards a more youthful, modern figure. It is in this context that what has
otherwise been regarded as Mix's juvenile image might be better understood.
Unlike Hart's cowboy, Mix never drank alcohol or smoked on screen. His
perfunctory romances tend to be defined by the odd kiss or the more
common climactic holding of hands, with 'Tom, the heroine and Tony
grouped together in harmonious symbiosis and mutual appreciation' (ibid.,
p.57). Rather than reading these slight romances as signs of immaturity and
sexlessness, it might be more productive to regard them as aspects of Mix's
different and more complex masculinity. Though desexualised in narrative
terms, perhaps as a consequence of commercial and censorship calculations
and requirements, Mix's film image is nonetheless sexually coded by film
form. Although he is a man of action, he is also gentle and emotional. As
Haskell says of Mix, 'The domestic person and the effective male are never
irreconcilable' (ibid., p.60).

After this opening scene in *The Fighting Streak*, Andy becomes a more conventional man of action. A typical Mix Western, the film is full of confrontations, chases and fights. Mix takes many opportunities to display his horsemanship, riding Tony across open locations, abruptly pulling up, turning and suddenly galloping again. The moves, reminiscent of Show horse-riding in the confined space of the circus arena, rapidly become a convention of the genre spectacle.

Elsewhere, Mix tends to soften gunplay, preferring fist-fights and cowboy displays, such as roping, to subdue and capture villains. In gunplay, guns are more likely shot from the hand rather than aimed to kill. But Mix is also in occasional scenes of violence that echo Anderson's lengthy and destructive fist-fights and Hart's beatings, especially in *Riders of the Purple Sage* (1925). There is also a scene in *The Fighting Streak* of greater psychological import when Andy is falsely accused and found ostracised from his community. In the gloom of the prairie night, a more wistful tone emerges to reflect the isolation of the cowboy life. Undoubtedly, the narrative organisation of Mix's Westerns simplifies the convoluted narratives of melodrama, harnessing the fast pace and variety form of the circus Show to the structure and drive of single narratives. Although Mix's cowboy persona and new action narratives are markedly distinct from those of the experienced Westerners at the time, there is also a more general generic process developing, widening, deepening and combining old and new generic conventions.

Mix's influence on the development of the Western genre is evident in a career longer than his contemporaries. His first appearance may be as a cowboy extra in Selig's early *Ranch Life in the Great Southwest* (1909). Like Hart and Anderson, Mix controlled his own image, eventually producing and directing his own films during the production of the first 100 shorts for Selig in the six years from 1911. In 1917 he signed for Fox, with which company he made more prestigious features, including indicative titles like *Western Blood* (1918), *The Daredevil* (1920), *Rough-Riding Romance* (1919) and *The Lone Star Ranger* (1923).

Mix's audacious showmanship was the model for many series Western stars. Among these, Ken Maynard is renowned for even greater horse-riding skills than Mix; Fred Thomson entered films, incredibly, from the priesthood, and brought a greater physical glamour than most; and the athletic Yakima Canutt, though better known for his advanced stunt-work on later Western features, performed stunts for others and for his own characters as a silent series cowboy star. It is Canutt who jumps ninety feet from a cliff top on horseback in *The Devil Horse* (1926) and who doubles for the Ringo Kid (John Wayne) by leaping along the line of stagecoach horses in the climactic chase in *Stagecoach* (1939). Of this generation of action cowboy stars who brought youthful vigour, glamour and athleticism to their films, Mix was the most successful for the longest period. He was also one of a few who managed the transition from the silent era to sound film. *Destry Rides Again* (1932) was the first of Mix's several sound films, made for Universal after his contract at Fox ended.

Many series Western stars found film employment before, during, but especially after their careers in any of the numerous touring Wild West Shows (Rainey, 1996, pp.260–81). Many of these brought skills first learned in the rodeo and circus rings to the screen. Mix was no different. Towards the end of his career in 1931, he was attracted by a lucrative offer from Sells Floto Circus and later ran his own touring Tom Mix Circus. He made fewer films thereafter, though he gave his name to a radio broadcast series that was repeated for a further fourteen years after his death in 1940. He appeared in over 300 films, the last of which was a cheap serial, *The Miracle Rider* (1935), for the Poverty Row studio, Mascot, 'leaving the riding-range free for a new breed of talking and singing cowboys' (Flynn, p.7).

SERIES WESTERNS AS PULP FICTION

In Ken Worpole's formative analysis, *Dockers and Detectives* (1983), he argues the importance of what he terms 'pulp fiction' in the lives of its putative working class male readership. Despite the evident differences between the lives of the readers and the fantasy world of the characters in cheap fiction such as the dime novel and genres like the crime thriller, pulp fiction for Worpole carries a potent meaning for its readers. First, it reflects a popular taste for male action stories in which the hero experiences difficulties he is obliged to face yet eventually surmounts. He is a man of action rather than words. When words are required of him, a pithy vernacular remark serves best to resolve the situation. Worpole finds a displaced working class male experience in these narrative structures and character personae, and in the use of vernacular language. Working class men frequently find themselves in employment in which their labour is subject to the command of senior figures, perhaps employers on whose decisions their employment and therefore livelihood may depend. They tend to be unschooled and uncomfortable in the use of language to control situations and emotions in ways practised by élite groups. Pulp fiction heroes share the same conditions and qualities as their readers, yet offer fantasies of control to those who precisely lack control over the conditions of their everyday lives.

Many of the plots pit their protagonists against economic villains, figures who represent big business, wealth or conspiracy. Even where conflicts are reduced to competition between the strong and the weak, the reader can imaginatively identify with the hero's defence of weaker interests since this mirrors his own life experiences. Following this argument Worpole sees pulp fiction as a possible vehicle for radical social criticism, central to its readership's emotional experience, yet the more attractive and powerful in not directly addressing the conditions readers may find themselves in.

Alternatively, for Ariel Dorfman, the regular and repetitive narrative structure of series Westerns featuring the Lone Ranger acts to obscure possibilities for change among its readership. The central conflict between Virtue and Money (but only 'money gotten in excess of certain limits') does not pit Labour against Capital but only against the acquisition of money that threatens the natural order, including an idealised Nature. Dorfman finds that the Lone Ranger offers support for social change by siding with the physically weak, but effectively obscures possibilities for change by separating them from the socially needy. The Lone Ranger, in metaphysical disguise (he appears to have no work and no need for money), emphasises the individual, the personal, the competitive and the paternal. When he talks, he speaks not in a working class vernacular but in 'the rhetoric of the bourgeoisie' (Dorfman, 1983, p.99). Dorfman's notional audience for the series is not Worpole's urban working class male, but the Third World television audience, the recipients of a series sold cheaply as a loss leader for popular American culture in the poorest national economies. The only inspiration that Dorfman finds to challenge his audience is the hope that, one day, the Lone Ranger's Native American companion, Tonto, will talk back.

Dorfman's estimation of the Lone Ranger, as a particular instance of the television series Western, differs markedly from Worpole's pulp fiction analysis. Worpole is more attracted to 'vernacular writing' (1983, p.47) for British readers, even if it is American literature, and less suspicious of Dorfman's fear of cultural imperialism. Worpole does, however, express concern for the 'ferocious virility' and oppressive male bravura of a pulp literature that alienates many women readers, even working class women. His critique of an exclusive masculinity that marginalises and rejects women is balanced against his valuation of a fiction that challenges the social marginalisation of working class men. Worpole therefore acknowledges a misogyny in pulp fiction that qualifies its attractions.

As these accounts indicate, there are many similarities between pulp fiction and the series Westerns examined so far in this chapter. The heroes prefer action over speech which, when used, tends to the laconic and vernacular. They are rough, independent male figures in comparable narrative situations. Yet both critics assume their pulp literature heroes display a traditional masculinity. If Worpole's analysis may hold good for series Westerns with experienced Westerners, it has been shown here that it is less evident of action cowboy stars. It is even less evident of other types of cowboy star. Moreover, neither critic analyses the role these films played for their intended audiences.

In the case of the third type of series Western cowboy star, the singing cowboy, both matters can be addressed.

SINGING COWBOYS

The musical and gangster film emerged with the coming of sound to cinema. They are genres rooted in cinema's new technical ability to record synchronised sound on film. The percussive sounds of tap dancers and machine-guns equally identify the moment of film sound. Most musicals and gangster films of the late 1920s and early 1930s are located in the city, the hub of modernity. The backstage musical, set in the musical theatre centre of Broadway, extends the rhythms of the new popular music of the day to the huge audiences of cinema. The contrasting response of the Western to these new developments, however, was to negotiate relations between the modern world and America's rural past. While the Hollywood majors largely ignored the Western in the 1930s, this was the period in which B series Westerns were in the ascendancy. But it was a different kind of series Western from those of the 1920s, being one in which the cowboy heroes not only talked but also sang. Peter Stanfield locates the reasons for this development in Hollywood's interaction with recorded country and Western music and radio broadcasting in the period, to which might also be added the rise of the Western comic book and revived Show circus tours (Stanfield, 1996).

Like all music in the period, traditional music forms like country music were standardised by the commercial recording industry. The singing cowboy was an important element in the process through which a vast range of musical influences – including subcultural, sectarian and subversive – was brought together into a musical form suitable for a mass market. Modern music of the time entailed crooning to lyrical and melodic harmony and to the syncopated rhythms of big band sound. Country music was at least a fusion of European folk traditions, rural idioms like 'hillbilly' and blue grass (Williamson, 1995), and the blues of plantation slaves in the American South. Cowboy songs had their own peculiar tradition. The first collection of cowboy songs, published in 1897, is connected with touring medicine shows and vaudeville's blackface minstrelsy. The cowboy song sung by the Virginian in Owen Wister's novel is a minstrel song (Stanfield, 1998, pp.97–8).

The music of the modern, the traditional, the general and the particular combined in the songs of the first of the singing cowboys, Gene Autry, whose vocal skills also included the added gimmick of blackface yodelling (mercifully without the blackface). Through the popularity of Autry and other singing cowboys, Westerns became identified with country music to the extent that it has since been known as country and Western music. Subsequently, singers have performed in Western outfits in live stage shows and even on the leading radio show of the time, *The Grand Ole Opry*. By the mid-1940s, all Westerns were using riffs and refrains associated with the musical structures of the singing cowboys. Westerns directed by John Ford from this time commonly organise a range of song traditions on the soundtrack and in their diegeses through associations with the singing cowboys. In *Rio Grande* (1950), there are four original and several traditional songs, but all are sung on and off-screen by the Sons of the Pioneers, a close-harmony group that frequently backed Autry in his films. Thanks to the series singing cowboy, music and song entered fully into the fabric of the A feature Western.

Gene Autry was the first successful singing Western star. Like other singing cowboys, Autry was a singer first (in his case, a sponsored commercial radio star) and had to learn to act as a cowboy. He was a small man of stocky build whose broad, toothy smile flashed through the flamboyant Show costume of an action hero, disguising his limitations as an athlete as much as an actor (these traits were satirised by musical star Dick Powell in *Cowboy from Brooklyn*, 1938). From his first appearance in *In Old Santa Fe* (1934), Autry plays a character named after himself. Like action cowboys, he has a horse and the horse has a name, Champion (later to have his own television series as 'the Wonder Horse' in the 1950s). Like all the singing cowboys who followed him, Autry's masculinity was tailored to a family and juvenile audience. He was immensely popular, especially in rural America and with young matinée audiences (he led *The Motion Picture Herald* poll of top money-making Western stars 1937–42). His film career continued until *Last of the Pony Riders* (1953) and a television career with *The Gene Autry Show* until 1955.

Most critics of the Western deride the singing cowboy, often in ignorance of the films. Even among those critics who celebrate series Westerns, like Fenin and Everson, and Jon Tuska, Autry's films are decried for their lack of authenticity and a suspicious, softer masculinity. Alone among critics, Peter Stanfield has seriously researched Autry's films and their contribution to developments of the Western genre. He finds they 'defy both stereotypical gender readings and the dominant conception of the Western as a frontier narrative' (1998, p.115).

The first problem for Western critics is that the idea of a *singing* cowboy can affront a conventional Western masculinity. Autry and other singing cowboys usually begin a song at the very start of a film and sing several more at regularly spaced moments. In *Strawberry Roan* (1948), Autry is one of a number of cowboys stringing a fence whilst performing the theme song, and in *Mexicali Rose* (1939) he even sings accompanied by bandits (Rainey, 1996, p.32). The songs tend to the jaunty, clip-clop rhythms of a walking (or, at the most, trotting) horse with generic titles such as 'Home on the Range' to add to the likes of Autry's most famous song 'Tumbling Tumbleweeds'. Songs are

Singing cowboy star of series Westerns, Gene Autry, with guitar, his horse, Champion, and June Storey, in a publicity still from *Carolina Moon* (1940).

usually accompanied by diegetic group harmonies with one or more strumming a guitar, rapidly giving way to full extra-diegetic orchestral support. The convention is neatly parodied in the comedy Western, *Blazing Saddles* (1974), when singing cowboy, Cleavon Little, rides by a full accompanying orchestra on the open range. However, comedy is as much a part of singing cowboy Westerns. Gene Autry has a comic sidekick in Smiley Burnette, a Sancho Panza riding his donkey alongside Autry's benign Don Quixote. Moreover, the songs are not merely entertaining time-fillers, but function to attract and combine the films' marginal groups, frequently serving to unite people in democratic causes.

As far as the affront to Western masculinity is concerned, the titles of Autry's films, like the songs, indicate the gentle masculinity of the singing cowboy. For Stanfield, he is 'the Southerner who transforms himself into a cowboy' (2001, p.3). Autry's cowboy persona is that of an ascetic puritan, teetotal and non-smoking; slower to action, he is quick to replace violence with tact and diplomacy through song. The same persona was adopted by other successful singing cowboys who took their lead from Autry, among them Dick Foran, Monte Hale, Rex Allen and Tex Ritter (best known for singing the theme tune over the credits of *High Noon*, 1952). Another was Roy Rogers, who (originally as Leonard Slye) emerged whilst Autry served in the armed forces in 1942. In a career that extended into television series in the 1950s, Rogers became an icon of a maudlin strain of B Western cowboys when he had his horse, Trigger, stuffed for museum display, after its death. Despite this, the softer, even sentimental masculinity of the singing cowboys also represents a more feminised and domesticated Western masculinity, not least attractive to the huge female audiences for Autry's radio career.

THE INFLUENCE OF B WESTERN SINGING COWBOYS

The singing cowboys influenced the development of the Western genre, but their music and song is the least of their contributions. Although sound Westerns use music extensively, exploiting the success of the singing cowboys, they are as likely to return to the earlier vernacular of folk music, for instance in the minstrel songs of Stephen Foster (whose 'Oh, Susanna' is the emblematic song of *The Covered Wagon*, 1923) and traditional hymns like 'Shall We Gather at the River', in Westerns directed by John Ford. The range can be demonstrated in the title songs for Ford films, for instance *My Darling Clementine* (traditional), *She Wore a Yellow Ribbon* (military march) and *The Searchers* (ballad). In *Rio Grande*, there are several Irish songs associated with Republican resistance to British rule, including 'The Bold Fenian Man', rendered as a ballad. Apart from Ford, the most unlikely use of a song in a Western is surely the Welsh 'Men of Harlech' sung by a preacher to raise the spirits of his besieged flock in *Apache Drums* (1951).

The most important aspect of the films of the singing cowboys affecting the Western genre is less the singing than the plot situations. The majority of Gene Autry's films are located in an imaginary but contemporary West, with cars, airplanes, telephones, nightclubs and jet rockets as common as guitars, horses, cattle stampedes, gunplay and saloon fights. Since the films are set in an uncertain period after frontier settlement, crimes of violence take place within a system of regulated and policed law and order. As a result, conflict tends more towards commercial dispute and political intrigue rather than violent struggles to pacify Indians or to subdue aggression in lawless frontier conditions.

In *Tumbling Tumbleweeds* (1935), for instance, Autry is the son of a wealthy landowner disowned by his father when he sides with settlers. Returning after several years to discover his father's murderer, his songs are motivated by his situation, working for a medicine show, and records on a phonograph (including his sentimental song, 'That Silver-Haired Daddy of Mine'). His songs function to unite family and townsfolk – dressed as rural labourers rather than as Westerners – against villains who deride his masculinity and call him a 'lavender cowboy'. In *Colorado Sunset* (1939), Autry joins forces with a network of women radio listeners who urge their husbands and their community to support Autry as sheriff against an anti-farmer 'Protection Association'. As in all his films, Autry is the agent who brings farmers, townsfolk and women in political alignment against forces hostile to rural communities.

Stanfield argues that plots of films like these had a particular resonance with rural audiences of the time, especially those in the South: 'The 1930s B Western is marked by an obsession with ownership of the land . . . under threat of being repossessed by an underhand representative of capitalist interests, the land, unbeknown to its rightful owners, having some hidden value like gold or oil' (1996, p.26). Autry's role is crucial in these plots, the agent through whom communities are united and democratic principles are established. Autry saw his roles as 'a kind of New Deal Cowboy who never hesitated to tackle many of the same problems: the dust bowl, unemployment, or the harnessing of power. This may have contributed to my popularity with 1930s audiences' (quoted in Stanfield 1998, p.110). The films were popular during and after a time of extreme economic depression, which had strongly affected communities on the land 'who also perceived themselves to be under threat from Northern business conglomerates' (ibid., p.26). President Roosevelt's New Deal policies at the time were broadly socially reformist attempts to revive the economy. In this context, the series Westerns of the singing cowboys can be seen as political interventions in their time.

Ronald Butler sees the films of the singing cowboys as means of escape from 'grim realities of failure, bankruptcy, foreclosure, knuckle-scraping poverty, hungry ugliness' (1985, p.19), but for Stanfield, the attraction to their fans is that they actively engage in the political issues close to their own interests. According to Stanfield, they do so by codifying the contemporary struggle between North and South, in terms of a frontier relation between East and West: 'Hollywood, by looking back to a time when America was divided against itself, and suggesting how the country dealt with these divisions, could offer up a palliative for contemporary tensions' (1996, p.27). He concludes of Autry's films that they address 'the difficulties his audience confronted in making the socio-economic change from subsistence farming to a culture of consumption, from self-employment to industrial practices and wage dependency, from rural to urban living. Autry's films represent a confrontation, magnified by the Great Depression, with modernity' (1998, p.115).

These films are also significant for wider developments in the Western genre. Stanfield argues that their plots provide later A Westerns (and Hollywood more generally) of the 1940s with a body of thematic concerns about the meaning of the land. Questions about land ownership and who works it relate to films as disparate as the reformist *The Grapes of Wrath* (1940) and the epic *Gone With the Wind* (1939). Westerns made after *Jesse James* (1939), however, assume that the settlement of land is a Jeffersonian 'agrarian ideal of the self-sufficient farmer' (1996, p.27). Dispossession can thereby justify both outlawry and audience identification with criminality. Importantly, Westerns tend to offer a utopian solution to attacks on land, with settler communities organising to outwit villainous control, which comes in various guises; the offending railroad in *The Return of Frank James* (1940), land grabbers in *Destry Rides Again* (1939), the corrupt 'Judge' Roy Bean (Walter Brennan) in *The Westerner* (1940) and the 'McCord Corporation' led by gangster star Humphrey Bogart in *The Oklahoma Kid* (1939).

Land appropriation is a central feature of indegist histories of America's origins, especially when it concerns white appropriation of Indian territories. The Dawes Act of 1887 effectively allocated land away from the Native American nations and simultaneously dissolved their collective cultures by attempting to assimilate them as individuals through agricultural practices. Much of the racial conflict that structures Westerns stems from these historical conditions of land appropriation

As part of this thematic development, Westerns of the time develop populist heroes, who can resolve any potential contradiction between individualism and community in acts that equally serve self and society. Thus, outlaw Frank James (Henry Fonda) in *The Return of Frank James* gives himself up to save the life of an innocent servant. He magically turns the law on his side in a comic final courtroom drama, as he gradually comes to represent the dispossessed South against the lawful Northern capitalist interests. Tom Jefferson Destry (James Stewart) – perhaps most associated with the populist hero through his films for director Frank Capra such as *Mr Deeds Goes to Town* (1936) – surprises villainy in *Destry Rides Again* with his milk-drinking, gun-eschewing homespun humour, successfully out-thinking the violent threat of the opposition in the community's interests. Cole Hardin (Gary Cooper) in *The Westerner* (1940), draws on qualities of the populist ideal of small-town neighbourliness to impose his domestic masculinity (he wears a gingham shirt) on a rougher masculine villainy (this includes acts of dispossession such as the destructive scenes of cattle driven onto crops). In all these populist heroes, the gentler masculinity of the polite and feminised gentleman owes debts to the series Western cowboys who sing songs, particularly to Gene Autry's 'Southerner who transforms himself into a cowboy' (Stanfield, 2001, p.3).

Finally, Stanfield points up the active space for women in these films alongside the gentler images of masculinity. Echoes of Scarlet O'Hara, the central character of *Gone With the* Wind, and the central female protagonists of other women's films of the period rebound in the heroine's emotional loss, with similar acts of sacrifice made by companionate heroines in Westerns such as

Drums Along the Mohawk (1939). Yet the source of women's prominent roles in these Westerns can also be found in the series Westerns of the singing cowboys. Unusually in the genre, many series Westerns scripts were written by women (Stanfield, 1998, p.111), so it is not surprising to find female characters as active agents at the centre of their communities in these films (ibid., p.112).

Stanfield's major research into the series Westerns of the singing cowboys, and in particular into Gene Autry and his films, opens up substantial debate about their significance both to their contemporary audiences and to later developments in the Western genre. Their importance for him coincides with new historical accounts that raise 'the possibility of imagining a West that operates autonomously from the frontier myth . . . in which the frontier has long since gone and the modern world . . . sits comfortably alongside the old' (Stanfield, 2001, p.10). The series cowboy of the 1930s more generally has little to do with American frontier history but is instead 'produced by the tensions engendered by industrialisation' (ibid., p.12), through an 'ability to mediate between the past and present, the rural and the urban, the farm and the factory, the premodern and the modern' (ibid., p.4).

THE LAST DAYS OF SERIES WESTERNS

Series Western stars of the 1930s continued their careers into the 1940s. Although action stars rarely sang, the films of the singing cowboys – especially Autry and Rogers – varied between action and songs, increasingly dissolving earlier distinctions. From 1939, however, the major studios began to re-invest in A feature Westerns after the unexpected box-office successes of films such as *Stagecoach*. With an increase in A film production, series Western production gradually declined, replaced by fewer, bigger-budget B Westerns. Some series stars graduated to character roles and bit parts in these new, more expensive features: only John Wayne became a major box-office star, his name becoming an icon of the Western genre. No other series stars escaped their identification with Westerns, though Robert Mitchum, a Western series villain in the early 1940s, grew to stardom in the 1950s and is not so identified with a single genre.

The popularity of some series stars declined enough for them to be teamed together. The Three Mesquiteers series has a changing roll call, but the Rough Rider series more regularly combine Buck Jones, Tim McCoy and Ray Hatton, first in *Arizona Bound* (1940). From *Bells of Rosarita* (1945) onwards, it was also increasingly common for a Western hero to call on other series stars to appear in cameo roles to help out with tasks too big to overcome alone. The sons of series stars, Tim Holt and Harry Carey Junior, began to appear in their own series Westerns during the late 1940s, but rapidly shifted to character roles in feature Westerns from the 1950s, Carey distinctively, in films directed by John Ford.

Perhaps studios were also finding it increasingly difficult to create variation within the series form. They turned to series built around fictional characters, like Columbia's Durango Kid (Charles Starrett) and, famously, a serial, *The Lone Ranger* (1938) with Lee Powell and Chief Thundercloud as Tonto (though better remembered in a 1949 television series played by Clayton Moore and Jay Silverheels). The Cisco Kid, originally a character created by O. Henry in the story The Caballero's Way (1904), appeared in an early sound film, *In Old Arizona* (1929), revived in 1939 in *Return of the Cisco Kid*, with the character – played by Warner Baxter – continuing in a Western series through the 1940s. Later played by Duncan Renaldo in a 1950s television series, the Cisco Kid is significant as a corrective to the prevailing stereotype of the shiftless 'greasy Mexican' of Westerns before this time.

Although girlfriends of singing cowboys often join them in duets – notably Dale Evans, who went on to marry Roy Rogers – few cowgirls had their own series. Dorothy Page was one and Marin Sais starred in two early series, including *The American Girl* (1917), before marriage to 1920s series star Jack Hoxie and supporting roles in his Westerns. A minor serial star, Ruth Roland, played the central character in a Western serial, *Ruth of the Rockies* (1920) and Ruth Mix (daughter of Tom) appeared in three serials made by Big Four Productions (DeMarco, 1980, p.25). Other late variations include series starring children, like the twelve year old Buzz Barton. As series Westerns trailed off in the 1950s, a series began with juveniles (dubbed 'moppet oaters' by the film trade magazine, *Variety*), starting with *Buckaroo Sheriff of Texas* (1951). In a fitting tribute to the Western's regard for the horse, some series stars' horses had their own series. Although, in Britain, the dominant image of the horse is a domesticated 'My Little Pony' (Haymonds, 2000, p.57), in American culture the noble savagery of the horse is an extension of the masculine dignity of its rider: 'a man on a horse is spiritually as well as physically bigger than a man on foot' (Steinbeck, 1933, p.156). Whether the same gendered pattern relates to the dog stars of the period – like Rin Tin Tin (and on into television), Rinty and Peter the Great – is a matter for further research.

During the Second World War, many series Westerns became part of the war effort – some scarcely disguising government propaganda in stories whose villains became Nazi spies and fifth columnists – the frequent contemporary settings contributing to naturalise the new development. In the first, *Riders of the Northland* (1942), Charles Starrett is a Texas Ranger in Alaska exposing a secret airfield and enemy submarine refuelling base.

After the war, from 1945, saw the beginning of the end of cinema's series Western. Changing post-war cultures began to erode audiences. The new domestic medium of television replicated the continuous programming policy which had been such a strong feature of cinema's popularity before the War and that had provided the conditions for the success of the series form. Although the last film series was made in 1954, the form in cinema was effectively over by 1951, by which time the studios had sold their considerable back catalogues of series Westerns to television. Republic was among the first, and they were used primarily as daytime programme fillers. But the successful screening of Hopalong Cassidy films on children's television marked a dramatic new turn. Film studios began making television series Westerns, some of which were so popular that they led 1950s prime time programming.

TELEVISION SERIES WESTERNS

The success of the Hopalong Cassidy series sold to television and the production of 52 episodes of a new television series in 1951 encouraged television companies to invest in their own series Westerns. The first added new series to the Lone Ranger films (1949–57) and the Cisco Kid (1951–6). Roy Rogers had his own Show from 1952–7. True to the traditional spirit of austerity in series westerns production, many included footage taken from earlier films.

At first intended for the child audience, new series Westerns were rapidly developed for overlapping family and adult audiences, screened at prime time at a key moment in American television in 1955 (Boddy, 1998). New cowboy stars gave their names to their series titles: the dramatic *Cheyenne* (1955–63) has Clint Walker as an archetypal nomadic cowboy; *Maverick* (1957–62), (its first three episodes directed by Budd Boetticher), has James Garner playing a more comic hero, a scheming cardsharp; and, in the 1970s, *Alias Smith and Jones* (1971–3), with its eponymous outlaws perpetually on the run.

Other long-running popular series, which were successful on British television, centred more on ensemble players: especially the township-based *Gunsmoke* (1955–75); the journey series, *Wagon Train* (1957–65), for which John Ford directed 'The Colter Craven Story' and in which Ward Bond, longtime actor in Ford's stock company, found a leading role; and *Rawhide* (1959–62), a cattle-trail series from which Clint Eastwood graduated to film fame. Apart from the homestead-based *The Rifleman* (1958–63), created by Sam Peckinpah, gunfighter Westerns tend to be journey Westerns organised around their itinerant heroes: *Have Gun, Will Travel* (1957–63) is notable for Richard Boone as the grumpiest and possibly the most villainous of television Western series' heroes. Among final variations is one of the last Western series, the hybrid *Kung Fu* (1972–5), with 'the counter-cultural masculinity' (Tasker, 2001, p.123) of David Carradine as Kwai Chang Caine, 'an exiled Shaolin priest who roams the West with a price on his head' (ibid., p.115).

During the 1960s, the action hero is integrated into family melodramas like *Bonanza* (1959–73), the first of several series based on a ranch-owning family, commonly incomplete and all-male. The *Bonanza* family are the Cartwrights, a father and three sons living on the Ponderosa ranch in Texas; *Laramie* (1959–63), though set on a relay station, has a surrogate male family; *The Virginian* (1962–1970) is very loosely based on Owen Wister's character. Later series in the cycle developed into domestic melodramas with extended families. *The High Chaparral* (1967–71) is set on a wealthier ranch, with an extended white family of John Cannon (Leif Erickson), whose Mexican wife (Linda Cristal) and local Apache tribe provide opportunities for liberal explorations of inter-racial themes; *The Big Valley* (1965–9) has the wealthiest ranch-owning family of all, headed by matriarch Victoria Barkley (Barbara Stanwyck); *Little House on the Prairie* (1974–82) is the most domestic of this strand of series Westerns, derived from autobiographies by Laura Ingalls Wilder. Producer Michael Landon plays Little Joe, the youngest of the Cartwright family in *Bonanza*, before taking over as father of the first functioning family in any television series Western, and the only series Western to survive into the 1980s.

Like its cinema forebear, the television Western was poorly received critically, and the subject of moral panic and public investigation. In one of the few serious studies of the television Western, '*Sixty Million Viewers Can't be Wrong*', William Boddy argues that as a television phenomenon it is a reaction 'to the generalised pressures of both the corporate workplace and suburban domesticity in post-war America' (1998, p.134). He finds a consensus view among the few serious commentators of the time that the television Western 'spoke to the . . . pressures of post-war domesticity on the formation of socially-sanctioned masculinity' (ibid., pp.134–5). Pumphrey concurs, yet finds a new diversity that could also be more 'inclusive, flexible and ambiguous' when 'consumed domestically in the context of family relationships' and where it assumes 'a flowing, publicly available, cross-generational debate around the traditional conception of the Western hero' (2001, p.149). There is some evidence to suggest that such subtle shifts in the Western hero's character was a wider phenomenon in Western films more generally, and certainly in B Westerns produced during the same period as the television Westerns.

B WESTERNS

Although series Westerns began to fade in the early 1950s and were gone by 1955, their idea of the cowboy star remained central to the genre. Older actors like Joel McCrea and Randolph Scott sustained careers in B Westerns, in part through successful investment in their own production companies, making films sold on their star image. After careers in a range of genre films in the 1930s, they narrowed their range, making Westerns almost exclusively from the mid 1940s. They start by playing experienced Westerners in the Hart tradition, both imposing figures, though more genial and charming (for instance, McCrea in *Saddle Tramp*, 1950). As their careers develop into the 1950s, Scott's persona becomes increasingly austere, culminating in a cycle of playful journey films (made by his own production company, formed with producer Harry Joe Brown, director Budd Boetticher and scripted by Burt Kennedy), in which the stoicism of his characters conceals personal tragedy. Of this cycle, *The Tall T* (1957), *Ride Lonesome* (1959) and *Comanche Station* (1959) at least are all genre classics. Subsequently, both actors starred in the key elegiac Western, *Ride the High Country/Guns in the Afternoon* (1962) before enjoying long retirement, Scott raising horses and McCrea making cameo appearances in very occasional film and television Westerns.

The most prominent actor of the B Western in the 1950s and 60s is also among the most original. Aged just 24 when he made his first film in 1948, Audie Murphy was a baby-faced actor whose juvenile appearance initially prompted his casting in titles like *The Kid from Texas* (1950), in which he plays Billy the Kid, and *The Cimarron Kid* (1952). Though physically slight and softly-spoken, Murphy was a war hero, the most decorated soldier in the Second World War, whose life story was filmed as *To Hell and Back* (1955). As unlikely a Western action hero as a war hero, his Westerns commonly acknowledge his wartime heroics. Belying his appearance, his characters conventionally surmount difficult situations and overwhelming odds. In *The Guns of Fort Petticoat* (1957), for instance, he is a lone male marshalling the few resources of a fort, populated by women, to survive an Indian siege.

Murphy's Westerns require his characters to reason as much as fight a way out of jeopardy. They draw on the crime structure familiar from the series Westerns of Gene Autry and other singing cowboys, placing the hero in a detective role. There are also further thematic connections with series Westerns. In *Column South* (1953), for instance, Murphy is cavalry lieutenant Jim Sayle, stationed in a New Mexican frontier fort in 1861, just before the outbreak of the Civil War. Murphy's Sayle acts as mediator in disputes between Northern and Southern troopers in a society dominated by prejudice and fear, and negotiates the dangerous prejudices of other officers against the local Navajo. His detective skills are initially displayed when he deduces the identity of the killer of a miner, whose death is falsely attributed to Indians, before exposing the film's major conspiracy against the union within his own military hierarchy. Murphy's hero is a considerable healer of national rifts, between North and South and between white and Indian, culminating in successfully romancing an unusually racist heroine, who he re-educates throughout the film. That the hero in Murphy's Westerns is often sympathetic to the Indian cause – even as he must intercede in disputes that require action sequences of staged conflicts – is also a mark of Westerns of the 1950s. As early as Gene Autry's *The Cowboy and the Indians* (1949), but famously with *Broken Arrow* (1950), Westerns of the 1950s increasingly demonstrate greater sympathy for the plight and cause of the Native American. Sayle's anti-racism in *Column South* is attributed to a childhood trauma, witnessing his father and others massacre an Indian village. Murphy's films are as much a part of developments in Westerns at the time as the series Westerns in which they are rooted.

It is strange that in his few A features, Murphy plays far less sympathetic character roles, especially as the racist brother of a family of homesteaders, treacherously denying his Indian sister, in *The Unforgiven* (1960). His feminised masculinity made him an unexpectedly successful B Western star, but it may be this quality that made him seek to play against type in the smaller roles in his few A Westerns. Murphy's expressionless performances graced over thirty Westerns, mainly for Universal Studios, before his career began to fade in cheaper co-productions in the mid 1960s, concluding with *A Time for Dying* (1969) before his death in a plane accident. In this film, director Budd Boetticher's last Western, Murphy has a brief cameo role as outlaw Jessie James, offering advice to the adolescent heroes rather than killing them – as they and we expect – in a coincidental meeting. For once, Murphy looks tired in the saddle, his body scarcely concealing signs of middle age; whether due to the demands of the part or as a result of make-up is, diplomatically, unclear.

SERIES WESTERNS REVISITED

For most critics, the meaning of the series Western is nostalgic, recalling childhood fantasies, and yearnings for an earlier, pre-industrial age and individualist ethics. For these reasons, series Westerns have been mostly celebrated by fans and ignored by critics. For some critics, however, their popular resonance suggests that series Westerns embody powerful fantasies for groupings of working class male, rural and female audiences. Stanfield's major work, *Hollywood Westerns and the 1930s: The Lost Trail* (2001), explores the political relation of the singing cowboys and their films to modernity and industrialisation, in which the series Western can be understood with new significance, providing new frames of reference, otherwise unacknowledged, for further serious study.

CHAPTER SIX

The Epic Western

Duel in the Sun (1946) tells the story of Pearl Chavez (Jennifer Jones). When her white father is hanged for the murder of her Indian mother, she is raised on the vast, wealthy ranch of Texas Senator Jackson McCanles (Lionel Barrymore). However, her mixed race and her mother's promiscuity deny her equal status in the eyes of the family. Torn by the conflicting attentions of the two sons, she leans towards the respectable Jesse (Joseph Cotton), but concedes to the carnal Lewt (Gregory Peck), 'men who represent the struggle within herself between good and evil, wife and tomboy' (Cook, 1988, p.298). Though Lewt cannot commit himself to Pearl, he is unable to accept her commitment to another, and he kills the man who would marry her. Outlawed, Lewt holes up high in the remote mountains, at the aptly named Squaw's Head Rock, where Pearl seeks him out. She affects to succour him, but instead guns him down. In a bitter exchange of fire power across the landscape, the two realise their connection and, after Pearl crawls desperately to be with Lewt, they die in each other's arms.

The extraordinary emotional turmoil and violence of Pearl's story is an erotic fantasy set in a Western family melodrama (Mulvey, 1981). As if this were not enough for one film, the intimate story of Pearl is also set in a wider narrative context. For the McCanles' cattle ranch stands in the way of the building of a railroad crossing the territory, a crucial stage in connecting East to West coasts. The educated son, Jesse, supports the advance, but a stubborn McCanles wants only to protect his property rights. The dispute prompts confrontation with the authorities.

In a scene that appears to abandon Pearl's story halfway through the film, pealing bells summon the hired hands from across the million acres of the ranch, too vast for the irony of its name, Spanish Bit. The exaggerated sound-track of bells, train whistle and pounding horses' hooves build to a crescendo as McCanles' cowboys respond. At first a few riders join together, then small groups, until hundreds of horsemen ride across the rolling plains and converge on the boundary fence, where they 'spread out in a line from the west marker to Pinto Point', facing down the railroad men. The stunning spectacle is topped, however, by the arrival of the cavalry who – in neat visual symmetry – file along the fence on the railroad side, one by one pulling up to face a cowboy adversary opposite. Finally recognising a higher authority in a force even greater than his own, McCanles concedes.

At first sight, there seems scarce connection between this scene in the grand struggle of conflicting political interests and the more intimate tale of Pearl Chavez that it so spectacularly interrupts. But though its manner makes *Duel in the Sun* one of the most original of Westerns, the way in which it combines the general and the specific, the public and the personal is a defining characteristic of the form of the epic Western.

EPIC WESTERN FORM

Epic Westerns are big Westerns. They tend not to be constrained, as series Westerns are, by limitations on budget and production schedule. Epic Westerns are A features, frequently expensive 'prestige' Westerns that commonly exceed even standard A features in length, scale and spectacle. If the average length of a Hollywood feature film is taken as ninety minutes in the classical period and two hours in the post-classical period, epic Westerns exceed the average. While other Westerns may be precisely located (like *The Searchers*, 1956, which opens with the title card 'Texas 1865') or not, epic Westerns generally emphasise their time and place. Their dramas may extend over a long period, possibly over generations. Making their canvas as grand as possible, they will also range across an extensive geography. Epic Westerns, then, tend to explore the widest historical period and traverse the largest geography. The sweep of history and geography will also command the staging of events in the most sensational and spectacular ways possible at the time of their making. As a result, epic Westerns will commonly deploy the latest technological innovations, such as advanced colour and sound processes, and wide screen processes like CinemaScope and Cinerama.

Duel in the Sun is a good example of an epic Western since it is among the most expensive Westerns made (and incidentally the most profitable). It is nearly two and a half hours in duration. In location, the film is based at the Texas ranch, a million acres in size. Although that geography is epic enough, the film also travels at least to El Paso in Mexico and many scenes are set in a township, Paradise Flats. If its sense of place is wide-ranging, its time scale may appear more limited, merely encompassing the short life of the young Pearl. Yet the film is introduced by a framing narration – orated rather more than narrated by Orson Welles – that makes clear that this is a timeless story. The film is also about inheritance and implies the passing of generations; Pearl survives her parents, and the wild Lewt is as much the image of his father as Jesse is the image of his more sensible mother. *Duel in the Sun* also includes action scenes and excessive pictorial settings that rival for spectacle the central major confrontation between cowboys and cavalry, such as an explosive train derailment and many glass shots of impossibly glowering skies. Finally, the film was shot in Technicolor in 1946, a time when colour was still a novelty in cinema and when Technicolor was a cutting-edge technical process.

EPIC NARRATIVE FORM

At such greater length and on such grander scale, epic Westerns must also exceed conventional narrative frameworks. Customary individual protagonists at the centre of a single narrative are replaced by multiple protagonists in subplots that weave together into a complex narrative. Thus, in *Duel in the Sun*, the Senator's story is as central as Pearl's and interweaves with it, since the racism and chauvinism that informs his power over her and others around her shapes her destiny. This power is part of the same imperial ambition which aggressively drives McCanles' desire to protect the land violently acquired by himself. In the same way that he assumes ownership of the land around him, so he assumes control of the people on it. As Jesse says, he 'puts the seal of ownership on everything – on his sons too'. The complex of plots and relationships enables the film to explore the nature of power, its unequal disposition, lack and loss among its many protagonists. Pearl lacks social power in the family and she finds her only power as a woman, desired by the competing brothers. Her thwarted self-interested attempts to exercise that limited power is what leads to her fate on Squaw's Head Rock.

McCanles' leading role in the film's central spectacle is climaxed when a fall from his horse weakens his authority. Thereafter, he gradually realises the error of his ways. The death of his wife, Laurabelle (Lillian Gish), and the absence of his sons, leaves him bereft. Error at a personal and emotional level is also mirrored in his public role as Senator, in an inflexibility that refuses to recognise the civilising effect of the arrival of the railroad. In his final, bathetic scene – with a railroad lawyer played by Harry Carey, the series Western star of an earlier generation – McCanles' sense of divine right gives way and he humbly accepts the return of his surviving son, Jesse. McCanles' public and private stories are interrelated, and woven into the intimate story of Pearl. *Duel in the Sun* is typical of the structure of interweaving plot and characters in the form of the epic Western.

The multiplicity of protagonists in epic narratives may be individuals in successive generations (as is especially the case with Westerns like *Duel in the Sun*, which centre on a family dynasty) or in an even larger community such as a wagon train (as in *The Covered Wagon*, 1923). The multiple characters and relationships in epic Westerns encourage audience identification, not only with individuals, but also with groups and the abstractions they represent (such as authority, justice, the future, etc). In the most accomplished epic Westerns, protagonists represent larger forces and also seem to embody them, making the epic just as much an individual, human story as any other narrative form. In *Duel in the Sun*, Pearl's story stands for the fate of many Western heroines, torn between self and partners and (especially among the Bad Girls) between respectability and desire. McCanles' story is more classically epic, the man who must choose between politics and the personal, nation or family, past or future, Eastern Law by the book or the Western way of the gun. Despite the discrepancy in their power, both Pearl and McCanles equally have to learn that personal choices in the epic Western are subject to wider public constraints.

MELODRAMA AND THE EPIC WESTERN

The Western owes its dominant aesthetic to melodrama. In its earliest days, Hollywood identified its films as melodramas, attesting to the industry's acknowledgement of its debt to stage melodrama. There were different types of melodramas. In the 1910s, what are now recognisibly Westerns were called 'frontier melodramas', the generic term for all fictions set in the West, and testimony to the idea that the image of the West is bound up in frontier history. By the 1920s, a further distinction emerged. Frontier melodramas are about the first pioneers, like trappers and backwoodsmen, while 'Western melodramas' concern later generations of settlers that focus on white conflicts with Indians and township struggles with gunfighters. Such a development was part of a wider process in Hollywood Cinema at the time: 'The AFI (American Film Institute) Catalogue listing feature films made in Hollywood between 1921 and 1930 indicates that almost every film was understood at the time to be a melodrama. Page after page lists melodramas of every sort – rural melodrama, Western melodrama, Gothic melodrama, sentimental melodrama, and so on' (Lang, 1989, p.46).

The emergence of the series Western form by the 1920s and its prominence during the 1930s served to make a final distinction. The low status accorded to the series Western and its presumed rural and juvenile audiences distinguished the form from the prestige Western, which was aimed at the widest inclusive audience, centrally targeted at the female and urban market. Only at the end of the 1930s did Hollywood lose the distinction; prefixes were dropped and 'the Western' emerged. The first prestige Westerns set the terms and conventions of the epic Western, its large canvas drawing on the aesthetic mode of melodrama to render personal stories as representative of wider social forces. As the melodrama of *Duel in the Sun* tells the story of a racial minority woman and a powerful white male, so the melodrama of epic Westerns makes personal stories represent wider social forces and conflicts. Importantly, epic Western narratives are sympathetic to and celebrate characters who lack social power and therefore exist on the margins of official society. So, a wagon train journey west focuses on poor immigrant 'dirt farmers' in *The Covered Wagon*, while *The Iron Horse* (1924) centres on the railroad labourers over the politicians, planners and financiers who promote it. By the time *Duel in the Sun* was made in 1946, the melodrama of the epic Western was so well established that the film could reflect upon its own form; Pearl's epic melodrama is made all the more noble by its supremacy over the conventionally grander genre story of men forging the future of the nation.

AMERICAN HISTORY AS MYTH

The first epics are long narrative poems about the exploits of legendary heroes, like the Greek Odysseus or Roman Ulysses. Epic Westerns also share a legendary and mythical landscape. The voice-over narration that introduces *Duel in the Sun* eagerly establishes its story as a 'legend of the wild young lovers who found Heaven and Hell'. Pearl is 'a wild flower sprung from the hard clay, quick to blossom and early to die'. The hyperbole sensationalises the romantic melodrama, yet also authenticates the spiritual and material story of Pearl; it may be legend, but the legend bears a more general truth about life and living. The same might be said of the tale of McCanles' transformation from imperial dictator to tragic isolate; it is a story in Greek mythology of hubris, the ruined ambition of the mortal who believes in his own divinity. Pearl's tragedy leads to death and McCanles' journey to self-knowledge, but, despite different outcomes, they represent wider social and political narratives. McCanles must learn from his experience, Pearl must be punished for hers; the audience will benefit from both. The grand, complex narratives of epic Western form function like the moral tales of the Bible's parables or the lessons to be learned from the German *Lehrstucke*.

The most powerful force in *Duel in the Sun* is not McCanles nor the vast ranch, neither the railroad nor even the military, but an abstraction represented by the flag, the stars and stripes before which all bow. As McCanles says: 'I once fought for that flag. I'll not fire on it now'. The flag represents an idea of America the nation, that takes on the function of myth. As the epic Western's complex aesthetic form is necessary to its grand scale, so that scale is necessary to the ambition of its epic themes. When Doug Williams calls it 'the American Epic' (1998, p.93), he draws attention to the Western's cultural significance and its association with an idea of America so fundamental that it can be invoked by Western icons like a saguaro cactus, a Stetson hat, Levi jeans, a six-gun or John Wayne. For Williams, the Western's idea of America is 'a myth through which the collective desires and understandings of the United States evolved in relation to the world' (ibid., p.94). If, as Kitses claims, the Western *is* American history, then it is American history appropriated as national myth.

THE FOUNDATION MYTH

Virginia Wright Wexman claims that 'It was during the silent era that Westerns took on the project of delineating a myth of national origin' (in Bernardi, 1996, p.131). The epic Western in particular explores matters of American identity, with what it means to be American, through America's foundation myth (Schatz, 1981, pp.45–80; Cawelti, 1976, pp.221–5). This is the idea that America originates from the period of European settlement in the seventeenth century. The myth works ideologically to obscure other origins, effectively denying the cultures and rights of original Native American inhabitants. Yet as the title of the epic, *How the West Was Won* (1967), suggests, (and Roosevelt's *Winning of the West* (1889), on which it draws) the foundation myth is far from straightforward. Spencer Tracy's opening narration states that the West was won 'from nature and primitive man'. The West was not simply charted and settled, but fought for; 'there never was empty, virgin, free land . . . just there for the taking' (Worland and Countryman, 1998, p.185), but winners and losers among and within the Native American, Mexican and European nations. The Western is a fertile genre to explore the foundation myth since it offers both an historical setting and the epic canvas of cinema's large screen size (in the case of *How the West Was Won*, it was in its time the largest ever screen size, the three-screen process of Cinerama) (Sheldon Hall, 1996).

Although England was not the first of the European nations to settle in the Americas, nor the Pilgrim Fathers the first English settlers, the foundation myth begins historically on the eastern seaboard, with the civilising potential of Puritan settlement. The Puritans were a religious order seeking the biblical Promised Land in the New World of America as a refuge from religious persecution in Europe. The foundation myth continues with the first stages of European exploration across the continent, with early pathfinders like the backwoodsmen, Kit Carson and Daniel Boone, and with expeditions to map land routes such as the Lewis and Clarke exploration of 1804–6. The Westerns that deal with these early aspects of the foundation myth are few in number. *Unconquered* (1947), *Drums Along the Mohawk* (1939) and *The Last of the Mohicans* (1936, 1992) are among the few films set in the eastern states just before the wars of Independence. *The Far Horizons* (1950) tells a romanticised tale of the Lewis and Clarke expedition and *Northwest Passage* (1940) is based on a military expedition into Canada. The next waves of pioneers are 'westerers', fur trappers and mountain men in the 1820s and 1830s (Billington, 1956). Again, there are relatively few films set in this period, notably *The Big Sky* (1952), *Across the Wide Missouri* (1950) and *Jeremiah Johnson* (1972). Patrick McCarthy calls films made about these 'wild men' 'westers' rather than Westerns, for their heroes favour wilderness isolation over cultures associated with civilisation. Unlike many Westerns that suppress the multi-national origins of America, westers implicitly acknowledge earlier generations of at the least Spanish and French colonists.

The great wagon train journeys across the continent in the 1840s and 1850s by groups of pioneers provide opportunity to explore the foundation myth for many more Westerns. They dramatise a subsequent period of settlement in the Western states, especially agrarian settlement. The image of the wagon train in Westerns crucially binds an American history of imperial conquest and European settlement into the quasi-religious dimensions of the foundation myth.

THE GREAT TREK WEST

Among the first Westerns about families in wagon trains seeking a homeland in the West is Bison's *Blazing the Trail* (1912), a short starring director John Ford's elder brother, Francis Ford. He is Blake, a scout for the 'Cooper Family (that) Goes West to Settle'. In this captivity narrative, the journey West is seen as hazardous. Duplicitous Indians claim friendship before an attack (seen in a remarkably early example of a flashback, after it is signalled first by a fire, seen by the scout and the audience from a distance). Settlers then rescue the surviving 'orphans' of the attack, an adult brother and sister, from an Indian encampment. In a coda to the successful outcome of the film, a touching long take finds the surviving offspring leaving behind the crosses that mark their parents' graves to join the wagon train and continue their journey.

Blazing the Trail introduces in embryo some of the conventions of the Wagon Train Western developed in *The Covered Wagon*, one of the first major epic Westerns. Both films define the purpose of the journey as settlement, identify the journey as hazardous and emphasise a community of families as the core social nucleus; they equally feature a burial scene as a convention of the wagon train film. *The Covered Wagon*, however, explores the epic nature of settlement, hazard and social agency in greater complexity and not without some contradiction.

The Covered Wagon is one of just fifty Westerns made in 1923. Several hundred Westerns were made annually during the early 1910s, yet Fenin and Everson record a slump in Western production until *The Covered Wagon* (1997, p.132). Directed by James Cruze for Paramount and scripted by Dorothy Arzner (later to direct films central to feminist film criticism (Mayne, 1995) in the 1970s), the film was so financially successful that it led to the rejuvenation of the genre, with three times the numbers of Westerns produced the following year, including the equally popular *The Iron Horse*.

Vardac claims that *The Covered Wagon* relates to *The Drama of Civilisation*, 'a series of mammoth pictures illustrating the struggle of the growth and expansion of America' (1949, p.144) which in turn established a new type of American stage drama in the late nineteenth century, dubbed by Percy MacKaye the 'Masque of American Life' (quoted by Vardac, p.145).

The Covered Wagon tells the story of a great wagon trek from the East to the West Coast. The trek is seen in panoramic views over the broadest range of landscape (with locations in Snake Valley, Nevada), though equally represented in a series of written narrative cards. They tell that migrants from Ohio and Mississippi first gather together at 'Westport Landing – 1848 – since called Kansas City . . . eager to brave the 2,000 miles of hardship' on the dangerous route to their destination in Oregon. A laudatory viewpoint on the epic nature of this event is established in the first of over twenty cards, declaiming: 'The Blood of America is the blood of the pioneers – the blood of lion-hearted men and women who carved a splendid civilisation out of an uncharted wilderness.' The pioneer journey is then delineated as one of 'crushing hardship, discontent and homesickness . . . grinding toil' and 'staggering loss of wagons and stock'.

An early scene on the journey demonstrates how the foundation myth requires dedication to the task of 'making America' through hardship and sacrifice on the trail. Just 'two weeks out', many in the wagon train turn back, the journey 'breaking the pioneer spirit'. Those who continue must go on to abandon many of their treasured possessions and some make the ultimate sacrifice. At the funeral of one of these, old Mrs Wattle, the pioneers are advised to leave her grave unmarked to avoid the attention of Indians (though at risk of what potential desecration goes unmentioned). At that moment elsewhere in the train, a new baby is born. The coincidence of birth and death affirms the painful but essential pioneer journey as a microcosm of the natural cycle of life. This necessary cycle is signalled in a close-up of wagon wheels rolling over the site of the anonymous grave. Similar scenes recur in subsequent wagon train Westerns. Among the most moving is in a later variant, *Westward the Women* (1952), in which an all-female wagon train of mail-order brides heads West (Evans, 1996). Survivors of an Indian attack sing out the names of the dead in an emotional roll call, honouring the sacrifice of those whose lives are lost in the making of a defiantly female America. Such scenes typify 'the heart-rending contrast between the community-centred aspirations of settlers and the harsh and unforgiving qualities of the Western frontier' (Studlar & Bernstein, 2001, p.4).

The religious dimension of such scenes of stoicism, sacrifice and loss is made explicit in *The Covered Wagon*, when the wagon train finds signs of an earlier pioneer journey. As it reaches Wyoming, the wagon train runs out of food, but comes across a marker left by Brigham Young, the historical leader of the earlier great 1840s Mormon wagon train. Like a sign from God, the marker acts to reassure the faithful and to spur them on. Although religion is an important point of reference in many Westerns (McCanles in *Duel in the Sun* calls Jesse 'a Judas' and Hardy (1991, p.152) calls the brothers' plot a Cain and Abel story), it is a key dynamic in wagon train Westerns. In *Wagonmaster* (1950), the train is composed of Mormons. They regard their journey to settlement in 'the promised land' of the West in the same terms as the biblical flight of the Israelites from Egypt. Leader of the wagon train, Elder Wiggs (Ward Bond) tells the scout, Travis (Ben Johnson) that they journey to 'a valley that's been reserved for us by the Lord . . . for His people'. These path-finders are special because they feel 'sent out to mark the trail and prepare the ground for those who come after'. In Williams' words, this 'mythic accession of God's Community to the Promised Land is a fulfilment of prophecy. The accession requires not just strength but faith – an act of defiance against the material world' (1998, p.95).

Historically, the Mormons are a small segment of pioneer America (*Brigham Young – Frontiersman* (1940) is the only film to build a story around the man), but in the foundation myth their great trek is a religious touchstone justifying the manifest destiny of the pioneer journey. Crossing a dangerous landscape and surviving attacks from renegade Indians and bad men are all part of the tribulations to test and prove the mettle of America's pioneer founders. In *Wagonmaster*, the central scene of the journey is the fording of a river, from which some shots are deemed so exceptional that they are repeated under the opening and closing credits. The early sound Western, *The Big Trail* (1930), has a spectacular scene in which lifting gear contrived from nearby trees lowers wagons, livestock and even the pioneers down a cliff face. In both films, community celebrations serve to sanctify the task and the journey.

The pioneers must not only overcome natural hazards. In *Wagonmaster*, the Mormons must learn that their faith alone is not enough to enable them to succeed in their quest. They must accept assistance from Travis and his sidekick, Sandy (Harry Carey Junior), with their added knowledge of the trail and its dangers; they must embrace the nomadic faithless among the

Medicine Show of 'Doctor' Hall (Alan Mowbray), whose wagon they come across; and they must ultimately confront evil masculinity in the form of the motherless Clegg family. In each case, the Mormon group is divided over decisions to include or resist the incomers. In each instance, the film supports the judgement of the excitable but inclusive Wiggs over the suspicious and sectarian Elder Perkins (Russell Simpson). Even the most religious of wagon train films, like *Wagonmaster*, rejects fundamentalism for a tolerant community that aligns religious faith with a wider secular worldliness.

What the Mormons of history and the wagon train pioneers of Westerns have in common is farming. The pioneers in *The Covered Wagon* are no exception. The film's sympathies are with 'the men (sic) of the Plow (plough)' who 'held to their purpose' of journeying to the rich farmland of Oregon. The plough is the central image of the film, pointedly established as the symbol of the trek by Jesse Wingate (Charles Ogle), elderly 'captain of the hull (whole) shooting match'. The agricultural settlement is not, however, the only foundation of the nation in *The Covered Wagon* and the settlement it represents is not without problems. Later, when the wagon train splits in two – one group forking to settlement in Oregon's farmlands, the other to the goldfields of California – the tragic separation is illustrated by ploughs abandoned at the wayside. Jesse warns against the lure of gold dust: 'The pick and the shovel never built a country – you've got to have a plow.' Oregon is undoubtedly spoken as the ideal destination during the journey, yet it is not the expected visual paradise when Jesse's party finally arrives there. The farmland is covered in snow and therefore unrecognisable ('"How far is it to Oregon?" "Why, you're here right now!"'). Furthermore, the resulting celebration at the ending of their journey is perfunctory. Nor are the goldfields a fool's paradise. Although the hero, Will Bannion (J. Warren Kerrigan, a popular star of the 1920s and hero of other Westerns such as *The Silent Battle*, 1916), gives his all to assist the wagon train and leads its rescue from a climactic Indian attack, he is no farmer. Later discovered to have joined the gold rush, he makes his fortune from prospecting, finally returning to the family settlement for the hand of the heroine, Jesse's daughter Molly (Lois Wilson). Despite the film's affirmation of the farmer, the couple's final embrace sanctions partnership between agriculture and industry, land and money. The nature of the embrace is significant for Haskell since it disturbs conventional relations between the hero and heroine when 'he buries his head in her shoulder. It is the woman who gives solace, comfort and protection to her man, not the reverse' (1977, p.61). Perhaps the balance of value leans from gold to the plough after all.

The plough is a very different symbol for a group other than the pioneers. To the prairie Indians across whose homelands the wagon caravan must travel, the plough that 'buries buffalo and uproots mountains' is the symbol of white intrusion. The threat to their survival is seen as absolute; the 'white man must be slain or the red man will perish' provides a rationale (if not a justification) for the climactic Indian attack on the wagon train. However, the film is at pains to establish a range of pioneer relations with other groups of Indians. Some are peaceable relations with friendly Indians; traders pass unmolested because they 'carried no plow and sought no land', suggesting that land disputes are at the root of interracial conflict. Another group of commercially savvy Indians is treated differently again. When aware of the value of their ferry for the pioneers to ford a river, they claim an extortionate price. The subsequent shooting of one of their number – one of several despicable acts by the villain, Sam Woodhull (Alan Hale) – alarmingly proves Indian fears of the wagon train to be well justified. Our attitude to this group of Indians is made ambivalent by their exploitation of the pioneers, yet the killing is unjustified and shocking.

PIONEERS AND IMMIGRANTS

True to epic form, the wagon train in *The Covered Wagon* is composed of a cast of hundreds in the dramatic background. Though there are fewer central characters, they typify the collective. Yet, paradoxically, our awareness of their personal stories makes the leading characters exceptional. The story of the great trek is told through the romance of the central relationship between hero Will, heroine Molly and villain Sam. When the trek starts, Sam is courting Molly, though she is aroused by Will's more sympathetic masculinity as he tends a child upset at the loss of a doll's head (an unsettling presentiment of the risks that lie ahead on the journey). Sam's villainous status is stated not only in a litany of foul acts but in his dress. In contrast to the simple working clothes of the pioneers and Will's light buckskin outfit – respectively representing the authentic and the artifice of Western costume – Sam dresses formally. Will's Show outfit renders him romantic, but the besuited garb of the Eastern dandy visually disputes Sam's honesty.

Will first joins the group of pioneers as captain of the wagon train from Liberty. Although he 'knows every foot of the trail', Jesse demotes him to care for the horses at the rear, on bad advice from the jealous Sam. This is the first of a series of insults Will bears stoically until his name is ultimately cleared. Will is an archetypal Westerner; he knows the land and how to cross it, and as importantly, he behaves civilly when his knowledge is challenged. He calmly corrects the errors of the pioneers, organises parties to keep up their depressed spirits, refuses opportunities to dispose of Sam (though it would be beneficial for everyone if they were rid of him) and acts proportionately to provocation. His actions valorise him, even over the other pioneers. Indeed, the figure of the scout/wagon master is as invariably romanticised in wagon train Westerns

The leading cast with some of the company of *The Covered Wagon* (1923) take a break from location shooting in Snake Valley, Nevada. A buck-skinned J. Warren Kerrigan drinks from a cup in the foreground, seated before Lois Wilson, smiling at the camera. Alan Hale stands behind, holding a pie. Ernest Torrence is seated second from left, with Charles Ogle standing behind, both bearded for their roles.

as other Westerns romanticise the cowboy/gunfighter. While the Westerner shares and embodies the values of the pioneers, only he possesses the skills necessary for the journey to succeed.

Will has a comic foil in a tobacco-chewing sidekick, Jackson (Ernest Torrence), a conventional comic character who would gladly have Sam's eyes out in a 'bar nothin' fight, were it not for Will's finer sensibilities. Later, Jackson will rescue an anonymous man from quicksand before discovering it is Sam, at which point he prepares to throw the villain back until Will intervenes. Jackson's comic Old Testament morality (an eye for an eye) contrasts with both the New Testament faith of the pioneers and the hero's rugged secular liberalism.

Although the film's pioneers are from the nineteenth century, it is easy to see in them antecedents of the film's contemporary American audience, made up from later generations of European migrants. Cultural associations – in the working clothes and poverty of the pioneers, even the (possibly Dutch) national costume that Molly bizarrely wears at one point, together with the homely vernacular language in the dialogue cards – speak to the varied national origins of those who similarly travelled to seek their fortune in a late nineteenth and early twentieth-century America. The wagon train Western binds its contemporary audiences into the foundation myth of America as a spiritual homeland, a refuge from political and economic oppression, where ownership of land is desired less for its commercial value than its symbolic promise of economic independence. As Hawkeye (Daniel Day-Lewis), hero of *The Last of the Mohicans* (1992) poetically puts it: 'The frontier's the only land available to poor people. Out here, you're beholden to none, not living by another's leave.' The popularity of wagon train Westerns in their time can thus be seen to arise from the connections they make between the biographical journeys of their contemporary film audiences and America's pioneer history.

FROM TRAIL TO RAIL

The Western has as much affection for the journey West as it has for settlement there, for surviving the journey proves the worth of the settlers and the case for manifest destiny. The Western even celebrates journeys that are not necessarily westward, in films set on the great cattle trails north and east from Texas in the 1860s and 70s, notably *Red River* (1948), the epic *The Tall Men* (1955), *Cowboy* (1958) and *The Culpepper Cattle Company* (1972). Whichever direction the journey takes, the accompanying modes of transport have particular associations. The horse, 'the lyrical centre of the Western' (Dibb, 1996, p.161), connotes individual and free movement on an open range, but when tethered to a buggy, it becomes a domestic vehicle, often with romantic associations of heterosexual courtship. (The exception to this occurs when the newly-married wife played by Shelley Winters in *Winchester, '73*, 1950, will be abandoned by her frightened husband, who takes to his horse with hostile Indians in pursuit). Epic Westerns like The *Covered Wagon* valorise the wagon for its connotations of family and community. The wagon train, however, represents a transcendent agriculture. Wherever a wagon train turns up in the genre, it is likely to bear epic connotations, even incidentally and in more recent westerns, like *Silverado* (1985).

Modes of transport like these can be distinguished from others more associated with the communications systems of a later technological world. Even the horse and stagecoach can make a break from associations with the rural world when they serve the delivery functions of the Pony Express mail service and the Wells Fargo stagecoach line. (These have their related films with several films having *Pony Express* in the title, though the epic *Wells Fargo* (1937) has little to do with its notional subject.) The mode of transport most associated with the developing machine age in the Western is the railroad. It is a powerful symbol of a modernising America and a new industrialised order, as powerfully as the wagon train symbolises an essentially rural order.

The railroad is the subject of *The Iron Horse* (1924), the second of the two great epic Westerns of the silent period. What *The Covered Wagon* does for the wagon train, *The Iron Horse* does for the locomotive by placing the railroad within the foundation myth. The film's title comes from the name Native American Red Cloud reputedly gave the locomotive that took him to Washington; it seems to confirm the advanced and overwhelming forces of a newly industrialised America. The most expensive Western of the silent period, *The Iron Horse* quickly followed the success of *The Covered Wagon*. It tells a story of the building of the transcontinental railroad in the following stage of Western movement from the 1860s. The films share an episodic structure befitting their journey narratives. Both emphasise the spectacle of landscape and event, and feature a central romance plot, but *The Iron Horse* places all this within an explicitly national historical framework.

Thus, the personal story of the hero, Davy Brandon (George O'Brien), and a dream inspired by his surveyor father to build the railroad link, represents a national political will, as much as an individual desire. None other than President Abraham Lincoln (Charles Edward Bull) also shares the dream. Lincoln sanctions the building of the railroad in the face of public scepticism and military doubt about the wisdom of financing it at a time of Civil War. After Lincoln's infamous 1865 assassination (represented merely in a title card), the railroad becomes a symbol of national unity between the northern and southern states. At the end of the film, Davy's concluding personal triumph is also a national victory. As he drives the last, ceremonial rail spike to complete the 1869 transcontinental link, forming 'a shining path from sea to sea' between the Union Pacific westwards and the Central Pacific eastwards, he also completes a more personal union with his childhood sweetheart, Miriam (Madge Bellamy), described as a 'wedding of the rails'. A title card in a coda offers a photograph of the real Lincoln over the phrase 'His truth is marching on'. Contrasting the fictional melodrama with authentic historical characters underlines the film's titular claims to historical fidelity; the final meeting at Promontory Point re-enacts the famous photograph of the scene, using the original locomotives, in the frozen moment of a tableau vivant.

The narrative between these framing scenes charts the building of the Union Pacific. Though Davy eventually moves to work on the Central Pacific, it is westward movement to the Pacific Ocean that drives the film (and indeed most Westerns thereafter, as is demonstrated even by titles like *Union Pacific* (1939), directed by Cecil B. De Mille and *Western Union* (1941), directed by Fritz Lang). Title cards in *The Iron Horse* extol the epic nature of the westward task, as in *The Covered Wagon*. Track-building crosses difficult terrain and workers face dangers from marauding Cheyenne: 'Men and horses strain every nerve hauling locomotives and supplies over the mountains . . . (with) tunnels chiselled by hand . . . by superhuman effort and undaunted courage'. Even so, titles are far fewer than in *The Covered Wagon*. Instead, their poetic language is replaced by the visual poetry of dramatic scenes, vividly representing the epic construction task. Interspersing elaborate scenes in which gangs of labourers struggle to lay down track, and then compete to outdo the pace of others, there are spectacular stagings, which include: horses dragging locomotives across snowscapes; Indians clustered on skylines, racing across landscapes and attacking trains; a buffalo hunt and a huge cattle trail over eight hundred miles. They testify to the necessary endurance of the pioneer spirit in the foundation myth and to the glamour of Western spectacle.

The advance is troubled by human conflicts too. A huge cast of extras populate the railroad towns of North Platte and then Cheyenne. The successive rise and fall of these towns charts advance over the continent, as 'everything but the old houses moves on wheels'. There is development towards organised law and order, finally embodied in a town marshal who replaces the initial rough justice dispensed by a Judge Roy Bean character known as 'Judge' Jed Haller (James Marcus), from his 'Bar of Licker and Justice'. His authority even extends into the streets, where he comically sanctions the marriage of a couple in one town and as perfunctorily divorces them on arrival in the next. The gangs of workmen are even more particularised, divided by allegiance to North or South and racially divided into Chinese (authentically) working the Central Pacific route, with Irish and Italians on the Union Pacific. The stoical dedication of the workers to their task is tested comically by interracial rivalries and dramatically, by loss of pay (stolen in an Indian raid) and food (arriving late and still on the hoof from Texas). Mutineering workers respond to Miriam's patriotic plea to stay on 'for the sake of country' (a marked difference from the treatment of the union organiser who threatens a strike in *Union Pacific* and is simply beaten into submission by the hero) and 'shirkers' who refuse to join the final rescue are shamed by the willingness of the women of the town to take up the fight. Director John Ford's affection for comic and sentimental Irish in his films renders them model labourers, sustained by work songs, 'I've Been Working on the Railroad' and especially 'Drill, Ye Tarriers, Drill' that survive interruption by Indian attack and even Chinese translation. The ultimate success of the railroad construction unites all races within one nation.

At the centre of the film is the triangular romance that connects the particular and the general in an epic Western. Miriam's father, Thomas Marsh (Will Walling) is contracted to build the Union Pacific and the film's central struggle is the search for a short cut through the Black Hills before his capital runs out. Davy knows from a childhood experience shortly before his father's killing that such a pass exists. Denying it are the capitalist Bauman (Fred

Kohler), who owns land on an alternative but longer route through Smoky River, and Jesson, Marsh's duplicitous engineer and Miriam's fiancée. Together the two villains conspire to keep the pass secret, even attempting to kill Davy, who survives a plot to kill him in the pass and an ambush by Bauman's gang of gunfighters. The development of the romance relationship in *The Iron Horse* and *The Covered Wagon* bear comparison. Both heroes dress in light buckskin, display local knowledge and dedication to their task. Both heroines are aroused by the sensitivity, rather than the bravery of the heroes (in Davy's case, as childhood sweethearts, though the adult Davy is first spotted by Miriam from a train, as a man of action riding for the Pony Express and chased by Indians). The Western credentials of the hero and heroine are affirmed in opposition to Eastern villainy, and the hero must gradually overcome the heroine's false suspicions aroused by jealous competitors.

However, *The Iron Horse* complicates the triangular relationship by dividing villainy into two characters. Jesson is the conventional jealous lover, but Bauman represents powerful moneyed interests and personal greed, echoing the villainy in many series Westerns, including 'Handsome' Jack Pressley in William S. Hart's *The Silent Man* (1917). Bauman is a racially ambiguous villain, whose confused racial identity otherwise separates him from the film's appeal to racial harmony (comically, Italian railroad worker Tony finally claims Irish identity through marriage). Bauman first appears among a marauding band of Indians as a renegade white man. Davy's father foolishly believes this will save his life, but he is brutally murdered by Bauman's hand. The axe used for the execution is shot to reveal his 'Two Fingers' to the concealed child Davy, an identity flirting with his subsequent guise as Bauman, with his dark-toned skin and moustache combining to suggest the Western's conventional sly Mexican. Bauman's dual identity is neither explained nor motivated, however. When he loses his struggle to route the Union Pacific through his land, his response is to rouse the Cheyenne to a final, climactic attack on the workers, in a scene in which he is again identified as a 'white brother'. In a final fight with Davy during the battle, Bauman is exposed as the renegade 'Two Fingers' and the murderer of Davy's father. Though the film champions racial integration, villainy is nonetheless defined by racial ambiguity.

A similar pattern extends to the treatment of Indians in the film. Although the Cheyenne are the villains (and, unlike in *The Covered Wagon*, their attacks are unexplained and hence unjustified), the Pawnee scouts are cited as friendly Indians. Somewhat oddly 'employed to guard the workers', they even replace the more conventional cavalry as the last-minute rescuers of the railroad folk from the final mass attack of the Cheyenne.

Throughout, Brandon is supported by 'Three Musketeers' made up of Irish ex-soldiers who, like their namesakes, dwindle in number during the Indian attacks. Their comedy is paramount, not least in scenes of tooth-pulling and tobacco-spitting, but this does not deny them other scenes of sacrifice and mourning over the deaths of companions. Victims of bar-room brawls (one, from an 'orgy' of heavy drinking) are as honoured as those who die during battles with the Cheyenne. Remarkably, these include a group of women, mainly but not exclusively associated with the town prostitutes, who join the workmen on a train that sets out in a climactic rescue. One is a major character, Ruby, (introduced with some sexual explicitness as 'the bright but not too particular star of the "Arabian Nights" dance tent'), who is killed by a bullet intended for Davy. In all these cases, deaths are honoured, often in one of several mournful funeral scenes. Perhaps even more remarkably, one of these includes a puppy whining over the body of a fallen Indian brave. Honouring the dead in *The Iron Horse* extends to both genders and not only the white races, but also the Chinese, to friendly and even to opposing hostile Native Americans.

THE VISUAL LEGACY

Henry Nash Smith's major work on the American foundation myth argues that there is a contradiction at the heart of the duality between Garden and Desert. No Hollywood genre explores the contradiction more closely than the Western, and it is perhaps these first great epic Westerns of the silent period that graphically realise it. During the crossing, the Western landscape is a wilderness, but even though the contrary ideal of the West as Garden motivates the pioneer journey in *The Covered Wagon*, the snowscaped destination visualises it much like Smith's Desert. The West of these epic Westerns is both wilderness and Promised Land.

The Iron Horse informs the quality as well as the nature of images of the West. The high production values of *The Iron Horse* – said to be the personal favourite of the films John Ford directed (Fenin and Everson, 1977, p.136) – are evident not only in its scale and spectacle, but also in its visual style. The death of Davy's father is made horrific by the use of off-screen space. The first Indian attack is rendered ominous by silhouetting figures against a train. The tension of the bar-room fight is heightened by concealing its progress in shifting lamplight, and intercutting reaction shots into action shots of surrounding crowds. Burials and mourning are seen in long takes and subdued lighting. The attention paid to the mise-en-scène demonstrates 'a quality that Ford's sound-era films would also possess: evidence of the painter's eye for depicting human enterprise against the landscape of the West' (Studlar and Bernstein, 2001, p.4). *The Iron Horse* developed a visual style that informed the visual language – the rhetoric – of the Western genre.

Bazin observes that the form of Westerns before the 1950s bears 'the ethics of the epic and even of tragedy' with a style attesting to 'a predilection for vast horizons, all encompassing shots (with) virtually no use for the close-up' (1971, p.147). To the extent that this is so, it may be because Westerns until this time tend to place characters in landscapes in ways that isolate Humanity in and against Nature. As a consequence, natural features become exaggerated, taking on epic proportions. The most famous example is director John Ford's use of Monument Valley as backdrop to several of his Westerns, notably *Stagecoach* (1939), *Fort Apache* (1948) and *The Searchers* (1956). Ed Buscombe says of the powerful image of the Valley: 'no one can look at such a spectacularly eroded landscape without reflecting on the eons which separate us from the creation of the earth. The layered tiers of the great sandstone towers are eloquent testimony to the countless millennia which have been etched upon their surfaces . . . The human dramas Ford plays out against this backdrop gain in poignancy from our sense of their tenuous grip upon such an ancient terrain' (1992, p.45). The great buttes of the Valley are shot in ways that give the Western landscape a mythic force (Leutrat and Liandrat-Guigues, 1998). The location became so much a part of the iconography of the Western that few film-makers chose to work there again until Italian director Sergio Leone's epic *Once Upon A Time in the West* (1968), by which time it had come to represent and celebrate the films of Ford as much as the Western. It has since become the archetypal Western landscape: Marty McFly (Michael J. Fox) drives into it (and into a band of Indians chased by cavalry), when time-travelling from a 1989 urban present to an 1885 gold-rush past in *Back to the Future III*.

THE EPIC LEGACY

The Covered Wagon and *The Iron Horse* are formative epic Westerns. They emerge at a time of Western production decline in the early 1920s, coinciding with reductions in the production of short films, as the feature film became the standard in Hollywood. When production of Westerns picked up again during the late 1920s and in cycles through the 1930s, it was almost wholly series Westerns that were produced. The exceptions were Westerns among Hollywood's prestige A films. To find suitable sources for its new prestige production schedule, Hollywood turned to the melodrama stage, where many plays had been adapted from classic American literature and other original novels. Among the first is D.W. Griffith's early feature film about the Southern States and the Civil War, *The Birth of a Nation* (1915), based on Thomas Dixon Junior's epic novel, *The Clansman* (1906), and several stage adaptations. Innumerable film versions of Harriet Beecher Stowe's novel, *Uncle*

Tom's Cabin, set on a Southern slave-owning plantation, also drew on further stage adaptations. Although Hollywood drew equally on European sources, especially Shakespeare, these titles indicate an increasing turn to epic themes in American literature and theatre. Western fiction was central to this project. For instance, director Cecil B. De Mille filmed the Western, *The Squaw Man*, several times, as early as 1914, though most influentially in 1918. The script was adapted from a stage melodrama by Edwin Milton Royle, first performed in 1905.

Epic Westerns that followed the two great silent classics, *The Covered Wagon* and *The Iron Horse*, did not emulate their commercial success. The commercial failure of two big-budget Westerns in the early days of the sound period – *The Big Trail* (1930) and *Cimarron* (1931) – halted production of epic Westerns until the 1940s. *The Big Trail* covers the same journey to Oregon as *The Covered Wagon*, with its hero in the midst of an additional revenge plot. Its box-office failure returned its leading player, John Wayne, to B Westerns until his major success in *Stagecoach* (1939) cemented a productive relationship with director John Ford in a long career that – of all Western stars – is perhaps most associated with the Western genre. *Cimarron* builds a story around the 1893 land rush at Cherokee Strip, Oklahoma, first staged in William S. Hart's last film, *Tumbleweeds* (1925). Hart's version focuses on a cattle family whose leader renounces the ways of the trail for settlement. It is one of the first Westerns to deal with the last days of the frontier, its elegiac tone befitting the end of the star's film career and looking forward to a later cycle of elegiac Westerns from the 1950s onwards. *Cimarron*'s epic 'pageant of American history' (Newman in Buscombe, 1998, p.255) centres on the journey West of a Southern family. Later versions of the film proved the event of the land rush no more popular with audiences, including *The Great Man's Lady* (1942) with Barbara Stanwyck and Joel McCrea, and *Cimarron* (1960) with Glenn Ford.

EPIC WESTERNERS

In the face of these box-office failures, occasional prestige Westerns of the 1930s elevated a feature of many early Westerns by building stories around archetypal Westerners. In 1920s epic Westerns, fictional central characters meet authentic Western names lower down the cast list. Perhaps to add credence to claims of historical authenticity, mountain man Jim Bridger joins *The Covered Wagon*, while less conspicuously, Buffalo Bill hunts buffalo (dressed in circus outfit) and Wild Bill Hickock keeps law for the railroad in *The Iron Horse*. In 1930s Westerns, however, such minor characters move to the dramatic centre. All three turn up in leading roles – together with Calamity Jane and General Custer – in the epic, *The Plainsman*. Custer is also the hero of *They Died with their Boots On* (1941) and, less flatteringly, the epic *Custer of the West* (1968), though in the revisionist epic, *Little Big Man* (1970), the peripatetic hero survives several archetypal Western conflicts, including the Battle of the Little Big Horn, with an insane Custer played by Richard Mulligan ordering massacred troops to take 'No prisoners!' John Wayne produced and directed the epic *The Alamo* (1960), with Richard Widmark as Jim Bowie, who gave his name to the double-edged knife, and Wayne himself as frontiersman Davy Crocket. This film was one of several Westerns to recreate the 1836 resistance in a fortified mission of 187 men against the overwhelming military forces of Mexican dictator, Santa Anna. *The Alamo* turns an imperial struggle for Texas during an Hispanic civil war into a patriotic assertion of American democracy. Like all other American Westerns about the Alamo, it ignores the many Chicanos who died alongside the American defenders.

The majority of 1930s prestige Westerns named after or about Westerners concern law and order stories of marshals and/or outlaws. *Jesse James* (1939) is one of several popular Westerns made at the time and spawned several sequels about the outlaw James Brothers. Among less well-known biographies is that of the owner of the land of the first Californian gold rush, *Sutter's Gold* (Frayling, 1998, pp.3–5, 21–4). Other prestige Westerns of the period deploy historical groups like the Texas Rangers. Bizarrely, *The Texans* (1938) combines a story of the Chisholm cattle trail with 'the formation of the Ku Klux Klan and the impact of . . . the transcontinental railroad' (Hardy, 1991, p.88). A final trend advanced in the period is Westerns named after Western towns, such as *Dodge City* (1939), *Virginia City* (1940) (both starring Errol Flynn), and the minor *San Antonio* (1945).

THE EMPIRE PLOT

The epic Western dynamically returns in the period following The Second World War, in a cycle of films set on vast ranch spreads, beginning with *Duel in the Sun* (1946), a film that producer David O. Selznick planned to follow the great commercial success of the Civil War epic, *Gone With the Wind* (1939). The setting and subject of ranching motivates the centrality of the cowboy hero in post-War Westerns, enabling new conflicts within the foundation myth to emerge in troubling ways. Frank Gruber in *The Pulp Jungle* (1967), finds two associated plot structures, with the Empire plot developing from the Ranch plot. The character groups in conflict in Ranch plots are ranchers vs. rustlers or cattlemen vs. settlers/sheepmen, but the major conflict in the Empire plot is between the power blocs of 'The Ranch and The Forces of Civilisation Who Need to Advance Through It'. Both plot structures concern disputes over rights to and use of land, but the Empire plot places such disputes in a later national context, when monopolistic ownership of vast tracts of land becomes a threat to the noble cause of Western advancement.

These plots do not celebrate the colonisation of uncharted territory for farming, as in Westerns like *The Covered Wagon*, to 'reaffirm the act of foundation' (Cawelti, 1976, p.73). They concern access to rather than routes through land, an issue all but ignored during the forward march of the railroad in *The Iron Horse*. By the time of the production and the later historical setting of *Duel in the Sun*, the land is settled – for raising cattle – and the central issue becomes disputes over ownership. Senator McCanles in *Duel in the Sun* is at the centre of an Empire plot, but he also typifies cattle barons in the ranch plot; like an ancient feudal lord, he views his property as a fiefdom, though his conflict is not with local groups such as other ranchers, but with the national agencies of railroad, the law, the government and the military.

The Ranch plot localises this conflict of power and land rights. It is the centre of numerous Westerns of the 1950s, notably *The Man From Laramie* (1995), *Tribute to a Badman* (1956) and *Man in the Shadow* (1957). In each of these, a cattle baron heads a family dynasty, jealously guarding rights to his land and is in conflict with and between sons or son-figures over who is worthy of inheritance. In *The Man From Laramie* most complexly, the headstrong Dave (Alex Nicol) is unsuited to inherit the ranch of his father, ageing cattle baron Alex Waggoman (Donald Crisp), though his birthright will favour the son over the competing claims of ranch foreman, Vic Hansbro (Arthur Kennedy). A revenge plot intervenes into this ranch plot in the form of an outsider, Will Lockhart (James Stewart), whose search exposes the guilt of Dave and Vic, leading to their deaths. The revenge plot here acts as catalyst in the exposition and resolution of a dispute between father and competing sons (or a figure who substitutes as a son). Generational conflicts between older men and sub-cultural youth are common throughout Hollywood genres (and beyond Hollywood) in the post-War period, at a time when a new economic and social independence for teenagers posed threats to the patriarchy of older male generations. It is therefore no surprise to find such generational conflicts foregrounded in ranch Westerns and many other 1950s Westerns such as *The Tin Star* (1957), *Man of the West* (1958) – both, like *The Man From Laramie*, directed by Anthony Mann – and *Saddle the Wind* (1958), with perhaps the most 'delinquent' of Western youth played by John Cassavetes.

The most popular epic Western of the period, however, is *The Big Country* (1958), a minor film in criticism of the Western, but a revealing ranch Western in its narrative of two family dynasties feuding over land disputes. Major Henry Terrell (Charles Bickford) runs half a million acres of the Latimer

A publicity still of Gregory Peck as Jim McKay, the Eastern hero who brings justice to the epic Western ranch of *The Big Country* (1958).

Ranch, sanctioning needless acts of vengeance on a smaller neighbouring estate out of hatred for its dirt-poor owner, Rufus Hennessey (Burl Ives). The vista of vast plains seen from the vantage point of the grand mansion house of the Terrell ranch contrasts with the dusty rock basin of shacks in the Hennessey settlement. The contrast renders the land dispute grossly unequal and localised, far from the grand claims of manifest destiny in the foundation myth. Into this ugly confrontation, the hero, Jim McKay (Gregory Peck) arrives to marry Terrell's daughter, Pat (Carroll Baker). This is an unusual Western hero, an incomer whose breadth of experience on the oceans of the world as a Captain enables him to see through the small-minded local culture of the professed 'big country' and offer the hope of peaceable resolution to the dispute. Refusing taunts to his Eastern manners and schooled masculinity, he comes to a mutual but distant respect with the jealous ranch foreman, Steve Leach (Charlton Heston). After matching him in an evocative montage scene with long shots of their exhausting, dusty, moonlit fistfight, Jim wryly undermines a conventional notion of Western masculinity, even as he lives it out, saying through bloodied lip: 'Now, what did that prove?'

The narrative explores the pointlessness of the patriarchal dispute that threatens the livelihood of the smaller community and the lives of the working cowboys in both camps. The root of the conflict is personal hatred between the two men. Never explained, its destructiveness is incomprehensible (though the majesty of Burl Ives' performance as Rufus, especially in a scene when he interrupts a party to put Terrell's brutal power in its place, cannot help but underline his cause). In the first of a spectacular series of climaxes, Jim survives a pistol duel with Rufus' wastrel son (Chuck Connors) before his own father shoots him down ('All I wanted was for you to be the son I always wanted'). The eventual death of the old men in a rifle showdown among mountain rocks is made ignominious by an overhead high angle shot, that reduces them to insignificant figures. The coda scene, showing Jim riding off with Julie (Jean Simmons), a teacher and more Eastern (therefore, in the film's terms, more mature) alternative to Pat, together with the Terrell's Mexican wrangler, the sympathetic but comic Ramon, suggests a romantic resolution to the story in the founding of a new, more civilised ranch culture. However, the death of the heads of the dynasties leaves Pat, the raging spurned lover, isolated in the background. The ambiguous future is appropriate, for it demonstrates a more reflective view of the foundation myth, among other significant changes taking place in the Western genre from this period onwards.

THE LAST EPIC WESTERNS

The 1950s and 1960s is a major period for historical epics based on more European stories, often made by Hollywood studios overseas. There are connections between some Westerns and these 'sword and sandal' epics. *El Cid* (1961), for instance, is scripted by Philip Yordan who worked on occasions on a cycle of Westerns directed by Anthony Mann, frequently starring James Stewart, including *The Man from Laramie*. These films investigate the heroic in legend and ritual in individual ways (Kitses, 1969, pp.29–80) yet their flawed and fallible heroes are also representative not only of the director's films but also of wider changes in the Western at the time.

This is the final significant period of epic Westerns. The foundation myth becomes subject to even more thorough review than in the Ranch and Empire plots and, in some instances, to certain inversions. *The Way West* (1968) minimises the force and complexity of the preceding films about the great wagon train journeys West, including *The Covered Wagon*. In reducing its pioneers to a jumble of comically disparate and uncoordinated forces, *The Way West* more cynically celebrates the pioneer spirit. More substantially, *Once Upon a Time in the West* thoroughly undermines the positive role of the railroad in the building of America from earlier films like *The Iron Horse* by making it a force for evil. Its owner is empowered by the money capitalism corruptly provides him to hire gunfighters to violently clear the land of settlers. His moral vacuity is expressed through the contrast between the gunfighters' terrorism and his own physical weakness; a wasting disease requires he propels himself hand over hand around the confined space of a train carriage by a network of overhead rails. The otherwise complicated chase Western, *The Good, the Bad and the Ugly* (1966), has a spectacular scene in which the eponymous three suddenly arrive upon a Civil War battle at a moment of calm between the two sides. The three resolve the impasse unheroically by conniving mayhem in blowing up a bridge as a distraction from their escape. The sentiment of the film at this point is briefly anti-war – one of the three is momentarily deflected by the attention he feels obliged to give to a dying soldier – but the overwhelming sensibility is cynical in its depiction of a West ruled by individual self-interest, greed and corruption.

Once Upon a Time in the West and *The Good, the Bad and the Ugly* are Westerns directed by Sergio Leone towards the end of a cycle of Italian Western film production, so internationally popular that it changed the Western film in Hollywood thereafter. These were part of a movement of darker interpretations of the Western genre, in which Western heroism is subject to renewed scrutiny. The prestige Western, *The Professionals* (1966), is a good example of some of the narrative changes occurring. It is an action Western that takes the idea from *The Magnificent Seven* (1960) of a small group of mercenaries with individual skills who combine to overcome greater odds. Unlike the laudable cause in that earlier film – in which gunfighters risk their lives to aid a peon village to resist a seasonal visit by marauding bandits – the group of *The Professionals* learns that its romantic quest to rescue a kidnapped wife from a band of Mexican guerrillas is based on a lie. On her recapture, they discover that she has freely chosen to be with the leader of her supposed captors. In response, once the group satisfy the professional terms of their contract to return the wife to her husband, they also allow the lovers to ride away together. In common with heroes of other similar elegiac Westerns, the group realise that their days as hired guns are numbered and consider retirement.

The Professionals is one of several Westerns to ring changes indicative of major shifts in the genre from the 1960s onwards. Thereafter, the form of the epic Western is not substantially revised (though some films grow even greater in length, like the epics *Heaven's Gate* (1980) at 219 minutes and *Dances with Wolves* (1990), which increases in length from 180 minutes on first release to an incredible 236-minute 'director's cut'. Though epic form is less subject to revision, the foundation myth of the epic Western comes under increasing scrutiny. As all the conventions of the genre become subject to substantial revision in the latter half of the century, so formal distinctions grow less important. The most recent epic Westerns are among the most achieved of the revisionist Westerns explored in the final chapter.

CHAPTER SEVEN

The Romance Western

The epic Western explores American identity, confronting the nation's history in terms of the foundation myth. The central protagonist is the Western hero, a mythic figure who embodies an archetypal American identity forged in frontier history. Yet step back a little and see the same heroic figure at the centre of many Westerns. From the earliest Hollywood period, the hero of the silent short, feature and series Western is a hero of romance. The figure is extended in the first sound Westerns, *In Old Arizona* (1929) and *The Virginian* (1929) (Stanfield, 2001, pp.21–6) and becomes more complicated in the period of intense Western A feature production from the late 1930s onwards. At a time when cinema-going was as habitual a practice as watching television is today, series Westerns were targeted at rural audiences, but the audience for A Westerns was the urban family. The A Western was sold in part as melodrama and romance as well as providing male action and targeted women especially, thus broadening the appeal and increasing audiences for Westerns. Among these films are some of the most celebrated Westerns in film criticism.

THE ROMANTIC HERO

It is not immediately obvious to think about the classic Western hero as a romantic hero. Western heroes are central to Western narratives and romantic heroes tend to be secondary figures in the romantic novel of women's fiction. Nonetheless, romance Westerns are a clear variant of romance fiction in Hollywood Cinema and the wider culture. Songs in Westerns make this most explicit. Commercially, the theme song of *High Noon* (1952) is the most successful Western theme song and probably the most famous. It begins with the lines 'Do not forsake me, oh my darling, here on our wedding day.'

The lyrics of the theme song to the television series *Rawhide* (1959–62) conclude with the singer 'anticipatin' my true love will be waiting, waiting at the end of my ride.' In sentiments like these, romantic longing and the fear of separation is as palpable as in any popular song; the Western hero needs a mate like any other.

The heterosexual couple and the love triangle are more abundant in Westerns than popular memory and most male critics of the genre acknowledge. Romance Westerns conventionally feature heterosexual couples whose relationships develop through courtship, overcome problems troubling the relationship and conclude in the couple's partnership, classically signified by a final embrace. However, the romantic relationship is rarely central to the narrative of the romance Western; it is rarely a love story alone. The heterosexual relationship may be a pretext to motivate action, it may be marginal (the love interest), it may end in separation (a romantic tragedy) or it may even exclude the hero (the romantic subplot). The outcome of the romantic relationship is rarely certain in Westerns, in keeping with the treatment of romance in other male action genres. Partnership presumes a settlement with the heroine that contradicts the individualist, nomadic lifestyle of the hero. Romantic longing in Western song lyrics can express the unlikeliness of partnership as much as a longing for it.

As in Hollywood films more generally, the representation of romantic relationships in Westerns changes over time. In the classical period, under conditions of censorship, the nature of courtship is likely to be coded, appearing to be governed by compatibility rather than sexual desire. From the 1950s onwards, however, with increasing relaxation of censorship restrictions, the sexual nature of heterosexual relationships become more explicit, revealing that 'romance' codes sexual desire. From the period of social changes in the 1960s, which also saw the advent of a cycle of popular Westerns made by Italian film-makers, a new Western antihero emerges who is likely to eschew the courtship rituals of the romance hero in favour of an explicit sexual directness. In a similar move, the female object of desire who once was seen to work in a saloon becomes explicitly sexually available, often by formal payment.

The nature of the romantic relationship in Westerns may also differ from other forms of romance. In Wexman's account (1993, pp.113–29), the classical Western is likely to figure a traditional partnership, in which a patriarchal hero and a domesticated heroine combine eternal social divisions of absolute masculinity and femininity. She contrasts this with the greater equality and indivisibility of heterosexual relationships in what she terms the 'companionate partnership' that characterises more modern genres. However, the possibility of companionate relationships is often held out as an ideal for the central protagonists of romance Westerns. The realisation that the ideal is difficult or even unattainable for Western heroes is commonly experienced as tragic for characters and audiences alike.

Heterosexual relationships in Westerns are complicated by the importance the genre accords to central male relationships; between the hero and sidekick, father and son figures, and within the all-male group. Even where these are familial, they are always homosocial relationships, examples of male bonding. However, Paul Willemen has written about repressed homosexuality in the 'homosexual sub-text' that haunts the Western genre (1981, pp.15–17). The potential variety of gendered and sexual relationships complicates the nature, role and function of romantic relationships in romance Westerns.

THE ROMANCE NARRATIVE

The hero of the romance Western is also romantic in a more classical sense. The 'romance' of the romance Western lies as much in the *structure* of the narrative as in its drama. In classical literature, romance narratives are quest narratives, in which a hero sets out to obtain a prized object, overcome obstacles and return with the prize. In Vladimir Propp's analysis of the fairy tale, he finds two major variants in the quest. The hero is either tested by acts of villainy or by a weakness that requires gifts of support in order for him to achieve the task. Romance Westerns clearly inherit this structure. Many Western plots are based on journeys during which the hero encounters villainous acts requiring assistance from what Propp calls 'donors'. Foremost among these are journey Westerns like *Comanche Station* (1959), wagon train Westerns like *The Covered Wagon* (1923) and cattle trail Westerns like *Red River* (1948). Revenge Westerns also tend to be journey Westerns, in which the hero hunts down the perpetrators of heinous acts he must avenge. Examples include *The Bravados* (1958), *Chato's Land* (1971) and, with a female hero, *Hannie Caulder* (1971). *The Outlaw Josey Wales* (1976) starts as a revenge Western, but somehow loses its way, as the wandering hero picks up a disparate group on the journey and replaces the family he initially lost.

THE ROMANCE HERO

The romance Western is defined not only by heterosexual romance and the romance narrative but also by *validation* of the hero's action. Crudely but neatly, the romance hero is a hero because his heroism is justified (a character in *Ride the High Country*, 1962 is said to die well since he 'entered his house justified'). The hero of the romance Western will triumph over unlikely, implausible or impossible odds; he may be misunderstood, mistreated or condemned; he may appear to act out of misplaced allegiances or misjudgement; he may be a criminal or act unlawfully; regardless of these qualities, he will represent a higher order of morality, justice and social purpose. The narrative of the romance Western must be resolved by the absolution of the hero; even if he fails in his quest, he will fail because it is right that he fails, not that he is a failure. As in Greek legend or mediaeval myth, the hero of the romance Western is a 'knight of the true cause' (Bazin, 1971, p.145).

Of all the action genres, the romance Western actively investigates the meaning of heroism, since heroism must operate in imaginary conditions lacking established order. Threat is defended by one's self rather than by formal policing and justice is enacted in practice rather than through the exercise of the rule of law. The Western is thereby a genre that can provide a dramatic stage for a disquisition on the nature and morality of power and on the legitimacy of force. In romance Westerns, however, legitimacy concerns the struggle between the power of law and the force of justice, often in conditions of lawlessness or law unjustly applied.

The central and contradictory sign of this struggle is the gun, used ritually in Westerns in ways that make it a particularly powerful American genre (Fairlamb, 1998). There is romance in the display of a six-gun; unlike the handgun in crime films, it is not concealed about the body, but worn openly on a belt about the waist. The ritual of the gunfight modernises the tradition of honour in the duel, democratising conflict by making the outcome dependent on human skill rather than mechanical power. Behaviour that threatens the ritual of the gunfight – a concealed weapon such as a knife or a derringer up the sleeve – or contrasts with it – like the treachery of the assassin's ambush – exposes villainy. If the use of the Colt .45 handgun symbolises democratic justice, the rifle is equally subject to ritual. It may emphasise more the competition of marksmanship rather than speed to the draw; in *Winchester '73* (1950), the villain who cheats the hero of the prized rifle in competition ultimately forfeits his life. Exceptional individuals may be defined by equally exceptional use of weaponry; the hunted hero of *Valdez is Coming* (1970) eventually wins the respect of his hunters, in part through his skill at dispensing death over huge distances, with a Sharp's rifle loaded with a preparation of his 'own making'.

The Western hero's relationship to his gun (Cawelti, 1975) is as conventional to the Western as the biker's knowledge of his motorcycle is to the road movie. In *Backlash* (1956), the hero and villain 'measure the effectiveness of a gun by the way it rests in the hand' (Kitses, 1969, p.51). The process of mechanical or automatic replacement of spent bullet with live ammunition in a gun's chamber makes it a dynamic weapon. Unlike twentieth-century armoury, the severely limited capacity of the gun chamber in Westerns can measure the moral capacity of the gunfighter. 'Counting to six' in order to act during the time it takes to reload is a precise calculation for suspense. In *The Tall T* (1957) and *Comanche Station*, for instance, the hero tricks the villain into believing his gun is empty. As the count reaches 'six', the villain who rises to escape is fatally halted by a hidden second gun.

The visibility of the gun promising the dispensation of justice in the hand of the Western hero paradoxically threatens its violation in the hands of the villain. At the same time, it is essential to the iconography of masculine display, gracing the body and movement of the hero (Pumphrey, 1989). The skills of actors in the trick use of hand guns is often deployed in Westerns to narrative purpose. In *Vera Cruz* (1954), the climax requires star Burt Lancaster to die in a gunfight, but not before he shoots, smiles, trick-spins his gun back into its holster and gracefully falls back to die. The action pleasurably defines the vanity of the actor as much as the character. In *Tombstone* (1993), such vanity is parodied when Doc Holliday (Val Kilmer) repeats each move of an advanced display of trick-spinning by a villain intent on humiliating him, though this time with a miniature whiskey cup spun on a little finger. The role and function of the gun is not only part of the weaponry, but also part of the romantic masculinity of the hero of the romance Western.

THE COWBOY GUNFIGHTER AS HERO

The hero as cowboy gunfighter in romance Westerns develops from earlier formations in dime novels, possibly to heal the central contradictory threat of violence in the Western hero. Historical cowboys had little need for guns in their daily labours and no need for a fast draw. Gunfights were the stuff of circus rather than the streets; nineteenth-century armoury was so imprecise and unreliable that a gunfight was a lottery rather than a display of shooting prowess. Gunfights do, however, appear as a dramatic convention at the turn of the century in illustrations, like Frederic Remington's *A Fight in the Streets* (1902), and in novels, like Owen Wister's *The Virginian* (1902). The first film cowboy heroes display their guns openly but use them infrequently. Even series Western cowboys use guns more sparingly than might be expected of a genre with violent confrontation central to its narrative development. The demands of fiction rather than history inspire generic change over time, gradually merging the cowboy figure developed by the likes of Broncho Billy Anderson and William S. Hart – film-makers who were keen to authentic- ate their Westerners – with the trick-shooting theatrical Show figures such as Buffalo Bill Cody and Tom Mix. The result was the cowboy gunfighter as mythic hero but also as an everyman figure, whose speed on the draw sym- bolises his quickness to moral action, whose mental acuity is evident in a sharp eye and whose destiny is defined by the accuracy of his aim.

Stagecoach

Stagecoach is an ideal romance Western to demonstrate this range of ideas and is one of several popular Westerns that transformed the prestige of the genre at the end of the1930s. For Bazin, *Stagecoach* took the Western genre to a 'definitive stage of perfection' (1971, p.140) and Peter Stanfield's research suggests that the film's complex fusion of history, allegory and adult themes was a ploy of Hollywood's successful film marketing at the time (2001, pp.148–51).

Adapted by Dudley Nichols from a short story, *Stage to Lordsburg* (1937) by Ernest Haycox, *Stagecoach* is an allegorical tale of a stagecoach journey, during which a divided group of travellers develop more self-knowledgeable relationships. The hero joins the group last, by which time the travellers have formed 'divisions between polite society and the social outcasts' (Buscombe 1992, p.36). Relationships change around the hero, representing a shifting series of symbiotic partnerships within the group. The young hero realigns and settles conflicts within the group, finally emerging as a mature man of action, rewarded from among the group with the ideal companion as heroine.

The composition of the group crucially defines the romance hero. The driver is a comic figure, the cowardly fool, Buck (Andy Devine), joined atop the stagecoach by Curly (George Bancroft), Marshal of the town of Tonto, riding shotgun alongside him. They are connected by an honest approach to their functional roles that otherwise separate them more than just physically from the passengers. Among the passengers is the pregnant Lucy Mallory (Louise Platt), a snobbish gentlewoman whose Southern origins are 'the nearest thing in the United States to a landed aristocracy' (ibid., p.23). A more sinister Southerner, Hatfield (John Carradine), introduced as 'a notorious gambler' with a reputation for back-shooting, dotes upon her. They will remain close during the journey until the moment Hatfield is killed in a climactic Indian attack, the only passenger in the stagecoach not to survive the journey. He dies just as he is about to pull the trigger on the 'last bullet' intended to rescue Lucy from the Indians. It is a blessing, for the coach – complete with the honour and life of Lucy – will be rescued by a cavalry troop.

Also in the coach is Samuel Peacock (Donald Meek, an apt name for an actor stereotyped as eternally mild-mannered), a balding whiskey salesman whose samples are gradually denuded by the alcoholic Doc Boone (Thomas Mitchell). The impecunious Doc is travelling against his will, evicted from Tonto by his landlady along with Dallas (Claire Trevor), a prostitute escorted to the coach by an assortment of pinch-faced harridans of the local Law and Order League. Doc and Dallas recognise that they are equally considered what Doc calls 'the dregs of the town', jointly victims of the 'foul disease called social prejudice'. The first major division on the stagecoach appears as the Southern pair finds offence in the presence of the other passengers, especially Dallas and the loud Doc's easy sampling of the whiskies belonging to the nervous Peacock.

This is the group that leaves Tonto for Lordsburg, though two more are quickly added. The first is Henry Gatewood (Berton Churchill), a pompous, blustering banker whom the audience knows has robbed his own bank, who joins the coach as it leaves town to escape detection. Everything about him is the polar opposite of the second addition. Just outside town, the party is completed by the sudden eruption of the hero, the Ringo Kid (John Wayne). In 'one of the most stunning entrances in all of cinema', we 'hear a shot and cut suddenly to Ringo standing by the trail, twirling his rifle . . . The camera dollies quickly in towards a tight close-up . . . as the camera settles securely on Wayne's sweat-stained face Buck . . . calls out "Hey, look, it's Ringo"' (ibid., p.9). Image, sound, camera and performance combine to present character and actor as an iconic romance Westerner.

The group completed, the flawed gentlepeople conflict with the morally ambiguous social outcasts. Under pressure by the threat of Apache ambush, the pairs at first grow more intimate; Buck and Curly, Lucy and Hatfield, Doc and Peacock, Dallas and Ringo, with only Gatewood keeping his own company. Ringo is the key agent in a series of misunderstandings that help define his character and the nature of the hero of the romance Western. When the coach reaches a staging post, his courtly manners lead him to offer Dallas a seat at table. As he joins her, he mistakes the departure of the Southern pair for 'a table closer to the window' as a slight against himself: 'Looks like I got the plague, don't it?' So naive is he around women that he will continue to be unaware of Dallas' profession (Alexander Walker, 1970, p.303). He courts her, tentatively but tenderly, unsure of her affection for one as unworthy as he considers himself. Even at the end of the journey, he insists on the propriety of courtship, accompanying Dallas to her door, despite her anxious protestations. Director John Ford constructs the brothel town in Lordsburg as a sultry but seedy ghetto. Dallas is distressed by his insistence but accepts her fate. Yet the sights and sounds she fears will destroy Ringo's admiration for her serve only to reinforce his commitment. Free of bourgeois prejudice, his ability to see through Dallas' position to the sensitive, considerate soul she has proved herself to be during the journey is a mark of the hero of the romance Western.

Ringo, the hero, will recognise in Dallas an equal yet complementary heroine. More than social outcasts, both have survived hard times without losing their humanity. We learn early that Ringo has broken from jail to kill the Plummer Brothers in an act of revenge. As he must, Curly places the outlaw under arrest, a constraint from which Ringo has to escape to complete his quest. However, when an opportunity arises, he refuses it, knowing that without his guns, the stagecoach has less chance of surviving an Apache attack. The group now includes a baby born to Lucy, assisted by Doc and tended by Dallas. Such social action secures the moral centre of the film for the three social outcasts, Ringo, Dallas and Doc. At the journey's end, the narrative moves to an appropriate allocation of reward and punishment. Lucy and child will be reunited with her husband and a passing exchange of glances with Dallas affirms their new sisterhood; Peacock is taken off on a stretcher to have his wounds tended, now denuded of his samples by Doc; a sheriff steps up as if to arrest Ringo but instead satisfyingly handcuffs the now exposed Gatewood.

The problem of Ringo's quest must now be resolved. How can the criminal intent of the hero be justified? Cleared of the respectable folk, the morally virtuous and the functionaries combine (like Propp's worthy donors) to aid Ringo in his task. First, Curly must turn a blind eye, accepting complicity with the illegality of a gunfight. Secondly, Ringo will need assistance from Doc's wit to overcome the combined force of the three brothers. Finally, Curly and Buck must assist the romantic couple to escape from the lawful consequences of the successful killing. Before this, Ford constructs a suspenseful gunfight in which the outcome is delayed to audience and characters alike. Ringo strides towards the low camera and throws himself forward to the ground, shooting. Instead of reverse shots to reveal the gunfight's outcome, there are cuts to the virtuous others reacting to the sound of the guns. After which, Luke Plummer enters the same bar he had earlier abandoned, as if he is the sole survivor, only to fall, dead. Ringo returns to give himself up to Curly. Affecting to re-arrest him, Curly places Ringo on a buggy, alongside a bemused Dallas. Handing Ringo the reins, he joins Doc in sending the buggy on its way as Doc concludes: 'saved from the blessings of civilisation'. Against the odds, the hero has overcome all obstacles, satisfied his quest, and won heroine and freedom as his prize. And as the ideal couple head into the background sunset of Mexico and the Western landscape, he is deified as much for the manner of his victory as for the victory itself. Ringo is an archetypal hero of the romance Western.

My Darling Clementine

Stagecoach is one of a number of A Westerns produced from 1939 that popularise the romance Western for a new, wider audience for the next twenty years. The Ringo Kid is a romance hero of his time, a more youthful develop-ment of the Good-Badman in the William S. Hart tradition and a character of greater psychological depth than series Westerns could afford. In John Wayne, the film forged a developing Western hero in the persona of a troubled innocent, a man whose values are too easily misrecognised, and a loner deserving of an equal partnership. As a star of Westerns directed by John Ford, Wayne's characters are among Ford's most idealised heroes, although the persona evolves over his subsequent film career into one more readily prone to violence and thus more morally ambivalent. Concurrently, Ford's heroes become more complex figures of romance, in parallel with wider post-War developments in the genre.

Among the first of these is Wyatt Earp (Henry Fonda), the hero of *My Darling Clementine* (1946). The film opens with a sentimental scene between Wyatt and his brothers who take a break from the trail in Tombstone, leaving the youngest, James, to guard their cattle. On arrival, the easy skill with which Wyatt then settles a disturbance, combined with the revelation of his reputation as lawman of Dodge City, prompts the townspeople to offer him the town marshal's badge. At first, he declines, until James is discovered dead and the cattle rustled by the Clantons, an all-male family led by Old Man Clanton (Walter Brennan). Unlike Ringo in *Stagecoach*, Wyatt uses the law to avenge the crime. Audience expectation might demand that the revenge plot take over the narrative immediately, but Wyatt takes his time. Only after the evidence is gathered do the brothers finally confront and overcome the Clantons at the legendary Gunfight at the O.K. Corral. By that time, the revenge plot is all but forgotten, for quite new dynamics in the romance Western have replaced it.

The heroes of *Stagecoach* and *My Darling Clementine* equally satisfy generic expectations of climactic gunfights. However, Ringo's gunfight places him beyond the law and he must finally ride into the West to escape the consequences of his illegal action. Unlike Ringo, Wyatt is not criminalised, as his quest for revenge is subsumed within the framework of the law. Wyatt's Westerner becomes a necessary agent of Eastern advance, as opposed to Ringo, who is 'saved from the blessings of [Eastern] civilisation'. As Peter Wollen has argued, Wyatt stands at the intersection of Nash Smith's polarity between Garden and Desert, a character embodying Kitses' shifting antinomies between wilderness and civilisation (1972(69), pp.94–102). Though he is introduced as a cattleman (and hence a Westerner), Wyatt's credentials as lawmaker (of Eastern laws) are rapidly established. Yet he is an unwilling participant, accepting the public role of town marshal only to satisfy a private quest for revenge. As the personal quest gradually shifts from the centre of the film, however, Wyatt seems to 'keep the peace' by idly filling time. He whittles in a porch chair, visits the barbershop and accompanies the eponymous Clementine (Cathy Downs) to a dance. This hero is some distance from the conventional man of Western action and no-one seems to expect anything different of him (Simmon, 1999).

The frontier hero of *My Darling Clementine* is an unlikely and reluctant agent of Eastern advance, an 'ambivalent mediator' (Stowell, 1986, p.98) between East and West. Where Wyatt and his brothers represent positive Western values, the evil Clantons represent the negative. They are forces of lawlessness that must be expelled in order to make this imaginary West a place fit for the new, ideal community, encapsulated in the townsfolk and nearby settlers who meet to commemorate the construction of the town's first church in a celebrated pivotal scene (Hall & Whannell, 1964, p.108). In order to overcome the Clantons, the Earps need the gun of the refugee from the East, the Byronic figure of Doc Holliday (Victor Mature), 'a dissolute consumptive who rules the town' (ibid., p.107). Though both use Tombstone for their own purposes, the gauche, unschooled Wyatt contrasts with the self-pitying, cultured tyrant, Holliday. Whilst Wyatt walks the open air of the town, Holliday hides away in his noirish hotel room or escapes from the drama into an off-screen Mexico. His death in the Gunfight is almost a suicidal release from civilisation's diseases (not just tuberculosis but also drinking, stealing and gambling) that will otherwise kill him. *My Darling Clementine* kills off Holliday because the future it idealises needs his kind of civilisation like it needs the Clantons' kind of wild(er)ness.

Holliday's death opens the way for partnership between Wyatt and Clementine, the teacher who comes from the East to rescue Holliday but, rebuffed, remains in the burgeoning Western town to educate the next generation of Westerners. The public ideal that Clementine promises contrasts with the individualism both of Holliday and his wild woman of the West, Chihuahua (Linda Darnell). Chihuahua is the most racially and sexually stereotyped character in the film and the Western's sacrificial Good Bad Girl, the promiscuous non-white woman (like Pearl in *Duel in the Sun*, 1946), who will throw herself (like Ruby in *The Iron Horse*, 1924) in front of a bullet intended for Doc. At the end, when the wildness of both the Eastern Holliday and the Western Chihuahua has been expelled from the film, Wyatt and Clementine are available for the ideal union of positive Western and Eastern values. However, Wyatt takes his leave of Clementine, riding on and leaving her to her school teaching. The ending has been subject to conflicting interpretations (Lovell, Nichols). At one extreme, Wollen (1972(69), p.96) takes Wyatt's expressed desire to return to Tombstone 'some day' as a certainty, whereas Lee Clarke Mitchell and Tompkins see Wyatt's departure as absolute confirmation of the Western's masculine rejection of the feminine.

In many ways, Wyatt's role is reminiscent of other populist heroes in American Cinema, such as those featured in films directed by Frank Capra. Like George Bailey (James Stewart), in the small-town romance, *It's a Wonderful Life* (1946), Wyatt is a reticent leader of his community, an individual holding back from representing the group, torn between a natural inclination to move on (in George's case, to explore the world) and recognition that the town needs him. The populist hero generally does what is right by the community and finally accepts his allotted place within it. However, the Western hero is more disturbed by the social role allocated to him.

This is evident in the sad and troubled ending of *My Darling Clementine*. Even if the film were not named after its heroine, the expectation of a romance narrative is that the couple will eventually unite. Like all romance heroes, Wyatt succeeds in his quest by avenging his brother's death. Yet, unlike classical romance heroes, he does not get his prize – Clementine, the heroine – unless, like Wollen, we see Wyatt's leaving as a deferral. Perhaps there are conditions in the romance Western that give the hero reason for separation. In terms of the models of Nash Smith and Kitses, the hero acts as an agent of change from Desert/Wilderness to Garden/Civilisation. However necessary his role is to realise this change, he is not essential to the new circumstances he brings about. He has entered a violent, lawless community whose positive elements have found in him a saviour. But the violent qualities he brings to overcome lawlessness are the qualities unwanted by the new society his actions make possible.

The figure of the woman becomes crucial in this pattern. Unlike those critics who argue that the Western marginalises women or represents a traditional, conservative femininity, Studlar finds in Westerns directed by John Ford an 'accommodation of masculinity to feminine values' (Studlar & Bernstein, 2001, p.11). Wyatt is gauche and discomforted around Clementine, the sexually unattainable bourgeois woman, which is most starkly evident in the comic stiffness of his dancing style at the church meeting. In *My Darling Clementine*, Wyatt's role is to build a social order in which a civilised masculinity *and* femininity can survive. Since, in Buscombe's words, a Western 'society without violence, a society fit for women, can only be established *through* violence' (1992, p.59), the very agent of change must also becomes its first victim. Wyatt's violent masculinity can therefore have no place within the new order it has enabled. The hero of *My Darling Clementine* is thus a hero of romance, without the possibility of romantic partnership. This contradiction is what leads Bazin to characterise the Western hero as a tragic figure.

THE ROMANCE HERO ALONE

The isolate hero is central to Western romance fiction from the earliest times. Yet isolation may be more or less chosen. Among the antecedents, James Fenimore Cooper's wandering hero, Natty Bumppo, oscillates between wilderness and frontier settlement. Alternatively, the independent cowboy of Owen Wister's *The Virginian* – 'nature's aristocrat' (Davis, 1992) – embraces the possibilities of both society and partnership. In contrast to this, the roaming cowboy gunfighter who rides in, delivers justice and rides on has popular antecedents in the nineteenth-century dime novel, like Robert Montgomery Bird's *Nick of the Woods* (1837). Westerns of the 1950s commonly explore the terms of and reasons for such behaviour in the hero.

Some romance Westerns of the 1950s develop the mythic tendencies of the isolate hero to an extreme. Among the starkest is the hero of the most popular of 1950s Westerns, *Shane* (1953). The eponymous hero justly settles a feud between farmers and cattlemen by rescuing farmer Will Starrett (Van Heflin) from a gunfighter, Wilson (Jack Palance), menacingly hired by cattleman Ryker (Emile Meyer). Shane (Alan Ladd) first appears inexplicably in the film's landscape, seen from the point of view of Starrett's son, Joey (Brandon De Wilde), as if magically summoned by the lonely little boy (the original novel by Jack Schaeffer is first-person narrated by Joey). His buckskinned costume, blonde good looks and courtly manners also arouse Starrett's wife, Marian (Jean Arthur). If Shane seems the mysterious answer to an unacknowledged call for help from all members of the family, he also finds hope for himself among them. For a man who drifts 'here and there – somewhere I've never been', the family offers the possibility of settlement. However, the very skills necessary to overcome the family's adversary are also those that make it impossible for the hero to settle among and become like them. Once he has served his purpose and defeated the enemy, he must ride on. In the closing shots of *Shane*, there is a suggestion that the hero has taken a mortal wound as, unresponsive to Joey's call for him to return, his arm hangs limply from his body, slumped over his horse. Though Joey rightly expresses the family's love for Shane, his claim that the family also needs him is wrong. Shane would certainly return to a grateful audience, but also to a proud husband he has physically bested, a wife he may compete for and a son for whom he has become a hero ideal. However, what really prevents him from returning is his gunfighter status: 'There's no living with a killing . . . Right or wrong, it's a brand and the brand sticks. There's no going back'. *Shane* knows it is best that the romance hero return to the mythical space from whence first he came, in a 'subversive affirmation of the allure of solitariness' (Baker, 1996, p.220).

In contrast to this, the hero of *The Far Country* (1955) is less eager to act according to his social responsibilities. And it is that very denial which makes him less a figure of romantic myth like Shane and more the typical flawed hero of 1950's Western romance. Jeff Webster (James Stewart) wants only to attend to his herd of cattle and maybe also his sidekick, Ben (Walter Brennan). Caught up in border politics between the corrupt Judge Gannon of Skagway and the mining community of Dawson City, he finds himself called upon to act in the interests of the community. Despite this, 'looking out for myself' is Jeff's watchword, even when he is plainly disgusted by the treatment meted out to the miners by Gannon and his gang. The community is a ramshackle collection of drifters, dead beats and no-hopers. But its society is warmly idealised in a range of characters including two spinsters called Hominy and Grits who run a restaurant like an old people's home, with lashings of bear stew accompanied by songs on the piano. Jeff constantly denies them all, facing up to his social responsibilities only when Gannon's treachery touches him personally. An attempted escape down river from the increasing lawlessness of Dawson City leaves Ben dead and Jeff's gun-hand injured in an ambush. When Jeff recovers, he returns to single-handedly take on and kill the gang. Although it is unclear what combination of personal revenge and social justice motivates his action, his accommodation within the community is then made possible in a way not available to the heroes of *My Darling Clementine* and *Shane*. The final shot of the film has Jeff sentimentally ringing a bell suspended from the horn of his saddle, attending for the first time to the femininity instead of merely the youth of Renee (Corrine Calvert), who has insisted throughout that being a part of the social order is the only way to live. Jeff's alternative claim to an independent older woman, the sexualised Ronda (Ruth Roman), ends after her death in the street, shot in the back by Gannon. With the homely Renee literally in the frame, the Western hero can and will settle down.

THE IDEAL WESTERN COMMUNITY

The community of Dawson City represents a solid body of communities in Westerns, for whom the special skills of a Wyatt Earp, a Shane or a Ben Webster justly – more or less voluntarily – offer their services. Yet, as the first epic Westerns amply demonstrate, the pioneer community itself can be cast as heroic. Some of the most emotional moments in Westerns come from the sacrifices of pioneer families. In *Drums Along the Mohawk* (1939), an aged pioneer woman played by Edna May Oliver is comical in her fearless resistance to a Mohawk invasion of her bedroom. In *Rachel and the Stranger* (1948), the aftermath of an attack on a cabin by marauding Shoshone is made a humbling experience for an audience who has witnessed the settler family's labour invested in its building. No deaths of a pioneer family are more telling than the moment in *The Searchers* (1956) when Ethan Edwards (John Wayne) rides to the top of a sandy bluff and – in a reverse cut and with an orchestra striking the most heartfelt chord – confronts the burning cabin of his brother's family.

The most supreme of Western communities lies in the humanity of John Ford's Westerns. This even encompasses the forts of his cavalry Westerns like *Fort Apache* (1948), where the rituals of society such as meals and dances bring civility to the uncivil, hospitality to the new arrival and the weak, and resolution in the cause of justice. In defence of such societies, the romance hero will always recognise that the good of the community must triumph over every other cause, even if the cause conflicts with his own. The criminal hero (Joel McCrea) of *Four Faces West* (1948) – a remarkable Western in which not a single gunshot is fired – has a chance to escape from a chasing posse to freedom across the border. But he comes across a sickly Mexican family in an isolated cabin. Can he leave them to die of diphtheria? His conscience will not allow him to turn his back on his social responsibility. He sacrifices his only defence by extracting the gunpowder from his bullets to turn into sulphur to burn the disease from their throats. The family survive and the chasing sheriff, Pat Garrett (Charles Bickford), releases him. In communities whose cause is transparently just, the romance hero will find reward in his own sacrifice.

THE PROFESSIONAL

In films directed by Howard Hawks, the central focus is not the romantic individual but the professional group. In the Westerns, the group is either isolated, as on the cattle trail in *Red River* and in the backwoods in *The Big Sky* (1952), or elevated from the township community around it, as in his late Westerns like *Rio Bravo* (1959), *El Dorado* (1966) and *Rio Lobo* (1970). In these, 'Hawks' town consists of jail, hotel, saloons, and rows of inconspicuous house-fronts: inhabitants appear only when the narrative demands their presence, and there is never the least attempt to evoke that sense of community that is one of the finest and most characteristic features of the work of Ford' (Wood, 1998, p.178). Although the group effectively acts in defence of the community, it essentially operates in accord with its own internal professional code. The group acts not just for the good of the wider community but because they judge it justifies their own collectivity. For this reason, the professional group is exclusive, what Robin Wood calls the 'elect'. Hawks famously disapproved of the hero's behaviour in *High Noon*, disputing that a professional would chase round the town seeking the help of amateurs to support his cause. For Wood again, everything depends 'ultimately, on a matter of personal responsibility, not social duty' (ibid., p.181), though the social and personal need not be divisible.

The separation of the professional group from the community makes Hawks' Westerns disquisitions on the nature of heroism, 'the conditions necessary to it, and the human conditions that accompany those limitations' (ibid., p.185). The group might comprise individuals with the necessary skills for the job, but the essential qualification is their ability to work together, to trust and rely on each other. This also means that members of the group also have human failings. Acknowledging this, the hero invariably asks only if those who join the group are 'good enough'.

In Hawks' most celebrated Western, *Rio Bravo*, Sheriff John T. Chance (John Wayne) organises a ramshackle group to keep criminal Joe Burdett (Claude Akins) in the town jail to await the arrival of the federal marshal. However, they are pitted against a superior force of gunfighters hired by Joe's brother, Nathan Burdett (John Russell). Ranged against them are Chance's allies Dude (Dean Martin), an alcoholic with the shakes, Stumpy (Walter Brennan), an old man with a limp, Colorado (Ricky Nelson), a young cowboy who volunteers when the gang kill his boss in an ambush, and Feathers (Angie Dickinson), an itinerant gambler. The film centres attention on the dynamics of the group, their supportive yet critical interrelationships and how they manage the flawed heroism of the others. Wood argues that 'there comes a point when these friendships, valuable and creative as they are, reach the limit of their power to influence and affect, beyond which point the individual is alone with his own resources or sheer chance to fall back on' (ibid., p.185). At the start of the film, Chance rescues Dude from alcoholic self-pity, kicking from his reach a spittoon in which a villain has thrown a coin to feed Dude's drink problem. Later, when he is caught off guard while on sentry duty, his shame at letting the group down leads him to find solace in a bottle of whiskey. Dude is then left to find his own way back to self-respect. In a key moment in the film, as he reaches for a bottle, he hears the strains of the threatening tune that Santa Anna played at the Alamo, intending to demoralise the beleaguered defenders and to leave 'no quarter' in the battle ahead. While Burdett orders the tune played in the saloon as ironic comment on the small group in the jail, it has the opposite effect on Dude. Reminded of his professional obligations, to himself as much as to the group, he carefully replaces the cork in the bottle.

Hawks' heroes are marked not as isolates but as individual members of a collective. The group is sustained by the mutual benefit it offers to all its members. Dude's identification with the elect provides his sense of worth and identity. However, this is not something all in the group can easily recognise or acknowledge. Though Chance helps others to recognise their responsibilities, he fails to recognise that he needs help himself.

Chance's independence and self-sufficiency is illusory. He goes through the film systematically rejecting the help of others, yet every crisis . . . would end in disaster were it not for the unsolicited intervention of others. Without the cripple, the drunk, the comic Mexican, the teenage boy, a girl on hand to fling a well-timed flowerpot, the superman would be defeated before he had the chance to perform a single decisive action. Yet if the others are physically

*indispensable to him, it is never in doubt that Chance is spiritually
indispensable to them. Remove him . . . and you would be left largely with
human wreckage, for it is . . . Chance . . . who gives meaning, coherence and
integrity to the lives of those around him.*

(Wood, 1998, p.187)

The emphasis on the professional all-male group may seem to exclude
women. But, for Hawks, women who offer the possibility of romantic
partnership with such heroes are themselves professional – in attitude if not
in status. The male/female relationship echoes the fun and comedy in the
banter between members of the elect, giving rise to a humour that counteracts the dangerous conditions of 'death, rupture and loss (that) abound in
Hawks' world' (Thomson, 1994, p.322). David Thomson finds in Hawks'
films an 'optimism derived from a delight in people' (ibid., p.323), whereas
Wood finds that humour masks a stoical attitude to life, realised in the
'stylised austerity' of *Rio Bravo* (1998, p.177).

THE REVENGE HERO

In the final generation of romance Westerns in the late 1950s and early 1960s,
the hero is increasingly a personally troubled figure, not just divided by
loyalties to self, friends and a wider society, but also dealing with his own
generically new inner demons. The figure develops from the romantic agent
of change, like Wyatt Earp in *My Darling Clementine*, and the instrument of
justice in the West, like Shane. However, this new romance hero acts for
himself rather than acting for society, as in the Westerns of John Ford, or
for the group, as in Hawks' Westerns. Unlike Ringo in *Stagecoach*, this new
romance hero is emotionally damaged by the experience of loss in his past.
His quest for revenge is seen as destructive and it is necessary for him to
exorcise his neuroses before (like Jeff in *The Far Country*), he can become
whole again. No examples of the new revenge hero are more telling than in
the Westerns of directors Budd Boetticher and Anthony Mann.

Budd Boetticher directed a small group of B Westerns in the 1950s known
as 'the Ranown cycle', named after a production company formed by star
Randolph Scott and producer Harry Joe Brown. Their work with Boetticher on
Seven Men from Now (1956) brought them together with scriptwriter Burt
Kennedy, with whom they then made *The Tall T* (1957), *Ride Lonesome* (1959)
and *Comanche Station*. Where *Shane* is set in a lush pastureland spoiled only
by the muddy pioneer street in whose few buildings the villains idle their
time, the landscape in the Ranown cycle is 'a labyrinth of huge rounded rocks,
classic badlands terrain' (Russell, 1965, p.196) through which characters

travel, resting by verdant waterholes, where they settle to talk. The location for all the films is a few hours drive from Hollywood in the Alabama Hills of Lone Pine's small town, a popular site for Westerns from series like *The Lone Ranger* (1949–57) to the epic *How the West Was Won* (1962). But Boetticher renders the location as remote from any human society.

Boetticher claims that the Ranown cycle has 'pretty much the same story, with variants. A man whose wife has been killed is searching out her murderer'. This enables 'quite subtle relations between a hero, wrongly bent on vengeance, and outlaws who, in contrast, want to break with their past' (quoted in Russell, 1965, p.198). The hero is invariably 'a man with a mission, albeit a private one, morally ambiguous and . . . driven "to do what a man has to do", but . . . pretty pessimistic about the outcome' (Dibb, 1996, p.164). Typically,

> the hero . . . and his small group of travelling companions thrown together by accident, have to contend various hazards; bandits and Indians, etc. The films develop, in Andrew Sarris' words, into floating poker games, where every character takes turns at bluffing his hand until the final showdown . . . after the showdown, the hero rides off again through the same rounded rocks, still alone, certainly with no exultation after his victory.

> (Russell, 1965, p.196)

In this common narrative structure, heroics are so pared down that the hero becomes 'frightening, a man who cultivated the past at the expense of the present' (Hardy, 1991, p.251) such that, in comparison, the villainy around him is made more human.

The Tall T is the only one of the cycle to start light-heartedly, since the hero has at first no reason to be vengeful. Although the man who rides out of the rocks under the credits in Ranown Westerns is always actor Randolph Scott, here he is Pat Brennan, initially a more easy-going character than in the other films and perhaps the kind of man the others were before their loss and ensuing bitterness. Brennan rides by a swing station (a post for stagecoaches) and exchanges affectionate banter with the owner and his young son. Moving on to a ranch, Brennan stakes his horse on a bet for a seed bull. Following a slapstick scene in which Brennan is thrown by the bucking bull, he is abruptly found alone and footsore on the road home. At this point, fate takes a hand as he finds himself an unwanted hitchhiker on a private stagecoach hired by the newly married Willard Mimms (John Hubbard) and his wife. The film then takes on a darker tone as the camera reveals the silhouette of a gunman moving in the station shadows. The stage is held up at the way station and the driver is killed by a gang led by Usher (Richard Boone) expecting to rob the regular stage. It is the killing of the driver and the discovery that the bodies of the station family have been thrown contemptuously down a well that changes Brennan's character. Thereafter, with 'granite-like circumspection' (Kitses, 1969, p.97) and single-minded determination, he focuses on survival to avenge the deaths of the innocents.

Brennan becomes like the hero in the other Ranown films, one who knows that his life is precarious, that at any moment he could be killed, yet whose knowledge serves only further to narrow and make more resolute his purpose. Waiting for 'the opportunity of meaningful personal action' (ibid., p.198), these heroes are 'fallible and vulnerable; they make their way inch by inch, not at all with the sublime confidence of crusaders' (Russell, 1969, p.199). The hero comes up against the leader of a gang who finds in him qualities he covets. Critics invoke the rituals of the bullfight to explain the nature of the hero's relationship with the villain in the Ranown cycle. As Richard T. Jameson says, 'it is not hard to detect the rhythms of the corrida in the deadly, flirtatious style of encounter between these adversaries' (1980, p.1054), though which is the matador and which the bull gives pause for thought. In *The Tall T*, the gang hold Mrs. Mimms (Maureen O'Sullivan) to ransom. Despite there being no financial benefit, Usher keeps Brennan alive because he recognises in him an association he prefers to the young members of his gang, the ignorant Billy Jack (Skip Homeier) and vain Chink (Henry Silva). However, Usher disposes of the craven Willard Mimms out of disgust for a man prepared to sacrifice his wife for his own freedom. The line between heroism and villainy crossed, the villain is thus made as much a victim of circumstances as the hero. As Boetticher says, these villains 'made mistakes like everybody else: but they are human beings, sometimes more than (the hero)' (quoted in Russell, 1965, p.198).

At the end of each film, the villains will be dead, some by the forced hand of a leader who will then seek to avoid, but finally have to confront the hero. In *The Tall T*, Brennan gradually isolates and picks off the gang one by one until only the leader remains. In *Comanche Station*, we are saddened at the deaths of the 'young guns', so poorly educated and unknowing that even an admission of friendship in their relationship comes as a surprise. Here, as in other films in the cycle, a villain will risk death rather than continue a task he loses faith in. Again in *Comanche Station*, Dobie (Richard Rust) will fatally turn his back on the gang leader, Ben Lane (Claude Akins), tempting the shot that finally comes. Villains will die ignominiously. Frank (Skip Homeier) will be found floating down the river with an arrow in his back. Dobie's body – foot trapped in a stirrup – will be dragged by his horse across the rocky terrain. In *The Tall T*, Usher has the chance to ride off free, but a sense of honour and a shared integrity forces him to confront Brennan. He is buckshot in the face and dies absurdly, wildly, blindly, in the darkness of a cave, no different in death than his meaner companions. Although they are villains, men like Usher are too likeable to deserve such an end. As Lee Russell says:

> *Boetticher sympathises with almost all his characters; they are all in the same predicament in which the prime faults are inauthenticity and self-deception, rather than infringement of any collectively recognised code. The fact that some end up dead and some alive does not necessarily indicate any moral judgement, but an underlying tragedy which Boetticher prefers to treat with irony.*
>
> (Russell, 1965, p.199)

The Tall T is the only one of the Ranown cycle to offer the possibility of partnership with the heroine. Elsewhere, no relationship is possible because the hero himself is 'a man beyond all human ties' (Kitses, 1969, p.102). The hero's stoical acceptance that what is happening to him is all that there is to happen is evident in his dialogue. When Usher tries to express his own ambition that 'a man . . . ought to have something of his own, something to belong to, to be proud of', the hero who has lost everything can only reply:

The absurd romance of the majestic Ranown cycle is evident in this publicity still from *The Tall T* (1957), with Mrs. Mimms (Maureen O'Sullivan) and Brennan (Randolph Scott) surviving the threat of Usher (Richard Boone).

166

'They say that'. Though heroes still survive and villains must die in these Westerns, because 'everyone loses' (ibid., p.109), Boetticher obscures the line between heroism and villainy.

Kitses considers the Ranown cycle 'comedies, deeply ironic works . . . bittersweet reflections on the human condition' and thus 'parodies of the morality play' (ibid., p.96). Though for Russell, Boetticher's is 'an a-historical world in which each man is master of his own individual destiny' (1965, p.196), for Kitses 'violence and injustice are less the property of malignant individuals than of the world itself' (1969, p.96). The Ranown cycle offers about as dystopian a view of the Western imaginary as the romance Western can allow.

THE REVENGE TRAGEDY

Anthony Mann directed *The Far Country*, but its hero, Jeff Webster, is less bent on revenge than in Mann's others Westerns, whose heroes seem driven by the desire for personal vengeance. The heroes of *Winchester '73* (1950) and *The Man from Laramie* (1955) are scarred by vengeance from the start. In *Bend of the River/Where the River Bends* (1952), *The Naked Spur* (1953) and *Man of the West* (1958) – all but the last with James Stewart – the climax finds in the hero a compulsion to vengeance that threatens to make him more villainous than the villain: 'the revenge drive, which normally requires no validation within the genre, vibrates in Mann with primeval significance, operating as a flaw in the hero who is seen to raise himself up and to presume to judge' (Kitses, 1969, p.73). These films are central among those revenge Westerns that develop the romance hero, from being an unwitting agent of social change, towards an individual whose distance from society emotionally damages him. The films bring psychological depth to the Western hero, revealing a patina of reason and humanity overlaying an unconscious and uncontrolled passion and violence.

Mann's heroes are 'extreme men stretching out beyond their reach. Rarely is it a matter of choice; as if possessed, these men push ahead completely at the mercy of forces within themselves' (ibid., p.29). As Mann said of the hero of each of these films; 'he was a man who could kill his own brother' (Mann, quoted by Kitses, 1969, p.33), as indeed Lin MacAdam (James Stewart) in *Winchester '73* does. The ruthless, neurotic obsession of the hero is such that, like Howard Kemp (James Stewart) in *The Naked Spur*,

> *the revenge taken upon the character is taken upon himself, a punishment the inner meaning of which is a denial of reason and humanity . . . Mann's heroes*

behave as if driven by a vengeance they must inflict upon themselves for having once been human, trusting and therefore, vulnerable.

(Kitses, 1969, p.33)

The hero's reactions to humiliation and gross acts of villainy are among the most remarkable in the genre, as in *The Man from Laramie*, when the childlike Dave Waggoman, in an act of petty spite, makes his men hold Will Lockhart's hand out so that he can shoot through it. Will spits out 'You . . . scum' and the words overpower the action through the intensity of James Stewart's delivery. It is no surprise to find the hero as capable of acts that otherwise define villainy. In *Man of the West*, Link (Gary Cooper) tears the clothes from Coalie (Jack Lord), the brother he has unmercifully beaten, as retribution for similarly forcing the heroine, Billie (Julie London), to strip to save Link's life. The relentlessness of the humiliation contrasts with the dignified restraint of another brother, Claude (John Dehner), who stays with the family simply because 'I watch out for that old man. I love him, and I watch out for him'. In *The Naked Spur*, Kemp retrieves the body of his criminal quarry, the despicable Ben (Robert Ryan), from a rapid-flowing river in order to cash in on his bounty-hunting quest. As Lina (Janet Leigh) begs him to leave the body and the vengeance it signifies, the contradiction in the internal struggle between the decent man and avenging demon is manifested in Stewart's extraordinary performance, body twisting, face grimacing, language falling from his mouth, his face awash with genuine tears. In Stewart's performances, moments of manic frenzy are made all the more shocking by their stark contrast to the star's 'honourable man' persona.

The drive to vengeance makes the Mann hero irrational, breaking the code of decency he otherwise intends to uphold. This means that, 'in order to do what they know to be right, his heroes risk becoming the embodiment of all they hate' (Petley, 1980, p.1047). Villains seem to recognise something of themselves in the heroes on their first meeting. In *The Far Country*, the murderous Gannon quickly appreciates the qualities of his adversary: 'I'm gonna like you'. Often – especially in *Bend of the River* – 'the charming villain functions as a reflection of the hero, as his more or less unbalanced alter ego. This is what gives their confrontations such mythic power' (ibid., p.1048). This is a theme scriptwriter Borden Chase would return to in other Westerns such as *Backlash*, in the war-traumatised hero of *The Man From Colorado* (1948) and in the tyrannical hero of *Red River*, but Mann's Westerns offer its most powerful expression.

Mann's villains are less of a social than a personal threat to the hero; they tend to be criminalised by the hero as much as by their crime. The final confrontation between hero and villain becomes a monumental power struggle.

Located in high mountains, often requiring characters to scrabble up cliff-faces and squeeze into crevices, 'the terrain is so coloured by the action that it finally seems an inner landscape, the unnatural world of a disturbed mind' (Kitses, 1969, p.72). High up among the rocks, Lin confronts and kills his own brother, Dutch Henry Brown (Stephen McNally) in *Winchester '73*, and Will shoots Vic in *The Man From Laramie*, finally exorcising the need to avenge the sense of responsibility he bears for the villain's part in the deaths of their father and brother, respectively. In *Man of the West*, Link cannot escape his criminal past until he kills the father figure and all the sons of the family that raised him. Shades of Greek myth and Shakespearean tragedy are evident as the malevolent Doc Tobin (Lee J. Cobb) walks down the windswept mountain, 'firing widely and continuing the demented soliloquy that is his basic mode of expression, until he is finally silenced' (ibid., p.57) by bullets from Link's gun. These are Oedipal dramas, the family offering the only social dimension to the mythic struggles between the central protagonists.

Mann's Westerns render the romance hero as a psychologically flawed individual. Though conventionally different from society, the hero becomes asocial, not just reluctant but resistant to social and personal affiliation. His Western morality becomes tainted by internal contradictions, rather than by the external conditions that form the romance heroes of earlier periods.

THE UNBALANCED HERO

If Mann's hero 'borders on the unbalanced' (Kitses, 1969, p.35), the final stages in the development of the romance hero tip him towards forms of psychopathy; less the psychological than the pathological hero. In *The Left Handed Gun* (1958), 'a psychological study of delinquency' (Russell, 1965, p.196), Billy the Kid (Paul Newman) is driven to extremes by the killing of his mentor, Tunstall (John Dierkes). In gradually eliminating the killers, he endangers the lives of his more naive younger friends, and forces the hand of his solitary sympathiser, Pat Garrett (John Dehner). His temptation to violence, lack of self-control and self-knowledge is like that of several young gunslingers in Westerns of the 1950s, including *Saddle the Wind* (1958) and, especially, Budd Boetticher's Westerns. The delinquent gunslinger represents a displaced feature of the youth culture and Method acting style (Bignell, 1996) of the times.

Even older characters – like the protagonists played by Kirk Douglas in *The Last Sunset* (1961), Henry Fonda in *Warlock* (1959) and Gregory Peck in *The Bravados* (1958) – take the length of their films to realise their true nature and status. The hero of *The Bravados* will probably mend his ways, indicated by his final words to a crowd gathered to honour his homecoming, inviting prayer for the soul he lost in his revenge narrative. Clay Blaisdell (Henry Fonda) rides out of *Warlock*, stricken by conscience, abandoning his guns in the street at the feet of the hapless marshal. Douglas' character in *The Last Sunset* will die, like Billy the Kid, in an act of sacrifice, both recognising they are lost souls. Billy accepts his death in 'a Christ-like benediction of his killer, Garrett, and the abandonment of the gun that turned Billy into Billy the Kid, the mythic hero' (ibid., 1996, p.105). Western romance heroes of the 1950s realise that their fate lies in maintaining their commitment to violence and facing destruction or abandoning this and surviving. Whichever they choose, the consequence is personal loss.

THE MAD GUNMAN

The romance hero whose violence renders him obdurate prefigures developments in the Western hero from the 1960s and beyond. Two key films of earlier periods identify an important transition away from the hero of the romance Western. Both feature characters who find themselves in circumstances that test their sanity, and both characters are played by John Wayne. The first is the tyrannical Tom Dunson in *Red River*.

Red River is both the title of the film and the key site of its narrative. It is where the hero parts from his loved one, where he finds another object of affection to replace her and where he meets his nemesis on a journey. The film opens with a parting from Fen (Coleen Gray). Despite her pleas to leave the wagon train and go with him, Dunson is resolute that they must part. He lives to regret his decision, as she is killed by Indians. Despite this, his insistence on the rectitude of his decision demonstrates an obstinacy that the film then explores. Dunson builds a relationship with the small boy who grows into Matthew Garth (Montgomery Clift) and with whom he shares a herd of cattle. The emotional tie between them is symbolised by Fen's snake-bracelet, a gift from Dunson that Matthew wears on his wrist. The epic cattle trail they will embark on is a rite of passage for Matthew, but for Dunson it represents a legacy, as much emotional as financial, 'something to pass on' to this 'son'. During the journey, Dunson tests the relationship when he ruthlessly drives his cowboys. His behaviour grows ever more unreasonable until, sensing that Dunson will blindly put cattle before men, Matthew joins a mutiny. Though the group abandons the now impossible Dunson, they continue his task, leading the cattle to the railhead at Abilene. In the final climax, Dunson advances on Matthew – Wayne powerfully moving through the cattle whilst focusing on his quarry ahead – as if intent on killing him. Instead, they fight, a fight stopped by the heroine, Tess (Joanne Dru), because 'anyone can see you love each other'.

An action shot from *Red River* (1948), with the young Montgomery Clift as Matthew Garth and John Wayne as Tom Dunson.

The ending seeks to re-establish connections between Dunson and the audience as much as with the other characters, since both increasingly lose sympathy for the figure whose heroic role passes to the younger man. *Red River* is not only an 'examination of the limits of the acceptability of Dunson's ruthlessness' (Wood, 1998, p.185) but also a measure of the transitional hero as an identification figure. The film's romantic ending scarcely heals the wounds caused by the disruption to audience expectations of the romance hero.

The second transitional film, *The Searchers* (1956), develops the romance hero towards a conclusively pathological state. Ethan Edwards (John Wayne) steadfastly pursues the Comanches who slaughtered his family. Such is his rage that it drives him madly to seek the death of his only surviving relative captured in the raid, his niece, Debbie (Natalie Wood). There is a suggestion of a transgressive love between his brother's wife, Martha, and himself in an early scene in the family home (Bogdanovich, 1967, p.93) that critics argue defines the nature of Ethan's search for Debbie (Wollen, Henderson, McBride and Wilmington). At the end of a long, meandering hunt across the course of the film, Ethan does not kill the now 'full grown' woman, but lifts her up in his arms in a movement that echoes a previous gesture from the film's start when she was just a child. Despite the sudden change of heart, when Ethan returns Debbie to white society, he finds no place for himself within it. Visually abandoning him to the wilderness, director John Ford places the camera in the darkened home and closes the door on Ethan in a swirl of dust, leaving him to blindly 'wander forever in the wind', like the soul of the buried Indian whose eyes he earlier horrifically shoots out.

Like romance heroes of Westerns before him, Ethan appears necessary as an instrument to satisfy the social quest the community requires of him, yet extraneous to its domesticated culture: 'Edwards is ... too violent, too abrasive, useful only in times of crisis; he rejects but is also rejected.' (Baker, 1996, p.220). As a Western romance hero, he is singularly unsuccessful in his quest. He wanders around the changing landscapes and seasons, fruitlessly following clues to Debbie's whereabouts and sacrificing the lives of others with him. These include Brad (Harry Carey Junior), boyfriend to Debbie's raped and murdered sister and son of the Jorgensons who will presumably foster Debbie on her return, and Look, the Indian who 'marries' his nephew, Martin Pawley (Jeffrey Hunter), but runs away after she is threatened by Ethan, to end up killed in a cavalry massacre. It is Marty not Ethan who will rescue Debbie from the Comanche encampment and kill her captor, the chief, Scar (Henry Brandon). The activity of the Western hero as a man of action is rendered futile.

Ethan's only part in the rescue will centre on threatening Debbie's life, before accepting the fact of her rescue by others. Marginalised, he will scalp Scar instead, a transgressive act reminiscent of his treatment of the dead Indian whose eyes he shoots out. Ethan slaughters buffalo to stop them 'filling the bellies' of the Indians whose community Ford is at pains to depict as a village of men and women, young and old, similar to the white community. In such circumstances, Ethan's behaviour is seen as savage and irrational, deformed by an abiding racist hatred of the Indian. His criminal legacy is also unacceptable. Though he has fought in the Civil War on the losing side, he refuses to 'beat my sword into a ploughshare' and cannot be sworn in as a deputy since he already 'gave his oath' to the Confederate states. There is the suggestion that, before arriving on the scene, he survived by border raiding – violent theft – and we see him execute a plan that leads to him killing three men by turning the tables on their attempted ambush. His presence in the social life of the white community is always disruptive; too hastily 'putting an amen' to the funeral service for his own family and disrupting other rituals like a wedding. He is most like the villain, Scar, the Indian chief; both are consumed with hatred from personal loss and both are turned savage by their experience. Ethan bears too many qualities associated with villainy to be the hero; 'he is a wanderer, a savage, outside the law' (Wollen, 1972(69), p.96). And yet, the final closing of the door on his retreating figure is tragic. In Buscombe's affectionate analysis of the film, he finds that director John Ford 'shows Ethan for what he is, a murderous racist, and yet draws out our pity for him' (2000, p.69). It is as if the door closes not only on the character, but also on the very figure of the romance hero.

THE END OF THE ROMANCE HERO

The characters of Tom Dunson and Ethan Edwards stretch the definition of heroism in the romance Western to breaking point. In their obsessive quests, driven by hatred, they extend the revenge theme to the limits of the romance Western. From the early 1960s onwards, the Western hero becomes either an anti-hero, in a West imagined as chaotic and senseless, or an anachronistic figure of a West imagined as old fashioned. These two major developments are explored in following chapters, respectively on the dystopian and elegiac Western.

CHAPTER EIGHT

The Dystopian Western

The romance Western dominates the genre until well after the first half of the twentieth century. Even so, from the earliest times there are signs that not all Westerns are comfortable with its vision of a romantic hero and a utopian future. From the 1940s in particular, Westerns begin to push at the boundaries of the romance mythology. The imperialist assumptions about American frontier history and identity that inform the foundation myth of the epic Western are increasingly called into question. By the 1960s, critiques of the Western imaginary develop the genre in significantly new ways. Where the romance Western imagines a utopian future, this new strand of the Western imagines a dystopian present so bad that any future at all is unimaginable.

The sharp generic shift is evident in the contrast between *The Magnificent Seven* (1960) and *Westworld* (1973). In *The Magnificent Seven*, Yul Brynner plays Chris, hired by a poor Mexican village to assemble fellow professional gunmen to protect them from seasonal raids by bandits. Chris finds gunmen living through such lean times that only in places like Mexico do their violent skills still have a function. The film, however, still honours them as they make the peons' cause their own. The mercenaries become altruists, whose willingness to sacrifice their lives for a charitable cause makes them admired by travelling salesmen, townsfolk, their young raw recruit, the peons and the audience. At the end of the film, with the bandits dead and the quest validated, the young gunman, though now seasoned by battle, remains in the village with one of its young women. Chris tells the one other remaining survivor that, despite their sacrifice, 'Only the farmers won. We Lost. We always lose.' The gunfighters of *The Magnificent Seven* are romance heroes, champions of the weak, enablers of justice but, at the end, Chris recognises that the days of the Western romance hero are on the way out.

The leader of the seven is reprised in several sequels to *The Magnificent Seven*, but none prefigures the gunfighter in *Westworld*, no longer a figure to admire but only to fear. Yul Brynner plays both gunfighters and they look alike in the same black outfit. Yet, in *Westworld*, the gunfighter is neither the hero nor human, but the villain and a robot. The figure is no longer in his own drama nor in his own genre but in Westworld, the name not only of the film but also of its setting, a futuristic theme park. The hero is now not the Westerner, but an urban man on vacation, participating in sanitised, staged 'Western' scenarios in which robots are programmed to respond to a tourist's every need. At first, the urban hero delights in the pleasures of Westworld. He has sex with a robot saloon 'girl' and beats the robot gunman to the draw in a staged gunfight. Then, the computer system breaks down and the robots go wild. The conventions of the Western genre become disrupted by a convention of the dystopian science fiction film: technology inevitably goes wrong. The robot gunman refuses to lie down, to be carried off, repaired and put back into action. Worse, he shoots back, killing the hero's best friend and stalking the hero through the rest of the film. The hero survives the ending by discovering the robot's weakness; it is blind, programmed only to respond to body heat. After this discovery, defeating it becomes easy; it 'dies' in flames, the face ripped away to expose the electrical circuitry beneath.

By the 1970s, the heroes of romance Westerns like *The Magnificent Seven* become monstrous, disturbed figures in their own genre and pastiches in others. As in *Westworld*, the Westerner loses his humanity and thereby his role as the instrument of a utopian future.

SAYING GOODBYE TO THE ROMANCE WESTERN

Though the West of the Western imaginary is invariably a visually barren, unforgiving and hostile terrain, it may be redeemed by its aesthetic beauty and by the possibilities held out for the hero to secure its future, even at a personal cost. Romance Westerns are ultimately romantic in their view that the West will be settled for the better, through noble heroism. They promise a new America in the combination of the best values of Eastern civilisation and Western democracy.

However, the Western hero from Natty Bumppo to the Ringo Kid and beyond is ambivalent about the emergent civilisation. Though settlement is a symbol of civilisation, Westerns are full of towns that need cleaning up and clearing out to make way for decent society. William S. Hart's Western, *Hell's Hinges* (1916), refers in a title card to the town of Placer Center, 'a gunfighting, man-killing devil's den of iniquity', so corrupt that Hart's hero, Blaze Tracey, lives up to his name by burning first the saloon, the 'Palace of Joy', then the town, leaving the ground for the pious to build on. Blaze claims: 'Hell needs this town, and it's goin' back, and goin' pretty damn quick'.

Though romance Western heroes invariably succeed in 'cleaning up' towns that need it, the potential for powerful forces of corruption to triumph are latent in the genre and explicit in the dystopian Western.

In the romance Western, the Western hero's sacrifice is ultimately in the name of a future social order, a better America. Romance Westerns are a key part of America's coming of age in the modern world of the first half of the twentieth century. As Peter Stowell puts it: 'these post-Civil War romances provided the country with a foundation myth for its industrial era' (1986, p.96). In contrast to these, a strand of Westerns emerges more strongly during the 1940s which are distanced from the terms of the foundation myth. In these, the West is not only physically but also psychologically a barren, unforgiving and hostile terrain, in which towns are unremittingly weak or even corrupt.

The changes arise as a consequence of the passing of time – in the setting of the films and in Hollywood's contemporaneous conditions of production. Following the Paramount Decree of 1946 that gradually eroded studio control of American Cinema, the system of factory production that fuelled series Westerns was turned to the production of television programmes, including series Westerns (Boddy, 1998). B feature production declines and the proportion of A feature Westerns increases. As a consequence, a greater melodramatic sensibility develops in the genre to target a wider audience than the centrally rural male audience for series Westerns.

Dystopian Westerns tend to be set in a later period than romance Westerns, closer to the end of the nineteenth century – long after pioneers and land claims – when the West is settled. In these Westerns, the West is colonised by the sins of urban modernity and the worst of human values are evident in the greed, self-interest and injustice of its townsfolk. These are Westerns that 'depict the corruption and restrictiveness of the industrial era' (Stowell, 1986, p.97). In these new historical conditions, the cowboy gunfighter's function and purpose as hero becomes less certain. The conditions are such that the Western hero is unable and unwilling to act in the interests of justice. The human flaws in the character of the revenge hero enter more centrally into the dystopian Western, magnified by new social and legal arrangements. This makes the hero first a powerless victim of melodrama, finding survival difficult in a hostile human environment, and thereafter an anti-hero, conceding to the inevitability of new forces of darkness.

EARLY INDICATORS

That The 'Wild' West needs 'taming' is a given in the Western genre. Yet, from the very start, there are signs that all is not well with the Western hero whose function it is to tame it. In the silent Western, *Naked Hands* (1909), the hero Billy goes wild when he confronts the villainous lover of the heroine. He tears the villain's home apart in his fury, calming down only when a wife and child appear, staring aghast at the demon amid the debris of a room. W.S. Hart is known as the Good-Badman precisely because of his disposal towards villainy as much as heroism. These silent Western figures presage the darker figure of the hero of revenge Westerns. Yet, in most cases, such transgressions are redeemed by the hero's ultimate cause. In the emerging urban world of the dystopian Western, however, the fallible hero is treated more ambiguously and may even be denied the possibility of redemption.

THE FIRST DYSTOPIAN WESTERNS

The inability of the hero to right the wrongs of the West is the central theme of *The Ox-Bow Incident* (1943), a wartime Western that introduces a new social realism and an overt political liberalism to the genre. Its story of the hanging of three innocent cowboys by a lynch mob is a displaced interrogation of events in the white supremacist American South, where a culture tolerated a legal system that turned a blind eye to this ritual form of murder and terrorism of black people.

The Ox-Bow Incident is unconventionally heavy on dialogue and light on action, with time taken to debate the circumstantial evidence of criminal responsibility and the morality of sentencing without proper trial. Three wanderers, played by Dana Andrews, Anthony Quinn and Francis Ford, are accused of rustling. They speak passionately of their innocence and are eloquently defended by two cowboys – played by Henry Morgan and Henry Fonda (in a role prefiguring his juryman in the later *Twelve Angry Men*) – from among the posse that turns into a lynch mob. Despite their protests, they are powerless to prevent the lynching. When the innocence of the three is subsequently established, the townspeople and farmers return to their homes. The experience of savagery beneath the surface of their newly urbanised Western values renders some sheepish and others bullish. Even a woman is complicit (played by Jane Darwell, in an ugly twist on the earth mother she more usually plays, for instance in films directed by John Ford, like *Wagonmaster* and as Ma Joad in *The Grapes of Wrath*, 1940). The West of *The Ox-Bow Incident* is a wasteland of ignorance, intolerance and hysteria (with a town 'no more than a collection of ugly buildings' (Lovell, 1967, p.99)) that the most eloquent of Western heroes cannot control. Though *The Ox-Bow Incident* was not a popular film, its new darkness of style and theme had an immense impact on the subsequent development of the genre.

WESTERN FILM NOIR

The Ox-Bow Incident is shot entirely within a studio, using a high contrast monochrome lighting style developed in the 1930s to produce a sense of unease and paranoia more associated with film noir. Buscombe argues that 'in the 1940s . . . the western was ready to take on board adult themes which film noir and melodrama were exploring' (2000, p.23). Though set on the open range, the confined setting adds to the sense of the West as a space limited not just by geography, but also by sensibility. Other Westerns of the period use studio settings to represent the landscape as a space that confines rather than liberates the hero. A particular example is *Blood on the Moon* (1948), in which the loyalties of the gunman hero played by Robert Mitchum are so tested by a duplicitous friend, that not even a campfire can offer solace. Scenes set around brooding night-time campfires become a staple of the genre into the 1950s and even in colour Westerns like *The Law and Jake Wade* (1958). Here, campfires offer opportunities for the captive hero to mull over his fate, trapped between returning to the town where he faces false accusations or continuing his journey to certain death at the hands of the villains. In *Grim Prairie Tales* (1990), two cowboys compete to scare each other and the audience witless with a series of enacted horror stories, told – of course – around a campfire.

The noir style and its brooding sensibility of fear and suspicion penetrate all kinds of otherwise conventional Western locales. *Yellow Sky* (1948) and *Face of a Fugitive* (1959) both stage suspenseful shoot-outs in the dark enclaves of wilderness ghost towns, with oblique shafts of light casting false shadows that trick the unwary eye. *Rawhide* (1951) tells the story of a couple held captive in a swing station of that name by a sinister gang of jail breakers. Their threat is created as much by long interior spaces shot in deep focus from low camera angles as from the malign characters and sinister performances of the actors.

Other noir Westerns represent the wider landscape as a wilderness prison, the open range entrapping its subjects rather than releasing them. Some play with extremes of temperature, set especially in the winter cold. *Day of the Outlaw* (1959) finds its protagonists in a climactic battle high up in distant snowscaped mountains, their journey made more and more impossible by deep snowdrifts. The conditions unsettle the easy certainties of a gang of villains, turning them against each other. Freezing conditions ultimately make guns unusable, with fingers too frozen to pull triggers, thereby enabling the beleaguered hero to escape the brutish bad men he has led to their deaths. Barely surviving the conditions himself, he leaves their bodies to be engulfed by the wilderness snow. In *The Last Hunt* (1956), the villain will freeze to death overnight despite covering himself with a buffalo hide. In a ghastly but fitting punishment for his mindless slaughter of the herds (and, as a result, the

Indians who feed upon them), he unknowingly conspires in his own death by wearing the fresh hide with its skin rather than the fur next to his own; the slowly freezing blood of the animal thereby freezes his own.

DESIRE AND REPRESSION ON THE RANGE

In dystopian Westerns, the landscape can become the site of intense and threatening sexual tensions, like the urban locales of film noir. In *Thunderhoof* (1948), the ostensible search for the wild stallion of the title scarcely conceals the rivalry between characters played by Preston Foster and William Bishop for Mary Stuart's heroine. Intense passion in relationships can even be expressed in unusual film styles. In *Colorado Territory* (1949), Joel McCrea and Virginia Mayo play doomed lovers on the run from a chasing posse amid the 'bravura treatment of landscape . . . especially in the confrontation where the ant-size humans meet their malevolent destiny amid barren mountains. The final shot, an optical zoom of McCrea's death, is magnificent' (Hardy, 1991, p.178).

The noir landscape permeates the mood of a classic psychological Western, *Pursued* (1947), directed (like *Colorado Territory*) by Raoul Walsh. The story of Jeb Rand (Robert Mitchum), haunted by a traumatic childhood memory he cannot explain, is set among 'vast, precipitous walls of rock, dwarfing the riders below, which become associated symbolically with . . . the inescapable repressiveness of which the characters are simultaneously embodiments and victims' (Britton, 1996, p.196). The childhood trauma returns as a nightmare in which Jeb witnesses a massacre, seen from a child's view from under a bed and dominated by close-ups of jangling spurs and intermittent gun flashes. The enigma of the nightmare is gradually unravelled for both the hero and the audience.

The film starts with Jeb and Thorley Callum (Teresa Wright) who have run away from her family and holed up in a remote, burned-out farmhouse at Bear Paw Butte. Raised from childhood, together with her brother, Adam (John Rodney), they have developed a neurotic love/hate relationship. A series of revealing flashbacks gradually implicates the Callum family who have raised Jeb, yet denied his adult relationship with Thorley. The farmhouse was once the home of the Rand family, wiped out by Grant Callum (Dean Jaggers) because of an adulterous relationship between Jeb's father and Grant's sister, Ma Callum (Judith Anderson). As a consequence, Ma had sought to make good the crime by raising Jeb, the only survivor of the massacre. Selfishly repressing the memory of his origins allows Jeb to unknowingly repeat the sin of his father in his relationship with Thorley. 'The main narrative thread of *Pursued* is therefore the feud between two tight, nuclear

Deep focus monochrome photography and a wide angle lens serve to centre Jeb Rand (Robert Mitchum) in the disturbed world of the dystopian Western, *Pursued* (1947).

families, which is associated quite explicitly with the perversion, morbidity and repression of sexual impulses' (ibid., p.199). Through Grant Callum's murderous, authoritarian allegiance to the family, monogamy and patriotism, the values that the romance Western otherwise holds dear are corrupted and called into question.

The noir treatment of the family makes its members into monsters; Grant's paranoia and Ma's repression are responsible for Jeb's alienation. At the end, Ma kills Grant and – symbolically – the Western family ideal. Whether it can also release the hero from the trauma and neurosis of his repressed identity is another matter: Jeb's line, 'You've given me back my life' should sound affirmative but, delivered from the lips of Robert Mitchum, it is far less certain. The final image of the film sees the new couple ride away together. Any apparent celebration of the partnership is undermined by the taint of incest in the union of two people raised as brother and sister. And, despite their reconciliation, they bear the burden of a disturbed past. Thorley's earlier words on the night of her wedding to Jeb, 'The moment he thinks he has me, he'll lose everything', auger less than well for their future.

This dystopian strand of the noir Western derives in part from writers of the twentieth century Western novel. Douglas Pye refers to

> Zane Grey's Riders of the Purple Sage *(1912, first filmed in 1918 and remade . . . including the version with Tom Mix in 1925) in which the hero and heroine escape pursuit in a hidden valley that is finally sealed off from the outside world by a fall of rock – an Eden which is also an inescapable trap.*

> *(Pye, 1996, p.15)*

Such bleak scenarios inform the Western's development in the period following the Second World War. While other genres tend to celebrate post-War recovery and renewal, the possibility of romance in modern America is increasingly questioned in the dystopian strand of the post-War Western. For instance, the central protagonist played by Glenn Ford in *The Man from Colorado* (1948) suffers from the trauma of his (Civil) War military experience. Unable to cope with the honours heaped upon him on his return, he grows more and more unhinged until he sets fire to the very town that has welcomed him home, in order to destroy his wife and the friend he unreasonably suspects is her lover.

THE WESTERN AS MALE MELODRAMA

Noir Westerns are melodramas. True to the melodrama aesthetic, central protagonists in film noir face situations and experience emotions more familiar to the female protagonists of melodrama. In noir Westerns, the psychological pressure on the male hero to act in accord with social rather than individual need, or to live within unchosen moral contradictions, leads to the trauma of a *Man from Colorado* or a Jeb in *Pursued*. Such troubled heroes abound in 1950s Western melodramas. Noir Westerns tend to be B Westerns, made in the constrained conditions of production only slightly better resourced than series Westerns. Equivalents of their troubled heroes develop in A Westerns during the 1950s, where greater resources enable expression of a noir sensibility in full colour rather than in a monochrome high contrast lighting style. This is the period of some of the great Western melodramas, deploying a heightened mise-en-scène to express the inner turmoil of their characters and relationships.

In both *Jubal* (1956) and *The Hanging Tree* (1959), two Westerns directed by Delmer Daves, 'a hero, in flight from his past, enters a community bringing his own demons with him and triggers an eruption of desire and violence' (Michael Walker, 1996, p.123). In a plot transposed from the novel and film noir, *The Postman Always Rings Twice*, 1934, Jubal Troop (Glenn Ford) is the hero of the film of his name. He turns up on a ranch (immediately undermined as a Western hero by appearing exhausted and on foot), where he finds himself caught up in a troika of sexual tension. The ranch is owned by the sympathetic Shep Morgan (Ernest Borgnine), whose unsatisfied wife, Mae (Valerie French), is immediately aroused by Jubal. Since 'Shep is such a nice fellow', Jubal resists Mae's advances, like all the other cowboys working the ranch, except Pinky (Rod Steiger). Events conspire against Jubal, innocent in deed if not quite in thought of the desirable Mae. When Pinky, like Iago in *Othello*, plants seeds of doubt in Shep's mind, the spurned Mae venomously confirms his suspicions. Shep then confronts Jubal in a saloon and shooting wildly, he forces Jubal to defend himself until Shep is killed. The killing triggers a monstrous outbreak of a previously suppressed collective desire. Pinky attacks and rapes Mae, leaving her for dead, to whip up the resentments of the cowboys, who in turn form a posse to hunt Jubal down. Pursued by the posse, like furies in the night, Jubal returns to the ranch to find a barely surviving, but repentant Mae who lives long enough to put the posse to rights. As Jubal rides away free, 'a swinging pulley hints to us that Pinky will be the subject of the lynching that he has been demanding for Jubal' (ibid., p.151).

Michael Walker focuses on the Oedipal triangle in *Jubal*. Mae is the seductive mother figure and Jubal 'the unwilling killer of the father-figure' (ibid., p.151). In killing Shep, Jubal re-enacts his own traumatic childhood, in which his mother could not forgive him for his innocent part in her husband's death in a river accident. In this Freudian psychoanalytic account, Pinky becomes Jubal's id, expressing the suppressed illicit desire for the mother figure of Mae. The analysis is enticingly supported by the mise-en-scène of meetings between Jubal and Mae. In their first encounter in the ranch barn, the forge's smoke and hot branding iron visually express Jubal's arousal. In a later night-time scene, Mae stands provocatively at a ranch window, exchanging glances with Jubal in the bunkhouse. Mae suggestively parts the curtains and Jubal rolls a cigarette, as another cowboy knowingly observes: 'Tried to roll them cigarettes once but I couldn't learn to keep my finger out'. For Walker, 'the hero's Oedipal guilt has been displaced onto Pinky, but the film – through its incisive analysis of the hero's neurosis – still makes it clear that, in fantasy, he is nevertheless implicated' (ibid., p.151). The film's 'swooping camera' creates 'a sense of boxed-in tensions' (Hardy, 1991, p.24) and the deep blues of night-time scenes exaggerate the actors's physicalities and the sexual repression of their characters.

Jubal is one of several 1950s Western melodramas which centre on characters whose emotions are out of control and whose rampant desires cause social and psychological mayhem. For instance, in *The Last Sunset* (1961), directed by Robert Aldrich, the gunfighter hero played by Kirk Douglas commits suicide on learning that the object of his desire is his own daughter. His hysteria is expressed in the excessively long walk he takes to his death. Symbolising the trauma of the consequent loss of masculine power, the hero empties his gun of bullets, before facing a showdown that takes place off-screen; a consummate expression of ultimate humiliation for the Western hero.

MELODRAMA AND THE DYSTOPIAN WESTERN

Though neither is set in single towns, the psycho-sexual relationships of *Jubal* and *The Last Sunset* are also typical of a group of 1950s township Westerns. The most complex and excessive of these is surely *Warlock* (1959), directed by Edward Dmytryk. In a melodrama narrative, two gunmen, Clay Blaisdell (Henry Fonda) and Morgan (Anthony Quinn), are hired to pacify trouble-making cowboys led by local rancher, Abe McQuown (Tom Drake). The weak and naive townspeople find themselves powerless when the two set up a casino that attracts even more criminal elements. The powerful forces they have released and cannot control turn the townspeople into passive victims of melodrama. In a second romance narrative, cowhand Johnny Gannon (Richard Widmark) feels obliged to abandon his delinquent brother to McQuown in order to save the town from his banditry. In an opening scene, McQuown conspires to humiliate a brave but inadequate town sheriff by forcing him to ride bareback from the town in an act also intended to bring the township to heel. The action of the scene is echoed, though its outcome is inverted at the climax, when Gannon dons the sheriff's badge and organises the town to overcome the rancher's villainy. The romance narrative of the film repairs the earlier failure and renders heroic the humble Gannon, who becomes a figure of action and decisive resolve.

Meanwhile, in the melodrama narrative, the relationship between the gunmen becomes troubled when Clay enters into a romantic relationship with a local woman of the town, Jessie (Dolores Michaels). As Morgan sees his love for Clay threatened, the disabled sidekick grows increasingly emotionally disturbed. In peroxide blonde hair, elaborate floral waistcoats and the feminine décor of his rooms, Morgan's mounting hysteria leads him to finally confront his lover in a gunfight. Clay is obliged to kill him in self-defence and, in an ensuing scene, he abuses the townspeople, burning his boats socially and literally, as he dowses Morgan's body with oil from a lamp and sets it aflame on a gaming table. This hysterical parody of a Viking funeral is a supreme moment of melodramatic excess in the dystopian Western.

The two narratives come together at the very end of the film. The new sheriff and the surviving gunman confront each other in an unequal contest. The gunfighter's superior skill enables him to outdraw the cowboy sheriff. Instead of shooting him, Clay throws his guns into the sand of the street, takes the route of the humiliated sheriff, but this time rides away with dignity. The hero of melodrama is also its victim. Unlike the hero of romance, his excessive behaviour and emotions can find no place in the newly complex social order of the dystopian Western.

Warlock is not the only Western of the time to explore its homosexual relationship obliquely and as a symptom of hysteria. Richard Lippe finds another, in *I Shot Jesse James* (1948), that inspires formal excess. *The Singer Not the Song* (1961) is a rare homoerotic Western made in England with quintessential English stars; John Mills as a priest and Dirk Bogarde as a bandit. Such Westerns are evidence of a gradual loosening of censorship ties during the 1950s due to changing social mores and Hollywood's need to differentiate its films from the culture of its new television production. The result is that the Western hero of the period becomes more and more sexualised. In *Rancho Notorious* (1952), for instance, the heroine notices that the hero's gaze on her body is more than romantic: 'You're always standing in doorways and always using your eyes' she says, and comments on his seductive language in a fittingly generic manner: 'You're as smooth on the ground as you are on the back of a horse'.

THE BAROQUE WESTERN

Wood considers *Rancho Notorious* 'a noir Western in colour' (1988). It is the most baroque of this group of Western melodramas, emphasising its artifice in an ornate film style. It is, yet again, a revenge narrative in which the hero's troubled and insecure identity spills over into a wild mise-en-scène and an extraordinary music track. The lyrics of the most morbid and bizarre of Western ballads about 'the old story of hate, murder and revenge' frequently punctuate the narrative as comment on plot developments. In an establishing scene, Vern (Arthur Kennedy), rather too eager to advance his wedding day, is in prolonged embrace with his fiancée, Beth (Gloria Henry). A strange red suffusion fills the screen, in a foreboding of the red mist before the eyes and the bloody killings it will cause. When Beth is raped and murdered, Vern finds that the insecure townspeople are unwilling to break their daily routines and form a posse. Maddened by his loss and their rejection, he sets out alone to hunt down her killer. His desire for revenge turns into a detective story when he arrives in an outlaw town – following the lyrics of the song, incredibly named Chuck-a-Luck – in which a saloon is presided over by a grande dame, Altar Keane (Marlene Dietrich).

Vern has already proved unpleasantly self-serving, but his meeting with Altar sets 'his wound-up hysteria and aggression into relief' (Jacobowitz,

1996, p.94). As he searches for the murderer, Vern turns against Altar when he discovers her wearing Beth's brooch, stolen by her killer. He falsely swears allegiance to her, to cajole her into divulging the killer's identity. She is seduced by his empty promises, only to be cruelly cast aside. The dignity of her response to his insults contrasts with his accusations of her 'dirty life'; 'You think a dance hall girl was a dirty life . . . You ought to be proud of that compared to what you are now'. Far from the courtly manners of Ringo Kid towards Dallas' 'fallen woman' in *Stagecoach*, 1939, Vern is the antipathy of the romance hero; he is 'a man destroyed by his bitterness, and the violent rage misdirected onto Altar outweighs her crime of sheltering outlaws . . . No hero . . . is offered; the film has demystified the hero as despicable' (ibid., p.97). Altar's tragic story concludes the film, as she rides off with another man, leaving the despicable Vern's revenge narrative on the sidelines.

Vern finds nothing in the towns to hold a more positive alternative to his hate. The good people are indifferent to his tragedy and in the outlaw town gambling tables are rigged; criminals even cheat other criminals. Towns in dystopian Westerns 'are governed by corrupt politicians or fascistic law and order parties, and the only governing reality is the system of capitalist exchange – safety and independence are not inherent rights and can be bought for a price' (ibid., p.96).

CYNICAL COMEDIES

The dystopian Western becomes a general feature of the genre during the 1960s. Bob Baker dates the change between *A Fistful of Dollars* (1964) and *Waterhole 3* (1967), 'the time span during which the tone of the genre shifted decisively' (1996, p.217). Major social, political and cultural changes in the period undermine the dominance of values assumed by the romance Western. The new tone is expressed firstly in the predominance of comedy Westerns, frequently satirising the conventions of the Western genre as clichés. In *Texas Across the River* (1966), for instance, both cavalry and Indians are subjects for parody: a guileless cavalry troop rides back and forth across the screen in fruitless pursuit of one of two sparring heroes, while an Indian chief sets his own war bonnet on fire and – in a running gag – his son cannot fire an arrow from his bow.

In comedies like these, the Western hero is no longer taken seriously. In earlier periods, the comic hero of the Western tends to be a greenhorn Easterner, out of place in the manly masculinity of the West, like James Stewart's new town marshal in *Destry Rides Again* (1939) and Bob Hope's itinerant dentist in *The Paleface* (1948). In the 1960s, however, the comic hero is a Westerner, like Lee Marvin's drunken gunfighter in *Cat Ballou* (1965) and the philandering hero of *Waterhole 3*, a serial seducer perpetually chased by avenging fathers and husbands. Even law makers do not escape parody. In *Support Your Local Sheriff* (1968), James Garner plays a sheriff so idly self-confident that he can disarm a potential assassin from the desk chair in his office by sticking his finger in the threatening gun-barrel.

THE EUROPEAN WESTERN

Crucially, it was the international success of a new cycle of Italian Westerns in the 1960s which gave impetus to a new cynicism in the Western. Westerns were made in countries other than America – even in Britain – including international productions from the earliest times (Frayling, 1998, pp.29–33). In France, Pathé made one of the first Westerns, *Hooligans of the West* (1907), and many of the Indian dramas sympathetic to Indian interests, including *Indian Justice* (1911). German film companies made Westerns as early as 1936, with *The Emperor of California*.

A series of German Westerns, based on the novels of Karl May and shot mostly in Yugoslavia in the 1960s, were enormously popular in Germany and reached audiences elsewhere in Europe, starting with the first of the Winnetou series, *The Treasure of Silver Lake* (1962). The novels and films feature a central relationship derived from that of the white hero and Indian sidekick in Fenimore Cooper's *Leatherstocking Tales*. Though the novels have been under-stood as nationalist, (or even, fascist; they were Hitler's favoured fiction), the films are dissimilar. In Tassilo Schneider's analysis of the films, the white hero, Shatterhand, and the Indian, Winnetou, inhabit no wilderness, but an idealised garden in which 'the bond' between them goes 'far beyond the homoerotic subtext that is arguably at the heart of the western genre' (1995, p.56). The two greet each other with embraces and kisses, Winnetou looks at Shatterhand 'with the look of a woman' and when Shatterhand 'sees his brother, he has no eyes for anybody else' (ibid., p.56). For Schneider, the films offer 'a universal, ahistorical realm of exotic adventures and timeless heroes . . . Freed from the tensions generated by heterosexuality, capitalism and national identity, the German western is a "utopia of the adventure"' (ibid., p.57).

The films commonly starred an American actor (at first, an ex-Tarzan, Lex Barker) as Old Shatterhand, with an international cast. Italian Westerns followed the pattern, attempting to break into the American market by featuring a recognisable American face and Westernised names in the lead roles. Westerns made in Italy (or, as frequently by Italian film companies in Germany and Spain) were dubbed by critics 'Spaghetti Westerns', at first derogatively, then more affectionately as the cycle expanded considerably.

The styling continued with German 'Sauerkraut' Westerns and Spanish 'Paella' Westerns.

SPAGHETTI WESTERNS

Italy had a history of producing Westerns from the 1940s, with *Una signora dell'ovest/Woman of the West* (1942) and *Il fanciullo del West/Boy of the West* (1943). In the 1960s, a cycle of Westerns followed the successful break-through into European markets of 'sword and sandal' epics produced by the Cinecittà Studios in Rome. The huge international success of *A Fistful of Dollars/Per un pugno di dollari* (1964) – a remake of the Japanese samurai film, *Yojimbo* (1961) – established a pattern. In this, Clint Eastwood, star of the television Western series *Rawhide* (1959–62), is 'The Man With No Name', a laconic mercenary who sells his services to the highest bidder. Its director, Sergio Leone, then made a group of more elaborate Westerns, the most influential among a huge cycle of over four hundred films which funda-mentally changed the genre thereafter, including Western production in America.

Italian Westerns break away stylistically from the romantic American Western in action and tone. They shift attention from the sexual hysteria of Western melodramas to a dystopia of male action. Action in Italian Westerns is emphatic and brutal, an 'opera of violence' (Staig and Williams, 1975) and a 'ballet of the dead' (Leone, quoted in Buscombe, 1988, p.254), from which few are spared. They combine a new physicality with a cynical black humour, characteristic of Italian comic traditions like commedia dell'arte. Dirty bodies and stained clothing, chin stubble and body fluids are made painfully evid-ent, especially in prolonged close-ups. Though 'cavalier' with history (Frayling 1970, p.132), Leone's research into Western history and folklore led him to design sets based on historical photographs and to seek an authentic, aged look to costumes (ibid., pp.125–9).

The 'Latin' qualities of Italian actors inform the settings of the films. Spaghetti Westerns offer a wholly wilderness frontier 'Mexico' of the Medi-terranean imagination, sparsely populated by gangs of gunmen, with poor adobe towns and the occasional wealthy hacienda. The influence of *The Magnificent Seven* is evident in stories of 'gringo' heroes in 'Mexican' geo-graphy. No longer social spaces, the mud and snow flats in Westerns directed by Corbucci and arid deserts in Westerns directed by Leone and Sollima (the three Sergios) are mythic stages on which to interrogate Western conventions and meanings.

For some critics, this makes the genre available for wider mythologies that break its national boundaries. Marcia Landy finds the 'images of towns . . .

convey the sense of dirt, grime and poverty that apply just as easily to the undeveloped terrains of Latin America, Africa, Sicily or Sardinia as to the North American West' (1996, p.216). It is therefore less surprising to find some Italian Westerns explicitly politically engaged. *A Bullet for the General/ Quien Sabe?* (1966), for instance, is considered: 'a radical political allegory on the revolutionary situation in Latin America' (Wallington, 1970, p.32).

Italian Westerns tend to disconnect the Western hero from history and society; he operates 'as a completely marginal figure vis-à-vis the various social groups he encounters' (Frayling 1970, p.130). Such relationships as do exist are not to be trusted in a world where human life is cheap. The quest – if one exists – is purely for money. *For a Few Dollars More/Per qualche dollari in più* (1965) opens with the title: 'Where life had no value, death sometimes had its price. That is why the bounty hunters appeared'. As in the American Western *Vera Cruz* (1954) (an influence Leone recognises), Italian Westerns proceed like a series of vindictive games of one-upmanship. In *The Good, the Bad and the Ugly/Il buono, il brutto, il cattivo* (1966), the central protagonists, Blondie (Clint Eastwood) and Tuco (Eli Wallach) take turns to invent ever more elaborate tortures for the other.

Among the most extreme of Italian Westerns is a series of twenty films beginning with *Django* (1966), including the surreal, sadistically violent *Django Kill!/If You Live, Shoot/Sei sei vivo spara!* (1967), in which 'children are shot, outlaws roasted on a spit, animals disembowelled and a man is suffocated by molten lead' (Hardy, 1991, p.302). Scenes like these ensured that Italian Westerns like the Django series were banned or severely cut by censors on their release outside Italy. Christopher Frayling considers such gross violence 'comic strip', performed by protagonists who behave like invincible superheroes. Death is dispensed implausibly by an anachronistic array of armoury, with 'an almost fetishistic emphasis on . . . technological resourcefulness' (1998(79)). The Man with No Name uses dynamite and James Coburn's Irish republican rebel is armed with quantities of it in *A Fistful of Dynamite/Duck You Sucker/Giù la testa* (1971), Colonel Mortimer (Lee Van Cleef) in *For a Few Dollars More* has a bedroll of exotic guns strapped to his horse, whilst Django sports a modern machine-gun.

SERGIO LEONE WESTERNS

In *A Fistful of Dollars*, The Man With No Name (who everyone in the film nonetheless calls Joe) seeks no quest, but personal gain. Yet his arrival acts as a catalyst in the feud between two families. In *For a Few Dollars More*, Colonel Mortimer is a bounty hunter. These are protagonists who kill casually, yet their excesses bear some moral justification. The Man With No Name seems to work to reunite a mother, Marisol, and her son, separated by the feud. Mortimer is forced to become a bounty hunter by circumstances not of his choosing, obliquely referring to a life destroyed 'when the railroads came'. Such protagonists 'are not the adventurers of the American West, but gringos whose very presence . . . precipitates . . . opposition between the oppressors and the oppressed' (Wallington, 1970, p.33). In seeking self gain and freedom from oppression for others, these protagonists play a delicate survival game. They strategically shift allegiances and prompt confrontations between opposing forces until – as in Jacobean tragedy – the stage is finally littered with corpses. At that point, the survivor rides on, as if to start the game all over again.

A *Fistful of Dollars* is a characteristic Western of director Sergio Leone, the most internationally successful of Italian Western film-makers. Elliptical narrative structures are built around a series of absurd contests between the central protagonists, each in turn besting the other until a final confrontation. There is much visual humour in slapstick and situation comedy within the treatment of these tricksters and cheats as they continually double-cross each other and destroy the democratic rules of fair play in Western rituals like gunfights. In *The Good, the Bad and the Ugly*, Blondie and Tuco take turns to play the victim in a scam to win bounty money, relying on the other to save the 'thief' from the hangman's noose.

Climactic gunfights are elaborately choreographed and stretched out in time to observe reactions in close-up, often looking grotesque in the CinemaScope frame. The 'close-ups are not reserved for the protagonists alone but are dispersed, associated with antagonists and with silent observers of the action' (Landy, 1996, p.218). Conversely, 'camera movement – pans, tilts, the use of handheld equipment – conveys the sense of a world of energy and motion, a world of bodies that collide' (ibid., p.218). Dialogue is minimal (a necessary strategy to overcome problems of synchronising dubbed American voices over Italian actors in prints for overseas sales), replaced by aural themes (with grunts, whistles, whines or heightened natural sounds) for characters and situations. These are embedded in operatic orchestral scores such as those composed by Ennio Morricone for Leone's films and are influenced by Martin Botcher's music for the German Westerns, resulting in a 'a highly self-conscious referencing of the formal conventions of the American genre' (Schneider, 1995, p.53). These contribute as much to the dramatic affect of the films as the narratives and performances (Landy, 1996, pp.216–17).

All this is evidence of a formal play that draws attention to the process of storytelling and film-making: the camera and editing create 'ostentatious . . . spatial relationships brought about by excessive low (or high) angles, the use of special lenses, or the introduction of figures into the frame from unnatural directions or in uncomfortable close-up' (Wallington, 1970, p.34). The end of

Clint Eastwood as The Man With No Name in *For a Few Dollars More/Per qualche dollari in più* (1964), the film whose international success influenced the style and mood of Westerns made thereafter.

The Good, the Bad and the Ugly finds Tuco chasing around a cemetery searching out a name on a gravestone. The camera starts with his point-of-view until it hurtles around, out of focus, combining with Morricone's frenzied music track to express the character's fevered state of mind. In *My Name is Nobody/Il mio nome è Nessuno* (1973), a chase scene descends into farce as a posse rides back and forth across a rocky landscape, with an orchestral refrain erupting into prolonged silences between every reappearance. Flashbacks and dreams are frequent and often enigmatic. All this is 'cinematic hyperbole', exaggerating 'the language of the Western' (ibid., p.34), perhaps even a distancing device to make the spectator more aware of the experience of the fiction as 'fiction' (Frayling 1998, p.xxiii).

For Frayling, the most considerable writer on this subject, these Westerns self-consciously play with generic conventions (indeed, a bartender in *A Fistful of Dollars* says, 'It's like playing cowboys and Indians'). They 'deconstruct and rearrange the images and themes which comprise the reverence of puritan-liberal Hollywood Westerns' (ibid., p.35). In Leone's *Once Upon a Time in the West/C'era una Volta il West* (1968), Henry Fonda plays a villain, complete with innocent 'baby blue' eyes. Witnessing this gentlest of populist stars slaughter a sodbuster family early in the film – in a horrific reversal of the opening scene of *Shane* (1953) – is almost as shocking as seeing him spit as he returns his gun to its holster. However, more classical tropes can figure to contradict Frayling's argument. For instance, the trio who come across a Civil War battle for a bridge in *The Good, the Bad and the Ugly* find themselves in a scene that dramatically departs from the otherwise playful tone of the film. The bloody confrontation concludes with Blondie comforting a dying soldier in a 'time out of war' that resonates with antiwar sentiment.

Leone's Westerns are deeply implicated in and comments on the history of the Western genre. Many American Westerns are invoked, especially those directed by Robert Aldrich, Budd Boetticher, Sam Fuller and Nicholas Ray (ibid., p.136). In reference to Jeb's trauma in *Pursued*, a flashback structure in *Once Upon a Time in the West* has the revenge quest of Harmonica (Charles Bronson) punctuated by a blurred memory that is eventually revealed as his unwilling complicity in the hanging of his brother. Leone's Westerns invoke an alternative vision to the foundation myth of the West for Frayling and contribute to a subsequent movement of revisionist Westerns from the 1970s onwards. Leone has said: 'I see the history of the West as really the reign of violence by violence' (ibid., p.135).

For Landy, however, Spaghetti Westerns are most interesting as male melodramas that involve 'conflicts of identity and homosocial bonding' (1996, p.217). The films 'interrogate masculinity and its discontents, its complicity with violence and power' (ibid., p.215). Rather than interventions in the conventions of the Western or revisions to the foundation myth, Landy sees Leone's Westerns developing themes existing in Italian Cinema about 'protagonists who struggle to survive in societies that are hostile to change and to collective practices' and 'the clash between rural and urban life and between tradition and modernity' (ibid., p.215).

BACK TO AMERICA

Christopher Wagstaff finds that Italian Westerns return the genre to its serial roots (1992, p.58), targeted at audiences of working class male youth in Italian cities (Schneider sees the German Westerns also popular with German male youth). By the time the cycle declines in the mid-1970s, Italian Westerns set the tone and style of American Westerns and the action film more generally. Ironically, the increased stylisation of the genre, emphasising a rough masculinity from this time onwards – Yvonne Tasker calls them 'muscular movies' (1983, p.8) – may have contributed to its demise as a popular genre, by limiting its appeal to predominantly one gender of a mass audience.

A series of revenge Westerns that mark Clint Eastwood's return to America, with the formation of his own production company, Malpaso, demonstrate the influence of the Italian Western. The first, *Hang 'Em High* (1967) is influenced by his work with Leone, though by the time of *Pale Rider* (1985) – another reworking of *Shane* – Eastwood's own concerns as a director predominate, exaggerating the mythic hero at times into a supernatural being. In *Pale Rider*, a prayer for assistance is immediately followed by a cut to a distant rider on horseback, the figure of the avenging angel characteristically played by Eastwood in his Westerns. Between those films, Eastwood also worked with American director Don Siegel on a journey Western, *Two Mules for Sister Sara* (1970), and the immensely successful and influential police film, *Dirty Harry* (1971). As early as *High Plains Drifter* (1972), Eastwood's narrative style combines the abstract qualities of Leone and Siegel's commitment to genre conventions. Eastwood's debt is acknowledged not least by the actor/director himself: the final credit for one of the last great Westerns, Eastwood's *Unforgiven*, is a dedication 'to Sergio and Don'.

High Plains Drifter is the most supernatural of Eastwood's dystopian Westerns. It tells the story of a mysterious loner, played by Eastwood, who rides into Lago, a town with a secret, built on a seashore (apart from *One-Eyed Jacks*, 1961, the only Western to use such an unconventional location). The narrative of how this ghostly figure is both its victim and its avenger is told partly in revealing flashbacks up to the moment a sheriff is savagely whipped to death. The revelation that the hero is the reincarnated sheriff emerges as he bizarrely avenges his own killing; he inverts the town's hierarchy, humiliates the townsfolk and forces them literally to 'paint the town red'. Finally confronting and killing those responsible for his previous death, he leaves the town destroyed, revealing that the sign of Lago he ordered to be overpainted now bears the name of 'Hell'. As Hardy rightly says: 'The result is a stunningly confident, formalised, abstract work' (1991, p.338).

Eastwood's film career – both as star and director – develops distinctively, yet the lasting influence of the Italian Western style is evident not only in his many Westerns, but in American Westerns more generally. Graphic, stylised violence and killings become common, notably in the work of Sam Peckinpah from *The Wild Bunch* (1969) onwards. Peckinpah also developed the use of slow motion, first used by director Arthur Penn in the climax to the gangster film, *Bonnie and Clyde* (1967), to prolong and exaggerate the moment of violent death of the eponymous 'innocents' by the state. The mass slaughter of a Mexican army at the end of *The Wild Bunch* shares a new scale of destruction with other Westerns of the time, notably the Mexican-set *100 Rifles* (1968). While in these Westerns the Mexican military are the villains, comparable massacres of Indian villages in *Soldier Blue* (1970) and *Little Big Man* (1970) are sympathetic to the victims.

The Wild Bunch opens with an extraordinary scene of children cruelly laughing at a scorpion tormented by an army of red ants among a brazier's flames. The scene prefigures the film's final carnage, but also demonstrates the commonplace casual violence in the Western from the 1960s onwards. Charlton Heston's hero in *Will Penny* (1967) suffers the sadistic games of the villainous all-male Quint family, realising more graphically a tendency in the Western from its earliest days. A new development in the dystopian Western is that the hero is as likely to be the perpetrator of the violence as the villain. Will Penny's revenge may be motivated, but in *True Grit* (1969), for instance, a lowly villain has his hand ignominiously pinned to a table by a knife wielded by the hero, Rooster Cogburn, played by the star, John Wayne.

Female victims of violence are common in 1970s Westerns. In keeping with a liberalised, yet firmly misogynist sexuality in the period, Westerns commonly feature newly conventionalised rape scenes. Whereas the threat of unspecified attack and implied rape is not uncommon in Westerns before this period, from now onwards villainy is frequently defined precisely by its explicit sexual threat to women. Most sexual attacks are ugly, as in *Soldier Blue*, or mercifully reported or occur off-screen (though scarcely more bearable or justified) as in *The Last Hard Men* (1976). Incredibly, some are offered as comic, as in *High Plains Drifter*; in *Waterhole 3*, rape is indefensibly defined as 'assault with a friendly weapon'.

Although there are examples of such cynicism in Westerns before the emergence of the Italian Western, notably in *Great Day in the Morning* (1956), none are as bitter as those that follow. *Welcome to Hard Times/Killer on a Horse* (1966) is one of the earliest responses to the Italian Western. It typifies the extreme changes wrought on the American Western. The Man From Brodie (Aldo Ray) wreaks unmotivated destruction on Hard Times (the town of the original American release title) and, laughing manically, leaves it burning wildly. The intense, shocking opening is replaced by a more sombre mood as the town gradually restores itself, oddly recreating every original lost figure, from the undertaker, Hansen (Elisha Cook Junior), last seen shot in his hearse, to Zar (Keenan Wynn), complete with travelling saloon and female entertainment. At the moment the town seems settled, the killer returns. Two original survivors, Will Blue (Henry Fonda) and Molly Riordan (Janice Rule), this time resist. Molly has raised the young, orphaned Jimmy Fee (Michael Shea) to protect her, a morally ambiguous act revealed when she falsely lures Will to her bed to demonstrate Jimmy's willingness to use a gun in her defence on command. Will's reluctance to use violence in the opening scene is cruelly exposed as inadequate in the face of the killer's terrorism. With the killer's return, Molly's taunts urge Will to confrontation. At the end, the killer lies dead, together with Molly, who has become the victim of Jimmy's terror.

Scripted and directed by Burt Kennedy, *Welcome to Hard Times/Killer on a Horse*, has none of the wry humour and leisurely pace of his Ranown cycle work. Though its old testament story explores familiar generic themes of savagery versus civilisation, its confrontation between opposing rough and gentle masculine characteristics unfolds with morally ambivalent characters, amid scenes of unmotivated violence and in an exaggerated style only possible in a Hollywood Western after the rise of its Italian derivative.

No final comment on the period should pass without mention of two highly individual Westerns directed independently of Hollywood by Monte Hellman from scripts by actor Jack Nicholson, *Ride in the Whirlwind* (1966) and *The Shooting* (1966). Called 'existential Westerns' by critical supporters, their misunderstood, doomed heroes seem to reject both the harsh frontier life of settlers and the only alternative of outlawry. In 'pared-down, fragmented' narratives (Hardy, 1991, p.299) and an editing style probably borne of their quick, cheap production conditions, the films have an original dystopian mood.

THE VIETNAM WAR

In the late 1960s and early 1970s, such extremes of violence and cynicism also mark combat films about the Vietnam War, an unresolved conflict that devastated a national landscape and left dead over 1 million North Vietnamese, 200,000 South Vietnamese and 50,000 Americans. The war had profound effects in America, 'shattering ... the ideological consensus that had governed the post-Second World War era (and) reverberated throughout the realm of popular culture' (Worland and Countryman, 1998, p.186), not least in news media and Hollywood fiction (Buxton, 1989). John Wayne exceptionally celebrated America's role in *The Green Berets* (1968), the only combat film made during the war. Others were produced (though commonly made in the Philippines) after America's ignominious 1973 withdrawal, claimed by the

President at the time, Richard Nixon, as 'peace with honour'. These combat films are critical of an American political machine that waged war unreasonably and a military machine that waged it madly (Comber and O'Brien, 1988). *Apocalypse Now* (1979) deals with the war's madness and *Platoon* (1986) is not untypical in its support for the soldiers as 'grunts', battle-hardened innocents abandoned to survive in an alien culture and terrain. In particular, the battle-scarred veteran (the Vietnam 'Vet') emerges as a central hero of films like *Platoon* and the *Rambo* (1982, 1985, 1988) series.

Interrogations of the Vietnam War were displaced into Hollywood genres like the crime film and the Western at the same time as the war was being waged (Slotkin, 1992, p.441) and also when action genres were increasingly trading conventions and narratives (Tasker, 1993, p.69). Though Jeanine Basinger argues that the Vietnam War 'killed off' the Western as a popular form (1986, p.213), the genre already embraced certain conventions of the combat film. In turn, the Vietnam combat film owes debts to the captivity narratives and tragic heroes of romance Westerns.

Dystopian Westerns of the late 1960s and early 1970s trade conventions with combat films to question both the foundation myth of frontier history and the more modern myths that dominate ideologies of American power at the time of their making. Far from Carlos Clarens' position, that 'the Western suddenly stood for everything imperialistic and genocidal about America' (1980, pp.13–14), the dystopian Western became a generic space for critical reflection on America and its history. This is nowhere more incisive than in the cavalry Western.

THE CAVALRY WESTERN

The convention of the cavalry rescue is as old as the Western, figuring prominently in Selig films from 1909 and defining the meaning of the cavalry in Griffith's Westerns from *The Last Drop of Water* (1911). By the time of one of the first Western feature films, *In Old Arizona* (1929), it is a staple convention of the genre (Abel, 1998, p.83). The horse soldier of the US cavalry has possibly been the most common hero of Westerns together with the cowboy gunfighter. John Ford's cavalry trilogy of the late 1940s, *Fort Apache* (1948), *She Wore a Yellow Ribbon* (1949) and *Rio Grande* (1951) exemplify the central characteristics of the cavalry Western. All these films concern events that impact on life in a frontier fort. The central focus is the cavalry itself, especially relations among the officers who, with their families, comprise the community celebrated in the films. The ostensible conflict in these cavalry Westerns is between the soldiers and the Indians over whom they seek to control an uneasy peace. But, as Pye has argued (1996c, p.155), the central conflict is more between the military community and an absent authority that exerts a remote and arbitrary rule over it.

The films are all set at some point after the Civil War, where a Washington authority – often alluded to but never seen – governs an unlikely chain of command. In *Fort Apache*, the decision of 'an ungrateful War Department' to send West a vainglorious Lieutenant Colonel Thursday (Henry Fonda) leads to the destruction of the entire command (Tony French, 1998). *She Wore a Yellow Ribbon* devotes much of its narrative regretting the imminent retirement of Captain Nathan Brittles (John Wayne) whose skills in command are as pertinent as ever, despite his age. Within the trilogy, incomprehensible official decisions are made that reduce seasoned officers with much-needed experience to the ranks, because of their prior Confederate associations. *She Wore a Yellow Ribbon* has a touching scene in which a trooper killed in an Indian raid is honoured at his funeral. The soldiers who previously fought on both sides of the Civil war join together to pay respects to one who was a Major many proudly served under in the Confederate army.

In common with the conventions of the war film more generally, Ford's cavalry trilogy features familiar generic events including: breaking in new recruits, an initial successful sortie followed by a larger conflict which depletes the group, and the final honouring of the dead. The idea that a suspect authority will sacrifice the ordinary Joe is as conventional to the cavalry Western as it is to the combat film (Gallagher, 1986a, pp.246–54). In Ford's cavalry trilogy, however, such sacrifice will not allow the institution to be condemned. At the end of *Fort Apache*, Captain Kirby Yorke (John Wayne), newly promoted to Major, salutes the memory of the fallen as he upholds the tradition of the military.

Other cavalry Westerns of the period are more concerned to dramatise conflicts within and between the ranks. In the end though, they come to celebrate the cavalry as an institution as much as Ford, ultimately overcoming divisions in individual acts of sacrifice and collective action. In *Only the Valiant* (1951), for instance, Gregory Peck's cavalry officer brushes aside the hatred of his undisciplined soldiers to unite them against a common foe, the Apache. Here, however, two captured soldiers representing North and South are finally seen fighting themselves rather than the Apache. In *Escape From Fort Bravo* (1953), a cavalry troop hunt down a group of escaped Southern prisoners of war, only for unity to be forced on them when attacked by Indians. In a magnificently staged final scene, the Indians mount a siege with military precision on the dwindling group holed up in a sunken gulch.

In later cavalry Westerns, however, the cavalry as an institution is more likely to be an evil than a peaceful force, the cause of conflict rather than its solution. Ford's cavalry trilogy was made in the period immediately following the Second World War, when the war against European fascism provided just cause to unite against a common enemy (Slotkin, 1992, pp.334–43). Cavalry Westerns produced following the very different Korean War in the 1950s tend to condemn not only the political and military institutions but also the serving soldiers. The actions of the cavalry who ride into Indian villages to rescue white captives is sanctioned in films directed by John Ford like *The Searchers* (1956), *Two Rode Together* (1961) and *Cheyenne Autumn* (1964). Yet, by the time of *Little Big Man* and *Soldier Blue* in the early 1970s, the military atrocities of the Vietnam War inform new visions of a bloodthirsty, sadistic cavalry, indiscriminately mutilating and massacring women and children. The disturbing re-enactment of the Washita River Massacre of 1868 in *Little Big Man* in particular is part of a critique, both historical and contemporary. The historical revelation of a frontier atrocity also exposes a contemporary American foreign policy that destroyed Vietnamese villages – 'in order to save them', as one militarist of the time reportedly put it – in the name of democracy, and a military authority unable to control many of its units, as in the infamous massacre by American soldiers of an entire Vietnamese village, My Lai.

Major Dundee

The epic *Major Dundee* (1964) is a key transitional cavalry Western in the period between the Second World War and the Vietnam War. Kitses calls the film 'a . . . landmark in the Western' (1969, p.139). Major Dundee (Charlton Heston) is an obsessive cavalry officer who runs a prisoner-of-war camp for Confederate soldiers captured during the Civil War. He leads a ramshackle group of volunteer troopers, bribed confederate prisoners and cavalier frontiersmen to hunt down a band of marauding renegade Indians led by Sierra Charriba (Michael Pate). The success of the quest is undermined from the start by Dundee's intransigent command over a force whose uneasy unity is established as the troop leaves the fort; the Confederates sing 'Dixie', the bluecoats 'The Battle Hymn of the Republic' and the civilians 'My Darling Clementine'. Dundee's obsessive pursuit of the Apache continues even after its objective – to rescue captured white children – has been achieved. In keeping with the conventions of the combat film, the group is gradually depleted by external attack, but it is also weakened by recurrent internal conflicts between Northerners and Southerners, blacks and whites, soldiers and civilians. These conflicts are frequently initiated by Dundee, for instance when he hangs the Confederate soldier, O.W. Hadley (Warren Oates), for desertion, in defiance of protesting fellow confederate soldiers.

The leader of the Confederate group, Captain Tyree (Richard Harris), is Dundee's alter ego. They are constant antagonists, yet Tyree also rescues Dundee when he falls from grace in a drunken depression. Tyree initially refuses allegiance to the flag: 'It's not my country, Major. I damn its flag and I damn you. I would rather hang than serve'. As the narrative develops, he secures the affections of the motley troop, until his final sacrifice unites them around the flag to overcome the common enemy. In the thick of battle midstream, Tyree is shot as he clasps the American flag with Dundee. His response is to ride suicidally into the enemy, which provides time for the rest of the troop to escape. By this point, the Apache have already been disposed of, tricked into an ambush. The final confrontation is rather with a detachment of French Lancers, barring the route across a river bordering Mexico, into which the troop knowingly strayed in pursuit of the Apache. Few survive this ultimate 'European' conflict, but those who do represent all groups within the troop, now united under the bloodied flag of America and the bugle tune of militarism.

Throughout, the Apache represent an arrogant savagery ('Who will you send against me now' chants Sierra Charriba) that can only be overcome by a comparable savagery among the heroic group. Kitses sees in this, however, 'a savage direction open to all men' (ibid., p.149), making the Indians into Dundee's id. Savagery is not all Indian, however. The French mistreat Mexicans and Americans mistreat both. The Apache action is even justified: in Dundee's insistent words, 'It's their land, all of it.' National and racial identity is rarely simple or settled. Dundee is a Southerner who fought for the North, Tyree an Irishman who fought for the South. Even minor characters among the troop, such as Riago, a Christian Indian scout, and Sergeant Gomez, a Mexican, share in the confusion of national identity.

For Kitses, *Major Dundee* is 'a monumental attempt to lay bare the roots of America as a nation' (ibid., p.145). He sees in Dundee's 'quest for personal identity' an interrogation of American national identity, seeking 'a meaningful confrontation with the past, and a tortured struggle to achieve mastery over self-annihilating and savage impulses' (ibid., p.141). The past is America's imperial history and immigrant legacy. The troop is a disempowered group from the European and African diasporas, competing with a powerful WASP culture, personified in Dundee, to define their roles in America's future. The film savagely undermines the foundation myth in its depiction of the birth of America in needless sacrifice, wholesale slaughter and ruthless conquest.

Paul Seydor claims that the script for *Major Dundee* was 'intended to be about how men in war soon forget their ideals and become lost in the lust for blood and glory' (1980, p.69) but, as he and Kitses explore, the film was subject to major production difficulties that deformed the intentions of its director, Sam Peckinpah. For this reason, Kitses considers it 'a great broken monument' (1969, p.139). Though symptoms of production difficulties are found in moments of incoherent plotting and editing, they are perhaps of a piece with a story about 'a company divided by itself' (Seydor, 1980, p.75). A film about the forging of a national identity in savage acts also looks forward to later Westerns that question more explicitly an institutional need for violent masculinity. In an oddly prescient phrase at the time of its writing, Kitses claims 'what is striking – for the command as much as us – is that we are watching men secure enough in themselves to be able to choose violence as a mode of behaviour, an expression of feeling' (1969, p.151). Seydor, however, finds the violence neither individual nor gendered, but social: 'the more civilised a society, the more capable it is of barbarity' (1980, p.76).

THE VIETNAM WESTERN

Kitses describes *Major Dundee* as 'a bitterly artful parody of the traditional cavalry picture' (1969, p.146). The savagery in *Major Dundee* is both individual and collective, rooted in the Western hero and in an American national identity derived from 'the blood-bath from which America is born' (ibid., p.151). Often dystopian Westerns produced at the time of the Vietnam War share this sense of an unjust conflict, whose only consequence is the lives of its combatants. Leaders in Vietnam fictions are extreme figures like Dundee, who 'suffer from . . . (a) moral rectitude' (ibid., p.143) that may validate the hero of Western romance, but emotionally disables the dystopian Western hero. In extreme conditions of combat, the rules of war become clouded and military objectives questionable when they place lives at unnecessary risk. The result in the Vietnam Western is psychological and emotional breakdown.

THE DYSTOPIAN WESTERN AS GOTHIC HORROR

Vietnam Westerns explore ironically the dystopian spectacle of pointless, savage conflict. None more demonstrates the turn of the Western to gothic horror than one of the last great cavalry Westerns, *Ulzana's Raid* (1972). The West of *Ulzana's Raid* is all blasted wilderness and no garden, a land 'inimical . . . to any human life' (Pye 1996b, p.266). It is set in an Arizona that one of its characters, in words from Alan Sharp's intelligent dialogue, describes thus: 'If the devil owned Hell and Arizona, he'd live in Hell and rent out Arizona.' The desolate landscape is riven by horrific violence, whose arbitrariness is gradually exposed as a product of the colonial relationship between the powerful and the powerless, an abstract authority and those it subordinates. Set some time after the major Indian campaigns in the early 1880s, it concerns the escape from a reservation of a small band of Apaches, led by Ulzana of the film's title. Military convention requires that a troop of cavalrymen be sent after them from a nearby outpost, Fort Lowell. Before this, however, a proper assessment must be made of the Apache numbers and their intentions. The military has its procedures, which the authorities, embodied in the figure of Major Cartwright, will rigorously apply. Delay, however, threatens the lives of isolated, local settlers. This dilemma establishes the conflict at the heart of the cavalry narrative, between those who apply the rules and those whose lives are put at risk by the obligation to live within them.

Unlike other leaders such as the martinet Colonel Thursday in *Fort Apache* or the mad frontier officer in *Dances With Wolves*, Cartwright is not an insensitive commander and he 'freely acknowledges' his ignorance of the Apache. However, he feels 'obliged' to favour regulation over expediency. The troop, conversely, is made up of seasoned campaigners who know from experience the intention of the renegade Indians. Among their party, a scout, McIntosh (Burt Lancaster), explains that the band will form a raiding party, intending to 'burn, maim, rape, torture and kill . . . anything that crosses its path'. This early statement prefigures the horror to be meted out on a troop that, deployed to protect settlers, will not be able to protect itself. The fiction echoes conditions faced by the American military during the war against North Vietnam, later to become a convention of the Vietnam combat film.

Although the 'forthright' McIntosh lacks military authority, the greenhorn troop leader Lieutenant DeBuin (Bruce Davison) at first defers to the older man's seasoned knowledge. However, as he bears witness to the 'Apache leavings' of the tortured, mutilated, raped and killed, his Christian faith in the redemption of the 'heathen' Indian is increasingly tested. The experience scratches away at the surface of his liberalism, revealing a racism ultimately and only reconciled by accepting the scout's greater pragmatism (as McIntosh says of DeBuin's hatred of the Indians, 'it might not make you happy, but it sure won't make you lonely. A lot of folk in these parts feel that way').

The inappropriateness of Christian faith in such circumstances is cruelly demonstrated by events in one of the Apache raids on a homestead. A settler, Rukeyser (Karl Swensen), shares DeBuin's naivety. Unprotected, he is grotesquely punished for refusing to give up his land to the seasoned guerrilla fighters he judges as 'drunk Indians'. Rukeyser and the audience are tricked into believing a bugle call heralds a conventional last minute cavalry rescue. As Rukeyser praises the Lord for his salvation, a sharp cut indicates that this is not the same bugle hanging from the waist of the bugler some distance from the scene, but the one that hangs from the neck of Ulzana's small son. Rukeyser's mutilated body is subsequently found by the troop, the genitals burned over a fire and, in some original prints uncut by censorship, the remains stuffed in his mouth. The excessive horror of the punishment graphically exposes the outer limits of humanity explored by the Vietnam Western.

Soldier, settler and renegade reservation Indian are all subordinated by colonial authority and equally subject to arbitrary attack. They have no place in this deathly landscape in which survival is a lottery. The idea is established from the start of the film, with DeBuin distracted from umpiring a casual baseball game among the soldiers that seems wholly incongruous in a Western landscape. The resulting near mutiny identifies DeBuin's inability 'to keep his eye on the ball', both here and later, when his shattered faith puts the troop at risk.

An inadequate military authority contrasts with the utter seriousness of adhering to the rules of the mission. Two gallopers sent to find tracks of the fugitive Apache do not return. One neglects his instruction not to 'bring the settlers in' to the fort, resulting in his suicide in an Apache ambush before which he shoots Rukeyser's wife in the forehead as she pleads for her life. The shock of such events only makes generic sense when we subsequently learn in the most graphic ways (such as Rukeyser's death) of the horrors of which the Apache are capable. We are left to muse on the fate of the second galloper, a young boy left screaming for his life as he is dragged off, not to be seen again in the film.

Tracking down the Indian 'hunting party' is seen as a game governed by rules in which, as McIntosh wisely reminds DeBuin, 'first one to make a mistake gets to bury some people'. But this knowledge does not stop McIntosh and the other men from toying with DeBuin's naivety. Information is withheld from him and his questions are deflected. After witnessing the results of the attack on the galloper, DeBuin asks why the Apache spared the life of Rukeyser's son. McIntosh rightly reponds: 'Spared him what?', but offers no explanation other than 'Apaches have whims'. McIntosh's tired response stems from the same sense of powerlessness that motivates and explains the Apache's cruelty.

The explanation for the cruelty of the Apaches comes from the specialised knowledge of McIntosh's friend, the Indian scout Ke-Ni-Tay (Jorge Luke). With DeBuin, the audience learns the social and cultural rationale for what otherwise seems a sadistic pleasure in killing. In oppressive conditions of reservation imprisonment and poverty, Ulzana and his men must break out to 'taste freedom'. The manner of the killing arises from the conditions they find themselves in; 'in this land, man must have power', obtainable only from the painful death of those marked as their enemy. In a central explanatory scene around a campfire, Ke-Ni-Tay, in an even more laconic manner than McIntosh, identifies the nature of this power not as any innate racial characteristic, but as a monstrous deviancy caused by the psychic damage of imperial oppression. The rules of the game are that men are killed, women are raped and children survive, all relative to the value of their power in the colonial hierarchy. And, as in *Major Dundee*, the same rules do not only govern the behaviour of the

Gothic horror comes to the Western: the scouts Ke-Ni-Tay (Jorge Luke) and McIntosh (Burt Lancaster) about to discover the mutilated body of a settler in *Ulzana's Raid* (1972).

Indians. Later, soldiers will mutilate the fallen body of Ulzana's son, justifying their own barbarity to DeBuin by claiming 'Apaches don't like it if you do this to their dead. Kind of spooks them.' The colonial context produces atrocities on both sides of the racial division of power.

In circumstance of 'institutional disintegration' (Pye, 1996b, p.266), committed relationships represent powerful statements about human endurance. The parting of Rukeyser and his wife is ennobled by the exchange of looks that acknowledges their terror but sensitively masks it from their son. We subsequently learn from their massive diary of the love for one another that must have sustained the long ocean journey and overland trek from Europe to this bleak environment. And we recall the mutual affection and loyalty of their parting words: 'I fix that swinging door that makes you curse so much, you betcha'; 'You look to yourself, Willie'. The quality of their relationship contrasts with the desolate terrain they seek to farm.

The two scouts equally exchange knowing looks in frequent shot/reverse shot structures that serve to affirm the depth of their friendship. Teasing DeBuin is a kind of safety valve for their own fears; McIntosh defers to his friend when tracking, because he will not 'argue with no Indian about horse shit' and Ke-Ni-Tay recalls a notional kinship with their prey. They also accord by the rules of the military game, however absurd, illustrated when a maddened DeBuin orders an obedient Ke-Ni-Tay to forfeit his horse to McIntosh. The order implicitly questions Ke-Ni-Tay's allegiance because of his shared racial origins with the terrifying Ulzana. McIntosh's response is not protest, but the quiet offer of his rifle in exchange, thereby making clear his subservience to military rule yet his abiding trust in their friendship.

At the end, with extreme loss of life and the raid over, McIntosh lies dying. Ke-Ni-Tay kneels and lifts a limp arm, as if to check the life of his friend. Gently returning the arm, the final exchange of looks is a touching affirmation of nobility in the most extreme of circumstances. The relationship across the racial divide between McIntosh and Ke-Ni-Tay is the film's central and most subtle, echoing a vestigial relation between McIntosh and an Indian wife suggested at the start of the film. Interracial relations have a long history in the Western, echoing that of James Fenimore Cooper's Chingachgook and Leatherstocking. Though, in the words of Pye (1966b, p.267), *Ulzana's Raid* carries 'strong suggestions of an ideal meeting between the two races . . . any residual echoes . . . are compromised or even invalidated by the historical situation'. When Ke-Ni-Tay commits himself to the cause of the cavalry – 'I sign the paper' – he also commits himself to the destruction of his own people.

The complex nobility of such private moments even extends to Ulzana. Though an audience wishes to see proper end to the horrific violence he perpetrates, by the suspenseful climax of the film, responsibility for the violence has stretched beyond any of the characters to the historical conditions of colonial war. As among heroes of romance Westerns, and in the gothic horror of this film, Ulzana becomes as much victim as criminal. With the raid over, his son dead, facing capture and return to the reservation, Ulzana chooses to sing a death song before sacrificing himself to Ke-Ni-Tay's gun. This is yet another scene that invokes the new redundancy of such Western conventions as the cavalry rescue and, here, the democracy of the stand-off.

Although, without Ke-Ni-Tay, the chase would end differently for the surviving troopers, McIntosh is the central figure. In Burt Lancaster's performance of weary resignation, it is not only McIntosh who is dying, but also a Western hero now on his last legs, exhausted by the effort of survival and resigned to his fate in the dystopian Western. There are more than a few traces of an elegiac Western hero in McIntosh. He recognises the limitations of his own power, knowing that his advice is unlikely to be heeded, yet always 'just saying my say'. He is ennobled by his knowledge and sensibility, his acceptance of anOther culture, his respect for Ulzana and friendship with

Ke-Ni-Tay. *Ulzana's Raid* is a Vietnam Western that digs deep into the genre tradition to transcend the conventions of the combat film. But, finally, its hero is a Westerner in the meaningless, random world of a dystopian Western, where personal action is pointless. *Ulzana's Raid* is indeed a bleak, pessimistic vision for such a worthy character.

CHAPTER NINE

The Elegiac Western

The classical Western offers romance in its character relationships, quest narrative and the validation of its hero. In the dystopian Western, all this is troubled and, at its most extreme, undermined or even denied. The response of the elegiac Western is to turn romance into tragedy and the hero into a victim of dystopia.

An elegy is a lament, an expression of sorrow, often in the form of a song or poem mourning the dead. Westerns are elegiac when their dominant mood is a pervasive sadness, inspired by the passing of ways associated with a culture no longer fashionable or valued. In this new Western imaginary, times are changing as a modern urban world takes over. The elegiac Western tends to be set near to or after the official closing of the frontier, variously between 1890 (after the final surrender of the Native Americans of the plains nations) and the turn of the twentieth century. It views the earlier rural culture nostalgically, justified by experiencing the past as better than a dystopian present. In terms of the foundation myth, the Promised Land has turned into Paradise Lost. Where the romance Western is full of hope for a youthful future, the elegiac Western harks back to a romantic past. The elegiac Western is about historical and personal ageing, and the problems of people and societies growing old.

Although symptoms of a nostalgic attitude towards a West of the past are evident from the first days of the genre, they intensify from the 1950s onwards. Elegiac Westerns of the 1960s and 1970s coincide with the final film performances, retirement from the screen and deaths of the great Hollywood film stars most associated with Westerns of the classical period (Gallafent, 1996a, p.241). Concurrently, the production of Westerns dramatically declines. Hardy estimates over five hundred Westerns were made at the height of the genre's production during the 1950s, compared with just over two hundred in the 1960s (including the European Westerns released outside their domestic markets). The 1970s is the last decade of mass production of

Westerns, though less than two hundred are made, followed by a dramatic reduction in the 1980s to less than forty. The audience demography shifts as dramatically in this period, with the loss of the mass audience to new domestic attractions like television and a consequent new focus on the youth market as Hollywood's target audience.

Yet statistics for the 1950s underestimate Western film production in the decade. There is massive production of Westerns for television series in the 1950s. The rise of the dystopian and elegiac Western in cinema was one response made by the film industry to differentiate A Westerns from the predominantly romance form of television series Westerns. However, the sharp decline in Western film production in the following decades is certainly a result of the shift in generation and cultures of the film audience. Elegiac Westerns are therefore not only responses to but also comments on the ageing of the genre. Romance Westerns establish the film conventions of the Western. Dystopian Westerns interrogate them, but elegiac Westerns mourn their passing.

FROM ROMANCE TO ELEGY

The hero of the elegiac Western exaggerates those tendencies in the romance hero to separation from the community. The archetypal Western hero is socially isolated by his identification with violence. Shane, for instance, or Will Kane (Gary Cooper) in *High Noon* (1952) ride (or ride back) into their narratives, face villainy alone, settle conflict, and ride on. For many such romance heroes, the final movement is explicitly westward. At the climax of *My Darling Clementine* (1946), the hero, Wyatt Earp, moves further west after settling scores with the Clantons who killed his younger brother, in the process pacifying the lawless town of Tombstone. Personal vengeance and public duty both satisfied, one might expect romance to dictate that the hero remain in the township to enjoy a promise of partnership with Clementine, the woman of the East, in a conventional 'happy ending' of heterosexual romance. Instead, his departure heightens the romance in another sense, by suggesting merely the possibility of delay in the union or a problem to overcome in achieving it. Though not finally a romantic partner, Wyatt remains just as much a romance hero as Will in *High Noon* and Ringo in *Stagecoach* (1939) who do end their quests with the heroine.

When Will and Amy (Grace Kelly) take their leave, it is out of disgust with the town's failure to support Will's quest for justice, Will symbolically grinding his marshal's badge underfoot. Ringo and Dallas ride on West, escaping the 'benefits of civilisation', in Doc's ironic words. The audience has seen 'civilisation' dramatised in the primly moralistic women who force Dallas from the town of Tonto at the film's opening and in the 'wide open town' of Lordsburg, complete with the brothel ghetto from which Dallas finally escapes.

Will and Ringo are romance heroes because of their romantic relationships and narrative quest. Though Wyatt, like Shane, ends up alone, he remains a romance hero because he shares the romance *function*. They are all agents of change whose actions enable civilising Eastern values to enter the burgeoning but troubled settlements of the West. Despite contrasting personal outcomes, all these characters are romance heroes because they are equally validated by the function of their actions.

DYSTOPIA AND ELEGY

The narratives and mood of these films made around the period of the Second World War (*Stagecoach* at the start of the European conflict in 1939, and *My Darling Clementine* at the end, in 1946) and the Korean War (*Shane* and *High Noon* in 1952) are closely connected to expectations between these times of future social and political reforms. The 1950s are marked by a powerful political conservatism and relative economic affluence in America and Europe. By the 1960s, heroic resolutions in Westerns change, along with the wider development of more cynical responses to post-War hopes explored in dystopian Westerns.

For instance, the eponymous heroes of the epic *The Professionals* (1966) are mercenaries who carry out a contract to return a kidnapped wife, only to release her when they discover her a willing captive. Though they deny their contracted quest, they succeed in a higher, moral quest for justice. They are therefore heroes of a romance narrative, since they release not a relieved captive wife but a resentful thwarted lover. But, as characters, they are marked by the cynicism of dystopian heroes, surviving as best they can in a world of self-interest. Faced with the failure of his plan to destroy the couple's romance, the furious, thwarted and tyrannical husband swears 'You bastard' at the leader (played by Lee Marvin) of the four professionals, who responds: 'In my case, an accident of birth. But you, sir, you're a self-made man'. The cynical humour corresponds with the social and political mood at the time of the film's production.

As the quest of 'the professionals' is explicitly mercenary, not social and moral like their romantic predecessors, they gain nothing for their pains beyond personal honour. Their quest is born of a lie and their function has no meaning beyond their violent skills. These heroes thus bear within them, more explicitly than before, the seeds of their own redundancy. Though the romance hero may or may not end up in settled partnership, the plight of the elegiac hero is that he ends his quest with nothing beyond his own society and pride. This is often despite his best efforts, because he must remain true to a code of honour seen as untenable in a changing world. The elegiac Western calls into question not only the action of the hero, but also his function. At the end of *The Professionals*, the eponymous four ride on, true to generic convention, but their direction is not specified, nor is their continuing affiliation confirmed. They appear as men out of time, their values separating them from the dominant attitudes of the world around them.

THE LIMITS OF ROMANCE

Heroic function seems to make for an uncertain romance, even where characters seem less than heroic. Cattle trail boss, Tom Dunson, in *Red River* (1948) behaves so badly that his cowboys mutiny. Yet his ostensible quest still succeeds, as they take his place in getting the cattle to market. It is only the manner in which the quest is pursued that is questioned, not the quest itself. The climax reveals that the true function of the quest is Dunson's spiritual journey to a self-knowledge previously lacking. Once he can acknowledge his obstinacy, the romance of his relationship with Matthew can be restored and the two can move on to a shared heroism. Even so, Pye argues that 'after *Red River*, Dunson-like characters become more and more common – anachronistic, morally problematic figures stranded in some sense by historical change, whose assertions of identity are increasingly undermined' (1996a, p.20).

This is certainly the case in the preponderant revenge Westerns from the 1950s onwards. In these, the hero acts for self rather than for greater social good. In *The Bravados* (1958), the hero (Gregory Peck) aggressively hunts down and kills a gang of criminals he wrongly believes raped and murdered his wife. At the end, when he learns of his mistake and acknowledges his crime, his conscience rather than the law exonerates him. His call for the prayers of townspeople, who congratulate him for ridding them of villainy, elevates him morally, despite his crime. Such 'Dunson-like characters' of revenge narratives become social heroes of romance because they are finally integrated into communities.

In this context, *The Searchers* (1956) presents the most severe test for the romance Western, since the revenge quest of its hero, Ethan Edwards (John Wayne), is driven less by an understandable if misguided righteousness than by a psychotic racism. Ethan seeks to avenge the death of a brother's unattainable wife, not by rescuing her captive daughter, Debbie (Natalie Wood), but by killing her. The quest is so foul that no romance Western could sanction it. Nor does *The Searchers*. Ethan's heroic role is displaced onto Martin Pawley (Jeffrey Hunter) (ibid., 1996b, p.262). Conventionally, as the sidekick, Martin has the secondary dramatic role. Against convention, however, he is made structurally central through his heroic actions. It is Martin who is always there to remind Ethan that the hero's task is to rescue the damsel in distress and to ensure that he returns her home intact. It is Martin who finally rescues Debbie and kills the villain.

Ethan's character and behaviour makes his final change of heart psychologically unfathomable (as indeed, does Debbie's change of heart, from desiring at first only to 'stay with my people', the Comanche, to next appearing happy to be rescued). Both changes of heart are explicable only in terms of the conventions of romance. The character of Ethan is ultimately softened in order to make his function support the just cause. However, the journey is as uncomfortable for the audience as it is for the characters. The psychology of the romance hero in revenge Westerns can render his function dangerously close to villainy, but in *The Searchers*, Ethan's heroism is ultimately restored by his subordination to the true cause of returning the prize, Debbie. When Ethan lifts the rescued Debbie in his arms and later carries her from his horse to her substitute home and family, there is no doubt it is he and not Martin who plays out the heroic role.

The Searchers is a landmark transitional Western, at the limits of romance dominating the genre in the first half of the twentieth century and an indication of the future genre developments in its latter half. From the 1960s onwards, the conventions of the romance Western are definitively altered. The genre changes under the impact of transformations in the wider culture and society, and the arising contradictions within itself. The seeds of the turn towards the dystopian Western are evident in scenes in *The Searchers* in which Ethan behaves more like a villain than a hero. But it also lies at times in exaggerations in the form of the film. A fast track in to a choker close-up on a character's response mark key moments within scenes, for instance when Ethan's family prepare for the Indian attack in his absence and when Ethan searches for Debbie among a group of captive white women.

The ending of the film, however, looks forward to the elegiac Western. Recall again the door closing on the retreating figure of the hero, abandoning him outside the new family home. As the dust rises, he walks away, destined to 'wander forever between the winds' like the soul of the dead Indian whose eyes he earlier shot out. The final image of *The Searchers* pre-empts the tragic irony of heroism in the elegiac Western – the hero is not just alone, but unwanted and unnecessary.

THE END OF THE OLD WEST

Cawelti argues that the 'basic premise of the classic Western was a recognition of the inevitable passing of the old order of things, reflected in the myth of the 'old West', together with an attempt to affirm that the new society would somehow be based on the older values' (1976, p.251). That the 'Old West' must some day die out is the cause of sentimental regret in romance Westerns from the earliest days. At the start of William S. Hart's last Western, *Tumbleweeds* (1925), he 'prophetically remarks . . . as the cattle herds leave the Cherokee Strip: "Boys, it's the last of the West"' (Parkinson and Jeavons, 1973, p.21). The elegiac Western moves beyond the occasional sentiment of 'a recognition', to represent centrally the experience of a changing culture and society. What determines the elegiac mood is that, in Cawelti's terms, the new Western society comes to reject not only older values, but also those who represent it. Or, as Pye puts it, 'The Wild West could produce heroes of romance . . . while the settled west could not' (1996a, p.20).

THE END OF THE GUNFIGHTER

Slotkin's monumental trilogy traces the history of the idea of the frontier in the production of America's national myths. The culmination of structuralist criticism of the Western, he firmly establishes the binary opposition between savagery and civilisation at its heart. The model is most applicable to the romance Western, where the hero's function is to subdue savagery and pave the way for civilisation. The elegiac Western subtly shifts that dynamic as the Old West comes to embody a 'lost civilisation' and the New West a savage modernity. The title of Slotkin's final volume, *Gunfighter Nation* (1992), places the image of the gunfighter at the centre of American identity. The gunfighter is also the first subject of the elegiac Western's interest in the process of change.

Among the first Westerns to interrogate the figure of the gunfighter is, fittingly, *The Gunfighter* (1950). The hero is the ageing, tired Jimmy Ringo (Gregory Peck), seeking to escape from his violent past into peaceful retirement, but unable to avoid confrontation with a succession of young gunfighters eager to make a quick reputation by killing him. The township in whose saloon bar he decides to stop drifting and await his fate is defined not only by the peaceful establishment of law and order but also by the trappings of a modern world. People shop and tend their front gardens. Children go to school, play in the streets and inquisitively stare through windows at this notorious man of the gun. The mise-en-scène of family and home is a cruel and ironic comment on Jimmy who waits, patiently clock-watching, for the appearance of a wife and child he previously abandoned. Just as his hopes are raised by the possibility of sanctuary in settlement, he is assassinated. In his death lies a moral. The killer's joy is momentary, for as 'the man who killed Jimmy Ringo', he now embarks on the same lonely, haunted career as his victim. *The Gunfighter*

John Wayne takes rifle, cushion and final leave from a distinguished film career, as John Books in the elegiac *The Shootist* (1976).

establishes a governing idea of the elegiac Western, that violence breeds not peace but only further cycles of violence, not romance but only death.

A similar plot situation and theme is evident in John Wayne's final role, as gunfighter John Books, in *The Shootist* (1976). The hero aims to end his days, not pining for a lost life on public display in a saloon like Ringo, but in quiet dignity in a respectable private house in Carson City, owned by single mother, Bond Rogers (Lauren Bacall). The gradual revelation that he is dying from cancer of the bowel leads her to put aside her reservations about housing a man of violence. The hero carries about with him both the symbols of his violent life and his new compact with death; a pistol and an embroidered cushion to ease his pain when at rest. But as the past reasserts itself, he chooses a more fitting way to die. First, an old girlfriend turns up, ostensibly to nurse him in his last days, but actually to extort what little money he has left, because, she claims, 'you owe me that, at least'. Secondly, the son of the house, Gillom (Ron Howard), shows too keen an interest in following in the hero's footsteps. Finally, he acknowledges that a life lived by the gun must sensibly die by it too. He sends out an invitation to three local villains to a stand-off in the local saloon.

His final trip to town makes character and actor seem monstrously out of place, with John Wayne's 'monumental' (Thomas, 1996, p.76) frame in wide-brimmed hat and dark suit. The township has modernised even more than in *The Gunfighter*, with milk delivered to the door on a float and the trip to the saloon taken by trolley car along a main street. In the grandly furnished saloon with a long, shaped bar, Books eventually shoots and kills three villains, but is himself finally shot in the back from an unsuspected quarter, the bartender. Gillom, observing the gunfight from the saloon doors like Joey at the climax to *Shane*, runs to assist the now debilitated hero by shooting the bartender. The future of the youth hangs in the balance, but Books persuades him to cast aside the gun to avoid having to live the life of violence like he, Jimmy Ringo and his assassin have led. The date is January 1901, the month of the death not only of John Books, but also of Queen Victoria and the end of a nineteenth century whose cultural values are lost to the modern age.

THE END OF JOHN WAYNE

The Shootist is as much 'a personal elegy' (Hardy, 1991, p.351) to John Wayne, the archetypal Western film star of so many classic Westerns, as an elegy to the passing of an associated culture. Wayne was suffering from the same cancer as the character he portrays in the film and died shortly after it was completed. The film opens with the violent biography of the character reflexively illus-trated by a montage of shots of Wayne firing guns in some of his earlier films. More than these explicit references, the nature of the hero in *The Shootist* is connected even more substantially to the actor's film career. The stereotype of the Wayne persona is of an independent, unbending action hero, with conservative politics allied to Wayne's own acknowledged Republican sym-pathies (Walker, 1970, pp.302–13). Yet, as Deborah Thomas has shown, the characters he played in a long and substantial film career inform a more complex and contradictory persona.

Wayne's characters tend to eschew the romance of female partnership, frequently because the women they love are dead before the films start (*She Wore a Yellow Ribbon*, 1949) or die at the start (*Red River, The Searchers*), the loss marking their characters in ways that determine the subsequent narrative. In Westerns directed by Howard Hawks such as *Red River* and *Rio Bravo* (1959), Wayne is one among the all-male group, the Hawksian 'elect' (Wood, 1998), with a task requiring professional skills to succeed. Throughout these roles, his 'toughness' comes not from a conventional physical strength but from psychological qualities: 'a massive assurance, an indomitable solidity' (Buscombe, 2000, p.25), self-reliance (Alexander Walker, 1970, p.304), a resolute 'sincerity of purpose' and a willingness to accept responsibility

(Thomas, 1996, p.79). However, in the films he made just before *The Shootist*, such as *Cahill* (1973), *The Cowboys* (1973) and *True Grit* (1969), he plays grandfatherly characters with younger characters in tow, a paternalist rather than a patriarch. These characters are protective, almost motherly, teaching a new generation the subtleties of honest survival. In all of these the young learn qualities of personal responsibility and endurance that mark not just the characters but also the career of the star. The Westerner as teacher and role model for callow youth is a feature of Westerns elsewhere, but markedly so from the 1970s onwards, notably in *The Culpepper Cattle Company* (1972) and *Barbarosa* (1982).

THE WEST AS ANACHRONISM

In the most elegiac of Westerns starring John Wayne, *The Man Who Shot Liberty Valance* (1962), these qualities in Wayne's persona bear the greatest meaning and emotional affect. Where the heroes of *The Gunfighter* and *The Shootist* are seen as out of time and place, director John Ford takes to tragic extremes the idea of the man of the West whose way with a gun excludes him from the civilised society he has helped to create. The film also exemplifies a shift within the elegiac Western from the gunfighter to the more generalised Westerner as tragic hero, a figure that combines associations of the ordinary (working (on) a ranch), the extraordinary (skilled with a gun) and the theatrical (dressed as a cowboy).

The heroic role is split into two characters in *The Man Who Shot Liberty Valance*. One is the good Westerner, Tom Doniphon (John Wayne), who destroys his own way of life when he secretly kills his alter ego, the wild bad Westerner, Liberty Valance (Lee Marvin). The killing leaves the way for the other hero, the good Easterner – teacher, lawyer and later state senator, Ransom Stoddard (James Stewart) – to reap the reward. The death of Valance enables the community, statehood and other civilising influences to flourish. Yet, in killing Valance, 'Doniphon has created a space for the growth of a civilised society in which he himself is unable to participate' (Wexman, 1993, p.116). Tom loses his status and the heroine, the woman of the West, Hallie (Vera Miles), to Ranse.

The irony is that it is the man of the East who is thought to have killed Valance in a gunfight, the act building a reputation that sees him go on to represent the town and the state in the senate. The truth is revealed in flashback, with Ranse finally acknowledging Tom's responsibility for the killing in a framing admission to journalists at Tom's pauper's funeral. Yet the newspaper editor uncharacteristically refuses to print the truth, saying: 'When the legend becomes fact, print the legend'. Despite the apparent suppression of truth, director John Ford reveals his own sadness at the necessary sacrifice. With Tom freed in death from his solitary misery, the final scene finds Ranse and Hallie returning home back east on a train. Their comforts satisfied by the railroad man, the tragic irony of his final line: 'Nothing's too good for the man who shot Liberty Valance' fills characters and audience alike with hurt.

The pervasive mood of *The Man Who Shot Liberty Valance* is sombre, a sense of enclosure expressed by interior studio scenes, largely standing in for the township. Tag Gallagher claims that 'everything speaks of age' (1986a, p.385), assisted by a slow narrative pace, extensive scenes of dialogue and choreographed, weary movements of the actors. Everything seems covered in dust, like the old stagecoach Ranse exposes as the one that originally brought him to town, or in ruins, like Tom's farmhouse that he burns in a drunken rage on losing Hallie. While the actors are aged by make-up in the framing sequences, no attempt is made to make them look as correspondingly young as the characters they play in the flashback central sequence. The tolling bell that calls the community together to celebrate the founding of the church, so full of promise for the future in *My Darling Clementine*, is here a death knell. Hallie talks about 'churches, high school, shops' but they are invisible to the spectator.

A central symbol of life amidst this decay is the cactus rose. The only plant life able to survive in the parched environment of the film's desert West, it is first given by Tom to Hallie as a gift of courtship. Hallie's gratitude puzzles Ranse, who compares it to the 'real rose' cultivated 'back East'. It is the first stage in a relationship that will eventually lead Hallie to choose Ranse and the oncoming modern world over Tom and the Old West. Years later, Hallie places a cactus rose on Tom's cheap coffin. Though returning the sentiment of the original gift, its meaning has now changed. Originally a symbol of a desert that irrigation and modernity will change into a Garden, it now stands for human values lost in legend. The only evidence of the modern world in the film is the train that opens and closes it, churning out thick black smoke that blots the landscape. Ford's commitment to the end of savagery is evident in the satisfaction of Valance's disposal, but a greater sentiment for the necessary passing of the Old West is reflected in the image of the cactus rose. Ford is not like the editor, perpetuating myths of the Old West, but committed to more complex truths within the legends. Ford's achievement is to accept that old ways must change even as he regrets their passing.

ELEGIAC WESTERN TOWNSHIPS

The new urban towns in *The Shootist* and *The Man Who Shot Liberty Valance* are mostly indifferent to the passing of their Western heroes. Only remaining associates bear witness and care. As with generations of working people whose achievements in life are rarely commemorated in death, the meaning of the Westerner in the elegiac Western is feared lost to history and merely a relic of personal memory. Significantly, in *The Shootist* and others of Wayne's final films, it is youth who bears the truth, so that the issue becomes more one of learning from, rather than protecting, the memory. The central conflict in the elegiac Western is the struggle between honouring traditions and the figures that embody them whilst also recognising the need to move on. In township Westerns, that conflict is often between the hero and a town cast as villain.

The town in *The Gunfighter* is curious about the gunfighter but not the man, and is therefore indifferent to Jimmy's plight. The exceptions are the marshal, who wants him to leave to avoid trouble, and the bartender, who wants him to stay for the extra business his reputation attracts. Such characters, full of self-interest rather than social responsibility, represent whole townships in later dystopian Westerns. In elegiac Westerns, when town leaderships rather than a larger, more compliant populace take exception to the ageing hero, it is evidence of an increasing self-interest among the larger, anonymous population created by that urban development.

Towns in elegiac Westerns of the 1960s are commonly governed by established law and order, yet continue at moments of crisis to display the worst attributes of their lawless past. Townspeople may respond to a crime against them like a mob rather than a community, resorting to their own defence by illegal means, especially lynch law. The situation is repeated in films directed by Delmer Daves, including *The Hanging Tree* (1959), *White Feather* (1955) and *The Badlanders* (1958). Perhaps the foulest township corruption is in *Death of a Gunfighter* (1969). Here, the hero is an ageing town sheriff, Patch (Richard Widmark), explicitly a 'hired hand' of the town council. Patch's violent frontier ways are considered in council meetings obstructive to profitable investment in the town. At first, the worthy local politicians unsuccessfully attempt to persuade and, thereafter, to bribe Patch to retire or move on. They then legally conspire against him in a failed attempt to use the territorial marshal to arrest him on fanciful charges. All legal means having failed, the last recourse is to assassination. When an ambush in a saloon bar leaves him scarcely alive, he staggers into the street, to be confronted and killed by the guns of surviving members of the town's council. The final death scene is extraordinary, as guns firing down from every concealed place in the main street set the town as a stage for a spectacular killing on the scale of Jacobean drama. With close-ups to identify every local councillor as a marksman, *Death of a Gunfighter* critically examines the new politics of a modernising America and finds it wanting. At the end, Patch, the victim of a dystopian township, is identified as the body in the coffin in the enigmatic opening scene. As the final credits roll, life on main street goes on.

In Steve McQueen's final Western, he plays the eponymous hero, *Tom Horn* (1980). Based on a real life character, opening titles sketch in Tom's considerable frontier history as a man who rode shotgun for a stagecoach line and who, as a cavalry scout, captured Geronimo in the Apache wars. However, at the opening of the film, the ageing Tom is searching for any work on offer, 'a vestige of that heroic era we've just about lost' as the opening title card suggests. When he comically misjudges his skills against the national heavyweight boxer he antagonises, Gentleman Jim Corbett (a further authentic name, but of urban legend), his natural skills of self-defence are too rusty, unschooled and lacking in modern method. Realising that he has overreached himself, he is happy to accept a simple cowboy job as the only employment on offer. Rancher John Coble (Richard Farnsworth), another old-timer, recognises Tom's worth and encourages him to accept a job offered by a confederation of local farmers to hunt down rustlers. Though the wealthy and besuited farmers at first tacitly agree to his frontier ways of violence, they turn against him in the face of press and public panic once the task is completed, and they encourage the law to take its course.

After a dubious trial, Tom is imprisoned and hanged. McQueen's performance dignifies the character, even as he makes him an enigmatic figure. Tom yearns for the landscape of an open range that is being parcelled up under the impact of modern farming. When he makes a forlorn escape from jail, he is quickly corralled like a wild horse before he reaches the outskirts of town. He then appears to conspire in his own death ('Suicide? Is that what I've been doing all these years?'), declining to defend himself at his trial and stoically, perhaps even wryly, accepting his fate on the scaffold. Though the authorities here, as in *Death of a Gunfighter*, require his death, there is a difference. Among the townsfolk, there is a reluctance to punish Tom that finally turns into an uneasy resistance at the hanging. Yet the Law and the Times overcome the will of the people, as if the structures and systems of the modern world, rather more than human agency, conspire to rid themselves of Tom and the Old West he represents.

THE DEATH WISH

Tom Horn would roam freely were it not for the intervention of modern systems of law and settlement. Yet, once caught up in a corporate world, Tom almost wills his own death. A violent death wish is explicit in other elegiac Westerns, particularly in heroes who are outlaws. *Butch Cassidy and the Sundance Kid* (1969) treats its itinerant robbers and tricksters in mostly comic mode. However, it freezes them in mid-frame and legend under the final credits as they rush from their hiding place, firing their guns towards the camera and the hordes of Bolivian soldiers they know lie in wait for them. Though the historical roots in the Hole-in-the-Wall Gang are common (Seydor, 1980, p.182), the light-hearted comedy of *Butch Cassidy and the Sundance Kid* contrasts with the graphically savage *The Wild Bunch* (1969), which explores the passing of a similar violent masculinity in epic form. Director Sam Peckinpah's dystopian vision of America in *Major Dundee* here turns into tragedy in the more local story of a group of ageing thieves who come to choose the manner of their own deaths.

The Wild Bunch opens with an attempted bank robbery in a small town just before the First World War. Signs indicate that the town is changing its name from San Rafael to Starbuck, an ironic comment on both the Americanisation of Texas border towns in 1912 when the film is set and the triumph of American capitalism in the twentieth century. The robbery goes badly wrong, and not just for the ageing outlaw gang whose criminal career gives the film its title. Bounty hunters and railroad detectives lie in wait on the rooftop above. Eager for the spoils that the bodies of wanted men with prices on their heads will bring, they fire indiscriminately into a crowd of passing churchgoers and bystanders around the retreating robbers. In the ensuing carnage, 'escalating past horror into a kind of feral exultation' (ibid., p.139), filmed in Peckinpah's characteristic slow-motion style, the gang's central figures escape. The opening scene establishes a modern world obsessed with financial gain, but unable to move beyond primitive savagery.

The depletion of the 'Bunch' in the failed robbery tests the faith of the survivors in their leader, Pike Bishop (William Holden). Yet the camaraderie of the thieves, on discovering their haul contains washers and not gold, contrasts with the primitive bickering among the degenerate bounty hunters, 'egg-sucking, chicken-stealing gutter trash', according to their leader, Deke Thornton (Robert Ryan). Deke longs for alliance again with the gang he must chase ('We're after men, and I wish to God I was with them'), especially with Pike, the former companion whose carelessness we learn from flashbacks led to Deke's capture. A condition of Deke's parole from imprisonment is his aid in the current pursuit. Uncomfortable with the task from the beginning, he will abandon it long before the end.

The film's central concern is how to preserve unity and honour, even among thieves, in a modern world that encourages individualism and deception. Pike's belief is in 'giving your word' and standing by it regardless, despite the common failures, errors of judgement and personal loss of everyday life. When tested, Pike powerfully insists 'We're going to stick together, just like it used to be. When you side with a man, you stay with him, and if you can't do that, you're like some animal. You're finished.' Paul Seydor writes affectingly of how the film intricately weaves character relations between the positive and negative poles of trust and deception, yet never simply affirms Pike's sentiments (ibid., pp.158–70). Dutch (Ernest Borgnine), 'the conscience of the Wild Bunch' (Peckinpah, quoted by Seydor, 1980, p.153), for instance, emphatically suggests that it is not giving one's word that counts but 'who you give it to!'

Far from being a man out of his time, like most heroes of elegiac Westerns, Pike is willing to adapt in order to survive. His answer to the stresses on the gang's unity is to 'start thinking beyond our guns. Those days are closing fast . . . What I don't know about, I sure as hell am going to learn.' In order to make one last heist before retirement, the gang ride into Mexico's revolutionary war, where they contract to steal rifles from a US munitions train for an army of Mexican bandits disguised as federales (Mexican military), led by the slow-witted but savage Mapache (Emilio Fernandez). This time, a successful and magnificently staged hold-up emboldens the gang, and they deal circumspectly with the treacherous Mapache at his camp in Agua Verde by trading the guns for money in stages.

In a central, gentle section, the gang take stock and rest up as 'guests of honour' (ibid., p.153) in the village of their youngest member, Angel (Jaime Sanchez). This touching scene suggests a haven is possible, but the final trade that will lead to it finds Angel detained in Agua Verde, now a limp body dragged grotesquely behind Mapache's car. Once again, the modern world brings a horror to equal any in the day of the horse. Outwitted and outnumbered, the gang can only offer to trade back their spoils for Angel. Mapache refuses, offering to pacify them with the pleasures of the flesh that so define his own life. When Pike responds with 'Why not?' it appears that he and the remaining three gang members concede.

In a tender scene bathed in morning light, Pike leaves all his money with a prostitute and her tiny baby. Exchanging glances among Dutch, Tector Gorch (Ben Johnson), and his brother, Lyle (Warren Oates), Pike reflexively echoes the last words of Wyatt Earp before facing the Clantons at the O.K. Corral in *My Darling Clementine*: 'Let's go'. There is a pause, pregnant with uncertainty and fear, then Lyle repeats Pike's earlier: 'Why not?' to signal mutual understanding. They strap on holsters and shoulder modern pump guns (their one concession to modernity), before striding purposefully, side by side, back into Mapache's army. The walk is accompanied by a suspenseful military drum roll that is suddenly silenced as they demand the return of their young friend. Under threat of the gun, Mapache seems prepared to acquiesce before cynically and horrifically slitting Angel's throat. In response, Pike shoots Mapache. The gang crouch and wait, prepared for an onslaught, until slowly appreciating that it need not come. They could safely walk away. They again look deep into each other's eyes and laugh as they realise their power. Pike stands up

Tector (Ben Johnson), Lyle (Warren Oates), Pike Bishop (William Holden) and
Dutch (Ernest Borgnine) of *The Wild Bunch* (1969) walk to their deaths.

straight and pointedly shoots a German Officer (Peckinpah's improbable
but symbolic European intruder, like the French lancers in *Major Dundee*),
triggering a slow-motion blood bath. The gang take their last stand around the
prized machine-gun from the train robbery, that earlier Mapache had sprayed
indiscriminately and comically. In a climax of unremitting violence, it leaves
the ground littered with bodies, including those of the Wild Bunch. Pike's
hand remains fixed around the trigger of the machine-gun pointing with
phallic and religious import at the sky, like a mythic Viking warrior, dying
with weapon in hand. Dutch, Tector and Lyle are splayed around him. This
extended sequence is mesmeric, intercutting action with slow motion shots
and a soundtrack at times diegetic, at others slowed down, with a chilling
manic laughter.

That the gang offer their lives in this violent manner is 'less an act of
heroism than a statement of their identity' (Hardy, 1991, p.319). The Wild
Bunch seek redemption through loyalty to friendship. Therefore, tragically
but inevitably, they face their deaths. Their cause is also reckless (Watson,
1998, p.10) and absurd: when Pike shoots the German officer, Angel (their
ostensible prize) is already dead. Seydor argues (1980, p.164) that Pike's
flawed agency in this is crucial 'to fulfil his reputation in spite of himself'. Pye
finds it typical of all Peckinpah's heroes 'who are frequently conventionally
morally dubious and/or whose values achieve positive force, sometimes

paradoxically, against a background of grotesque institutional violence and corruption' (1996b, p.262).

The film does not end here, but with a scene of black comedy, as the bounty hunters descend on the bodies, 'delighted the job will now be so easy', in a 'grotesque little spectacle of human avarice and opportunism at its most carnal' (Seydor, 1980, p.175). Deke is outside the walls of Agua Verde, at first alone (except for a couple of appropriately perching vultures) and then among the peons who harboured the gang with such tenderness. They will see to the other bounty hunters later and off-screen. As Deke wanders with the peons into a sandstorm, accompanied also by old-timer Sykes (Edmond O'Brien), who has been running horses for the gang, Sykes has the final line: 'It ain't like it used to be, but it'll do'. Their laughter merges with that of the gang, resurrected in earlier images reprised from the film. Old age survives as a subculture of 'reluctant . . . idealists' (ibid., p.180), outside and distant from the mainstream. Those who inhabit the condition knowingly must make their choices about the best way to live it out with honour and dignity. Even though the manner of their death is hidden from other characters in the film, the audience knows how the gang came to die. As the closing credits begin, the gang are reborn to ride into a fade to black and personal memory. The film looks back 'with romantic longing at characters who in turn are perpetually looking back' (Kitses in Kitses and Rickman, 1998, p.237).

A HYMN TO THE PASSING ORDER

The Westerns of director Sam Peckinpah are key elegiac westerns. *Guns in the Afternoon/Ride the High Country* (1962) is an earlier film that explores 'the tragic implications of the growth of civilisation' (Kitses, 1969, p.56) on the individual. For Pye: 'The power and control (over himself, others, the narrative) of the Western hero are . . . challenged . . . at its most extreme in Peckinpah's films, in which the protagonists are subject to the destructive and anonymous forces of a changing American society, their range of action finally limited in some cases to a choice of how to die . . . (1996a, p.18). Peckinpah expresses that choice in *Guns in the Afternoon/Ride the High Country* in terms of how best 'to enter your house justified', a religious expression cited by the hero, Steve Judd (Joel McCrea), as his father's guiding principle of living with dignity and honour.

Steve and Gil Westrum (Randolph Scott) are 'old men who only old men remember' (Lovell, 1967, p.99), anachronisms in the modern Western town, and they know it. But they deal with it in different ways. When Steve rides in, he is immediately out of place, shooed off the street by a policeman and nearly run over by a car; law and the modern world have come to the West. Humiliations do not stop there. His advanced years and threadbare clothes discourage his imminent employers, despite his reputation as a town tamer: ('I was expecting a much younger man.' 'I used to be. We all used to be'). Times may be hard for Steve but he retains his pride. Lured to the town by the prospect of work protecting a gold shipment ('it's better than tending bar'), he is disappointed to learn that its value is far less than predicted. Despite this, he keeps his failing eyesight private, waves aside objections, swallows his dignity and forces the commission.

Steve contrasts with Gil, who is first seen dressed up in Show outfit and running a crooked rifle range in a fairground. Falsely claiming to be the Oregon Kid, 'the last of the town tamers', Steve exposes his charade. If Steve's way of dealing with hard times in a new world is to continue righteously at his craft, Gil's approach is to deny his own biography and trade on myths of the Old West: 'It's easier than punching cows'. Out of an earlier respect for each other, the two team up, the more successfully to transport the gold from high up in the mountains, (the 'High Country' of the film's American release title). But Gil also intends to take the gold for himself, either by persuading Steve to his side or by force, 'if necessary'. For this purpose he takes along his unappreciative sidekick, the young Heck Longtree (Ronald Starr).

The film then becomes a journey Western, the three picking up Elsa Knudsen (Mariette Hartley), a runaway from her abusive father, Joshua (R.G. Armstrong), whose fundamentalist faith is treated as a sinister corruption of the pioneer spirit. Elsa claims the right to join the travellers, intent on marrying Billy Hammond (James Drury), a miner in Coarse Gold, their destination. On arrival, 'the Sodom and Gomorrah of Coarse Gold' (Kitses, 1969, p.156) turns out to be a slum of tents, with the savage and carnal Hammond Brothers intent on sharing Elsa on her wedding night in a brothel of surreal gaudiness. In the resulting rescue, Gil wants to confront the township, but Steve relies on the law to settle the dispute over the legitimacy of Elsa's marriage. Though principled, Steve's position leaves Elsa's fate in the balance, but Gil's pragmatic solution is to threaten the 'judge' who spoke the marriage vows, and hence effect Elsa's release; 'the delivery of the innocent from the savage forces' (ibid., p.158).

In pursuit, the Hammonds fail in their attempts to retrieve Elsa and kill her escorts. More seriously, though, will be a major confrontation between Steve and Gil. As the estimated sum of money expected from the miners decreases at stages of the journey, so Gil seems more and more determined to secure it for himself, even if it means stealing it from Steve. The friendship that was renewed, through easy talk of ageing gracefully with aching bones and tired bodies, turns sour as Gil questions the debt he feels society owes men like him. Steve's stand with the angels and Gil's with the devil is visualised in a scene in which the two bed down in Knudsen's barn, Steve in white long-johns and Gil in bright red, and in Gil's dialogue which refers to 'The Lord's bounty (that) may not be for sale, but the devil's is, if you're willing to pay the price'. The conflict between friendship and self-interest comes to a head when Steve prevents Gil and Heck from taking the gold at gunpoint: 'It all pointed this way, all that talk about . . . what we had coming but never got paid. I knew in my bones what you were aiming for, but I wouldn't believe it. I kept telling myself you were a good man, you were my friend.'

On the return journey home, the emphasis shifts from the maturing relationship between a chastened Elsa and a subdued Heck, to Steve's growing ill-treatment of Gil. Out of a sense of wounded pride, he refuses Gil his gun and keeps him handcuffed. The climax reunites the two, however, as they combine to face the Hammonds, who are holed up in Elsa's farmhouse after killing her father while at prayer at his wife's grave, and bent on further retribution. They are 'stung into defending their family honour openly' (ibid., p.156) by Steve's insult: 'You red-necked peckerwoods, damn dry gulchin' Southern trash' that inspires one of the brothers, Hector (Warren Oates), to

The ageing gunfighters of *Guns in the Afternoon/Ride the High Country* (1962), Steve and Gil (Joel McCrea and Randolph Scott) plot to confront the Hammond Brothers, with Heck and Elsa (Ronald Starr and Mariette Hartley) in the background.

shoot frenziedly but uselessly into a chicken coop. The brothers face Steve and Gil 'just like the old days', in a final stand-off, composed with the two groups facing each other at the most extreme edges of the CinemaScope frame. When it is over, the brothers are dead, redeemed somewhat by their willingness to leave the safety of their hiding places for a face-off, out of a sense of 'family pride'.

Steve also lies dying. The injured Heck is aligned now with Elsa, so the young have a future. Steve's earlier judgement, 'Boys nowadays, no pride, no self-respect. Plenty of gall but no sand', like so many other hasty judgements on the journey, is now denied. Gil promises to return the gold, 'just like you would have'. Steve responds: 'Hell, I know that, I always did. You just forgot it for a while, that's all'. As Seydor comments: 'The journey into the past is thus triumphantly completed, and with it Gil's redemption, which with almost classic inevitability, has taken the form of a rebirth in the wilderness' (1980, p.59). The final image has Steve, lying down, looking back 'out past the yellow and russet leaves of the forest to the far horizon, where the high country in all its savage majesty stands' (Kitses, 1969, p.159), before slipping out below the frame and into death.

Kitses' judgement that 'the elegiac tone of an autumnal world marks the passing of the old order' (ibid., p.159) refers as much to other Westerns directed by Sam Peckinpah. In the gentle *The Ballad of Cable Hogue* (1970), the cantankerous Cable (Jason Robards) is left for dead by his partners in a barren desert but literally falls upon scarce water. He turns his oasis into a watering hole for a stagecoach line that brings him the incredible devotion of a good woman (Stella Stevens) to assuage his desire for revenge. Just at the moment he realises he cannot carry out the deed, and decides to return to his lover, so fate steps in; 'he dies trying to stop a car as he would stop a horse' (Hardy, 1991, p.322). The prayers said over his grave provide a eulogy to Peckinpah's heroes: 'Take him, Lord, but knowing Cable, I suggest you don't take him lightly'.

In the 'languorous dirge, a drifting death-poem' (Kitses in Kitses and Rickman, 1998, p.224) of the much darker *Pat Garrett & Billy the Kid* (1973), the young outlaw, Billy (Kris Kristofferson) is killed by Sheriff Pat (James Coburn) against his better judgement and in the face of Billy offering himself, Christ-like, to his guns (an image echoing the final scene of the earlier *The Left Handed Gun*, 1958, with Paul Newman as Billy and John Dehner as Pat Garrett). Billy represents an Old West that must be killed off because of the threat it poses to the modern corporate world. But Pat's uneasy role in the death is also unacceptable to those who hired his guns. He is assassinated by the same corporation that hired Pat to kill Billy. Richard Combs speaks for all Peckinpah's heroes when he claims that: 'Peckinpah's Westerns . . . are not tied to a sentimental conception of history but to needs and choices that always confront Peckinpah's Westerners as they age . . . Garrett's struggle with freedom and integrity, age and change, survival and adaptation, are what make him (a) tragic hero' (Combs, 1989, p.262).

THE SOCIAL HERO

Pye argues that: 'Peckinpah has plenty of less extreme antecedents. There is less and less sense of the West offering freedom or escape – because of the encroachment of civilisation and/or because there can be no escape from the contradictions of the self. The hero becomes . . . the product of a social past, not the asocial, archetypal worlds of the "West"' (1996a, p.18). This is most evident in elegiac Westerns of the 1970s, like *Wild Rovers* (1971) and *Monte Walsh* (1970), which focus on the working life of the cowboy, rather than on the mythic figures of gunfighter, outlaw or 'town tamer'.

In *Monte Walsh*, scenes echo classic paintings by Frederic Remington and Charles Marion Russell (the latter explicitly, behind opening credits). Lee Marvin and Jack Palance play cowboys, initially among ranch-hands, whose easy-going camaraderie celebrates the cowboy life. But work dries up as Eastern capital displaces their labour with new methods and machinery. As more and more men are laid off, one old-timer at risk of losing even the meagre livelihood that comes from mending fences, ends his days by riding his horse over a cliff. Others resort to rustling cattle or petty thieving to make a living. Palance's character joins the petit-bourgeoisie and opens a store. Marvin's character can no more face the indoor life than accept a job offered as 'Texas Jack Barrat' in a Wild West Show. Unlike Gil in *Guns in the Afternoon/ Ride the High Country*, this hero 'ain't spitting on my whole life'. Social observation then recedes as genre conventions take over. Palance is shot and killed by an unemployed cowboy, whereupon Marvin becomes a gunman and seeks revenge. The climactic confrontation takes place in a dark abattoir, an ironic metaphor for the general working conditions of the cowboy labourer and also for the low value society places on that labour.

That being a cowboy is no more than just a menial labouring job for working class men is made explicit in *The Culpepper Cattle Company* (1972), where one cowboy says that what he does is 'what you do when you can't do nothing else'. Here, life on the cattle trail in its last days starkly contrasts with the romantic images in the head of the young hero, the cook's apprentice, dubbed 'Little Mary' (Gary Grimes) by the cowboys. That the cowboy life is unremittingly hard, with long hours, saddle sores and routine labour, is suggested in earlier romance Westerns like *Cowboy* (1958). *The Culpepper Cattle Company*, however, is one of the 'mud and rags' school (Buscombe, 1988, p.51) of Westerns, and further authenticates the cowboy's lot in scenes of common workplace harassment and bullying of men and cattle. Some cowboys leave the trail when violence is threatened ('I ain't no gunman') and others die haunting, explicit deaths in random accidents as much as in the final gunplay.

A variation of the social hero features in *The Hired Hand* (1971), a 'superb evocation of the rigours and essential aimlessness of frontier life' (Hardy, 1991, p.332). Director Peter Fonda also plays the nomadic cowboy, Harry, who, witness to the macabre sight of the body of a young girl floating down a river, decides to return to his settled wife (Verna Bloom) and son several years after abandoning them. Scenes of movement through stunning, verdant Western vistas are presented in almost abstract montages of dissolves. The visual elegy continues through scenes of farm work, including mending the sails of a watermill and clearing the land. The initial uncertainties of the wife about her husband's return are allayed by his work as the hired hand of the film's title, which convinces her of his intention to stay. He moves from bunking out in the barn to return to the marital bed. This is the signal for his sidekick, Harris (Warren Oates), to move on.

In amongst these bucolic scenes, the film has two sequences of visceral violence. Early, the two cowboys wreak revenge on the killing of a friend in a clumsy assassination attempt that leaves the killer with bullet holes in his feet. Later, the incident returns to haunt both men, when a messenger bears Harris' little finger, torn from his hand in order to smoke Harry from his haven and back to the scene of the crime. The wife fears he intends to abandon her again, but his intentions mean little when he is killed in the ensuing gunfight. Harris survives to return, with the impression left that he will take Harry's place. Even the names suggest that, in the end, one cowboy is much the same as another. As the wife says: 'It could as well as have been either of you'. The film's elegy lies in its haunting mood of ordinary life amidst rural beauty, arbitrarily disrupted by horror and violence.

THE LAST COWBOYS

Heroes of elegiac Westerns, whether gunfighters or lawmen, outlaws or cow-boys, are more consciously figures of their time and role, often aware of their own history and society. Unlike the mythic heroes of romance Westerns, whether nomads like Shane or town tamers like Wyatt Earp in *My Darling Clementine*, their social function in a modern world is invariably called into question and found wanting. From the 1960s onwards, a cycle of contem-porary Westerns – set in the period in which they are made – tell stories about the last Westerners, barely surviving the twentieth century on the edges of society, in a limited culture sustained by a select few. Gallafent considers them films that ask questions about a modern America. After 'the process of settlement has long been concluded', choosing to be 'some kind of Westerner' poses problems when 'the penalties imposed on those who try to make it are becoming so great that they cannot be endured, or entail sacrifices that seem not to be worthwhile' (1996a, p.243).

Some of these modern Westerns are comedies, like *The Rounders* (1965), whose cowboy heroes desire settlement, but always find the lure of the open range too attractive, even if their attempts at bronco-busting descend into farce. Others are dystopian Westerns, like *Hud* (1962), whose eponymous hero would rather sell his diseased cattle for a quick financial killing than burn and bury the herd to prevent an epidemic, as his father has done. Most contemporary Westerns, though, take their elegiac cue from the honourable father rather than the cynical son.

Such films attracted writers and directors interested in social criticism more than the challenges of generic convention, such as celebrated dramatist Arthur Miller in his script for *The Misfits* (1961). The story concerns a group of cowboys, reduced to earning a living by chasing down wild horses, worth in a modern world only the price of their meat for dog food. The animals are the 'misfits' of the film's title, but only as much as 'the ill-assorted group of loners and no-hopers who live from rounding them up' (Petley in Buscombe, 1988). The all-male group attempts to maintain a cowboy lifestyle in what little open range is left in a modern America, sectioned off into urban, agricultural and national parkland areas. But the addition of a woman on one of their chases acts as a catalyst to their all-male culture, exposing their cowboy craft as an offensive, archaic cruelty. *The Misfits* represents the ways of the Old West as corrupting those who seek to sustain them out of time and place in a modern world.

The film features the last performances of two great stars of the classical Hollywood period, Clark Gable and Marilyn Monroe. In his youth, Gable's star persona was that of the quintessential modern man but as he aged, he brought gravitas to roles in Westerns like *Across the Wide Missouri* (1950) and *The Tall Men* (1955). By the time *The Misfits* was released, his death from cancer made his role more tragic in the film, as a failure looking for one last success before retirement. Monroe's well-publicised emotional breakdowns on set foreshadow her subsequent death and putative suicide from a drug over-dose. Knowing this makes her final extraordinary outburst in the film more poignant. She seems to be attempting to free herself from the same ropes that the exhausted male group have thrown around a horse to bring it to its knees. The sense of entrapment in her performance is perhaps as much a comment on her own life as it is on her character, a woman finding a voice to resist the controls of a male-centred culture. Her role and persona function in the film as a force of nature and innocent sexuality (Dyer, 1987, pp.37–8), making the character a female embodiment of the untamed rural landscape that Western heroes are always posited against. In *The Misfits*, however, woman, horse and landscape together reject the culture of the traditional Western hero.

Where *The Misfits* plays out the action of its story on stark salt flats, the drama in *Lonely are the Brave* (1962) contrasts images of urban consumerism against a more neutral natural environment. The film is scripted by Dalton Trumbo, one of several Hollywood writers whose careers were stalled during political investigations of suspected communist sympathisers in the 1950s. Unsurprisingly, therefore, *Lonely are the Brave* deals with a man out of place in and harassed by his society. It opens with the hero, Jake Burns (Kirk Douglas), waking under an airplane's vapour trails in the skies of the morning, and then tricking his horse into its saddle. That the animal is hobbled suggests the untamed wildness of the creature; that a cowboy is no longer able so easily to control it suggests a new loss of power in the Western hero. This is confirmed when the rider barely manages to prompt his frightened, rearing horse across a carriageway, to pull up beside a scrap metal yard piled high with cars. The opening images establish the film's major conflict between free movement and the constrictions of a wasteful modern consumerism.

The film tells the story of a hero unable to settle in an urban society. With few social ties, his attempt to free a friend imprisoned for assisting illegal Mexican immigrants leads to his own imprisonment. Unable to tolerate incarceration, he breaks free and finds himself in a cat and mouse chase over the mountains with the police, led by a lugubrious police chief, Morey Johnson (Walter Matthau). Though hunted by the superior transport of a force in cars, jeep and helicopter, the cowboy always manages to outthink the modern 'posse', keeping his horse one step ahead. Just as he has Mexico in his sights, he comes to another road, where the animal that has provided the means to elude the law on the open range now brings about his literal downfall.

The final scene is set in the dark and pouring rain, the headlamps of oncoming vehicles blinding the rider. A lorry, whose journey enigmatic-ally punctuates the action throughout the film, knocks Jake from his skittish horse. Scarcely conscious, the cowboy hears the animal's agony, as he realises the truck contains lavatory bowls. The chase is over and a lesser modern world has won, 'a world so fragmented, so composed of impassable borders . . . in which no one achieves sustained contact with anyone else' (Gallafent, 1996a, pp.244–5). The hero is 'the last real cowboy, lost in the realities of the jet age' (Hardy, 1991, p.281).

ELEGIAC COMEDIES

Two contemporary Westerns of the 1970s explore the comedy rather than the tragedy of 'the last real cowboy'. *Kid Blue* (1973) parodies his existential plight, with Dennis Hopper as a modern Westerner who fails to emulate his ancestors, either as an outlaw (his attempt to rob a train ends with him falling from the roof) or as a businessman (he ends up checking a conveyor belt of Santa Claus ashtrays). The more whimsical *Rancho Deluxe* (1974) finds the hero and his mixed-race sidekick (played by Jeff Bridges and Sam Waterston) as small-time rustlers hunted down by an old-timer played by Slim Pickens. Underlying the comedy of both films, however, is a sadness about the decline of the Old West, with an encroaching commercialism of which even old Western films and television series are seen as a part.

THE LAST WESTERNERS

Gallafent argues that the West of modern Westerns 'is a natural world that is strangely diminished and unable to sustain itself' (1996a, p.254). The rodeo film, a sub-genre of the Western, tackles the same subject. There are occasional contemporary Westerns about modern rodeo from the 1940s onwards. Some are romantic comedies, like *A Lady Takes a Chance* (1943) with John Wayne, and *Sky Full of Moon* (1952), set in the gambling city of Las Vegas. Among notable dramas in the 1950s, *Bronco Buster* (1952) is an early film directed by Budd Boetticher. Another, *The Lusty Men* (1952) directed by Nicholas Ray, explores the character and narrative conventions that make the rodeo Western a supreme variant of the elegiac Western. It features Robert Mitchum as an ageing rodeo competitor, eager to settle down, but unable to retire from the arduous demands of the competition circuit. The fragility of life on the circuit is visualised in Ray's treatment of a rodeo ring perpetually shrouded in dust lifted by swirling wind. Around the ring are other professionals, such as circuit managers and administrators behind the scenes. Their interests are commonly seen to coincide more with that of a voyeuristic audience, 'an anonymous mass . . . one large component of a machine whose appetite is spectacle and danger, and which runs without regard for the particular human material it devours' (Perkins, 1981, p.1145). The hero is trapped in the Show world of the rodeo ring, a man whose life is defined by the dangerous risks he takes in rendering his virile masculinity as an entertainment spectacle. He 'is like the bull in being contained within the structures of the rodeo; his image too is framed, hemmed in, by the wooden posts of the bull-pen' (ibid., p.1145). Mitchum's character will finally die in the ring, his name immortalised by the manner of his death rather than in any worthy mortal achievement.

In a cycle of rodeo Westerns in the 1970s, the tragic rodeo narrative develops even greater elegiac force. James Coburn plays an egocentric rodeo star in *The Honkers* (1971), whose commitment to the masculine culture of the ring isolates him from a domestic world; he abandons his marriage, and is in turn abandoned by family and best friend. In *J.W. Coop* (1971), Cliff Robertson's equally obsessed character sees the winning of a national rodeo competition as an aim that will exonerate him from a life of crime. *When the Legends Die* (1972) sees Richard Widmark as a rodeo veteran teaching a young Frederic Forrest 'the ways of the world as well as of the rodeo ring' (Hardy, 1991, p.341). In all these films, the masculine lure of a rodeo circuit diminishes the hero, making him a relic of the Old West he represents.

A central rodeo drama is *Junior Bonner* (1972), in which Steve McQueen plays the hero of the title, 'set squarely in an unheroic present' (ibid., p.339). Like heroes of rodeo Westerns elsewhere, Junior's body is riven with pain from broken bones and other recurrent injuries caused by falls in the ring. Like them too, he longs for release and settlement away from the demands of exposing his ageing body to further and more permanent injury. But Junior's past behaviour and reputation constantly thwart his good intentions. When he returns to the family home, old associates are typically suspicious. An old girlfriend has long given up on the promises he makes when regularly returning to renew their relationship.

His terminally ill father is the wastrel Junior will become in just a few years time. Against his family's advice, Junior releases the old man from a nursing home, intent on returning some dignity to his father's declining days. But in the familiar surroundings of their old home, things rapidly go wrong. Like son, the father soon returns to dissolute ways. Like father, the son reverts to nomadic ways and Junior abandons his responsibilities yet again.

THE END OF THE WESTERN

The cycle of rodeo Westerns of the 1970s represents a summative comment on the elegiac Western. The masculinity of the rodeo hero is of a kind that distances him from modern society and female culture. A single-minded focus on winning or excelling in the ring brings only the reward of lost allegiances beyond it. He may have the experience and wisdom of age but is invariably foolish, in a state of perpetual arrested development. To survive, he must become a parody of his former self, seen at its extreme in the hero (Robert Redford) of *The Electric Horseman* (1979). Here, he earns a living dressed in a Show outfit bedecked by sparkling lights, parading on his horse through the gambling casinos of Las Vegas, advertising a breakfast cereal. Even without the absurd visual trappings, the hero of the elegiac rodeo Western turns into a cruel parody of a past frozen in commercialised myth.

The form and conventions of the elegiac Western appear fitting comment on the last stages in popularity of a previously mass popular genre. The Western hero is out of time and place, psychologically and socially reduced because 'the authentic life, the autonomous self, are no longer possible. Style has replaced substance, the frontier a stage with a cast of drifters, unhinged, heroes without a referent' (Kitses in Kitses and Rickman, 1998, p.224). The modern Westerner adopts the role 'as a form of retreat or withdrawal . . . aware of the possibility of . . . irrelevance to the modern world' (Gallafent, 1996a, p.249). Both the modern Westerner and so too the Western genre become history in a modern world. Fortunately for the continuation of the genre, however, that's only how it feels to the elegiac Western.

CHAPTER TEN

The Revisionist Western

Revisionist Westerns are 'films that in whole or part interrogate aspects of the genre such as its traditional representations of history and myth, heroism and violence, masculinity and minorities' which Jim Kitses (in Kitses and Rickman, 1998, p.19) then goes on to argue 'can be seen now to make up the primary focus of the genre.' How can films that 'interrogate' 'traditional representations' 'make up the *primary* focus' of the genre? Since all Westerns (like all genre films) must be both recognisably similar to and yet different from others (as Neale, 1980, p.40, says, functioning 'to produce regularised variety'), all Westerns must to some extent revise. Perhaps this 'primary focus' on films that 'interrogate . . . traditional representations' is more a consequence of film criticism than the empirical history of the genre. Though some Westerns are inevitably more reflexive than others, more reflective and self-conscious about manipulating generic form and meaning, it is criticism that detects significant generic changes that make any western 'revisionist'.

Take the case, for instance, of one of the most popular Westerns in the last decade of the twentieth century, *The Last of the Mohicans* (1992). The interracial heroes and active heroine could be considered revisionist when compared to 'traditional representations' of interracial conflict and passive heroines (to say nothing of Hollywood's more recent anglophobia, shown in its characterisation of English aristocrats and officers as ignorant and intolerant). Yet *The Last of the Mohicans* is otherwise a Western squarely in the romance tradition. Its spectacular scenery and events are the setting for romantic character relationships, with a thrilling quest narrative that validates its hero upon the successful rescue of the heroine. In the final death of Chingachgook's son, the last Mohican of the title, the sense of loss and regret also makes it an elegiac western. The pleasures of *The Last of the Mohicans* owe more to the traditional splendour of these generic qualities, and to the original novel and film of the same name, than to any substantial generic revision.

The Last of the Mohicans is a recent Western, but that does not make it re-visionist. What is more remarkable is that its traditional generic pleasures can still command the attention of a contemporary audience. This final chapter examines a tradition of notable revisionist Westerns that dot the landscape of the genre. Like all the preceding chapters, it is again concerned with history, with those Westerns that make significant revisions to developments in the genre such that a film like *The Last of the Mohicans* can take the form it does.

REFLEXIVE WESTERNS

Among the most popular of 1990s Westerns, *City Slickers* (1991) and its sequel, *City Slickers II: The Legend of Curly's Gold* (1994), reprise the classic genre comedy, founded by actors such as Buster Keaton in *Our Hospitality* (1923), Bob Hope in *The Paleface* (1948), and even Kenneth More in the British *The Sheriff of Fractured Jaw* (1958). In all of these, urban 'greenhorns' adrift in the rougher masculinity of the West learn to accommodate themselves to cowboy ways. Another comedy Western of the 1990s, *Maverick* (1994), reproduces the spirit of the much earlier television series, providing cameo roles for the actor in its original title role, James Garner, and a string of aged Western character actors from earlier times, like James Coburn and Denver Pyle. It is also a homage to Yakima Canutt, the series Western star best known for devising and performing some of the most spectacular stunts in Westerns. Yet more reflexive is *Three Amigos!* (1986), with a trio of singing cowboys from a 1930s Western series mistaken by a Mexican village for genuine gunfighters and called upon to perform heroics on a par with those of *The Magnificent Seven* (1960). More explicitly, *Rustler's Rhapsody* (1985) satirises the singing cowboy, with anachronistic jokes such as the hero commenting with surprise on the film's opening shift from monochrome to colour and his charming display of faith that his fate will 'turn out alright' because it always does in Westerns.

None of these films is as affectionate, satiric or penetrating in its comedy, however, as the earlier *Hearts of the West/Hollywood Cowboy* (1975). Set in the 1930s, Jeff Bridges plays a character hiding among a Western film crew to escape pursuit from gangsters. There, 'gazing at the tawdry neon spires of Hollywood' (Hardy, 1991, p.347), he learns that the tricks of acting and performing stunts for series Westerns is no glamorous occupation, but requires skill and hard labour. The culture of movie-making is finally validated in the climax when the appearance of the veteran star actor (Andy Griffith), dressed in full Show costume, sees off the armed gangsters with a gun loaded only with blanks. These reflexive Westerns demonstrate that Hollywood itself holds the series Western in affectionate memory.

CORRECTING THE MYTH AFTER THE ELEGY

Although the elegiac Western 'loudly declared the final closing of the frontier, both literal and metaphorical, and . . . left their protagonists dead or pathetic vestiges of a vanished time' (Worland and Countryman, 1998, p.187), the Western survived the decline of the elegiac cycle by the 1980s in more than reflexive comedies. Since then, the mythology of Western folklore has been returned to with a new spirit. The subsequent cycle of Westerns owes debts to revisionist histories of the foundation myth, in particular to the framework of critical approaches found in New History. Revisionist Westerns find less to celebrate and more to condemn in American history, which makes them inclined to deal more circumspectly with the history of the Western imaginary. Though not every revisionist Western has a figure like Beauchamp, the dime novelist in *Unforgiven* (1992), to witness the action, they do deploy strategies to deal just as reflexively with both American history and the history of the Western film.

LEGENDARY WESTERNERS

Revisionist Westerns re-scrutinise the reputations of Western legends. The cast list includes familiar lawmen, outlaws, gunfighters and even Western film actors from a century of Westerns. Among lawmen, the figure of Wyatt Earp, so celebrated as an agent of civilisation in 1946 and *My Darling Clementine*, whose reputation is reinforced in *Gunfight at the O.K. Corral* (1956), becomes a man who bends the law to his own purposes by 1967 and *Hour of the Gun*. The famed Gunfight that climaxes the former films opens the latter in a squalidly one-sided affair, presaging its staging in *Doc* (1971), where the Clantons are presented not as villains but innocent victims of the Earp's guns. In this film, Wyatt (played by a sloe-eyed Harris Yulin) seeks to use his reputation only to further a political career.

New history claims that just one Clanton son was present at the Corral and that Old Man Clanton died several months before, so other figures must emerge to confront the Earps in more recent films like the epic *Wyatt Earp* (1994). Though 'the Earps' trajectory towards Tombstone through a series of business deals involving saloons, gambling, prostitution, professional protection, and mining suggests more than most Westerns are willing to admit about the settlement of the West as an entrepreneurial rather than a civilising endeavour' (Dowell, 1995, p.7), the film does not avoid the celebratory tone that the earliest film versions took from biographies of the late 1920s. Director Lawrence Kasdan claims that the Earp clan operate in the film like the mafia family of Mario Puzo's *The Godfather* (1969), as the words of Wyatt's father (Gene Hackman) indicate: 'The closer you keep your family, the better. Nothing counts so much as blood. The rest are strangers.' Wives are sidelined in *Wyatt Earp*, as they are in *The Godfather*, but whereas Michael Corleone is corrupted by the culture of machismo and family honour, Wyatt ends up apparently unaffected by the cult of family.

In yet another recent exploration of the Earp legend, *Tombstone* (1993), the Gunfight neither opens nor climaxes the film but is buried about the middle. It is a squalid affair, the Earps massacring cowboys with little will to fight (and incidentally, an inability to shoot straight). The film opens with the clearest statement of the economic and social conditions behind Western expansion, in Robert Mitchum's narration: '1879. The Civil War is over and the resulting economic explosion spurs the great migration West'. Then, fiction takes over, in reference to: 'the earliest example of organised crime in America. They call themselves The Cowboys'. As in *Wyatt Earp* the West of *Tombstone* shares the culture of the modern urban crime film. At the end, the surviving Earps turn vigilante.

Successive versions of the Wyatt Earp story (Gallafent, 1996b, pp.302–11) are clearly critical responses to new histories of the Earp brothers: *Tombstone*, in particular, 'suggests that the West wasn't won by collective morality but by greed and violence' (Grist, 1996, p.294). They are also reflexive responses to earlier films and explorations of changing mores of their day. *Tombstone* refers to its own generic history by framing its story with shots from the early tableaux film, *The Great Train Robbery* (1903). The relationship between Wyatt and the consumptive Doc Holliday grows more intense with each film in this history until, in *Tombstone*, Doc's dedication to the friendship verges on the homoerotic.

At the end of *Wyatt Earp*, Kevin Costner's Wyatt, with a new wife, looks forward to a Hollywood career, surely a reference to Earp's reputed time befriending early Western film-makers. *Tombstone* ends with silent Western stars William S. Hart and Tom Mix as pallbearers at Earp's funeral. Earp is alive and in Hollywood in the modern Western, *Sunset* (1988), set in 1929 during the transfer to sound cinema. More a critique of Hollywood than of the Western, James Garner plays Wyatt, hired as technical adviser on a Western production starring silent star, Tom Mix (Bruce Willis). Garner plays Earp as a game-playing hedonist and Willis offers Mix as talentless and narcissistic. History and legend are equally, comically, bankrupt.

ROMANTIC OUTLAWS

If the Wyatt Earp legend is treated over time with increasing cynicism, successive films about outlaws like Jesse James and Billy the Kid have found it harder to lose the romantic legend. The reputation of the criminal James Gang was reported sympathetically in a book by John Edwards, *Noted Guerrillas or the Warfare of the Border* (1877) and provides the approach in the most popular version, *Jesse James* (1939), and as late as *The True Story of Jesse James/ The James Gang* (1957). By the time of *The Great Northfield Minnesota Raid* (1971), Jesse (Robert Duvall) is clearly unhinged and a selfish criminal, far from the earlier Robin Hood image. The poor old widow who the classic Jesse saves from destitution is here murdered for her money. Most recently, *The Long Riders* (1980) returns brothers Frank and Jesse (played also by brothers, Stacy and James Keach) to romantic outlawry.

William Bonney fares better, but that may be because there was little initial sympathy for him. He is a villain in the biography written in the year of his death, but romance Westerns are more influenced by Walter Noble Burns' *The Saga of Billy the Kid*, published in 1926 (Buscombe, 1988, p.66). The Billy of *Billy the Kid* (1930) is an innocent. Paul Newman plays him 'as a martyred illiterate' in *The Left Handed Gun* (1958), while in *Pat Garrett and Billy the Kid* (1973), Kris Kristofferson makes him a working class hero, terrorising only wealthy landowners, who accepts 'the consequences of his own myth, no matter how unreal, even though it means his death' (scriptwriter Rudolph Wurlitzer, quoted by Combs, 1989, p.262). In *Young Guns* (1988), however, Billy is once more the romantic hero, leader of a gang of lawmen fated to ride into elegiac myth. Oddly, in the lesser sequel, imaginatively titled *Young Guns II* (1990), Billy (Emilio Estevez) becomes a psychotic killer.

New history establishes that the legends of Western figures like Wyatt Earp and Billy the Kid emerge from their association with one of several range wars during the later periods of Western settlement. Range wars inform many outlaw Westerns, especially, but also settlement Westerns, like *Shane* (1952), and ranch Westerns, like *Man Without a Star* (1955). In the latter, barbed wire becomes a symbol for the violence involved. In all these films, though, the social forces that produce the range wars tend to be repressed. This is not the case with one of the last great epic Westerns, *Heaven's Gate* (1980). The film is a major revisionist Western, exploring the Johnson County War, not through legends like Earp or Bonney, but through ordinary people caught up in the political conditions that underlie the conflict.

THE LAST GREAT EPIC WESTERN

The number of epic Westerns inevitably diminishes with the decline in Western genre production from the 1970s onwards. Of the few, *Heaven's Gate* is remarkable. The film's production difficulties and huge over-expenditure famously bankrupted United Artists and, at 219 minutes in its director's cut, its length did not help it find a popular audience. Despite this, the film is a major tragedy, subversively exploding the foundation myth of America's frontier history.

The film opens unconventionally, with a graduation ceremony at America's prestige university, Harvard, in 1870. The new élite graduates revel in their manifest destiny to spread a 'civilisation' explicitly identified as their own WASP culture across the country. The appeal to 'Go West, young man' is not lost on either of the two most popular students, James Averill (Kris Kristofferson) and Billy Irvine (John Hurt). Averill is a favourite among women, attracted to him by his manly courtesy and sensitivity, whereas Irvine is admired for his wit and rebellious way with words. Like the Douglas Fairbanks characters in Westerns some sixty years earlier, Averill goes West for youthful masculine adventure. Irvine's effeminacy offers a contrary masculinity, but his zeal scarcely conceals a greater conservatism: in a valediction to the immediate educational class that hears him and the privileged social class he speaks for, Irvine claims to see no need for change in a world 'on the whole well arranged'. Their gentle masculinities and élite class position make them unlikely heroes of a Western.

The naive complacency of the pair is exposed when, some twenty years later, they are both caught up in the notorious Johnson County Wars. Averill's journey to Wyoming reveals that all is not equal on the frontier. He arrives at the station in an empty first-class carriage, while others travel on the roof of a cattle wagon and in a carriage labelled 'emigrant car'. The scene neatly establishes an alternative to the pioneer equality of the foundation myth in unequal power relations between racial and social classes. The emigrants are Eastern European families enticed West by false government promises of the 'heaven's gate' they will find there. A following scene makes evident the hard time to come, in which Nate Champion (Christopher Walken) casually shoots an emigrant butcher in the stomach. The town that Averill finds himself in is like no makeshift frontier town of other Westerns, but an urban sprawl, complete with smoke-filled industries and packed streets. This is no pastoral scene, no promised land, but a setting of industrial nightmare.

It emerges that the killing of the butcher is a response to attempts by an immigrant farming community to establish their own internal economy, working for themselves rather than as wage labourers for the Stockgrowers' Association, an organisation of wealthy and unscrupulous WASP employers. The Association hires gunmen like Nate to carry out a terrorist campaign against the immigrant economy. Averill is the US Marshal bound by duty, though not by consent, to enforce the law that sanctions the campaign. His ambivalence is echoed in Nate. Although killing the butcher suggests savagery, his subsequent refusal to kill a boy caught stealing a steer produces a

By the 1980s, the West of the Western has become an industrial nightmare:
Averill (Kris Kristofferson) arrives at *Heaven's Gate* (1980).

brief moment of conscience, possibly inspired by recognising in the boy his
own immigrant origins and childhood.

As Brian Wooland notes (1996, p.282), both the ambivalent hero Averill
and anti-hero Nate are denied heroic action since they are equally bound up
in the social and economic forces that power the destiny of the immigrants
and other small people around them. *Heaven's Gate* offers its audience no
respite from the consequences of this awful logic. Despite the temporary hope
raised in a spectacular roller-skating scene, which draws the entire community
together to celebrate the unity their labours promise, they are slowly starved
into submission. When some take to stealing cattle for food, all are massacred
by the gunfighters, mercenaries paid for the task, in virtual class war. Following the massacre, Nate is ambushed by other mercenaries sent by the
Association to deal with dissenting voices. Witness to the horrors, Irvine
proves to have the conscience, but not the power or will to act, taking to the
refuge of alcohol to bring him the anonymity his despair requires.

In a coda to the film, Averill, now an old man, is seen servicing a wealthy
female partner on a ship far away from the horror, staring into his past and
lost illusions. The film is a dystopian Western, considered even by some
nihilistic, denying the possibility of hope for an America founded in such
bloodshed, crime and oppression. If the epic Western conventionally explores

a progressive story of America in terms of the foundation myth, the America of *Heaven's Gate* is a murderous, class-ridden, racist order in which individual, personal and intimate relationships are impossible. No other Western offers such an interpretation of the foundation myth with such shocking majesty.

Steven J. Ross's extraordinary research into early film reveals the existence of a working class cinema directly engaged in exploring social class struggles in America before Hollywood's rise to dominance and its suppression in the 1920s. In its damning attack on America's class system, *Heaven's Gate* looks back to that time of an overtly politically-engaged cinema. However, this book has also been informed by an understanding that the Western can be understood to codify and thereby inscribe a working class consciousness, especially in its representations of masculine labour and identity (Lusted, 1996); that the genre conventions of the Western act as displacement strategies inscribing socio-political investigation from the point of view of groups on the social margins. Where social class is conventionally implicit in the genre and explicit in rare revisionist cases like *Heaven's Gate*, the politics of race and gender has been central to the revisionist western.

FROM INDIAN TO NATIVE AMERICAN

One of the most significant features of the revisionist Western is the changing representation of its central cast of characters. Of all its dominant relations of gender, social class and ethnic/racial identity, none has been more contentious than its representation of the Native American (Baird, 1996). By the end of the nineteenth century, two ideas of the indigenous population then known as Indians (or, more colloquially, red Indians or redskins) prevailed among white Americans. One was the primitive savage, incapable of civilisation, and the other was the noble savage, still primitive, but also uncorrupted by European civilisation. The first provided justifications for that century's racial genocide, informing institutionalised racism and white supremacist movements well into the twentieth century. The second offers alternative conservationist appeals, in memory of 'the Vanishing American' (Leslie Fiedler's resonant book title) and some terms of debate over ethnic civil rights movements.

The origins of film are bound up in a moment which fused fictional and ethnographic modes in these two essentially political constructions of racial difference. From the earliest times, fiction cinema in Hollywood and elsewhere was in struggle with these competing ideas in its representation of Native Americans. The Western, as it emerged with its refractions in the foundation myth of American history, especially in ideas of manifest destiny and of land appropriation in frontier history, was a primary site of that struggle. As interracial conflict and the Indian Wars of the second half of the nineteenth century dominate Westerns, it is no surprise that Indians in Westerns are mainly those who historically resisted white expansion, notably the Apache, Sioux, Cheyenne, Comanche and Seminole.

PRO-INDIAN WESTERNS

From the very beginning of cinema, Pro-Indian themes supporting assimilation compete with conflicts between white expansionism and Native American resistance, often within the same film. Among influential early films concerning white injustices to pacified Indians as individuals or tribes is *Ramona*, Helen Hunt Jackson's 1884 novel filmed four times 'about the victimisation of Indians who have become both farmers and Christians' (Michael Walker 1996, p.124), a theme supremely explored some decades later in *Apache* (1954). For Linda and Michael Woal, these early Indian dramas present the Indian as a tragic figure, whereas Romaine Fielding's *Chief White Eagle* (1912) 'dared to present an Indian character who, although he gives way to lust and murder, is sympathetic and worthy of respect' (1995, p.17). Reservation Indians are conventionally mistreated and exploited by whites as early as *The Covered Wagon* (1923), and justify Indian resistance in films from *Fort Apache* (1948) to *Ulzana's Raid* (1972). Indian reprisals are commonly motivated by previous attacks by whites, at least as early as *Two Flags West* (1950) and as recently as *Geronimo: An American Legend* (1994). Motivated or not, however, historical inevitability requires white suppression.

Occasional pro-Indian Westerns appear in the period following the Second World War, with A features like *Fort Apache* (1948), series Westerns like *The Cowboy and the Indians* (1949) with Gene Autry, and B features such as *Apache Chief* (1949). In a cycle of liberal pro-Indian Westerns made during the 1950s, Indians take more central roles (Lenihan, 1980; Slotkin, 1992). *Broken Arrow* (1950) was recognised as groundbreaking in its time (Everson, 1992(69), p.201). It explores the causes of Indian hostility and deals seriously with Indian culture. The film opens with Tom Jeffords (James Stewart), riding under the credits, his distinctive voice heard non-diegetically telling of a first meeting with the Chiricahua Apache. He tends a wounded Indian child, an act that subsequently spares him from being killed by adults from the same tribe. In the ensuing debate about scalping, it is made clear that whites scalp for the money that comes from their resale, while Indians do not scalp. The liberal corrective to the prevalent stereotype of the time does not deny the brutality of the Indians, since in the following scene three trespassing miners are ambushed, two subsequently hanged and one buried alive. The scene implies the horror of torture and mutilation, elements that would be made more explicit in later dystopian Westerns. Though the act is motivated by the discovery of Indian scalps on the miners, the film importantly offers new moral distinctions within as well as between white and Indian culture.

The influence of *Broken Arrow* is immediately evident in subsequent romance Westerns, including *Tomahawk* (1951). Interrogations of white racism feature in related Westerns of the 1950s directed by Delmer Daves, including *Drum Beat* (1954), *White Feather* (1958) and *The Last Wagon* (1956) in which Richard Widmark plays an Indian responsible for safely conducting a white family through hostile territory. For Michael Walker, this is a 'distinctly progressive anti-White narrative' (1996, p.123) for in 'Daves' West, it is white society that gives birth to monsters' (ibid., p.49). The liberal appeals of this cycle of films for Indian assimilation into white society and, in variation, for tolerance of separate development, are posited on twentieth-century arguments inscribed in the 1930s Indian New Deal (Neale, 1998, p.18) and the 1946 Indian Claims Commission (ibid., p.19). These posited that Native Americans had their own cultures, and that these were to be understood as different rather than, as before, inferior to the dominant white cultures.

Perhaps most interesting in this respect is *Devil's Doorway* (1950), directed by Anthony Mann, in which Shoshone chief Lance Poole (Robert Taylor) returns from service with the Union Army in the Civil War to find he is dispossessed of his homelands by white racist institutions. Julian Petley argues that the film demonstrates 'with merciless logic that the purpose of (white) law is repression and exploitation, and that political power does indeed flow from the barrel of a gun' (1980, p.1048). Poole's initial assimilation into white society denied, he sheds his urban clothes and, with long hair and bandana, justifies a shift from assimilation to Indian rights (Slotkin 1962, p.333). Neale sees in Poole's final death, wearing 'Union army uniform and his Congressional Medal of Honour *and* his Indian head-band' a new claim for ethnic diversity, in a revised notion of national identity, making it possible to think of Indian-American identity (1998, p.18). In *Run of the Arrow* (1957), the same theme is inverted when the white hero played by Rod Steiger braves both white and Native American prejudices to proclaim an American-Indian identity. At least the hero of this film is allowed to settle down with his Indian wife at the end. However, racial tolerance in pro-Indian films does not usually extend to acceptance of mixed race relationships. Where fears of miscegenation do not kill off the hero, as in *Devil's Doorway*, for instance, they kill off the hero's Indian wife, as in *Broken Arrow*.

Slotkin terms the generic revisions brought by this cycle 'the Cult of the Indian' (1992, pp.366–78). Neale demonstrates its thoroughgoing subsequent influence, even on television Western series (1998, p.13) and, in a footnote, on organised Indian civil rights movements (ibid., p.23). The cult of the Indian raised the profile of Indian rights in the genre, particularly in a cycle of revisionist epics that followed in the 1960s.

REVISIONIST EPICS

Epic Westerns from the 1960s bear the variant tone of the dystopian Western, from the cynical comedy of *The Way West* to the horrific *The Wild Bunch*, and form part of a significant period of revisionist ideas in the Western genre. A group of epic Westerns in the period openly challenge the foundation myth by reviewing the treatment of Native America in frontier history. Foremost of these are two that invert the conventional racial role of heroism and villainy. In the cavalry Western based on Mari Sandoz' novel, *Cheyenne Autumn* (1964), John Ford directs an epic trek of a tribe of three hundred Cheyenne. Unlike the Indian nation in *Ride out for Revenge* (1957), who are forced to route march, those in *Cheyenne Autumn* choose to leave starvation on their reservation to return to their homelands in the Dakota Mountains. The troubled journey is presented in religious terms similar to the pioneer trek in wagon train Westerns. As in *The Covered Wagon* (1923), trekkers express doubts about the journey, though Quaker schoolteacher Deborah Wright (Carroll Baker) provides the voice of white liberal commentary as she accompanies the walking Indians, with children in her buggy.

Other groups in antagonistic relation to the trekkers may express doubts about the justice of their role but they cannot interfere with their quest. The chasing cavalry troupe, for instance, led by Captain Thomas Archer (Richard Widmark), is uneasy about its assignment to return the Indians to the reservation. The trek poses a problem for government diplomacy, with Secretary of the Interior Carl Schurz (Edward G. Robinson) seeking inspiration from a portrait of Abraham Lincoln. The reaction of the local populations on the journey is treated more ironically. In a central comic scene set in Dodge City, a sarcastic Wyatt Earp (James Stewart) refuses to leave his poker game to rescue an hysterical local population from unlikely massacre by the 'savage Indians' of their imagination, a contrast to the sorry mass of dispossessed on the march.

Cheyenne Autumn is certain in its support of the Native American cause but less sure about how to deal evenly with both sides of the racial conflict. In contrast, *Little Big Man* (1970) has no qualms about attacking the foundation myth. Directed by Arthur Penn, *Little Big Man* is the epic story of novelist Thomas Berger's 121-year-old hero, Jack Crabb, whose incredible reminiscences may exaggerate his role in frontier history but still function to reveal 'the worthlessness of White civilisation and its juxtaposition with the idealised world of the Cheyenne' (Pye, 1996b, p.263). Drawing on images of the contemporaneous Vietnam War, the film viscerally reconstructs the infamous Washita massacre of 1868, in which a village of old men, women and children were massacred and their bodies mutilated by soldiers of the Seventh Cavalry. The film's inversion of the conventional white/red relationship is absolute. It extends to a pastoral construction of Native American culture, tolerant of social and sexual difference (of even warmly integrating homosexuality) and pacifist (Indians attack with buffalo bladders on sticks and take up arms only in shocked response to the unsportsmanlike behaviour of cavalrymen who shoot at them).

THE ENVIRONMENTALIST EPIC

Little Big Man posits its Indian characters as innocent victims of white aggression, defending a vanishing culture of greater moral worth than the better-resourced 'civilisation' that destroys it. This theme is given an ecological/environmentalist twist in the most popular Western of the 1990s, *Dances With Wolves* (1990). It tells the story of John Dunbar (Kevin Costner) who survives a suicidal battlefield ride to escape into the West. The narrative then adopts a diary form, with the hero narrating the story we witness, a common device in revisionist Westerns allowing a more reflexive narrative. After a period of isolation, Dunbar gradually assimilates into the counter-cultural life of the local Sioux, ultimately denying his American identity. Worland and Countryman splendidly describe how it comes to happen:

> Dances With Wolves *begins by imagining white American society as wholly bent on self-destruction. From (its) guignol opening, white society will be steadily denigrated until it is identified almost solely and literally with excrement – from the decadent, incontinent [and, in the director's cut, masturbating (author's addition)] officer who dispatches Dunbar to the distant frontier post to the brutish cavalry troopers who use pages from the journal of his life with the Sioux for toilet paper. The Sioux nation is soon posited as an alternative, indeed superior society – the human incarnation of the frontier landscape that completes Dunbar's physical and spiritual regeneration, as the Indian serves in the traditional Romantic role as 'noble savage'.*
>
> (Worland and Countryman, 1998, p.189)

The film attacks the aggressive white exploitation of the fauna of the land. In a key scene, Dunbar is repulsed by the sight of a deer carcass abandoned by previous white occupants in the only watering hole of his solitary frontier outpost. His exaltation at being part of a Sioux buffalo hunt contrasts with the barbarity of white buffalo hunters whose slaughter for hides leaves carcasses littering the landscape.

In contrast, as in *Little Big Man*, the Sioux are represented as conservationists in their landscape and social in their village community. Dowell finds this phenomenon a general trend amongst later revisionist Westerns:

> *Native Americans as new conservatives. Supportive family structures, ecological sensitivity, clan solidarity, pervasive spirituality, fundamental non-violence (iconic compensation for all those years depicted as terrorists) – and, above all, status as an endangered species.*
>
> (Dowell, 1995, p.9)

REPRESENTING THE INDIAN

> *In the American frontier myth created and refined by whites over three centuries, Indians, despite their historically and narratively central role, seldom represent themselves . . . rather, the Indian is foremost a metaphor manipulated to address . . . the shifting historical circumstances, problems and values of dominant white culture.*
>
> (Worland and Countryman, 1998, p.188)

In contrast, a significant development between *Cheyenne Autumn* and *Dances With Wolves* is the casting of Native Americans actors as Indian characters. In *Broken Arrow*, the leading Indian characters are played by whites in 'red-face' (a Greek Jeff Chandler, Lithuanian Charles Bronson and WASP Debra Paget), with the only credited Native American, Jay Silverheels, playing the single Indian villain. None of the leading Indian characters in *Cheyenne Autumn* are played by Native Americans, but by Mexican-Americans like Ricardo Montalban as Little Wolf and Dolores del Rio as Spanish Woman, and Italian-American Sal Mineo as Red Shirt, though, as in all Westerns directed by John Ford in Monument Valley, Navajo residents are Indian extras.

There are rare exceptions, like the B feature, *Navajo* (1952), in which all but the central characters are amateurs and played by Navajo, but *Little Big Man* is among the first A features with Native Americans in prominent Indian roles.

Some Native Americans become genre character actors during the 1970s, like Chief Dan George (actually Chief Nawanath of British Columbia's Burrard tribe) who plays the wiseacre Old Lodge Skins in *Little Big Man*, off to the mountains prepared to meet his maker but rising from his deathbed when rain prompts him to reconsider his God's wishes. In *The Outlaw Josey Wales* (1976), George plays a survivor of national political negotiations with white politicians whose advice to the pacified Indians – to 'endeavour to persevere', in exchange for broken treaties and land-grabbing – he treats with the cynical disdain it deserves. George is also at the centre of the gently mocking tone of interracial banter within the motley group that forms around the hero. Besieged by hostile Indians, an old white woman at his side bravely declares 'We'll show those redskins something' before turning to George: 'No offence meant'. 'None taken,' comes his avuncular reply. George's comic wisdom contrasts with the solemnity of Will Sampson. As Chief Bromden, he escapes from the asylum in *One Flew Over the Cuckoo's Nest* (1975) to find genre roles in *The Outlaw Josey Wales*, *The White Buffalo* (1977) and the controversial television series, *The Mystic Warrior* (1984). There is still no Native American star equivalent to 'people of colour' like Whoopi Goldberg or Denzel Washington, though clearly the Western is the most likely genre in which one might in future emerge.

By the time of *Dances With Wolves*, Westerns are informed by 'serious co-operation from modern-day descendents of the historic Indians they portray' (ibid., p.186). Native Americans speak in subtitled authentic cultural languages. Lakota dialogue dominates *A Man Called Horse* (1970), about an English lord's initiation into Sioux culture, including an unbearable reconstruction of the rites of passage Sun Vow ceremony, in which he is lifted by ropes attached to his chest. Perhaps a new boundary has been crossed in the casting of a Native American political activist, Russell Means, as the hero's sidekick, Chingachgook, in *The Last of the Mohicans* (1992).

In contemporary revisionist Westerns, Native Americans also play heroes and villains alike. For every friendly Indian, like the charismatic Chief Dan George in *Little Big Man*, there is a pock-marked Wes Studi as the evil Magua in *The Last of the Mohicans*. However, Studi is also the heroic victim of the title role in *Geronimo: An American Legend*. Importantly, Indians are both heroes and villains within each film, and their action psychologically explained rather than offered as a product of a primitive racial savagery.

THE RACE QUESTION

Hollywood's interest in interracial relations in the 1950s and 1960s was also explored in Westerns in the period. *Flaming Star* (1960) has Elvis Presley as the mixed race hero subjected to prejudice on both sides of the racial divide. *The Unforgiven* (1959) has Audrey Hepburn as a Kiowa Indian raised by a white settler family ostracised by their own community and falling victim to internal dissention when Indians return to claim her. At the end, the racial dispute the film earlier brought into sharp focus gets lost in the climactic mêlée. Such family melodramas are forgotten by the time of the elegiac

Tell Them Willie Boy is Here (1969) in which Robert Redford's modern day sheriff reluctantly shoots 'Willie Boy', the derogatory racist epithet attached to the renegade Paiute hero played by Robert Blake. Stalked by a posse, more victim than criminal, the Indian gradually casts aside his American-Indian identity with his modern clothing, to return to the ethnic identity of his racial origins.

More recent revisionist Westerns, influenced by New History, reject the terms of assimilation from earlier periods and the image of the passive 'cigar store Indian', exploring instead the racial politics of Indian resistance to white expansionism. *Geronimo: An American Legend* is a cavalry Western that tells its story of the Apache Wars in the Southwest of the 1860s and 70s once more through the flashback device of a diary written by Lt. Britton David (Matt Damon). The whites are represented by three kinds of Westerners: Lt. Charles Gatewood (Jason Patric), charged with negotiating Geronimo's 1886 surrender; Brigadier General George Crook (Gene Hackman), whose career is prematurely ended when Washington discovers the respect he gives his foe; and Al Sieber (Robert Duval), a pragmatic scout. All are agents and victims of political and military deceit in the treatment of the Apache. Wes Studi plays Geronimo as a man desperate to maintain individual dignity within a culture he grows to acknowledge cannot be preserved in the face of white imperialism. The episodic narrative structure includes long speeches from Geronimo and often redundant voice-over from David, punctuating spectacularly staged conflicts, initiated by white bigotry. Sieber's elegiac death in a saloon gunfight is a case in point. After surviving 'gunshot, arrowshot seventeen times', he dies in defence of an Indian, one of a race he has paradoxically spent his life killing. Conflict between and within both white and Indian cultures enables the film to explore the deceitful treachery of the historic political forces of the time.

The contemporary issue among Native Americans at the time of the film's making concerns the 'tension between the attraction of separate rights and equal rights for Indians' (Richard White, 1991, p.585). *Geronimo: An American Legend* explores this tension through its characters' experience of both resistance and assimilation. The film is bitterly angry at the historic treatment of the Indian, particularly at the end when the cavalry scout regiment, instrumental in securing Geronimo's surrender, are arrested after conflict ceases and 'with chilling parallel to the Nazi Holocaust . . . bundled into box-cars and shipped to imprisonment in Florida' (Worland and Countryman, 1998, p.193). Equating white America's treatment of the Indian to the Holocaust goes back at least to the cavalry officer, Wessels, played as a fascist Prussian by Karl Malden, in *Cheyenne Autumn*.

Beyond Hollywood, efforts have been made to provide Indian groups with the means of producing their own films. With a famous precedent in the experimental group of films known as *The Navajo Films* (1966), Rob Sabal's account of the making of *Indian Summer* (1992) provides a production record of a fiction exploring repressed aspects of an Apache culture likely to be lost within a generation.

More commercially, *The Broken Chain* (1993) is about the earlier alliance of the Iroquois Confederation of nations with eighteenth-century colonial powers. Although Dowell claims it is far more historically accurate than any Hollywood Western, it is still related to Hollywood's contemporary recon-struction of the Native American as a New Age mystic. This image stretches back to the counter-culture Indians of *Little Big Man* and the 'Vanishing American' of the nineteenth century. Though the image 'redresses a movie slur of the past, the charge of heathenism ... (it) feminises, or at least un-man's the Native American, and thereby implicitly neutralises him as a social or political threat ... Westerns about Indians continue to occupy the elegiac phase' (1995, p.10). This is borne out even by pro-Indian Westerns that seek to avoid the elegiac form, like *Journey Through Rosebud* (1972), the chase Western *Eagle's Wing* (1978), and the haunting and subversive *Windwalker* (1980), in which, uniquely in a captivity narrative, a Cheyenne hero tracks down his son kidnapped by Crow Indians.

BLACK WESTERNERS

Many critics have written about the changing role of the Indian in Westerns as an indirect commentary on changes in the position of America's black population. The pro-Indian films of the 1950s, for instance, have been read as responses to the black civil rights movement of the time. Though the argument is tempting, Neale cautions that it effectively results in effacing the Indian from history, a group with its own history of struggles for political representation (Neale, 1998). In a genre so bound up in the frontier myth of white imperialism, there is a fine irony in a critical argument that promotes the visibility of one racial minority group at the expense of another.

Black Americans have their own presence in Westerns. Despite historical evidence of black Americans in frontier culture as slaves (including runaways, often turning outlaw), labouring cowboys and in 'Negro' cavalry regiments, their presence in Westerns until the 1960s is minimal. In early Hollywood films, blacks are represented by whites in 'blackface', a cultural legacy of the minstrel show (Pines, 1975), and a product of an outrageous historical racism and oppression of black civil rights by white America until the 1950s (Null, 1975). Even when black actors begin to appear in Hollywood films from the 1930s onwards, they continue to appear most regularly as servants and slaves in plantation fiction, popularised in the influential nineteenth-century anti-slavery novel, *Uncle Tom's Cabin*, and later in women's fiction like *Gone With the Wind*. From this tradition of fiction emerges the domestic stereotypes of the 'Tom', 'coon' and 'mammy', three terms in the title of an early critical investigation of blacks in American Cinema by Donald Bogle (*Toms, Coons, Mulattoes, Mammies and Bucks*, 1974). The cultural legacy is evident in Westerns of the time. In *Cimarron* (1931), for instance, the Southern aristocrat family heading West discovers a stowaway black domestic servant child, but are too far away to return him home; he then provides comic relief on the journey. As late as *The Man Who Shot Liberty Valance* (1962), Woody Strode plays adult Pompey, still the 'boy' to John Wayne's hero, his slave origins suppressed by a working relationship presented as interdependent.

Set against this history, there are remarkable early attempts to counter the dominant stereotypes. In *The Trooper of Troop K* (1916), Noble Johnson 'plays the "shiftless Negro" who becomes the redeemed hero, a role which reverses the popular racial stereotype into a more positive figure' (Pines, in Buscombe, 1988, p.69). In the 1920s, black rodeo star, Bill Pickett, performs his ring skills in two fictions, *The Crimson Skull* (1921) and *The Bull-Dogger* (1922). In the 1930s and 1940s, as a result of attempts to draw on the revolutionary arts produced within the Harlem Renaissance of the 1920s (Huggins, 1971), notable musicals with all-black casts are made in Hollywood, including *Cabin in the Sky* (1943). As part of what Jim Pines calls this period of 'race movies', there are also all-black Westerns, produced independently for black urban audiences, among them *Harlem on the Prairie/Bad Man of Harlem* (1937) with Herbert Jeffries' singing cowboy, and the satirical *Look Out Sister* (1949).

RACE WESTERNS

From the 1950s onwards, Westerns contribute to a cycle of Hollywood social dramas in otherwise modern settings, exploring black civil rights and race relations through conflicts between black and white groups. Notable among these is director John Ford's *Sergeant Rutledge* (1960), providing the first substantial role for a black actor in an A feature Western. The statuesque Woody Strode plays the soldier of the title, wrongly accused of raping a white woman. Its revision of conventional black/white relations in fictions even beyond the Western genre forces *Sergeant Rutledge* to undermine audience support for the cavalry more characteristically evident elsewhere in films directed by John Ford. The military tribunal that tries Rutledge is the core of the film but, punctuated by long flashbacks, it is exposed as part of a military community that has lost sense of the rightness of its role in supporting white expansion. Following Rutledge's release when proven innocent of the charge, the end of the film enables him among other black soldiers. By then, the more conventional celebration of cavalry soldiery rings hollow. The film can be seen as a crucial stage in the revisionist Western, transforming the generic meaning of the cavalry in reimagining roles for black characters. As such, it provides an important connection to reversals in the imagining of militarism in revisionist epics like *Cheyenne Autumn* and *Little Big Man*.

Interracial conflict becomes a subject in many 1960s Westerns. In *Major Dundee* (1964), Brock Peters leads a group of black soldiers among mixed racial and ethnic groups in a campaign against Apaches, adding an important new racial conflict (importantly, *within* the movement of Western expansion). There is also a new racial moral centre: when a Southern redneck insults one of the black soldiers, there is no doubt where the film's sympathies lie. Black characters take more central roles in other films of the period. In the eccentrically-titled *The McMasters . . . Tougher than the West Itself* (1969), Brock Peters, again, 'is the black Union soldier who has to fight the Civil War all over again when he returns home to the South' (Hardy, 1991, p.314). In *The Scalphunters* (1968), a comedy Western, Ossie Davis has a central role competing with Burt Lancaster for stolen furs. At the climax, the film's liberal plea that we are 'all the same under skin colour' culminates in a fight in a mud hole that makes it impossible to distinguish between black and white.

Towards the end of the decade, political moves towards racial integration make it possible for black actors to appear in films without reference to their race or colour. One of the big stars of the period, Sidney Poitier, is a gunfighter in *Duel at Diablo* (1966), and Woody Strode, again, skilled with bow and arrow, is one of *The Professionals* (1966). Neither their racial origins nor their skin colour attracts mention. The age of 'integrated casting', since common-place in Hollywood and on American television, has begun.

BLAXPLOITATION WESTERNS

In the 1970s, a 'blaxploitation' cinema emerges, featuring predomin-antly black casts. Though made by Hollywood whites, the films engage with contemporary black themes, particularly with a developing popular black urban street, music and drug culture that, in the argot of the time, was fashionably 'hip'. Renewing inversions of conventional black/white relations, with black heroes and white villains, they are mainly crime thrillers, but include some Westerns. Influenced in style and levels of violence by Italian Westerns, the cycle begins with a cavalry Western, *Soul Soldiers/Red White and Black* (1970) (Cawelti, 1976, p.257). Thereafter, the central character of blax-ploitation Westerns is more like the most famous of the black superheroes of the cycle, Shaft, as in the popular *The Legend of Nigger Charlie* (1972) and its sequel, *The Soul of Nigger Charlie* (1973). As these titles suggest, (another is

Boss Nigger/Black Bounty Killer, 1974), these Westerns more overtly confront race issues from the position of a resisting black politics, aggressively returning the derogatory epithet in the titles to a white culture accustomed to its use as a term of racist abuse. Such confrontation declines along with the cycle, however, replaced by gentler parodies like *Adios Amigo* (1975).

The most accomplished Western to emerge from this period combines elements of the liberal and blaxploitation films. In *Buck and the Preacher* (1971), Sidney Poitier plays Buck, leading a wagon train of black ex-slaves West, following the defeat of the Confederate states at the end of the Civil War. Pursued by bounty hunters, they rely for aid upon a tribe of Indians hostile to white incursion. In a central scene that reveals a complex racial politics at work, Buck appeals for assistance from an Indian chief, claiming they share a common enemy. The chief responds that his support must be limited since the Indian cause needs all the meagre food and bullets it has. The Indian cause, he pointedly reminds Buck, is one against which black soldiers fight alongside whites. A humbled Buck answers, 'I don't do that no more', neatly invoking the responsibility of the individual as well as the collective identity amidst the historical forces that govern everyday lives. The film ends with one of the wittiest inversions of a cavalry rescue in a Western. As the wagon train is about to be overwhelmed by the small force of bounty hunters, the Indians ride cavalry-style to the rescue.

THE GANGSTA WESTERN

Black Westerns disappear as the blaxploitation film and the Western genre decline in the late 1970s. Black actors occasionally appear as sidekicks in subsequent Westerns, notably Mal(achi) (Danny Glover) in *Silverado* (1985), whose race drama is subsumed within the romance adventure of its four heroes, and with Morgan Freeman's performance as Ned Logan, sidekick to the hero, an example of uncertain integrated casting in *Unforgiven* (1990). A rare exception is *Glory* (1989), with early starring roles for Denzel Washington and Morgan Freeman. The Civil War story concerns a troop of black infantry led by a white officer played by Matthew Broderick. The troop suffers prejudice and ill-treatment from the white military establishment and ordinary troopers alongside them, but they prove their worth and finally meet a magnificent death in battle, implied at the end as they face an overwhelming enemy.

The sole title of the 1990s is the gangsta-rap Western, *Posse* (1993), accompanied by an insistent soundtrack of rap artists. It opens with a now aged Woody Strode, black icon of the Western, reminiscing to young film-makers about the historical West, as if connecting modern street culture to the days of the Colt .45. Evoking a history of black settlement in the Old West, the film then flashes back to the story of Jesse Lee (Mario Van Peebles) and his 'posse' of renegades from the Spanish-American War. They hole up in the black town of Freemanville, but rapidly become implicated in its conflict with the nearby white supremacist Cutterstown. The film acknowledges the history of the black Western in 'the kinship between black cowboys and Native Americans who have in common a well-founded suspicion of whites' (Bingham, 1994, p.242), as they join forces against a white sheriff and deputies who hang an Indian woman for 'trespassing'. The film also references a distinctive black social history, with Ku Klux Klan terrorism of the black community neatly inverted when Jesse and the gang, disguised in the distinctive white sheets and hoods, spring others from jail. The genre history is also evident in a plot taken from William S. Hart's *Hell's Hinges* (1916), with Jesse burning the town in order to rebuild it, though rather more in his own gangsta image than by the original's forces of moral purity.

Posse takes the convoluted trials of its narcissistic hero to extremes of the masculine gangsta culture, but its style is generic, influenced particularly by the Italian Western. Jesse's traumatic flashbacks echo those of Harmonica (Charles Bronson) in *Once Upon a Time in the West* (1968) and the ghostly hero of *High Plains Drifter* (1972). There is a similar cynicism about the value of life, as the posse and Freemanville are gradually depleted, and about the trustworthiness of relationships, when a black sheriff commits the ultimate betrayal of his people.

WOMEN WESTERNERS

In the same way that new histories have unearthed evidence of a far more extensive and varied black presence in westward expansion, they have also revealed a neglected female presence (Myers, 1982; Jeffrey, 1979). Though few of the 'suffragettes, farmers, professional women' in the authentic West appear alongside the more conventional 'mother, schoolteacher, prostitute, saloon girl, rancher, Indian squaw' (Cook, 1988, p.293), women are significant in Westerns. Though, for some critics, the landscape of the Western is hostile to women (Tompkins, 1992; Cook, 1988), their generic role has recently been reconsidered more sympathetically (Studlar, in Studlar and Bernstein, 2001; Lucas).

When the agency of the romance hero is to civilise the West, the figure of woman becomes key to a successful transition. Heterosexual partnership is a common resolution when it combines the best values of the East and the West in national union. In Westerns directed by John Ford, in particular, women are central to the civilising task set by the active male protagonists. In Studlar's analysis, Ford's women make sacrifices 'to ensure the birthright of future generations of Americans' that requires 'an accommodation of masculinity to feminine values' (Studlar and Bernstein, 2001, p.11). Women can be as stoical as men in the face of hardship on the frontier (like Lana (Claudette Colbert) in *Drums Along the Mohawk*, 1939) and men are frequently shown to be less capable of the adaptations necessary to survive (like Brad Jorgenson/Harry Carey Junior in *The Searchers*, 1956). Commonly in frontier Westerns, women display 'the courage, determination, independence and incredible capacity for endurance' Jenni Calder otherwise overlooks in the genre (1974, p.158).

If Ford is 'matchless in his appreciation of mature women' (Lucas, 1998, p.304), they abound elsewhere in the genre. In *The Hired Hand* (1971), for instance, the hero's wife who has fetched for herself, raised her child and tended the farm when abandoned by her husband, requires him on his return to prove his worth as the hired hand of the title, before taking him back. In a central scene, he questions her fidelity during his absence. She responds with a semi-comic speech about her rights to desire when and where she pleases, while not questioning his fidelity as it is no business of hers. The tragedy of dystopian Westerns is often that the ageing hero cannot resolve the problem of his isolation in potential settlement with a mature woman. *Will Penny* (1967) provides a fine example in Joan Hacket, the single mother full of unfulfilled yearning for a relationship the hero ultimately refuses.

Westerns directed by Raoul Walsh feature the most companionate partnerships (Wexman, 1993) in the genre, with adventurous women equal to men, who admire their independence. Rosie (Julia Adams) in *The Lawless Breed* (1952) and Colorado (Virginia Mayo) in *Colorado Territory* (1949) forge their own pathways alongside their men and make their own final choices; Rosie as a defiant mother, Colorado in a tragic suicide pact with the hero. Heroines in director Anthony Mann's Westerns have to be strong-willed to survive the extreme experiences they undergo. Both Lina Patch (Janet Leigh) in *The Naked Spur* (1953) and Rénee Vallon (Corinne Calvert) in *The Far Country* (1955) rescue the hero by offering him an alternative to a destiny otherwise consumed by hatred and despair and a denial of social commitment respectively. In the Ranown cycle, the heroine causes the hero to rediscover his lost humanity, as in *Comanche Station* (1959), when Cody (Randolph Scott) tells Mrs. Lowe (Nancy Gates) that she is the first person he has been able to talk to openly since the capture of his wife several years before.

Competing ideas of femininity are also evident in Westerns. The 'fallen woman' of melodrama is most commonly offered as the ideal partner (Dallas in *Stagecoach*, 1939, for instance, and Kay (Marilyn Monroe) in *River of No Return*, 1954) in preference to a bourgeois Easterner like Lucy Mallory (Louise Platt) in *Stagecoach*. Women from élite classes (conventionally, women with 'airs') can be persuaded to democratic ways by Western heroes, especially if music prompts them to dance, as in *The Outriders* (1950). The sexualised form of the female body can be an object of threat as much as desire for the male hero of the Western in the classical period, though more commonly an object of misogyny in the post-classical period. In a key transitional film, *Westward the Women* (1952), Peter William Evans argues that the brutal treatment of the feisty heroine, Danon (Denise Darcel) by the traditional hero, Buck (Robert Taylor) enables 'the causes of the conventional male's neurosis' about women in the Western to be interrogated in new ways (1996, p.209). At the film's end, the wagon train of mail order brides confronts the men who have paid for them to travel West. A new-found power derived from the hazardous journey emboldens one to resist the male gaze thus: 'You can look us over, but don't think you're going to do the choosing'.

Paradoxically, the sexualised woman of the West frequently loses out to a more demure femininity, as Chihuahua learns to her cost in *My Darling Clementine* (1946). Cross the woman with a racial minority, and the price she pays is frequently the ultimate one, as with Chihuahua again, Pearl in *Duel in the Sun* (1946), and almost any Native American woman in a Western.

In Landy's study of women in Italian Westerns, she argues that heterosexual romance:

> is subordinated to the motif of homosocial bonding . . . Sex between men and women is circumscribed in this environment, and when present it is likely to be coercive and brutal. When women are present, they are usually carriers of economic value as kept women, prostitutes, or heirs to property, like Jill in Once Upon a Time in the West, or figures of nostalgia, as in Duck You Sucker. Maternal figures are either conspicuously placed in the background or entirely absent, or they violate conventional notions of service. Eroticism is conveyed primarily through scenes of eating, sparring or killing.
>
> *(Landy, 1996, p.218)*

This also applies to Hollywood Westerns influenced by Italian Westerns, though there are enough exceptions. For one, Constance Miller (Julie Christie) in the nihilistic *McCabe and Mrs. Miller* (1971), directed by Robert Altman, is a saloon girl surviving by 'replacing any vestige of warmheartedness with cold-blooded pragmatism and emotional vacancy' (Lucas, 1998, p.312).

A WOMAN WITH A GUN

The female role in the narrative structure of the films in all these cases is invariably secondary to the male. Pam Cook argues that the woman in Westerns 'relinquishes her desire to be active and independent, ceding power to the hero and accepting secondary status as mother figure and social mediator'

(1988, p.295). A defining strategy of revisionist Westerns is to provide the central 'active and independent' roles for women otherwise lacking in the genre. As soon as this happens, the central protagonists invariably meet with resistance from men. In Freudian terms, nothing could be more threatening to masculinity in a Western than the castration fear of The Woman with a Gun. As early as *Belle Starr* (1941) with Gene Tierney, and *Tall in the Saddle* (1944) with Ella Raines, female stars can be found as feisty heroines who dominate their men, though Hardy claims that it is not until *Oklahoma Woman* (1956) with Peggy Castle, and *Gunslinger* (1956) with Beverly Garland, that 'the full potential of a woman gunslinger would be explored' (1991, p.117).

Nash Smith is alert to early dime novels centring on gunslinging female protagonists, as in *Wild Edna, the Girl Brigand* (1878) and *Denver Doll, the Detective Queen* (1882). But central female protagonists in Western films commonly need no gun to control their men when ownership of towns or ranch spreads make them powerful. In *Outlaw Women* (1952), Marie Windsor plays a woman who owns a casino in the border town of Las Mujeres. Attempts by local men to cede control result in them marrying all the women who work there, only to find that marriage does not inhibit the women from continuing their rule. In *The Furies* (1950), Barbara Stanwyck plays a daughter contesting her father's ownership of their ranch, the internecine struggle leading to the deaths of relatives and friends. In an hysterical central scene, the daughter stabs in the eye with a pair of scissors her father's new wife, played by the malevolent Judith Anderson. Earlier, Stanwyck is the title role in *Annie Oakley* (1935), a romance Western, but subsequently plays more formidable heroines in Westerns like *Cattle Queen of Montana* (1954) and *The Maverick Queen* (1956). In the latter, she is finally and shockingly gunned down as she uses her body to shield her lover, her gender no bar to the democracy of the gunfight. Stanwyck is a major female star of the genre, appearing with a whip rather than a gun in one of the most formally experimental of Westerns, *Forty Guns* (1957), directed by Sam Fuller, and finishing as a grand matriarch in the television series *The Big Valley* (1965–9).

THE BATTLE OF THE SEXES

Elsewhere, Westerns with central female protagonists are allegories of burgeoning female independence movements. In *Strange Lady in Town* (1956), Greer Garson plays a doctor who arrives in Santa Fe in 1899 to set up a practice. The film tells the story of how she gradually overcomes the prejudice of the locals, especially the men of the town, so she can get to tend the wounds of figures such as Billy the Kid and even Geronimo. The character is a forebear of the later television series, *Dr. Quinn, Medicine Woman* (1993–8).

Female stars do not need to be heroes to engage in battles of the sexes. Lucas explores ten strong female performances as dynamic heroines of Westerns (1998, pp.313–20) and others are equally worthy. Characters played by Susan Hayward, for instance, forcefully claim the right to change allegiance from one man to another in *Canyon Passage* (1946), and in *Garden of Evil* (1954), when she tricks a group of men into trekking across hostile Indian territory to rescue a worthless husband.

Female stars of the classical period are identified with the genre through characters associated with the self-sustaining, independent persona of their star image. Jane Russell's first film is the notorious Western, *The Outlaw*, made in 1940 but not released until 1946, due not least to censorship difficulties over the erotic objectification of her voluptuous body. By the time of *Montana Belle* (1952), however, her image as a sassy, wise-cracking spirit makes her Belle Starr as aggressive as any male outlaw. In two comedy Westerns, *The Paleface* (1948) and *Son of Paleface* (1952) she is the wordly-wise Westerner taking Bob Hope's infatuated Eastern dentist for a (literal as well as meta-phorical) ride. In her most substantial performance, in *The Tall Men* (1955) directed by Raoul Walsh, she is 'no prize to be given to the best man; rather she deflates the bravado of (the aggressive hero) and the wealth of (the mature hero) . . . it is she who chooses' (Hardy, 1991, p.243). Riding along-side the male protagonists, singing 'I want a tall man, don't want a small man', with its moral claim and sexual innuendo, the film 'celebrates the moment when strong men and strong women find each other' (Lucas, 1998, p.306). Russell finishes her film career as boldly in two B Westerns, the considerable *Johnny Reno* (1966) and the lesser *Waco* (1966).

Russell's mature modernity contrasts to the 'girl next door' image of Doris Day. This actress plays the title role in the first part of the classic musical comedy Western, *Calamity Jane* (1953), in filthy (though tailored) buckskins, before she is trained in more domestic ways and into skirts. In the narrative, her role as an independent woman is contested, until she forms a negotiated peace with Wild Bill Hickock (Howard Keel). Though the resolution finds her married and in white dress, it is she and not Bill who holds the reigns and drives the buckboard on their honeymoon. *Calamity Jane* is also one of the few Westerns that Jeanine Basinger (in relation to another, *Westward the Women*) could argue 'present overt, positive sister-hood' (1993, p.470) through Calamity's relationship with Katie Brown (Allyn McLerie). In *The Ballad of Josie* (1967), a comedy Western, Day is Josie Minick, a woman working to maintain herself after the death of an abusive husband (this much is biographical). The central conflict in the film lies in her attempt to raise sheep in cattle country, the conventional contest turned into a battle of the sexes as Josie stubbornly refuses to concede to cattlemen, who see her as a soft touch because of her gender. Cook calls the film an 'attempt to capitalize on an emerging women's movement' of the 1960s (1988, p.298).

Brigitte Bardot starred in three Westerns towards the end of her career: *Viva Maria!* (1965), inventing striptease in 1907 revolutionary Mexico with Jeanne Moreau; a European 'on safari' in the west in *Shalako* (1968) (in which the aristocrat played by Honor Blackman is incredibly but aptly asphyxiated by an Apache with her own string of pearls); and her final film, *The Legend of Frenchie King* (1971), a comedy Western. In all of these, Bardot brings edgy qualities of the foreign and exotic to disturb the conventional world of the romance Western, even revealing the comedy in the first and last films at the expense of the genre itself. Dowell's argument that more recent Westerns indicate that 'the root language of the genre is gender' (1995, p.10) seems particularly acute in these films and from this period of the 1960s onwards.

FEMALE AVENGERS

Cook argues that a different kind of femininity appearing in revenge Westerns owes much to the femmes fatales of film noir (1988, p.296). In *Two Gun Lady* (1956), a young woman searches for the men who killed her parents and, in *The Dalton Girls* (1957), four daughters become outlaws when their criminal father is killed. The eldest sister has to negotiate between the lust for revenge and the desire for settlement among her younger sisters, a conflict only resolved by the death of all but the sister seeking settlement. *Hannie Caulder* (1971) introduces a discordant comedy into its bitter story, in which Raquel Welch plays the woman of the title, bent on avenging her rape and the killing of her husband by three of the most depraved villains to grace a Western, played by genre stalwarts, Ernest Borgnine, Strother Martin and Jack Elam. Thereafter, flaunting rather than concealing her sexuality, dressed in little more than a poncho and gun belt, she learns the arts of gunfighting from a bounty hunter, played by Robert Culp, and hunts down the men. As with male avengers, the intensity of her quest makes her heroic role border on villainy. Their squalid deaths, though influenced like the rest of the film by the graphic violence and cynicism of the Italian Western, are oddly gendered, as Hannie kills them in a brothel, a perfume store and a derelict prison. Refusing to acknowledge intimacy with any man she meets results in the death not only of the villains but also of her mentor. In an enigmatic ending, a mysterious man in black who has haunted the film like a figure of death suddenly confronts her. Cook claims that 'women can never be heroes in Westerns' (1988, p.297), but despite the variations wrought by her unconventional gender, Hannie conforms to the narrative role of the hero of revenge Westerns.

Bad Girls (1994) is also a revenge Western of sorts, though its circular narrative dissipates any suspense in the chase. Its team of four female outlaws, dressed and armed like men, are alternately raped, threatened with rape, captured and rescued before the final massacre of male authority figures, from which, unlike their counterparts in *The Wild Bunch* (1969), 'they emerge alive to head on further West' (Dowell, 1995, p.9).

THE SOCIAL POSITION OF WOMEN

Two major female stars of classical Hollywood appear in the most notable Westerns to explore the social and generic position of women. In *Destry Rides Again* (1939), Marlene Dietrich is Frenchy, a feisty saloon performer, despite being in thrall to its owner. Structurally, she is released from her subordinated role by the feminised masculinity of the hero, Destry (James Stewart). Yet, as Florence Jacobowitz argues (1996, p.89), the potential for perversity and decadence in Dietrich's star image transcends this exceptional narrative function; she is aware of her sexual power as a woman and taunts her male

Marlene Dietrich as the feisty heroine, Frenchy, giving James Stewart as good as any man in *Destry Rides Again* (1939).

audience with it: 'the longer they wait (for her to perform), the better they like it'. At the end of the film, like many other strong Western heroines, she steps into the path of a bullet intended for her lover. But the image of her riding on Destry's back in a saloon bar game and brawling with another woman is a powerful evocation of female power that transcends her narrative.

Jacobowitz argues that, in contrast to *Destry Rides Again*, the subsequent revenge Western, *Rancho Notorious* (1952), becomes a woman's film, exploring woman's position in a patriarchal culture by asking: 'How does an independent woman survive if she rejects the male-defined options of wife/mother or property for the male pleasure? Where is her place if she demands rights denied to women?' (ibid., p.93). When the film was made, Dietrich was a star twenty years after the peak of her film career, operating in an industry that looks unkindly on signs of female ageing, especially on a face subject to the most interrogating gaze of the camera in close-up. The film self-consciously explores the problem of ageing for women, and not only in the film industry. As Altar Keane, running a criminal hide-out, she is only too aware of time passing. She says of the hero: 'I wish you'd go away and come back ten years ago'. Dietrich's star image is used by the film to analyse 'the limitations of the power achieved by the Dietrich persona through her glamour and her confident, bold sexuality' (ibid., p.93). Though Altar is a woman with unusual female power in a Western (she owns real estate), she is still cruelly mistreated by a hero who seduces, abuses and abandons her. Jacobowitz claims that '*Rancho Notorious* is . . . subversive – it utilises the "blinded" excessive melodramatic hero to analyse the strict regulation of gender underlying the Western's overt concerns of settlement and nationhood, and places the hero's troubled identity and actions within the demands of the social worlds' (ibid., p.89).

Johnny Guitar (1954) further interrogates the masculine world of the Western. Cook considers it 'the nearest Hollywood has come to a feminist western' (1988, p.298). The film is set in a baroque saloon house owned by Vienna (Joan Crawford), located in a wasteland whose development is promised with the coming of the railroad. The wealthy Vienna provokes the envy of a local township as she invests in land whose value they know will increase with railroad expansion. Their envy grows extreme, fronted by the 'truly hysterical' (Peterson, 1998, p.327) Emma Small (Mercedes McCambridge). Several scenes on horseback show this solitary woman dressed like a widow with black weeds flying in the wind, like a demon from Hell, culminating in a stunning close-up, as she turns to face the camera, in exaltation at setting fire to Vienna's place. This is the climax to a film in which Vienna has tried to mediate among conflicts 'dominated by death, betrayal and revenge' (Cook, 1988, p.299). By offering outlaws hospitality and finally harbouring an injured youth, the tolerant female world she stands for is condemned. Surviving a failed attempt to hang her and a gunfight with Emma, Vienna washes her hands of the assorted ranchers, outlaws and the posse from Hell: 'still in pants, still more than equal to any man . . . Vienna bids farewell to the western' (Cook, 1988, p.299).

Despite the film's title, the hero and villain of *Johnny Guitar* are both women. This has led to considerable critical debate about the film's 'competing discourses about gender' (Peterson, 1998, p.323) and its feminist identity. For Jennifer Peterson, Emma's villainy is located not in a rampant conservative hatred but in a stereotypical lesbianism. Finally abandoned by the male posse to her death in a gunfight with Vienna, Emma dies a magnificent villain, taking as many men with her as she can. Peterson sees in the resolution not a conflict between good and bad women but between good and bad sexuality. Yet Vienna understands Emma's motivation as sexual jealousy of her relationship with the Dancing Kid (Scott Brady). While Emma remains throughout the film in her black weeds, Vienna shifts from competing black trouser suits to dresses and abandons the magnificent white costume she wears to signify her purity when it is set alight during her escape. At that point, she removes it to reveal the trousers beneath. Vienna 'has it all, both breasts and a gun' (ibid., p.322).

While the gender identity signalled by Emma's unchanging habit remains stable, it is fluid for both the female hero and the male heroine. Both at times sport and use phallic guns, both use and refuse physical violence, yet these signifiers of masculinity contrast with feminine counterparts in the musical instruments that both play. In contrast to Vienna, who motivates action, Johnny (Sterling Hayden) is invariably passive, observing the action from the dramatic sidelines at the edges of the frame. However, 'Johnny is not completely feminised, nor is Vienna characterised as unhealthy for her androgyny; they are clearly sexually involved and there is no ambivalence on Johnny's part about his attraction to Vienna' (ibid., p.334). The song that opens and closes the film suggests that the story is told from Vienna's point of view, since 'There was never a man like my Johnny, like the one they call Johnny Guitar.' This combination of role-playing and female point-of view makes it possible to view Vienna as one of the few 'self-sufficient individualistic' female Western heroes, 'triumphantly affirmed by the narrative' (ibid., p.336) of *Johnny Guitar*.

Critics have been exercised by the melodramatic excess of the film's style. For Pamela Robertson, the film's 'feminist camp' contains a misogyny implied by the hatred between two women that 'yet, by its very excess, undermines and critiques' the misogyny (1995, p.33). In the same way that *Rancho Notorious* draws on its star's persona to inform the character of Altar Keane, so Joan Crawford's changing persona at a time of a similar career decline informs the qualities of masculinity and professionalism she brings to Vienna's phallic power (ibid., p.34). Crawford's female image at the time as a 'domineering shrew' also complicates what Robertson perceives as 'the kinky eroticism of

Vienna (Joan Crawford) wears the trousers and rules the roost over the Dancing Kid (Scott Brady) (right) and his gang (from the left, Ernest Borgnine, Ben Cooper and Royal Dano) in *Johnny Guitar* (1954).

the relationship' with Emma (ibid., p.41). Her concluding argument is that dissonances of character, the melodrama narrative and the film's baroque style enable 'all women, lesbian and straight . . . to create an alternative and oppositional reading' (ibid., p.46).

FEMINIST WESTERNS

Role-playing and disguise is also the strategy of the independent film, *The Ballad of Little Jo* (1993), one of the few Westerns scripted and directed by a woman, Maggie Greenwald. Although Janet Thumim considers that 'the Western and feminism seem to be contradictory terms' (1998, p.353) and Dowell claims that the film suggests that 'the only way a woman can succeed in the West(ern) is to become a man' (1995, p.9), Greenwald counters by saying that the film shows 'we belong' (Modleski, 1998, p.360). The central character is Jo Monaghan (Suzy Amis) who escapes from her Victorian melodrama as an Eastern unwed mother, to find that life West is no better for a woman. So Jo masquerades as a man, 'at first a circumstantial necessity, then an inspiration for survival and finally, of course, a tragic kind of heroism' (Dowell, 1995, p.9). Horrifically, Jo decides to scar her face in order to conceal and protect her gender from the male population around her. Yet it paradoxically allows for 'the pleasure and freedom enjoyed by a woman who cross-dresses as a man' (Modleski, 1998, p.356).

Like her namesake in *The Ballad of Josie*, Jo sets up a sheep farm, which she has to defend from the marauding employees of the Western Cattle Company. Jo's relationship to the landscape is tender and intimate and goes further than property ownership. She learns to live in a difficult but beautiful terrain in the same way as she sets about learning to live in disguise. As she grows more at ease with herself, she welcomes into her home Tinman (David Chung), a Chinese railroad worker she saves from lynching. At first their relationship is one of master and servant, but as Tinman gradually reveals himself to be more than the stereotypical 'chink' behind which he hides intelligence and sensitivity, Jo reveals her true identity and they fall in love. Aware that if their love was found out, they would be 'unquestionably, brutally' killed, they keep it private.

Jo's gender is revealed only at her death, with the local townsmen surrounding the body as it is laid out. Badger, a neighbour who has done his best to help out a resistant Jo during hard times, is incandescent with rage at the deceit, but most are more amazed or amused.

One of the film's original pleasures is its ability to bring into the foreground the gendered labour that otherwise goes on in the background of so many domestic scenes in Westerns, such as cooking, sewing and washing. These form part of the everyday material conditions of life in the film, historicising its Western imaginary in makeshift and provisional buildings set in a harsh but sensual natural setting, echoing Greenwald's own 'very primal connection to the landscape of the West' (ibid., p.359). Westerns as early as *The Trail of the Lonesome Pine* (1916 and 1936) suggest that the West is a place where women can break away from family constrictions to find their identity independently, but *The Ballad of Little Jo* is one of the few to explore the theme so affirmatively.

GENDER AND RACIAL MINORITY

Revisionist Westerns which take Native Americans and women as the central subjects to rethink the genre, invariably choose male Native Americans and white women. Though Indian women have been a 'central feature of the popular imaginary since . . . [p]opular literature evolved the stereotype of the docile squaw who tragically falls in love with the white man, often sacrificing herself for him or her tribe' (Jay, 2000, p.6), few have benefited from revisionist attention. The Indian woman at the centre of early films such as *The Girl and the Outlaw* (1906) and *Iola's Promise* (1910) differs little from those in revisionist films like *Broken Arrow* and *Little Big Man*, all of whom end up dead. Disney's animated feature, *Pocahontas* (1995), at least, has the woman as the central protagonist. She is also one of the few to survive partnership with whites in Westerns. It is telling that Stands-with-a-Fist, partner to the hero of *Dances With Wolves*, also remains alive at the end, but she is not a native but a white captive of the Dakota Sioux. Miscegenist assumptions die hard.

The condition of Native American women has yet to be fully explored in revisionist Westerns. Although there was hope of this, when Sacheen Littlefeather delivered Marlon Brando's Best Actor Oscar acceptance speech at the 1972 Academy Award ceremony and later acted in the pro-Indian film, *Winterhawk* (1975), but this was to be her only screen performance. Perhaps the most enjoyable role and performance for any female Native American in a Western is the Navajo Geraldine Keams in *The Outlaw Josey Wales* (1976) who evades beatings by white traders to join the hero's growing band of outcasts, and claim her share of fighting, laughing and loving among them.

Other American racial minorities fare little better. Among other Westerns to subtly subvert conventional racial relationships is *Walk Like a Dragon* (1960), in which a Chinese woman is rescued from a slave market by the hero, only to be subjected to the racism of the Western cattle town he takes her to.

Historically, Mexicans in Westerns are devious 'greasers', violent revolutionaries or exotic heroes like Zorro and the Cisco Kid (Frayling in Buscombe 1988, pp.184–8). Yet Mexico is as commonly a refuge for Americans on the run, as in *Wonderful Country* (1959) and *The Wild Bunch*, and Mexican actors like Pedro Armendáriz, Katy Jurado and Gilbert Roland frequently rose above the limitations of their generic roles (Armendáriz especially, as one of *Three Godfathers* (1948)). The history provides evidence of America's deeply ambivalent relationship to its old enemy on the Texas border. As early as 1912, however, two of Romaine Fielding's films, *The New Ranch Foreman* and *A Romance of the Border*, 'went against prevailing conventions to present Hispanic characters not as "greasers" and bandits but in a favourable light' (Woal and Woal, 1995, p.15).

The Mexican government and public grew sensitive to negative representations of its people and sought strategies to ameliorate the worst excesses. The making of *The Magnificent Seven* (1960) in Mexico, for instance, was subject to the censorship of an appointee of the Mexican government, alert to any negative representations of its nationals in the script and during production. One consequence was the immaculately white appearance of the peons, a strange contrast to the dusty clothing of the Seven.

Viva Zapata! (1952) is among the first sound Westerns to deal with a Mexican as a serious central protagonist, though the figure played by Marlon Brando is still a revolutionary and the film a social realist drama more than a genre film. However, Burt Lancaster's Mexican sheriff in *Valdez is Coming* (1970) is an honourable liberal attempt to turn the racial tables within the genre form. Seeking justice for an Apache woman widowed by an arrogant gun-runner (John Cipher), Bob Valdez seeks compensation in the form of just one hundred dollars. For his pains, he is tied to a symbolic wooden cross and sent away. Valdez then kidnaps the gun-runner's wife, and the film escalates into an exciting chase Western. The wife slowly comes round to the hero's cause, learning of his military history, killing Indians for whites, as he says, 'before I knew better'. At the end, dragged across country, many of his men killed, and left to confront Valdez alone, the villain tells Valdez 'Next time'. Valdez holds out his hands for 'one hundred dollars'. There is a cut to an overhead shot and a freeze frame, as the end credits roll, leaving an audience to wonder on the outcome.

Although this is a racially well-intentioned genre film, a white American star again plays its Mexican hero. In such a context, *The Ballad of Gregorio Cortez* (1982) stands out. The Mexico of this film is a pastoral idyll from which the eponymous hero is chased after killing a sheriff. As the hero is hunted down, the posse inflates the reputation of their prey by attributing to him crimes perpetrated by others. When he is finally captured on a dusty border, Gregorio (James Olmos) is saved from hanging but imprisoned for twelve years. Events in the film turn on misunderstandings of language and culture between the Texas posse and indigenous communities (Hispanic, Chicano (Mexican–American) as well as Mexican). As with the Indian victim of the chase in *Tell Them Willie Boy is Here*, Gregorio's crime grows less important as the narrative proceeds, the film developing into a condemnation of America's institutionalised imperialism of minority racial identities.

REVISIONIST WESTERN FORM

Perhaps the most frequently represented legendary Westerner in Westerns is Buffalo Bill. In *Buffalo Bill* (1944), he is celebrated as a man of peace, forced to become an Indian fighter only because of the prejudices of others. In a coda at the end of the film, Bill (Joel McCrea) appropriately announces his retirement in a Show ring: a voice from the audience – a little boy on crutches – cries: 'God bless you, Buffalo Bill'. The final melodrama sanctifies Bill as an American hero. By the time of *Buffalo Bill and the Indians, or Sitting Bull's History Lesson* (1976), the 'humorously self-conscious show-business hype of the title is at odds with the traditional archetypal western' (Simon and Spence,

1995, p.67). Bill (Paul Newman) runs his Wild West like a man who believes his own publicity, 'a consumer of his own image' (ibid., p.67) who 'no longer has a firm grasp on his own identity' (ibid., p.68). Gregg Rickman claims 'the film's movement is circular, around and around Bill's arena, even as Buffalo Bill never learns anything. His psyche remains stunted, his ego expanding as his soul withers' (1998, p.390). Ned Buntline (Burt Lancaster) is the dime novelist who has created Bill's legend. Unlike Beachamp in *Unforgiven*, Ned has no illusions. He is as cynical as the film about the denial of history and justice in the promotion of the Wild West, both as myth and Show.

Bill's delusion contrasts with Sitting Bull's serene and implacable refusal to promote Western myths. The final scene recreates the legend of Custer's Last Stand in the Show arena, but Sitting Bull refuses to play the game as the hostile Indian of white fears, instead 'performing a modest horse act' (Simon and Spence, 1995, p.72). Bill's furious response exposes the conventional history that makes Bill the winner: 'In one hundred years, I'm still gonna be Buffalo Bill, star, and you're gonna be the Indian!' Yet the film 'deploys ambiguity, contradiction, and interference to destabilise' Western conventions, drawing our attention 'away from the story towards plotting . . . to how a nation and a hero have been built by their histories, endowed with illusory coherence by the way their stories have been told' (ibid., p.75). Bill's reputation as heroic Westerner is undermined in order to examine the Western 'both as a national myth and as a commercial entertainment' (ibid., 65).

It is not only the content of *Buffalo Bill and the Indians, or Sitting Bull's History Lesson* that is revisionist, but also its unconventional narrative form. The film is based on a play, *Indians*, by Arthur Kopit, that refuses simply to 'tell its story' but insists on requiring an audience to be sensitive to how the story is told. This is typical of the formal organisation of the modernist Western, seeking to expose the ideological work of illusion and myth in the genre by disrupting its conventional narrative form.

THE MODERNIST WESTERN

Modernist Westerns appear in many guises, since their primary concern is to explore the formal limits of the genre. They experiment with narrative structure, refusing genre expectations, conventional editing and lighting systems. The play with form in modernist Westerns is therefore less to do with what an audience sees, but how it is invited to see it. For instance, among B Westerns, *Forty Guns* (1957) and, to a lesser extent, *I Shot Jesse James* (1948), both directed by Sam Fuller, deploy a distinctive film style that Nicholas Garnham calls 'kino-fist'. The formal style then melodramatises the emotional relationships in those films (Lippe, 1998). Fuller's films seem hysterical not

The bamboo camera symbolises the self-referential, modernist play with the conventional form of the Western in Dennis Hopper's *The Last Movie* (1971).

only because of the melodrama of their stories, but also because their film form is excessively confrontational. Despite a conventional iconography, their unusual form makes these Westerns almost unrecognisable as genre films. Modernist Westerns are rare in Hollywood, however. In many ways, the bizarre *The Last Movie* (1971) is the most subversive of these, an indictment of the Western and its racial history. The film was made by Dennis Hopper after the popular success of *Easy Rider* (1969), which he co-directed with Peter Fonda. The film was barely seen on its first release until Hopper 'prised the film from Universal (Studios) and re-released it himself' (Hardy, 1991, p.333). Whilst it provides no central roles for Indians, it investigates indigenous interests more fundamentally than the majority of its predecessors. Hopper plays a wrangler working on a Hollywood Western filmed in contemporary Peru, who remains after the crew returns home. His subsequent adventures leave several companions dead through accidents or suicide. This morbid scenario has less revisionist significance than the climax that seems to belong to another 'experimental' film. The Peruvian Indians transform the apparatus of movie-making (with bamboo cameras, lights, tracks, etc.) into a religious ritual. Apparently interpreting the filmed action they previously observed as a sacrificial offering, it begins to look as if not only the characters will be killed, but also the cast of actors who play them. At the climactic moment, however, the film abruptly stops being a fiction: the cast break from their roles and are joined by the technical crew of *The Last Movie* who appear from behind the camera to romp around the set with them. Exposing the film as fictional in this way is a modernist critique of commercial film-making and Western storytelling. Hardy considers that its subversive form undermines the Western's conventional racial relations; it becomes a film that 'chronicles America's and Hollywood's continued abuse of power over the natives' (1991, p.33). This provocative critique of American imperialism and the Western genre is expressed in a self-conscious narrative and hallucinatory images, probably inspired by the on- and off-screen drug-taking that led to the film's reputation as what Jonathan Rosenbaum calls an 'acid Western'.

THE POST-MODERN WESTERN

Dead Man (1995) was made wholly independently of Hollywood. It is equally formally enigmatic but a wholly dramatic Western, structured by director Jim Jarmusch in two parts. In the first, Johnny Depp is the conventional hero, William Blake, yet another Eastern innocent in the Western tradition stretching from Douglas Fairbank's hero in *Wild and Woolly* to Jack Crabb in *Little Big Man*. In this current guise, he plays an accountant seeking work in a nightmare vision of a township West. The town of Machine is one vast factory served by narrow streets of thick mud, a visual counterpart of the 'dark satanic mills' of industrialisation versed by Blake's more famous namesake, the English poet. When Blake is rejected by his prospective employer, the mill owner, Dickinson (Robert Mitchum) (an Old Testament patriarch complete with shotgun, fat cigar and long, white hair), he seeks solace in the arms of prostitute Thel. Forced to defend himself against Dickinson's jealous son, a gunfight leaves Thel and the son dead and Blake seriously wounded. He finds himself on the run from bounty hunters and he is easily identifiable in what Dickinson calls a 'goddamn clown suit'.

Beyond the town, the West turns out to be a Garden despoiled by the detritus of failed white expansion. Abandoned wagons and a sewing machine, piles of buffalo bones and burnt-out Indian tepees litter the trail. Wandering aimlessly, Blake is rescued by a Native American called Nobody (Gary Farmer) in preference to 'He Talks Loud, Says Nothing' as the Makah community, who reject his white-educated ways, call him. Nobody becomes Blake's guide and saviour. Fantastically, Nobody takes Blake for his English counterpart, quoting from his poems, and tending to his life-threatening wounds. At the end of the film, Nobody places the dying Blake in a canoe that drifts on the current of a river, 'taken up to the next level of the world – the place where William Blake is found – where his spirit belongs'.

The irony of Nobody's name is complex. He introduces himself by the title of the Italian Western, *My Name is Nobody* (1973), the comic reflexivity contrasting with the tenor of the grammatical sense that as 'nobody' does these things to the white man, the white man must take responsibility himself. The further irony is that the Native American is, indeed, an American 'nobody', effaced from American history and marginalised in American society. The final irony is in the destination Nobody sees for Blake, a spiritual escape for a character whose identity has become confused by overlaying his cartoon city suit with feathers and face paint, the signs of the indigenous Native American.

The moment of their first meeting marks the second half of the film from which point Nobody gradually takes over the hero's role from a more and more passive Blake. As if exacting revenge for all those 'faithful Indian companions' in the history of the Western, consigned to secondary status beside the white hero, 'Nobody uses Blake as a means of re-entering Native American culture, selling his vision of Blake as a spiritual heir of William Blake (the poet) to the Makah community of the Pacific Northwest' (Rickman, 1998, p.395).

Dead Man is 'built around a classic journey across the American West' (ibid., p.390) seen as 'the land of the dead' (ibid., p.400). This inverts the meaning of the setting and also the common allegorical function of the journey. Unlike most heroes of the journey Western, for whom the West provides a learning experience, Blake's quest is not spiritual. The 'Vanishing' American of frontier history is not only symbolised by Nobody, who dies in a duel with the only surviving bounty hunter, but by Blake and the white legacy.

Some critics find the film's revisionism limited because the Indian is again the elegiac figure of the Vanishing American, depending 'for authoritative representation on white discourse' (Hall, 2001, p.3) or 'a double Other: his Indianness is complete, yet he is also more than Indian, for he so perfectly embodies all the high virtues in which we confirm civilisation's best' (Prats, 1996, p.25). However, Nobody, is the sole figure who, against all the historical odds, is resilient and self-aware. The revisionism of *Dead Man* counteracts both the 'white triumphalist view' (Rosenbaum) of the romance Western and the pro-Indian Western theme of the Indian as victim. Nobody's centrality provides a point of view which observes that killing others (and Others) leads only to the death of self. Destructive in its unknowing, foolish innocence and smug certainties, white culture, like Blake's body, drifts downstream to oblivion.

Dead Man is also an allusive Western, its narrative meandering and episodic. In its resolution, which sees both Blake drifting down river, and

The confused identity of Johnny Depp's William Blake, the 'Vanishing American' of *Dead Man* (1996), is symbolised by the 'goddamn clown suit' overlaid by Native American signs.

Nobody and his assassin dead, the film questions more than its representations of traditional Western characters and situations. Drawing on New History themes of aimless quest and environmental destruction, Rickman concludes: 'what is promulgated in previous poetry, myth or films in the Western genre is upended and reversed – cancelled out' (ibid., p.384). *Dead Man* invites us to ask what making a Western after New History could mean, especially in a post-modern world where meaning is said to be no longer fixed, singular or reliable (Jameson, 1985).

THE POST-REVISIONIST WESTERN

Rickman's view is that even as *Dead Man* suggests that, like its heroes, the Western is dead, 'under erasure' (1998, p.401), its dependency on the genre's form and conventions confirms a continuing vitality. In the mainstream commercial cinema of Hollywood, Clint Eastwood is the last film-maker to persist in re-imagining the traditional illusionist form of the Western. His revenge Westerns have developed the romance hero into a supernatural avenger (*High Plains Drifter*, 1972, *Pale Rider*, 1995), who is still human enough to be redeemed when released from his obsessive quest by a company of angels (*The Outlaw Josey Wales*, the more modern *Bronco Billy*, 1980). Over thirty years, Eastwood the director has questioned the persona of Eastwood the actor, the figure of the Man With No Name and the masculinity it represents. Concurrently, the simultaneous celebration and questioning of the genre and its subject's American identity, makes Eastwood's Westerns exceptional. In *Bronco Billy*, for instance, Billy (Eastwood) is the only character with faith in his image as a Western hero in a cheap travelling Wild West Show even derided by its performers. He finally overcomes their cynicism, performing in a circus tent made up of a patchwork of American flags. For all their faults, America and the Western are celebrated.

The surprising popular and critical success of *Unforgiven* (1992), 'the most rigorous and cohesive of nineties' Westerns' (Grist, 1996, p.294), scripted by David Webb Peoples, is testimony to the continuing vibrancy of Eastwood's revisionist tendencies. The narrative of *Unforgiven* is set in Big Whiskey, Wyoming, in 1880 and is motivated by a crime in which a prostitute's face is slashed by one of two cowboys after laughing at his 'teensy little pecker'. In the aftermath of the scene, Little Bill Daggett (Gene Hackman), the 'genial and engaging but menacing' (Bingham, 1994, p.233) sheriff and highest authority in town, negotiates a settlement in the interests of the male owner of the brothel, saloon and 'billiard parlor'. Enraged that the cowboys have merely been fined and that the human face behind what the men consider 'damaged property' has been disregarded, the prostitutes take matters into their own hands. As in many Westerns, the narrative of *Unforgiven* begins with an injustice that must be put right. However, the law in this case is made explicitly patriarchal, serving only male interests, and avenging a conventional crime against a woman is initiated not by a male hero, but by an unconventional society of women.

Any political correctness in the feminist challenge is soon subverted by the extreme violence it provokes. The price on the cowboys' heads is $1,000. The first taker soon arrives, the arrogant English Bob (Richard Harris). Backed by his deputies, Bill confronts, savagely beats, imprisons, humiliates and finally releases him. If the treatment is a warning not to bring violence to the town, Bill's subsequent savagery towards others seeking the reward merely releases his further sadistic impulses. He beats William Munny (Clint Eastwood) and whips to death his friend, Ned Logan (Morgan Freeman). The representation of violence in *Unforgiven* is 'brutal, dreadful, squalid; anything but noble or ennobling' (Grist, 1996, p.297), stressing the 'fear, anxiety, suffering' (Thumim, 1998, p.347) for all involved. Grist relates the violence to 'destructive phallic energy and the male psychosexual urge to dominate' (1996, p.297).

Information spreads by word of mouth in *Unforgiven*. Like Chinese whispers, the retelling of the mutilation story distorts the original, until the version that inspires Munny is the disfigurement of face, eyes, fingers and 'tits' of the prostitute. The way in which myth enters into the genre is made explicit through the role of Beauchamp, the dime novelist who chronicles English Bob's gallant heroics with a gun. When Little Bill reads to his prisoner from Bob's 'biography', mispronouncing 'The Duke of Death' as the humiliating 'Duck of Death', we learn that if ever there was a gunfight with 'Two Gun Corcoran', then the name derived from 'a dick so big, it was longer than the barrel on that Walker Colt'. Beauchamp's role exposes the unreliability and dangers of myth-making, questioning 'the morality and the veracity of propositions about America's past as delivered in Western myths' (Thumim, 1998, p.341).

This is a world in which men make false claims, hiding behind reputations to avoid the risk of exposure. Grist claims that their savagery arises from anxiety at 'the loss of male potency' (1996, p.299). Thumim argues that the strangely ramshackle home Bill is building so badly ('not a square corner anywhere') expresses a male inadequacy he shares with other characters unsuccessfully masked by his savagery. William Munny's case is more complex. At the start of the film, he abandons pig farming, sick of chasing sick pigs. Leaving his homestead, placing his children in care, finding it difficult to mount his horse, this domesticated figure seems anything but a Western hero, and certainly no gunfighter. But his awesome reputation as a 'cold as snow' 'killer of men' is slowly revealed. It is related in an opening title card and familiar to all he meets. But Eastwood underplays the role, making it unclear if Munny's past is as violent as the reputation claims or whether, as for others around him, it is the product of myth. Susan Jeffords terms the contrast as one between 'hard bodies' and 'soft men'.

The uncertainty plays on the Eastwood persona, laconic and enigmatic, reflexively invoking a film career as an avenging killer. Munny's past is repressed, not least by the memory of a wife, Claudia, now dead from smallpox, whom he constantly claims reformed him, cured him of 'wicked-ness'. When he reaches Big Whiskey, he is sick with fever, a sign of his inability to deal with the present, as if unable to return to his reputation or even in fear of living up to it. In this context, the film's conclusion seems a decisive 'moment of moral ecstasy' (Tompkins, 1992, p.229) and, at first, a return to the more familiar Eastwood persona. Bent on avenging Ned's death and fuelled with whiskey, Munny enters the Big Whiskey saloon, surprising Little Bill and his deputies with the insult: 'Who owns this shit hole?' In the ensuing bloodbath, Munny kills everyone, armed and unarmed, innocent and guilty, except Beauchamp, left as witness and continuing myth-maker. 'I don't deserve this', says the dying Little Bill. 'Deserve's got nothing to do with it', says Munny. For Thumim, 'It is no longer clear, by the end of the film, who were the heroes, villains or bystanders, nor even, perhaps, what a hero is' (1998, p.347).

Unlike the slow-motion deaths in Peckinpah's Westerns, death and killing in *Unforgiven* is not a spectacle of aesthetic beauty. Grist argues that 'the carnage is such as to overwhelm any moral validation and constitutes perhaps the film's most significant revision of Western violence, which is thus reduced to a matter of power and circumstance rather than justice and right' (1996, p.300). Furthermore, 'the moral indignation that justifies violence in classical Westerns is shown as a construction of men' (Bingham, 1994, p.238). For Grist, also, the casting of older actors associated with the genre implies that it is 'the destructive attitudes of the older generation (which are) forcefully attacked' (ibid., p.301).

Munny's survival is incredible, supernatural. His threatening final words, spoken into the darkness and rain of the street, returns the reformed hero to villainy: 'You better not cut up nor otherwise harm no whores, or I'll come back and kill every one of you sons of bitches'. Yet a final title surreally declares that Munny and his children 'disappeared, some said to San Francisco, where it was rumoured he prospered in dry goods'. Hero or villain, the title leaves open the relationship between myth and history: 'In this way the audience itself is implicated in the recording, preservation and recycling of stories and their transformation into myths . . . of the Western . . . and of the masculine. (The film) demands that its audiences consider the politics of storytelling as well as its consequences for culture and history' (Thumim, 1995, p.350).

The final spectacle, undercut by the whimsy of the title card, risks undermining the film's revisionist achievement. For Susan Kelley, the film ultimately reconfirms the genre's traditional celebration of a tough masculinity, 'that the despair engendered by the recognition of the impossibility of a permanent and stable male identity encourages and condones violence' (1995, p.95) with the saving grace that 'the fiction finally tells us that the image of exemplary manhood *is* fiction, an imaginary construct' (ibid., p.99). But, as Thumim says, 'it is not only a classic Western, it is about the Western' (1998, p.342).

On the journey to Big Whiskey, Munny and Ned discover that their companion, the Schofield Kid (Jaimz Woolvett), a boy who claims a history of killing, is unable to shoot anybody, and not merely because he can see no further than his hand. His denial of the way of the gun may be conventional (when he abandons the quest with 'I'd rather be blind and ragged than dead', he echoes the realisation of mortality amongst conventional youth in Westerns like *Comanche Station*, 1959 and *Bad Company*, 1972). In contrast to this, the violence unleashed by the conspiracy of patriarchal abuse in the name of female justice is unconventional. One of the cowboys is innocent of the crime, and even seeks to make further reparation for his friend, but that does not spare him from an undeserved killing. Throughout, the injured woman (mistaken for 'an angel' by a delirious Munny), stands in silent condemnation of 'the action taken in her name' (Grist, 1996, p.301). She becomes identified with Munny when, after his beating, he tells her that 'I must look kinda like you' and yet she appears nothing like the subject of the horror stories he has heard about her disfigurement. The film thus offers a critique of the power of the gun even as it explores the conditions that produce it, working to reveal 'the complex and unsettling links between male sexuality and gender, their centrality to the Western genre (and) the uncertain and provisional understandings of reality embodied in both contemporary and historical accounts of Western history' (Thumim, 1998, p.350).

Armando J. Prats considers that *Unforgiven* 'reaffirms the moral role of the Western hero and, if only within the flash of the shootout, announces the resurgence, perhaps even affirms, the enduring relevance of the western' (1995, p.102). In the post-revisionist Western, myth returns in the full knowledge of revisionist history (Babiak, 1998). *Unforgiven* persists with 'the magic and moral purpose' (Prats, 1995, p.117) of the Western, the promise of a continuing capacity for further creative questioning of its fabulous fusion of history and myth: 'history . . . which is so self-assured in the finality with which it declares the end of the myth, has after all ensured the return of the hero . . . back once again from the sunset' (ibid., p.119).

No more hope nor justification for the survival and continuing life of the Western imaginary could be expressed than in this final sentiment.

FURTHER READING

Bazin, A. (1971b) 'The Evolution of the Western' in *What is Cinema?* Vol.2 (University of California Press, Berkeley) reprinted in Kitses, J. and Rickman, G. (eds) (1998) *The Western Reader* (Limelight, New York).

One of the two founding essays in film criticism of the Western. Where Warshow focused on the hero of the Western film, Bazin distinguished between the classical form of films such as *Stagecoach* and 'supra–Westerns' like *High Noon*. For him, the social and moral comment of the latter regrettably replaced the myth, history, drama and mise-en-scène of the former. At a time in the 1950s when authorship in American Cinema was denied, Bazin promoted a pantheon of directors whose work established the genre's tradition, including John Ford, Howard Hawks and Anthony Mann. Bazin opened the way to taking the classical Hollywood Western seriously.

Buscombe, E. (ed.) (1988) *The BFI Companion to the Western* (André Deutsch, London).

Buscombe's lavishly illustrated tome is a treasure chest of frontier history and folklore, with entries ranging from Abilene to Emiliano Zapata, and taking in cultural analyses of masculinity and the meaning of the railroad in the Western genre. Its myriad potted revisionist histories inform the frontier legends in Westerns. Following a deft introductory history of the genre, there are brief biographies of leading Western film-makers, lists of all their films, thumbnail analyses of selected Westerns and a rare survey of television Western series. This is an admirable work that satisfies both fans and scholars.

Buscombe, E. and Pearson, R. (eds) (1998) *Back in the Saddle Again: New Essays on the Western* (British Film Institute, London).

A collection of original writing in film studies and cultural studies of the Western. It includes important new interventions in Western archaeology (especially Studlar on Douglas Fairbanks and Schneider's jaw-dropping account of male relations in German Westerns), cultural studies of the Western in advertising and costume, New History applied to the Western film and Boddy's seminal research into the 'rise and fall of the TV Western'. Buscombe's opening analysis of the decline of the genre is definitive.

Cameron, I. and Pye, D. (eds) (1996) *The Movie Book of the Western* (Studio Vista, London).

This collection of important essays in contemporary film studies of the Western was among the first to suggest that the genre could still elicit challenging scholarship. It contains some hardy perennials from writers associated with the long-standing British journal of mise-en-scène criticism, *Movie*, new critical works and reprints of notable cultural studies. Foremost amongst these is Pumphrey's accomplished analysis of masculinity in the Western, 'Why Do Cowboys Wear Hats in the Bath? Style Politics for the Older Man'.

Cawelti, J. (1971) *The Six-Gun Mystique* (Bowling Green University Popular Press, Bowling Green, Ohio) and (1976) *Adventure, Mystery and Romance: Formula Stories as Art and Popular Culture* (Chicago University Press, Chicago).

In these two books, Cawelti elaborates the conventions of the 'formula' Western as a popular genre of adventure, mystery and romance. Like Kitses, Cawelti notes the ambivalence of the frontier in the Western, 'a place where advancing civilisation met declining savagery' in a landscape where settlement in the wilderness symbolises 'the thematic conflict between savagery and civilisation and its resolution'. The detail of Cawelti's exploration of the recurrent generic plots, situations, settings and characters through which this thematic is explored identifies the texture and complexity of the genre's pleasures and meanings.

Cook, P. and Bernink, M. (eds) (1999) *The Cinema Book* (British Film Institute, London).

This authoritative film studies text contains a section on genre criticism and the seminal place of the Western within it. It is also a repository for generations of film educationists whose work lies buried within the writing of the academy's more prestigious names. The writing of acknowledged scholars in the field such as Neale, Cook, Gledhill and Buscombe bears testimony to generations of uncredited teachers in the mandatory sector and their dedication to the education of new and future generations of film students.

Denning, M. (1987) *Mechanic Accents: Dime Novels and Working-Class Culture in America* (Verso, London).

The dime novel is an important nineteenth-century antecedent of the Western film, with its sensational stories about the American West. For Cawelti, these are no more than 'a form of adolescent escapism' but for Denning, they provided their working-class readership with a 'symbolic form of class conflict'. Denning shows how a range of conventions in narrative and iconography found their way into twentieth-century Western films. He shifts attention from film criticism's concentration on the Western as frontier history to the social meanings of the genre.

Fiedler, L. (1968; 72) *The Return of the Vanishing American* (Paladin, London).

Fiedler traces the contradictory history of white America's treatment of the Native American. By the end of the nineteenth century, the indigenous population had almost died out, despite a powerful nineteenth-century desire to protect its original peoples and preserve their cultures. The book has had a huge influence on popular histories, ethnic civil rights movements and the Western's elegiac representation of Native Americans.

Frayling, C. (1981; 1998) *Spaghetti Westerns: Cowboys and Europeans from Karl May to Sergio Leone* (Routledge and Kegan Paul, London/I.B. Tauris, London).

This is the major archival work on the European Western. It centres on the Italian 'Spaghetti' Westerns of the 1960s, providing a detailed study of their origins and development in Italy's social, political and film industrial context. Frayling argues that Italian Westerns not only challenge the hegemony of the Hollywood Western but also critique the classical genre form. He defends what detractors consider the sado-masochistic violence of the films as a comic strip genre parody, in the Italian tradition of commedia dell'arte.

Hardy, P. (ed.) (1991) *The Aurum Film Encyclopedia: The Western* (Aurum Press, London).

After a brief introductory survey, Hardy's encyclopedia explores each decade of sound Westerns with enlightening sketches of selected films, fully illustrated with evocative film stills. The entries are critically informed, especially valuable on inaccessible and neglected series Westerns of the 1930s and B features in the 1940s and 1950s. Appendices provide a range of tables of most popular Westerns, box-office Western stars, Academy Award winners and other diverting trivia. A final checklist of films and a comprehensive index makes the book exhaustive.

Kitses, J. (1969) *Horizons West* (Thames and Hudson, London).

Kitses' 'ambiguous cluster of meanings and attitudes that provide the traditional thematic structure' of the Western film is organised into an influential binary model. His 'shifting antinomies' between wilderness and civilisation, the individual and community, nature and culture, the East and the West is developed from Smith's central garden/desert dichotomy that both find at the root of American identity. For Kitses, 'the Western is American history', but a history refracted through the 'narrative and dramatic structure' of the genre's 'fabulous' world, especially of the Westerns of his three directors, Anthony Mann, Budd Boetticher and Sam Peckinpah.

Kitses, J. and Rickman, G. (eds) (1998) *The Western Reader* (Limelight Editions, New York).

This reader includes founding essays in film criticism of the Western resurrected from 'out-of-print' limbo. Crucially, Warshow, Bazin, Willemen, Russell and Kitses are contained within. Key essays buried away in small journals are reprinted, notably Lehman's 'Looking at Look's Missing Reverse Shot: Psychoanalysis and Style in John Ford's *The Searchers*'. There is also a string of new essays which include Thumim's generous analysis of *Unforgiven*, Rickman's definitive account of *Dead Man* and Kitses' gentle exploration of *The Ballad of Little Jo* among many others.

Limerick, P.N., Millner, C. and Rankin, C. (eds) (1991) *Trails: Toward a New Western History* (University Press of Kansas, Lawrence).

Among new revisionist histories of the American frontier myth, this book provides a platform for a selection of the major approaches and arguments. It offers a range of studies which argue a return of suppressed categories of race, class, sexual identity and capitalism to frontier histories. Although the work is revealing about history, it is less informed about how Westerns deal with it.

Smith, H.N. (1950; 71) *Virgin Land: The American West as Symbol and Myth* (Harvard University Press, Cambridge, Massachusetts).

Smith's cultural study informs all subsequent criticism of the Western. It concerns the symbolic meaning of the frontier in American society and popular culture. Smith argues that American national identity grew from a paradoxical idealisation of the American landscape as a biblical Garden and a wilderness Desert, to be 'tamed' for settlement and agriculture. For Smith, the formation of American identity lies in a tension between nature and culture, an ideological tension structuring fiction about the West, exposed by his analysis of the common concerns of Western literature.

Slotkin, R. (1992) *Gunfighter Nation: The Myth of the Frontier in Twentieth Century America* (Atheneum, New York).

Slotkin's third and final volume in his structuralist account of the meaning of Western narratives in the conflict between savagery and civilisation in American history, outlines the interacting relation of Western films and American political history. His extraordinarily detailed, painstaking scholarship and subtle argument traces the interacting role of frontier mythology in American culture and the Western, from its European origins to the administration of Ronald Reagan.

Stanfield, P. (2001) *Hollywood, Westerns and the 1930s: The Lost Trail* (University of Exeter, Exeter).

This is the major work on series Westerns, especially on the singing cowboy. Stanfield's thesis is that the series Western has little to do with frontier history and the formation of American identity and more with the politics of 'the land question' at the times when the films were made. His focus on 'the idea of the cowboy as a figure produced by the social tensions engendered by industrialisation' reveals much about the direction taken by Westerns of the late 1930s onwards and accounts especially for the popularity of the series Western with the rural audience.

Studlar, G. and Bernstein, M. (eds) (2001) *John Ford Made Westerns: Filming the Legend in the Sound Era* (Indiana University Press, Bloomington and Indianapolis).

Director John Ford's many Westerns are central to the genre. An introduction provides a skilled overview of the seminal critical writing about them. The book continues with several revisionist analyses. These are especially valuable in essays on Ford's representation of women (Studlar), ethnicity (Berg) and economics (Lehman).

Tompkins, J. (1992) *West of Everything: The Inner Life of Westerns* (Oxford University Press, Oxford and New York).

Among a group of literary scholars who have turned their kind attention to the Western, Tompkins' analysis of the Western canon has had the most impact. She denies appeals to frontier history, arguing rather that the genre 'is about men's fears of losing their mastery, and hence their identity, both of which the Western tirelessly reinvents'. She adds, 'the Western struggles and strains to cast out everything feminine.' Tompkins' analysis offers a feminist corrective to masculinist celebrations of the genre, though the book lacks a certain sensitivity to the films.

Warshow, R. (1954) 'Movie Chronicle: The Westerner', *Partisan Review* reprinted in Warshow, R. (1962) *The Immediate Experience* (Doubleday, New York), Nachbar, J. (ed.) (1974) *Focus on the Western* (Prentice-Hall, Englewood Cliffs, New Jersey) and in Kitses, J. and Rickman, G. (eds) (1998) *The Western Reader* (Limelight Editions, New York).

Together with Bazin's 'The Evolution of the Western', this is one of the two pioneering essays in the critical history of the Western film. Warshow's Western landscape is a wilderness environment and his wandering Westerner an American ideal, a man at ease with himself and the world about him. Yet he is one whose violence makes him a contradictory moral figure, even tragic and ultimately archaic, set apart from a society that, paradoxically, requires his skills. Warshow convincingly connects the Western hero and the Western landscape to ideas of masculinity, American history and American national identity, connections that were developed by subsequent critics.

Wright, W. (1975) *Sixguns and Society* (University of California Press, Berkeley).

Wright argues that the Western is 'part of the cultural language by which America understands itself'. This is a detailed structuralist study of the 'meanings viewers demand of the myth' of the West. Wright is less interested in historical connections than with what the most popular Westerns reveal about American society at the time of their making. He establishes the principle that while Westerns may deal with an American identity refracted through history, it is more crucially the contemporary world that they explore.

BIBLIOGRAPHY

Abel, R. (1998) 'Our Country'/Whose Country?: The 'Americanisation' project of
   Early Westerns' in Buscombe, E. and Pearson, R. (eds) *Back in the Saddle Again:*
   New Essays on the Western (British Film Institute, London) 77–95.
Agel, H. (1969) *Le Western* (Lettres Moderne, Paris).
Aleiss, A. (1995a) 'The Vanishing American: Hollywood's Compromise to Indian
   Reform', *Journal of American Studies* 25 (3) 467–72.
Aleiss, A. (1995b) 'Native Americans: The Surprising Silents', *Journal of Cineaste*
   21 (3) 34–6.
American Film Institute Catalogue (1995) *Film Beginnings 1893–1910* (Scarecrow
   Press, Metuchen, New Jersey).
Anderson, R. (1979) 'The Role of the Western Film Genre in Industry Competition
   1907–11', *Journal of the University Film Association* 31 (2).
Athearn, R.G. (1986) *The Mythic West in Twentieth Century America* (University Press
   of Arkansas, Lawrence).

Babiak, P.E.S. (1998) 'Rewriting Revisionism: Clint Eastwood's *Unforgiven*',
   CineAction 46 56–63.
Baird, R. (1996) 'Going Indian: Discovery, Adoption and Renaming Toward a True
   American, from *Deerslayer* to *Dances with Wolves*' in Bird, S.E. (ed.) *Dressing in*
   Feathers: The Construction of the Indian in Popular American Culture (Westview
   Press, Boulder, Colorado) 197–204.
Baker, B. (1996) '*Shane* Through Five Decades' in Cameron, I. and Pye, D. (eds)
   The Movie Book of the Western (Studio Vista, London) 214–20.
Barker, M. and Sabin, R. (1995) *The Lasting of the Mohicans: History of an American*
   Myth (University of Mississippi Press, Madison, Mississippi).
Basinger, J. (1993) *A Woman's View: How Hollywood Spoke to Women 1930–60*
   (Chatto & Windus, London).
Basinger, J. (1986) *The World War II Combat Film* (Columbia University Press,
   New York).
Bazin, A. (1971a) 'The Western or the American Film Par Excellence' in
   Bazin, A. *What is Cinema?* Vol.2 (University of California Press, Berkeley)
   140–8.
Bazin, A. (1971b) 'The Evolution of the Western' in Bazin, A. *What is Cinema?* Vol.2
   (University of California Press, Berkeley) 149–58.
Bederman, G. (1995) *Manliness and Civilisation: A Cultural History of Gender and Race*
   in the United States 1880–1917 (University of Chicago Press, Chicago).
Bellour, R. (ed.) (1966) *Le Western* (Union Général l'Editions, Paris).
Bellour, R. (1979) 'Alternation, Segmentation, Hypnosis: Interview with Raymond
   Bellour', *Camera Obscura* 314.

Berkhofer (Jnr), R.F. (1979) *The White Man's Indian: Images of the American Indian from Columbus to the Present* (Vintage Books, London).

Bernardi, D. (ed.) (1996) *The Birth of Whiteness: Race and the Emergence of U.S. Cinema* (Rutgers University Press, New Brunswick).

Bignell, J. (1966) 'Method Westerns: *The Left-Handed Gun* and *One-Eyed Jacks*' in Cameron, I. and Pye, D. (eds) *The Movie Book of the Western* (Studio Vista, London) 99–110.

Billington, R.A. (1981; 85) *Land of Savagery, Land of Promise: The European Image of the American Frontier in the Nineteenth Century* (University of Oklahoma Press, Norman and London).

Billington, R.A. (1956) *The Far Western Frontier 1830–1869* (Harper & Row, New York).

Bingham, D. (1994) *Acting Male* (Rutgers University Press, New Brunswick).

Bird, R.M. (1967) (repr.) *Nick of the Woods* (New College Press).

Bird, S.E. (ed.) (1996) *Dressing in Feathers: The Construction of the Indian in American popular Culture* (Westview Press, Boulder, Colorado).

Blackstone, S. (1986) *Buckskins, Bullets and Business: A History of Buffalo Bill's Wild West* (Greenwood Press, Connecticut).

Boddy, W. (1998) 'Sixty Million Viewers Can't be Wrong: The Rise and Fall of the TV Western' in Buscombe, E. and Pearson, R. (eds) *Back in the Saddle Again: New Essays on the Western* (British Film Institute, London).

Bogdanovich, P. (1967) *John Ford* (Studio Vista, London).

Bogle, D. (1974) *Toms, Coons, Mulattoes, Mammies and Bucks: An Interpretative History of Blacks in American Films* (Bantam, Books, New York).

Bold, C. (1987) *Selling the Wild West: Popular Western Fiction 1860–1960* (Indiana University Press, Bloomington and Indianapolis).

Bordwell, D., Staiger, J. and Thompson, K. (1985) *The Classical Hollywood Cinema: Film Style and Mode of Production to 1960* (Routledge and Kegan Paul, London).

Bowser, E. (1990) *The Transformation of Cinema 1907–1915* (University of California Press, Berkeley).

Brasner, W. (1977) 'The Wild West Exhibition and the Drama of Civilisation' in Mayer, D. and Richards, K. (eds) *Western Popular Theatre* (Methuen, London) 133–56.

Bratton, J., Cook, J. and Gledhill, C. (eds) (1994) *Melodrama: Stage, Picture, Screen* (British Film Institute, London).

Brauer, R. and Brauer, D. (1975) *The Horse, the Gun and the Piece of Property: Changing Images of the TV Western* (Bowling Green University Popular Press, Bowling Green, Ohio).

Bristow, J. (1991) *Empire Boys: Adventures in a Man's World* (HarperCollins, London).

Britton, A. (1996) 'Notes on *Pursued*' in Cameron, I. and Pye, D. (eds) *The Movie Book of the Western* (Studio Vista, London) 196–205.

Brooks, P. (1976) *The Melodramatic Imagination: Balzac, Henry James, Melodrama and the Mode of Excess* (Yale University Press, New Haven).

Brown, D. (1972) *Bury My Heart at Wounded Knee* (Pan, London).

Browne, N. (1975/6) 'The Spectator in the Text: The Rhetoric of *Stagecoach*' in *Film Quarterly* 29 (2) reprinted in Nichols, B. (ed.) (1985) *Movies and Methods 2* (University of California Press, Berkeley) 458–75.

Browne, N. (1998) *Refiguring American Film Genres* (University of California Press, Berkeley).

Brownlow, K. (1978) *The War, the West and the Wilderness* (Secker and Warburg, London).

Burns, W.N. (1926) *The Saga of Billy the Kid* (Grosset and Dunlap, New York).

Buscombe, E. (1970) 'The Idea of Genre in the American Cinema', *Screen* 11/12 33–45.

Buscombe, E. (ed.) (1988) *The BFI Companion to the Western* (André Deutsch, London).

Buscombe, E. (1992) *Stagecoach* (British Film Institute, London).

Buscombe, E. (1996) 'The Western' in Nowell-Smith, G. (ed.) *The Oxford History of World Cinema* (Oxford University Press, Oxford) 286–94.

Buscombe, E. and Pearson, R. (eds) (1998) *Back in the Saddle Again: New Essays on the Western* (British Film Institute, London).

Buscombe, E. (2000) *The Searchers* (British Film Institute, London).

Bush, C. (1977) *The Dream of Reason: American Consciousness and cultural achievement from Independence to the Civil War* (Edward Arnold, London).

Bush, C. (1988) 'Landscape' in Buscombe, E. (ed.) *The BFI Companion to the Western* (Andre Deutsch, London) 167–70.

Butler, R.C. (1985) 'What is a B Western?' in Wyatt, E.M. (ed.) *'B' Western: Cowboys of the Silver Screen* (Raleigh Chapter of the Western Film Preservation Society, North Carolina) 1.

Buxton, D. (1989) *From The Avengers to Miami Vice* (Manchester University Press, Manchester).

Cain, J.M. (1934) *The Postman Always Rings Twice* (Carnegie-Mellon University Press).

Calder, J. (1974) *There Must be a Lone Ranger: The Myth and Reality of the American Wild West* (Hamish Hamilton, London).

Cameron, I. and Pye, D. (eds) (1996) *The Movie Book of the Western* (Studio Vista, London).

Carey, D.S. (1975: 96) *The Hollywood Posse: The Story of a Gallant Band of Horsemen Who Made Movie History* (University of Oklahoma Press, Norman and London).

Cawelti, J. (1971) *The Six-Gun Mystique* (Bowling Green University Popular Press, Bowling Green, Ohio).

Cawelti, J. (1974) 'Reflections on the New Western Films' in Nachbar, J. *Focus on the Western* (Prentice-Hall, Englewood Cliffs, New Jersey) 113–17.

Cawelti, J. (1976) *Adventure, Mystery and Romance: Formula Stories as Art and Popular Culture* (Chicago University Press, Chicago).

Charney, L. and Schwartz, V.R. (eds) (1995) *Cinema and the Invention of Modern Life* (University of California Press, Berkeley).

Churchill, W. (1998) *Fantasies of the Master Race: Literature, Cinema and the Colonization of American Indians* (City Lights Books, San Francisco, California).

Clarens, C. (1980) *Crime Movies: An Illustrated History* (W.W. Norton, New York).

Collins, R. (1976) 'Genre: A Reply to Ed Buscombe' in *Screen* 11 (4/5) reprinted in Nichols, B. (ed.) (1985) *Movies and Methods* (University of California Press, Berkeley) 157–63.

Comber, M. and O'Brien, M. (1988) 'Evading the War: the Politics of the Hollywood Vietnam Film', *History*, The Journal of the Historical Association 73 (238).

Combs, R. (1989) 'A Fabulous Melancholy & A Greater Desire: *Pat Garrett & Billy the Kid*', *Monthly Film Bulletin* 56 (668) 262–5.

Cook, P. (1988) 'Women and the Western' in Kitses, J. and Rickman, G. (eds) reprinted from Buscombe, E. (ed.) *The BFI Companion to the Western* (British Film Institute, London).

Cook, P. and Bernink, M. (eds) (1999) *The Cinema Book* (British Film Institute, London) 137–56.

Corkin, S. (2000) 'Cowboys and Free Markets: Post-World War II Westerns and the U.S. Hegemony', *Cinema Journal* 39 (3) 66–91.

Coyne, M. (1997) *The Crowded Prairie: American National Identity in the Hollywood Western* (I.B. Tauris, London and New York).

Cronon, W., Miles, G. and Gitlin, J. (eds) (1992) *Under an Open Sky: Rethinking America's Western Past* (W.W. Norton, New York).

Davis, R.M. (1992) *Playing Cowboys: Low Culture and High Art in the Western* (University of Oklahoma Press, Norman and London).

Deloria, V. (1980) 'Foreword: American Fantasy' in Bataille, G. and Silet, C. (eds) *The Pretend Indian: Images of Native Americans in the Movies* (Iowa State University Press, Ames, Iowa).

DeMarco, M. (1980) *A Photostory of the Screen's Greatest Cowboy Star: Tom Mix* (Mario DeMarco Publications, Massachusetts).

Denning, M. (1987) *Mechanic Accents: Dime Novels and Working-Class Culture in America* (Verso, London).

Dibb, M. (1996) 'A Time and a Place: Budd Boetticher and the Western' in Cameron, I. and Pye, D. (eds) (Studio Vista, London) 161–6.

Dixon, T. (1905) *The Clansman: An Historical Romance of the Ku Klux Klan* (Doubleday, Page and Co., New York).

Dorfman, A. (1983) *The Empire's Old Clothes: What the Lone Ranger, Babar and other innocent heroes do to our minds* (Pantheon, New York).

Dowell, P. (1995) 'The Mythology of the Western: Hollywood Perspectives on Gender and Race in the Nineties', *Cineaste* xxxi (1–2) 6–10.

Drinnon, R. (1981) *Facing West: The Metaphysics of Indian Hating and Empire Building* (University of Minnesota Press, Minneapolis).

Dyer, R. (1984) 'Don't Look Now', *Screen* 25 (6) 61–73.

Dyer, R. (1987) *Heavenly Bodies: Film Stars and Society* (British Film Institute, London and Macmillan, London).

Dyer, R. (1992) *Only Entertainment* (Routledge, London).

Edmonds, I.G. (1997) *Big U: Universal in the Silent Days* (A.S. Barnes, New York).

Engelhardt, T. (1995) *The End of Victory Culture: Cold War America and the Disillusion of a Generation* (Basic Books, New York).

Evans, P.W. (1996) '*Westward the Women*: Feminising the Wilderness' in Cameron, I. and Pye, D. (eds) *The Movie Book of the Western* (Studio Vista, London).

Everson, W.K. (1969; 92) *The Hollywood Western: 90 Years of Cowboys, Indians, Trainrobbers, Sheriffs and Gunslingers, and Assorted Desperadoes* (Citadel Press, New Jersey).

Eyles, A. (1975) *The Western* (Tantivy Press, London).

Fairlamb, B. (1998) 'One in a Thousand: Western Stars, Heroes and their Guns', *CineAction* 46 18–25.

Fenin, G.N. and Everson, W.K. (1977) *The Western: From Silents to the Seventies* (Penguin, Harmondsworth).

Fiedler, L. (1968; 72) *The Return of the Vanishing American* (Paladin, St. Albans).

Fiske, J. (1885) *American Political Ideas Viewed from the Standpoint of Universal History* (Houghton Mifflin, Massachusetts).

Flynn, P. (undated) The Silent Western as Mythmaker, www.imagesjounal.com/issue06,infocus/silentwesterns2.htm

Frayling, C. (1981; 98) *Spaghetti Westerns: Cowboys and Europeans from Karl May to Sergio Leone* (Routledge and Kegan Paul, London/I.B. Tauris, London and New York).

Frayling, C. (1992) *Clint Eastwood* (Virgin Books, London).

Frayling, C. (2000) *Sergio Leone: Something to do with Death* (Faber and Faber, London).

French, P. (1973) *Westerns* (Secker and Warburg, London).

French, T. (1998) 'Bury My Heart at *Fort Apache*', *CineAction* 46 11–17.

Friar, R.E. and Friar, N.A. (1972) *The Only Good Indian . . . The Hollywood Gospel* (Drama Book Specialists, New York).

Gallafent, E. (1996a) 'Not With a Bang: The End of the West in *Lonely Are the Brave, The Misfits* and *Hud*' in Cameron, I. and Pye, D. (eds) *The Movie Book of the Western* (Studio Vista, London) 241–54.

Gallafent, E. (1996b) 'Four Tombstones 1846–1994' in Cameron, I. and Pye, D. (eds) *The Movie Book of The Western* (Studio Vista, London) 302–11.

Gallagher, T. (1986a) *John Ford: The Man and his Films* (University of California Press, Berkeley).

Gallagher, T. (1986b) 'Shoot-Out at the Genre Corral: Problems in the "Evolution of the Western"' in Grant, B.K. (ed.) *Film Genre Reader* (University of Texas Press, Austin).

Garnham, N. (1971) *Samuel Fuller* (Secker and Warburg, London).

Gledhill, C. (1987) *Home is Where the Heart is: Studies in Melodrama and the Woman's Film* (British Film Institute, London).

Goetzmann, W.H. (1966) *Exploration and Empire: The Explorer and the Scientist in the Winning of the American West* (Alfred A. Knopf, New York).

Goetzmann, W.H. and Goetzmann, W.N. (1986) *The West of the Imagination* (Alfred A. Knopf, New York).

Grant, B.K. (ed.) (1986) *Film Genre Reader* (University of Texas Press, Austin).

Green, M. (1979) *Dreams of Adventure, Deeds of Empire* (Basic Books, New York).

Green, M. (1984) *The Great American Adventure* (Beacon Press, New York).

Griffiths, A. (1996) 'Science and Spectacle: Native American Representation in Early Cinema' in Bird, S.E. (ed.) *Dressing in Feathers: The Construction of the Indian in American Popular Culture* (Westview Press, Boulder, Colorado).

Grist, L. (1996) '*Unforgiven*' in Cameron, I. and Pye, D. (eds) *The Movie Book of the Western* (Studio Vista, London) 294–301.

Grossman, J.R. (1994) *The Frontier in American History* (University of California Press, Berkeley).

Gruber, F. (1967) *The Pulp Jungle* (Sherbourne Press).

Gunning, T. (1990) 'The Cinema of Attractions: Early Film, Its Spectator and the Avant-Garde' *Wide Angle* 8 1986 reprinted in Elsaesser, T. (ed.) *Early Cinema: Space, Frame, Narrative* (British Film Institute, London).

Hall, M.K. (2001) 'Now You are a Killer of White Men: Jim Jarmusch's *Dead Man* and Traditions of Revisionism in the Western', *Journal of Film and Video* 52 (4).

Hall, S. (1996) 'How the West Was Won: History, Spectacle and the American Mountains' in Cameron, I. and Pye, D. (eds), *The Movie Book of the Western* (Studio Vista, London) 255–61.

Hall, S. and Whannell, P. (1964) *The Popular Arts* (Hutchinson, London).

Hampton, B.J. (1931) *A History of the Movies* (Covici-Friede, New York).

Hardy, F. (ed.) (1946) *Grierson on Documentary* (Collins, London).

Hardy, P. (ed.) (1991) *The Aurum Film Encyclopedia: The Western* (Aurum Press, London).

Hark, I.R. (1993) 'Animals or Romans: Looking at Masculinity in *Spartacus*' in Cohan, S. and Hark, I.R. (eds) (1993) *Screening the Male: Exploring Masculinities in Hollywood Cinema* (Routledge, London and New York) 151–72.

Haskell, M. (1977) *Big Bad Wolves* (Pantheon Books, New York).

Haycox, E. (1939) *Stage to Lordsburg, Cosmopolitan* (unattributed issue).

Haymonds, A. (2000) 'Rides of Passage: Female Heroes in Pony Stories' in Jones, D. and Watkins, A. (eds) *A Necessary Fantasy? The Heroic Figure in Children's Popular Literature* (Garland, New York).

Heilman, R. (1968) *The Iceman, the Arsonist and the Troubled Agent* (University of Washington, Washington).

Henderson, B. '*The Searchers:* An American Dilemma', *Film Quarterly* 34 (2) 1980/1 9–23 reprinted in Nichols, B. (ed.) *Movies and Methods 2* (University of California Press, Berkeley) 429–49.

Hilger, M. (1986) *The American Indian in Film* (Scarecrow Press, Metuchen, New Jersey).

Hilger, M. (1995) *From Savage to Nobleman: Images of Native Americans in Film* (Scarecrow Press, Metuchen, New Jersey).

Huggins, N. (1971) *Harlem Renaissance* (Oxford University Press, Oxford).

Hyde, A.F. (1990) *An American Vision: Far Western Landscape and National Culture 1820–1920* (New York University Press, New York).

Jackson, H.H. (1884) *Ramona* (Roberts Brothers, Boston).

Jacobowitz, F. (1996) 'The Dietrich Westerns: *Destry Rides Again* and *Rancho Notorious*' in Cameron, I. and Pye, D. (eds) *The Movie Book of the Western* (Studio Vista, London) 88–98.

Jameson, F. (1985) 'Postmodernism and Consumer Society' in Foster, H. (ed.) *Postmodern Culture* (Pluto Press, London) 113–18.

Jameson, R.T. (1980) 'The Ranown Cycle', *The Movie* 4 (53) 1054–5.

Jay, G.S. (2000) 'White Man's Book No Good: D.W. Griffith and the American Indian', *Cinema Journal* 39 (4) 3–25.

Jeffords, S. (1993) *Hard Bodies: Hollywood Masculinity in the Reagan Era* (Rutgers University Press, New Brunswick).

Jeffrey, J.R. (1979) *Frontier Women: The Trans-Mississippi West* (Hill and Wang, New York).

Jennings, F. (1993) *The Founders of America* (W.W. Norton, New York).

Jones, D. (1978) *The Dime Novel Western* (Bowling Green University Popular Press, Bowling Green, Ohio).

Kaplan, E.A. (ed.) (1998) *Women in Film Noir* (British Film Institute, London).

Kelley, S.M. (1995) 'Giggles and Guns: The Phallic Myth in *Unforgiven*', *Journal of Film and Video* 47 (1–3) 106–19.

Kitses, J. (1969) *Horizons West* (Thames and Hudson, London).

Kitses, J. and Rickman, G. (eds) (1998) *The Western Reader* (Limelight Editions, New York).

Klein, M. (1994) *Easterns, Westerns and Private Eyes: American Matters 1870–1900* (University of Wisconsin Press, Madison).

Kolodny, A. (1975) *The Lay of the Land: Metaphor as Experience and History in American Life and Letters* (Chapel Hill & University of North Carolina Press, Chapel Hill).

Kolodny, A. (1984) *The Land Before Her: Fantasy and Experience of the American Frontiers 1630–1860* (Chapel Hill & University of North Carolina Press, Chapel Hill).

Kopitt, A. (1969) *Indians* (Hill and Wang, New York).

Koszarski, R. (1990) *An Evening's Entertainment: The Age of the Silent Feature Picture, 1915–1928* (Scribner's, New York).

Lahue, K.C. (1964) *Continued Next Week: A History of the Moving Picture Serial* (University of Oklahoma Press, Norman and London).

Landy, M. (1996) 'He Went Thataway: The Form and Style of Leone's Italian Westerns', *boundary 2* (23) 1 reprinted under the title 'Which Way is America?: Americanism and the Italian Western' in Kitses, J. and Rickman, G. (eds) *The Western Reader* (Limelight Editions, New York) 213–22.

Lang, R. (1989) *American Film Melodrama: Griffith, Vidor, Minnelli* (Princeton University Press, New Jersey).

Lawrence, D.H. (1967) *Selected Literary Criticism* (Heinemann, London).

Lears, J.T.J. (1981) *No Place of Grace: Antimodernism and the Transformation of American Culture 1880–1920* (Pantheon, New York).

Lehman, P. (1981) 'Looking at Look's Missing Reverse Shot: Psychoanalysis and Style in John Ford's *The Searchers*', *Wide Angle* 4 (4) 65–70, reprinted in Kitses, J. and Rickman, G. (eds) *The Western Reader* (Limelight Editions, New York).

Lenihan, J.H. (1980) *Showdown: Confronting Modern America in the Western Film* (University of Illinois Press, Urbana and Chicago).

Leutrat, J-L. (1984) 'L'Histoire comme diffraction d'une identité' *IRIS* 2 (2) 57–67.

Leutrat, J-L. and Liandrat-Guigues, S. (1998) 'John Ford and Monument Valley' in Buscombe, E. and Pearson, R. (eds) *Back in the Saddle Again: New Essays on the Western* (British Film Institute, London).

Leverenz, D. (1991) 'The Last Real Man in America: From Natty Bumppo to Batman', *American Literary History* 3 (4) 753–81.

Lévi-Strauss, C. (1963) *Structural Anthropology* (Basic Books).

Levich, J. (1996) 'Western Auguries: Jim Jarmusch's *Dead Man*', *Film Comment* 32 (3) 39–41.

Levitin, J. (1982) 'The Western: any good roles for feminists?' *Film Reader* 5.

Limerick, P.N. (1987) *The Legacy of Conquest: The Unbroken Past of the American West* (W.W. Norton, New York).

Limerick, P.N., Millner, C. and Rankin, C. (eds) (1991) *Trails: Toward a New Western History* (University Press of Kansas, Lawrence).

Lippe, R. (1998) 'Samuel Fuller and the Western', *CineAction* 46 34–9.

Louvre, A. and Walsh, J. (eds) (1988) *Tell Me Lies About Vietnam* (Open University Press, Milton Keynes).

Lovell, A. (1967) 'The Western', *Screen Education* 41 reprinted in Nichols, B. (ed.) (1985) *Movies and Methods 2* (University of California Press, Berkeley).

Lucas, B. (1998) 'Saloon Girls and Rancher's Daughters: The Woman in the Western' in Kitses, J. and Rickman, G. (eds) *The Western Reader* (Limelight Editions, New York).

Lusted, D. (1996) 'Social Class and the Western as Male Melodrama' in Cameron, I. and Pye, D. (eds) *The Movie Book of the Western* (Studio Vista, London) 63–74.

McArthur, C. (1969) 'The Roots of the Western', *Cinema* (UK) 4 11–13.

McBride, J. and Wilmington, M. (1974) *John Ford* (Secker and Warburg, London).

McCarthy, P. (1995) 'Westers, Not Westerns: Exteriorizing the "Wild Man Within"', *Journal of Popular Film & Television* 23 (3) 117–29.

McCarthy, T. (1978) 'John Ford and Monument Valley', *American Film* 3 (7) 10–16.

McDonald, J.F. (1987) *Who Shot the Sheriff: The Rise and Fall of the TV Western* (Praeger, New York).

Maltby, R. (1996) 'A Better Sense of History: John Ford and the Indians' in Cameron, I. and Pye, D. (eds) *The Movie Book of the Western* (Studio Vista, London) 34–49.

Mast, G. (ed.) (1982) *The Movies in our Midst: Documents in the Cultural History of Film in America* (University of Chicago Press, Chicago).

Mauduy, J. and Henriet, G. (1989) *Geographies du western* (Nathan, Paris).

Mayne, J. (1995) *Directed by Dorothy Arzner* (Indiana University Press, Bloomington and Indianapolis).

Merck, M. (1980) 'Travesty on the Old Frontier' in *Move Over Misconceptions: Doris Day Reappraised* (British Film Institute, London).

Metz, C. (1982) *Psychoanalysis and the Cinema: The Imaginary Signifier* (Macmillan, London).

Miller, D. (1976) *Hollywood Corral* (Popular Library, New York).

Mitchell, L.C. (1981) *Witness to a Vanishing America: The Nineteenth Century Response* (Princeton University Press, New Jersey).

Mitchell, L.C. (1996) *Westerns: Making the Man in Fiction and Film* (University of Chicago Press, Chicago).

Modleski, T. (1995–6) 'Our Heroes Have Sometimes Been Cowgirls', *Film Quarterly* 49 (2) reprinted in Kitses, J. and Rickman, G. (eds) *The Western Reader* (Limelight Editions, New York).

Mulvey, L. (1975) 'Visual Pleasure and Narrative Cinema', *Screen* reprinted in Mulvey, L. (1989) *Visual and Other Pleasures* (Macmillan, London).

Mulvey, L. (1981) 'Afterthoughts on "Visual Pleasure and Narrative Cinema" inspired by *Duel in the Sun*', *Framework* reprinted in Mulvey, L. (1989) *Visual and Other Pleasures* (Macmillan, London).

Myers, S.L. (1982) *Westering Women and the Frontier Experience 1800–1915* (University of New Mexico Press, Albuquerque).

Nachbar, J. (1974) *Focus on the Western* (Prentice-Hall, Englewood Cliffs, New Jersey).

Nash, G.D. (1991) *Creating the West: Historical Interpretations 1890–1990* (University of New Mexico Press, Albuquerque).

Nash, R. (1967: 82) *Wilderness and the American Mind* (Yale University Press, New Haven).

Neale, S. (1980) *Genre* (British Film Institute, London).

Neale, S. (1990) 'Questions of Genre', *Screen* 31 (1) 45–66.

Neal, S. (1995) 'The Story of Custer in Everything but Name?: Colonel Thursday and *Fort Apache*', *Journal of Film and Video* 47 (1–3).

Neale, S. (1998) 'Vanishing Americans: Racial and Ethnic Issues in the Interpretation and Context of Post-war "Pro-Indian" Westerns' in Buscombe, E. and Pearson, R.

(eds) *Back in the Saddle Again: New Essays on the Western* (British Film Institute, London) 8–28.

Neale, S. (2000) *Genre and Hollywood* (Routledge, London and New York).

Newman, K. (1990) *Wild West Movies* (Bloomsbury, London).

Nichols, B. (1985) 'Style, Grammar and the Movies' in Nichols, B. *Movies and Methods 2* (University of California Press, Berkeley).

Nobles, G.H. (1997) *American Frontiers: Cultural Encounters and Continental Conquest* (Penguin, Harmondsworth).

Null, G. (1975: 90) *Black Hollywood: The Black Performer in Motion Pictures* (Citadel Press, New Jersey/Carol Publishing Group, New Jersey).

O'Connor, J. (1980) *The Hollywood Indian: Stereotypes of Native Americans in Film* (New Jersey State Museum, New Jersey).

Parkinson, M. and Jeavons, C. (1973) *A Pictorial History of Westerns* (Hamlyn, London).

Pearson, R. (1995) Introduction to *Journal of Film and Video* 47 (1–3) 4–6.

Pearson, R. (1998) 'The Twelve Custers or Video History' in Buscombe, E. and Pearson, R. (eds) *Back in the Saddle Again: New Essays on the Western* (British Film Institute, London) 8–28.

Perkins, V.F. (1981) 'Moments of Choice' *The Movie* 5 (58) 1142–5.

Peterson, C. (1994) 'Speaking for the Past' in Milner, C.A., O'Connor, C. and Sandelweiss, M.A. (eds) *The Oxford History of the American West* (Oxford University Press, Oxford).

Peterson, J. (1996) 'The Competing Tunes of *Johnny Guitar*: Liberalism, Sexuality, Masquerade', *Cinema Journal* 35 (3) reprinted in Kitses, J. and Rickman, G. (eds) (1998) *The Western Reader* (Limelight Editions, New York).

Petley, J. (1980) 'Mann of the West', *The Movie* 4 (53) 1046–8.

Pettit, A.G. (1980) *Images of the Mexican American in Fiction and Film* (University of Texas Press, Austin).

Pines, J. (1975) *Blacks in Films* (Studio Vista, London).

Prats, A.J. (1995) 'Back from the Sunset: The Western, the Eastwood Hero, and *Unforgiven*', *Journal of Film and Video* 47 (1–3) 100–19.

Prats, A.J. (1996) 'His Master's Voice(over): Revisionist Ethos and Narrative Dependence from *Broken Arrow* to *Geronimo*', *ANQ: A Quarterly Journal of Short Articles, Notes and Reviews* 9 (3) 15–29.

Prats, A.J. (1998) 'The Image of the Other and the Other *Dances With Wolves*: The Reconfigured Indian and the Textual Supplement', *Journal of Film and Video* 50 (1).

Propp, V. (1968) *The Morphology of the Folk Tale* (University of Texas Press, Austin).

Pumphrey, M. (1989) 'Why Do Cowboys Wear Hats in the Bath? Style Politics for the Older Man', *Critical Quarterly* 31 (3) reprinted in Cameron, I. and Pye, D. (eds) *The Movie Book of the Western* (Studio Vista, London) 50–62.

Pumphrey, M. (2001) 'The Games We Play(ed): TV Westerns, memory, masculinity' in Osgerby, B. and Gough-Yates, A. (eds) *Action TV: Tough Guys: Smooth Operators and Foxy Chicks* (Routledge, London and New York).

Puzo, M. (1969) *The Godfather* (Fawcett Crest, Greenwich).

Pye, D. (1996a) 'Introduction – Criticism and the Western' in Cameron, I. and Pye, D. (eds) *The Movie Book of the Western* (Studio Vista, London) 9–21.

Pye, D. (1996b) '*Ulzana's Raid*' in Cameron, I. and Pye, D. (eds) *The Movie Book of the Western* (Studio Vista, London) 262–8.

Pye, D. (1996c) 'Genre and History: *Fort Apache* and *The Man who Shot Liberty Valance*', *Movie* 25 reprinted in Cameron, I. and Pye, D. (eds) *The Movie Book of the Western* (Studio Vista, London) 111–22.

Rainey, B. (1996) *The Reel Cowboy: Essays on the Myth in Movies and Literature* (McFarland, Jefferson, North Carolina).

Rieupeyrout, J-L. (1952) 'The Western: a historical genre', *Quarterly Review of Film, Radio and Television* 3.

Rieupeyrout, J-L. (1964) *La Grande Adventure du Western* (Editions du Cerf, Paris).

Rickman, G. (1998) 'The Western Under Erasure: *Dead Man*' in Kitses, J. and Rickman, G. (eds) *The Western Reader* (Limelight Editions, New York) 381–404.

Robertson, P. (1995) 'Camping Under Western Skies: Joan Crawford in *Johnny Guitar*', *Journal of Film and Video* 47 (1–3) 33–49.

Robinson, D. (1996) *From Peepshow to Palace: The Birth of American Film* (Columbia University Press, New York).

Rollins, P.C. and O'Connor, J.E. (eds) (1998) *Hollywood Indian: The Portrayal of the Native American in Film* (University Press of Kentucky, Lexington).

Roosevelt, T. (1889; 1907) *The Winning of the West* (G.P. Putnam's Sons, New York).

Rosa, J.G. (1969) *The Gunfighter: Man or Myth* (University of Oklahoma Press, Norman and London).

Rosenbaum, J. (1996) 'Acid Western', 4.

Ross, S.J. (1998) *Working Class Hollywood* (Princeton University Press, New Jersey).

Rothel, D. (1984) *Those Great Cowboy Sidekicks* (Scarecrow Press, Metuchen, New Jersey).

Rowlandson, M. (1682) *The Captive*, available as *The Sovereignty and the Goodness of God* (1997) (Bedford Books, Boston).

Royle, E.M. (1926) *The Squaw Man* (Grosset and Dunlap, New York).

Russell, Don (1960) *The Lives and Legends of Buffalo Bill* (University of Oklahoma Press, Norman and London).

Russell, L. (Wollen, P.) (1965) 'Budd Boetticher', *New Left Review* 32 reprinted in Kitses, J. and Rickman, G. (eds) *The Western Reader* (Limelight Editions, New York) 195–200.

Ryall, T. (1970) 'The Notion of Genre', *Screen* 11 (2) 22–31.

Ryall, T. (1978) *The Gangster Film: Teachers' Study Guide* (British Film Institute Education, London).

Sabal, R. (1996/7) 'Making Contact: Working with the White Mountain Apache on *Indian Summer*', *Journal of Film and Video* 48 (4) 32–7.

Samuels, P. and Samuels, H. (1976) *The Illustrated Biographical Encyclopedia of Artists of the American West* (Doubleday, New York).

Sarris, A. (1976) *The John Ford Movie Mystery* (Secker and Warburg, London).

Savage, C. (1996) *Cowgirls* (Bloomsbury, London).

Saxton, A. (1990) *The Rise and Fall of the White Republic: Class Politics and Mass Culture in Nineteenth Century America* (Verso, London).

Schatz, T. (1981) *Hollywood Genres* (Temple University Press, Philadelphia).

Schneider, T. (1995) 'Finding a New Heimat in the Wild West: Karl May and the German Western of the 1960s', *Journal of Film and Video* 47 (1–3) 50–66.

Settle, W.A. (1966) *Jesse James was his Name* (University of Missouri Press, Columbia, Missouri).

Seydor, P. (1980) *Peckinpah: The Western Films* (University of Illinois Press, Urbana and Chicago).

Simmon, S. (1996) 'Concerning the Weary Legs of Wyatt Earp: The Classic Western according to Shakespeare', *Literature/Film Quarterly* 24 (2) reprinted in Kitses, J. and Rickman, G. (eds) *The Western Reader* (Limelight Editions, New York) 149–66.

Simmons, G. (1982) *Peckinpah: A Portrait in Montage* (University of Texas Press, Austin).

Simon, W.G. and Spence, L. (1995) 'Cowboy Wonderland, History, and Myth: "It Ain't all that different than real life"', *Journal of Film and Video* 47 (1–3) 65–77.

Singer, B. (1996) 'Serials' in Nowell-Smith, G. (ed.) *The Oxford History of World Cinema* (Oxford University Press, Oxford) 105–11.

Sklar, R. (1978) '*Red River*, Empire to the West', *Cineaste* IX (1).

Slotkin, R. (1973) *Regeneration Through Violence: The Mythology of the American Frontier* (Wesleyan University Press, Middletown).

Slotkin, R. (1985) *The Fatal Environment: The Myth of the Frontier in the Age of Industrialization* (Wesleyan University Press, Middletown).

Slotkin, R. (1992) *Gunfighter Nation: The Myth of the Frontier in Twentieth Century America* (Atheneum, New York).

Smith, H.N. (1950; 71) *Virgin Land: The American West as Symbol and Myth* (Harvard University Press, Cambridge, Massachusetts).

Smith, P. and Hulse, E. (eds) (1993) *Don Miller's Hollywood Corral: A Comprehensive B Western Roundup* (Riverwood Press, Burbana, California).

Staiger, L. and Williams, T. (1975) *Italian Western: The Opera of Violence* (Lorrimer, London).

Stanfield, P. (1987) 'The Western 1909–14: A Cast of Villains', *Film History* 1 97–112.

Stanfield, P. (1996) 'Country Music and the 1930's Western' in Cameron, I. and Pye, D. (eds) *The Movie Book of the Western* (Studio Vista, London) 22–33.

Stanfield, P. (1998) 'Dixie Cowboys and Blue Yodels: The Strange History of the Singing Cowboy' in Buscombe, E. and Pearson, R. (eds) *Back in the Saddle Again: New Essays on the Western* (British Film Institute, London) 96–118.

Stanfield, P. (2001) *Hollywood, Westerns and the 1930s: The Lost Trail* (University of Exeter, Exeter).

Stanfield, P. (2002) *Horse Opera: The Strange History of the 1930s Singing Cowboy* (University of Illinois Press, Urbana and Chicago).

Staples, T. (1997) *All Pals Together: The Story of Children's Cinema* (Edinburgh University Press, Edinburgh).

Steckmesser, K.L. (1965) *The Western Hero in History and Legend* (University of Oklahoma Press, Norman and London).

Steinbeck, J. (1933) *The Red Pony* (Heinemann, London).

Stowe, H.B. (1852; 1981) *Uncle Tom's Cabin* (Penguin, Harmondsworth).

Stowell, P. (1986) *John Ford* (Twayne, New York).

Strickland, R. (1997) *Tonto's Revenge: Reflections on American Indian Culture and Policy* (University of New Mexico Press, Albuquerque).

Strinati, D. (1993) 'The Taste of America: Americanisation and Popular Culture in Britain' in Strinati, D. and Wragg, S. (eds) *Come on Down? Popular Media Culture in post-War Britain* (Routledge, London and New York) 46–81.

Studlar, G. (1998) 'Wider Horizons: Douglas Fairbanks and Nostalgic Primitivism' in Buscombe, E. and Pearson, R. (eds) *Back in the Saddle Again: New Essays on the Western* (British Film Institute, London).

Studlar, G. and Bernstein, M. (eds) (2001) *John Ford Made Westerns: Filming the Legend in the Sound Era* (Indiana University Press, Bloomington and Indianapolis).

Taft, R. (1964) *Photography and the American Scene* (Dover Publications, New York).

Tasker, Y. (1993) *Spectacular Bodies: Gender, Genre and the Action Cinema* (Routledge, London).

Tasker, Y. (2001) 'Kung Fu: Re-Orienting the television Western' in Osgerby, B. and Gough-Yates, A. (eds) *Action TV: Tough Guys, Smooth Operators and Foxy Chicks* (Routledge, London and New York).

Tatum, S. (1982) *Inventing Billy the Kid: Visions of the Outlaw in America 1881–1981* (University of New Mexico Press, Albuquerque).

Teague, D.W. (1997) *The Southwest in American Literature and Art: The Rise of a Desert Aesthetic* (University of Arizona Press, Tucson).

Thomas, D. (1996) 'John Wayne's Body' in Cameron, I. and Pye, D. *The Movie Book of the Western* (Studio Vista, London) 76–87.

Thomson, D. (1994) *A Biographical Dictionary of Film* (André Deutsch, London).

Thumim, J. (1998) Maybe He's Tough But He Sure Ain't No Carpenter: Masculinity and In/Competence in *Unforgiven'* in Kirkham, P. and Thumim, J. (eds) *Me Jane* (Lawrence and Wishart, London) reprinted in Kitses, J. and Rickman, G. (eds) *The Western Reader* (Limelight Editions, New York).

Tompkins, J. (1992) *West of Everything: The Inner Life of Westerns* (Oxford University Press, New York and Oxford).

Trachtenberg, A. (1982) *The Incorporation of America: Culture and Society in the Gilded Age* (Hill and Wang, New York).

Truettner, W.H. (1991) (ed.) *The West as America: Reinterpreting Images of the Frontier 1820–1920* (Smithsonian Institution Press, Washington and London).

Turner, F.J. (1893) 'The Significance of the Frontier in American History' reprinted in (1986) *The Frontier in American History* (University of Arizona Press, Tucson) and (1962) American Historical Association Report (Holt, Rinehart and Winston, New York) 199–227.

Tuska, J. (1976) *The Filming of the West* (Doubleday, New York).

Vardac, N. (1949) *Stage to Screen: Theatrical Origins of Early Film* (Da Capo Press, New York).

Wagenknecht, E. and Slide, A. (1975) *The Films of D.W. Griffith* (Crown, New York).

Wagstaff, C. (1992) 'A Fistful of Westerns' in Dyer, R. and Vincendeau, G. (eds) *Popular European Cinema* (Routledge, London).

Walker, A. (1970) *Stardom* (Michael Joseph, London).

Walker, M. (1982) 'Melodrama and the American Cinema', *Movie* 29–30.

Walker, M. (1996) 'The Westerns of Delmer Daves' in Cameron, I. and Pye, D. (eds) *The Movie Book of the Western* (Studio Vista, London) 123–60.

Wallington, M. (1970) 'The Italian Western: A Concordance', *Cinema* (UK) 6 32–4.

Wallis, M. (2000) *The 101 Ranch and the Creation of the American West* (St. Martin's Press, New York).

Warshow, R. (1954) 'Movie Chronicle: The Westerner', *Partisan Review* reprinted in Warshow, R. (1962) *The Immediate Experience* (Doubleday, New York), Nachbar, J. (ed.) (1974) *Focus on the Western* (Prentice-Hall, Englewood Cliffs, New Jersey) and Kitses, J. and Rickman, G. (eds) *The Western Reader* (Limelight Editions, New York) 35–47.

Watson, G. (1998) 'The Western: The Genre that Engenders the Nation', *CineAction* 46 3–10.

Webb, W.P. (1931) *The Great Plains* (Ginn Waltham, Massachusetts).

Weinberg, A.K. (1935: 79) *Manifest Destiny: A Study of Nationalist Expansion in American History* (AMS Press, Brooklyn, New York).

West, E. (1994) 'The American Frontier' in Milner, C.A., O'Connor, C. and Sandelweiss, M.A. (eds) *The Oxford History of the American West* (Oxford University Press, Oxford).

White, G.E. (1968) *The Eastern Establishment and the Western Experience: The West of Frederic Remington, Theodore Roosevelt and Owen Wister* (Yale University Press, New Haven).

White, R. (1991) *It's Your Misfortune and None of My Own: A New History of the American West* (University of Oklahoma Press, Norman and London).

Wicking, C. (1969) 'Interview with Delmer Daves', *Screen* 10 (4/5) 55–66.

Willemen, P. (1981) 'Anthony Mann: Looking at the Male', *Framework* 15–17 (16) reprinted in Kitses, J. and Rickman, G. (eds) *The Western Reader* (Limelight Editions, New York) 209–12.

Williams, D. (1998) 'Pilgrims and the Promised Land: A Genealogy of the Western' in Kitses, J. and Rickman, G. (eds) *The Western Reader* (Limelight Editions, New York) 93–113.

Williams, R. (1973: 52) *Drama from Ibsen to Brecht* (Pelican, Harmondsworth).

Williamson, J.W. (1995) *Hillbillyland* (University of North Carolina Press, Chapel Hill).

Wister, O. (1902) *The Virginian: The Horseman of the Plains* republished (1992) in a reprint of a 1929 illustrated edition by University of Nebraska Press.

Woal, L.K. and Woal, M. (1995) 'Romaine Fielding's Real westerns', *Journal of Film and Video* 47 (1–3) 7–25.

Wollen, P. (1969; 72) *Signs and Meaning in the Cinema* (Secker and Warburg, London).

Wood, R. (1968) '*Rio Bravo* and Retrospect' reprinted from *Howard Hawks* (Secker and Warburg/British Film Institute, London) in Kitses, J. and Rickman, G. (eds) *The Western Reader* (Limelight Editions, New York).

Wood, R. (1988) '*Rancho Notorious*, A Noir Western in Colour', *CineAction* 13/14 83–93.

Wooland, B. (1996) 'Class Frontiers: The View Through *Heaven's Gate*' in Cameron, I. and Pye, D. (eds) *The Movie Book of the Western* (Studio Vista, London) 277–83.

Worland, R. and Countryman, E. (1998) 'The New Western American Historiography and the Emergence of the New American Westerns' in Buscombe, E. and Pearson, R. (eds) *Back in the Saddle: New Essays on the Western* (British Film Institute, London) 182–97.

Worpole, K. (1983) *Dockers and Detectives* (Verso, London).

Worster, D. (1992) *Under Western Skies: Nature and History in the American West* (Oxford University Press, Oxford).

Wexman, V.W. (1993) *Creating the Couple: Love, Marriage and the Hollywood Performance* (Princeton University Press, New Jersey).

Wexman, V.W. (1996) *The Family on the Land: Race and the Emergence of U.S. Cinema* (Rutgers University Press, New Brunswick).

Wright, W. (1975) *Sixguns and Society* (University of California Press, Berkeley).

Wyatt, E.M. (1994) *ABC's of Movie Cowboys* (Wyatt Classics Inc, North Carolina).

FILMOGRAPHY

Film titles below are commonly accompanied by production dates and director. Where these are uncertain, as in the case especially of many early films, missing details are replaced with production company and/or leading actor.

Aces and Eights (1936, Sam Newfield)
Across the Wide Missouri (1950, William Wellman)
Adios Amigo (1975, Fred Williamson)
The Alamo (1960, John Wayne)
Alien (1979, Ridley Scott)
The American Girl (1917, series starring Marin Sais)
The Americano (1916, John Emerson)
Annie Get Your Gun (1950, George Sidney)
Annie Oakley (1935, George Stevens)
Apache (1954, Robert Aldrich)
Apache Chief (1949, Frank McDonald)
Apache Drums (1951, Hugo Fregonese)
Apache Renegade (1912, Kalem Production Company)
Apocalypse Now (1979, Francis Ford Coppola)
Arizona Bound (1940, Spencer G. Bennett)
Backlash (1956, John Sturges)
Back to the Future III (1989, Robert Zemeckis)
Back to the Prairie (1911, A.K./American Kinema Production Company)
Bad Company (1972, Robert Benton)
Bad Girls (1994, Jonathan Kaplan)
The Badlanders (1958, Delmer Daves)
Bad Man of Harlem/Harlem on the Prairie (1937, Sam Newfield)
The Ballad of Cable Hogue (1970, Sam Peckinpah)
The Ballad of Gregorio Cortez (1982, Robert M. Young)
The Ballad of Josie (1967, Andrew V. McLaglen)
The Ballad of Little Jo (1993, Maggie Greenwald)
The Bank Robbery (1908, William Tilghman)
Barbarosa (1982, Fred Schepisi)
The Battle of Elderbush Gulch (1913, D.W. Griffith)
Belle Starr (1941, Irving Cummings)
Bells of Rosarita (1945, Frank McDonald)
Bend of the River/Where the River Bends (1952, Anthony Mann)
The Big Country (1958, William Wyler)
The Big Sky (1952, Howard Hawks)

The Big Trail (1930, Raoul Walsh)
Billy the Kid (1930, 1941, David Miller)
Billy the Kid Versus Dracula (1958, William Beaudine)
The Birth of a Nation (1915, D.W. Griffith)
Black Bounty Killer/Boss Nigger (1974, Jack Arnold)
Blazing Saddles (1974, Mel Brooks)
Blazing the Trail (1912, with Francis Ford)
Blood on the Moon (1948, Robert Wise)
The Bold Bank Robbery (1904, Sigmund Lubin)
Bonnie and Clyde (1967, Arthur Penn)
Boots and Saddles (1909, Frances Boggs)
Borderland (1937, Nate Watt)
Boss Nigger/Black Bounty Killer (1974, Jack Arnold)
The Bounty Killer (1965, Spencer G. Bennet)
Boy of the West/Il fanciullo del West (1943, Giorgio Ferroni)
The Bravados (1958, Henry King)
Brigham Young – Frontiersman (1940, Henry Hathaway)
Broken Arrow (1950, Delmer Daves)
Broken Blossoms (1919, D.W. Griffith)
The Broken Chain (1993, Lamont Johnson)
Broncho Billy (1909, G.M. Anderson)
Broncho Billy and the Buried Letters/The Buried Letters (1910, G.M. Anderson)
Broncho Billy and the Claim Jumpers/The Claim Jumpers (1915, G.M. Anderson)
Broncho Billy's Gratefulness (1913, Essanay, G.M. Anderson)
Broncho Billy's Love Affair (1912, Essanay, G.M. Anderson)
Broncho Billy's Redemption (1910, Reginald Barker)
Bronco Billy (1980, Clint Eastwood)
Bronco Buster (1925, Paul Terry; 1952, Budd Boetticher)
Buck and the Preacher (1971, Sidney Poitier)
Buckaroo Sheriff of Texas (1951, Philip Ford)
Buffalo Bill (1944, William Wellman)
Buffalo Bill and the Indians, or Sitting Bull's History Lesson (1976, Robert Altman)
Buffalo Bill and the Indian Wars/The Indian Wars (1914, Vernon Day, Theodore Wharton)
A Bug's Life (1998, John Lasseter)
The Bull-Dogger (1922, Richard E. Norman)
A Bullet for the General/Quien sabe? (1966, Damiano Damiani)
The Buried Letters/Broncho Billy and the Buried Letters (1910, G.M. Anderson)
Butch Cassidy and the Sundance Kid (1969, George Roy Hill)
Cabin in the Sky (1943, Vincente Minnelli)
Cahill/Cahill, United States Marshal (1973, Andrew V. McLaglen)
Calamity Jane (1953, David Butler)
The Call of the Wild (1908, D.W. Griffith)
Canyon Passage (1946, Jacques Tourneur)
Carolina Moon (1940, Frank MacDonald)
Cat Ballou (1965, Eliot Silverstein)
Cattle Queen of Montana (1954, Allan Dwan)
The Cattle Rustlers (1908, Frances Boggs)
Chato's Land (1971, Michael Winner)

Cheyenne Autumn (1964, John Ford)
Chief White Eagle (1912, Romaine Fielding)
The Chief's Blanket (1912, D.W. Griffith)
The Chief's Daughter/On the Cactus Fields of Southern California (1911, D.W. Griffith)
Cimarron (1931, Wesley Ruggles, 1960, Anthony Mann)
The Cimarron Kid (1952, Budd Boetticher)
City Slickers (1991, Ron Underwood)
City Slickers II: The Legend of Curly's Gold (1994, Paul Weiland)
The Claim Jumpers/Broncho Billy and the Claim Jumpers (1915, G.M. Anderson)
Colorado Sunset (1939, George Sherman)
Colorado Territory (1949, Raoul Walsh)
Column South (1953, Frederick de Cordova)
Comanche Station (1959, Budd Boetticher)
The Covered Wagon (1923, James Cruze)
Cowboy (1958, Delmer Daves)
Cowboy from Brooklyn (1938, Lloyd Bacon)
The Cowboy and the Indians (1949, John English)
The Cowboys (1971, Mark Rydell)
The Cowboy's Narrow Escape (1908, Bison Production Company)
The Crimson Skull (1921, Richard E. Norman)
Cripple Creek Bar-room (1898, Thomas Edison)
The Culpepper Cattle Company (1972, Dick Richards)
Curse of the Red Man (1911, Frank Boggs)
Custer of the West (1968, Robert Siodmak)
Custer's Last Fight (1912, Thomas H. Ince)
The Dalton Girls (1957, Reginald Le Borg)
Dances With Wolves (1990, Kevin Costner)
The Daredevil (1919, no details)
Day of the Outlaw (1959, André de Toth)
Dead Man (1995, Jim Jarmusch)
Death of a Gunfighter (1969, 'Allen Smithee' – Robert Totten/Don Siegel)
The Deerslayer (1911, Hal Reid; 1943, Lew Landers; 1957, Kurt Neumann)
Destry Rides Again (1932, Ben Stoloff; 1939, George Marshall)
The Devil Horse (1926, Fred Jackman)
Devil's Doorway (1950, Anthony Mann)
Die Hard (1988, John McTiernan)
Dirty Harry (1971, Don Siegel)
Django (1966, Sergio Corbucci)
Django Kill!/If You Live, Shoot/Sei sei vivo, spara! (1967, Giulio Questi)
Doc (1971, Frank Perry)
Dodge City (1939, Michael Curtiz)
Drum Beat (1954, Delmer Daves)
Drums Along the Mohawk (1939, John Ford)
Duck You Sucker/A Fistful of Dynamite/Giù la testa (1971, Sergio Leone)
Duel at Diablo (1966, Ralph Nelson)
Duel in the Sun (1946, King Vidor)
Eagle's Wing (1978, Anthony Harvey)
El Cid (1961, Anthony Mann)
El Dorado (1966, Howard Hawks)

The Electric Horseman (1979, Sydney Pollack)
Elmo The Mighty (1919, Henry McRae)
The Emperor of California (1936, Luis Trenker)
End of the Trail (1932, D. Ross Lederman)
Escape From Fort Bravo (1953, John Sturges)
Face of a Fugitive (1959, Paul Wendkos)
Il fanciullo del West/Boy of the West (1943, Georgio Ferroni)
The Far Country (1955, Anthony Mann)
The Far Horizons (1954, Rudolph Maté)
Fighting Blood (1911, D.W. Griffith)
The Fighting Streak (1922, Arthur Rosson)
A Fistful of Dollars/Per un pugno di dollari (1964, Sergio Leone)
A Fistful of Dynamite/Duck You Sucker/Giù la testa (1971, Sergio Leone)
Flaming Arrow (1913, Bison Production Company)
Flaming Star (1960, Don Siegel)
The Fly (1986, David Cronenberg)
For a Few Dollars More/Per qualche dollari in più (1965, Sergio Leone)
Fort Apache (1948, John Ford)
Forty Guns (1957, Sam Fuller)
Four Faces West (1948, Alfred E. Green)
The Furies (1950, Anthony Mann)
Garden of Evil (1954, Henry Hathaway)
Geronimo: An American Legend (1994, Walter Hill)
The Girl and the Outlaw (1906, D.W. Griffith)
The Girl from Montana (1907, G.M. Anderson)
Glory (1989, Edward Zwick)
The Goddess of Sagebrush Gulch (1912, D.W. Griffith)
Gone With the Wind (1939, Victor Fleming)
The Good Bad Man (1915, Allan Dwan)
The Good, the Bad and the Ugly/Il buono, il brutto, il cattivo (1966, Sergio Leone)
The Grapes of Wrath (1940, John Ford)
Great Day in the Morning (1956, Jacques Tourneur)
The Great Man's Lady (1942, William Wellman)
The Great Northfield Minnesota Raid (1971, Philip Kaufman)
The Great Train Robbery (1903, Edwin S. Porter)
The Green Berets (1968, John Wayne)
The Grey Fox (1982, Phillip Borsos)
Grim Prairie Tales (1990, Wayne Coe)
Gunfight at the O.K. Corral (1956, John Sturges)
The Gunfighter (1950, Henry King)
Guns for Hire: the making of 'The Magnificent Seven' (2000, Louis Heaton,
    transmitted Channel 4, 13/05/00)
Guns in the Afternoon/Ride the High Country (1962, Sam Peckinpah)
The Guns of Fort Petticoat (1957, George Marshall)
The Gunslinger (1956, Roger Corman)
The Hand that Rocks the Cradle (1992, Curtis Hanson)
Hang 'Em High (1967, Ted Post)
The Hanging Tree (1959, Delmer Daves)
Hannie Caulder (1971, Burt Kennedy)

Harlem on the Prairie/Bad Man of Harlem (1937, Sam Newfield)
The Heart of an Indian (1912, Thomas H. Ince)
Hearts of the West/Hollywood Cowboy (1975, Howard Zieff)
Heaven's Gate (1980, Michael Cimino)
Heller in Pink Tights (1960, George Cukor)
Hell's Hinges (1916, Reginald Barker)
High Noon (1952, Fred Zinnemann)
High Plains Drifter (1972, Clint Eastwood)
The Hired Hand (1971, Peter Fonda)
The Hold-up of the Rocky Mountain Express (1906, Edwin S. Porter)
Hollywood Cowboy/Hearts of the West (1975, Howard Zieff)
The Honkers (1971, Steve Inhat)
Hooligans of the West/Les Apaches du Far-West (1907, Pathé Frère Production
     Company)
Hopi Snake Dance (1893, Thomas Edison)
Hour of the Gun (1967, John Sturges)
How the West Was Won (1962, Henry Hathaway, George Marshall, with John Ford
     directing 'The Civil War' episode)
Hud (1962, Martin Ritt)
The Indian Brothers (1911, D.W. Griffith)
Indian Justice (1911, Pathé Frère Production Company)
The Indian Massacre (1912, Thomas H. Ince)
The Indian Runner's Romance (1909, D.W. Griffith)
Indian Summer (1992, Rob Sabal)
The Indian Wars/Buffalo Bill and the Indian Wars (1914, Vernon Day, Theodore
     Wharton)
In Old Arizona (1929, Raoul Walsh, Irving Cummings)
In Old Santa Fé (1934, David Howard)
The Invaders (1912, Thomas H. Ince)
Iola's Promise (1910, D.W. Griffith)
I Shot Jesse James (1948, Sam Fuller)
The Iron Horse (1924, John Ford)
It's a Wonderful Life (1946, Frank Capra)
Jeremiah Johnson (1972, Sydney Pollack)
Jesse James (1939, Henry King)
Johnny Guitar (1954, Nicholas Ray)
Johnny Reno (1966, R.G. Springsteen)
Journey Through Rosebud (1972, Tom Gries)
Jubal (1956, Delmer Daves)
Junior Bonner (1972, Sam Peckinpah)
J.W. Coop (1971, Cliff Robertson)
Keno Bates, Liar (1915, William S. Hart)
Kid Blue (1973, James Frawley)
The Kid from Texas (1950, Kurt Neumann)
Killer on a Horse/Welcome to Hard Times (1967, Burt Kennedy)
Kit Carson (1903, no details; 1911, Bison Production Company; 1928, Alfred Werker;
     1940, George B. Seitz)
The Knickerbocker Buckaroo (1919, Albert Parker)
A Lady Takes a Chance (1943, William Seiter)

The Lamb (1915, Christy Cabanne)
The Last Drop of Water (1911, Biograph, D.W. Griffith)
The Last Hard Men (1976, Andrew V. McLaglen)
The Last Hunt (1956, Richard Brooks)
The Last Movie (1971, Dennis Hopper)
The Last of the Mohicans (1936, George B. Seitz; 1992, Michael Mann)
The Last of the Pony Riders (1953, George Archainbaud)
The Last Sunset (1961, Robert Aldrich)
The Last Wagon (1956, Delmer Daves)
The Law and Jake Wade (1958, John Sturges)
The Lawless Breed (1952, Raoul Walsh)
The Left Handed Gun (1958, Arthur Penn)
The Legend of Frenchie King (1971, Guy Casaril)
The Legend of Nigger Charlie (1972, Martin Goldman)
The Life of an American Cowboy (1906, Edwin S. Porter)
Lightnin' Bill Carson (1936, Sam Newfield)
Little Big Man (1970, Arthur Penn)
The Little Train Robbery (1905, Edwin S. Porter)
Lonely are the Brave (1962, David Miller)
The Lone Ranger (1938, William Witney, John English)
The Lone Star Ranger (1923, Lambert Hillyer)
The Long Riders (1980, Walter Hill)
Look Out Sister (1949, Bud Pollard)
The Lusty Men (1952, Nicholas Ray)
McCabe and Mrs. Miller (1971, Robert Altman)
The McMasters . . . Tougher than the West Itself (1969, Alf Kjellin)
The Magnificent Seven (1960, John Sturges)
Major Dundee (1964, Sam Peckinpah)
A Man Called Horse (1970, Elliot Silverstein)
The Man from Colorado (1948, Henry Levin)
The Man from Laramie (1955, Anthony Mann)
Man in the Shadow (1957, Jack Arnold)
Man of the West (1958, Anthony Mann)
The Man Who Shot Liberty Valance (1962, John Ford)
Man Without a Star (1955, King Vidor)
The Massacre (1912, D.W. Griffith)
The Matrix (1999, Andy Wachowski and Larry Wachowski)
Maverick (1994, Richard Donner)
The Maverick Queen (1956, Joseph Kane)
The Mended Lute (1909, D.W. Griffith)
Mexicali Rose (1939, George Sherman)
The Miracle Rider (1935, Armand Schaefer, B. Reeves Eason)
The Misfits (1961, John Huston)
Mr Deeds Goes to Town (1936, Frank Capra)
A Mohawk's Way (1910, D.W. Griffith)
The Mollycoddle (1920, Victor Fleming)
Montana Belle (1952, Allan Dwan)
Monte Walsh (1970, William Fraker)
My Darling Clementine (1946, John Ford)

My Name is Nobody/Il mio nome è Nessuno (1973, Tonino Valerii/Sergio Leone)
Naked Hands (1909, G.M. Anderson)
The Naked Spur (1953, Anthony Mann)
Navajo (1952, Norman Foster)
The Navajo Films (1966, Susie Benally, Maxine and Maryjane Tsosie, Mike Anderson, Johnny Nelson, Al Clah)
The New Ranch Foreman (1912, Lubin Production Company)
Northwest Passage (1940, King Vidor)
The Oklahoma Kid (1939, Lloyd Bacon)
Oklahoma Woman (1956, Roger Corman)
Once Upon A Time in the West/C'era una volta in West (1968, Sergio Leone)
One-Eyed Jacks (1961, Marlon Brando)
One Flew Over the Cuckoo's Nest (1975, Milos Forman)
100 Rifles (1968, Tom Gries)
Only the Valiant (1951, Gordon Douglas)
Our Hospitality (1923, Buster Keaton)
The Outlaw (1940, Howard Hawks, Howard Hughes)
The Outlaw and the Child (1911, Gilbert P. Hamilton)
The Outlaw Josey Wales (1976, Clint Eastwood)
Outlaw Women (1952, Samuel Newfield, Ron Ormand)
The Outriders (1950, Roy Rowland)
The Ox-Bow Incident (1943, William Wellman)
Paint Your Wagon (1969, Joshua Logan)
The Paleface (1948, Norman Z. McLeod)
Pale Rider (1985, Clint Eastwood)
Pat Garrett and Billy the Kid (1973, Sam Peckinpah)
The Perils of Pauline (1914, Louis J. Gasnier)
Perils of the Wilderness (1956, Spencer G. Bennet)
The Phantom Bullet (1926, Clifford Smith)
The Phantom Empire (1935, Otto Brower, B. Reeves Eason)
The Plainsman (1936, Cecil B. De Mille)
Platoon (1986, Oliver Stone)
Pocahontas (1995, Mike Gabriel and Eric Goldberg)
Poker at Dawson City (1898, Thomas Edison)
Pony Express (1925, James Cruze)
The Pony Express (1953 Jerry Hopper)
Posse (1975, Kirk Douglas)
Posse (1993, Mario Van Peebles)
The Postman Always Rings Twice (1946, Tay Garnett; 1981, Bob Rafelson)
The Prairie Pirate (1925, Edmund Mortimer)
The Professionals (1966, Richard Brooks)
A Pueblo Legend (1912, D.W. Griffith)
Pursued (1947, Raoul Walsh)
Rachel and the Stranger (1948, Norman Foster)
Rage at Dawn (1955, Tim Whelan)
Ramona (1910, D.W. Griffith; 1912, unknown; 1916, Donald Crisp; 1928, Edwin Carewe; 1936, Henry King)
Ranch Life in the Great Southwest (1909, Francis Boggs)
Rancho Deluxe (1974, Frank Perry)

Rancho Notorious (1952, Fritz Lang)
Rawhide (1938, Ray Taylor; 1951, Henry Hathaway)
The Redman's View (1909, D.W. Griffith)
Red River (1948, Howard Hawks)
Red White and Black/Soul Soldiers (1970, John Cardos)
Rescued from an Eagle's Nest (1907, D.W. Griffith)
Return of the Cisco Kid (1939, Herbert I. Leeds)
The Return of Draw Egan (1916, William S. Hart)
The Return of Frank James (1940, Fritz Lang)
Ride in the Whirlwind (1966, Monte Hellman)
Ride Lonesome (1959, Budd Boetticher)
Ride out for Revenge (1957, Bernard Girard)
Ride the High Country/Guns in the Afternoon (1962, Sam Peckinpah)
Ride with the Devil (1999, Ang Lee)
Riders of Death Valley (1941, Ford Beebe, Ray Taylor)
Riders of the Northland (1942, William Berke)
Riders of the Purple Sage (1918, Frank Lloyd; 1925, Lynn F. Reynolds;
    1931, Hamilton McFadden; 1941, James Tinling; 1996, Charles Haid (TV))
Rio Bravo (1959, Howard Hawks)
Rio Grande (1938, Sam Nelson; 1951, John Ford)
Rio Lobo (1970, Howard Hawks)
River of No Return (1954, Otto Preminger)
Robin Hood (1922, Allan Dwan)
A Romance of the Border (1912, Lubin)
A Romance of the Western Hills (1910, D.W. Griffith)
A Romantic Tale of the West (1911, unknown)
Rough Riding Romance (1919, Arthur Rosson)
The Rounders (1965, Burt Kennedy)
Run of the Arrow (1957, Sam Fuller)
Rustler's Rhapsody (1985, Hugh Wilson)
Ruth of the Rockies (1920, George Marshall)
Saddle the Wind (1958, Robert Parrish)
Saddle Tramp (1950, Hugo Fregonese)
San Antonio (1945, David Butler)
Satan Town (1926, Edmund Mortimer)
The Scalphunters (1968, Sydney Pollack)
The Searchers (1956, John Ford)
Sergeant Rutledge (1960, John Ford)
Seven Men from Now (1956, Budd Boetticher)
The Seven Samurai (1954, Akira Kurosawa)
Shaft (1971, Gordon Parks)
Shalako (1968, Edward Dmytryk)
Shane (1953, George Stevens)
The Shepherd of the Hills (1941, Henry Hathaway)
The Sheriff of Fractured Jaw (1958, Raoul Walsh)
She Wore a Yellow Ribbon (1949, John Ford)
The Shooting (1966, Monte Hellman)
The Shootist (1976, Don Siegel)
Show People (1928, King Vidor)

Una signora dell'ovest/Woman of the West (1942, no details)
The Silent Battle (1916, Jack Conway)
The Silent Man (1917, William S. Hart)
Silverado (1985, Lawrence Kasdan)
The Singer Not the Song (1961, Roy Baker)
Single White Female (1992, Barbet Schroeder)
Sky Full of Moon (1952, Norman Foster)
Soldier Blue (1970, Ralph Nelson)
Son of Paleface (1952, Frank Tashlin)
The Soul of Nigger Charlie (1973, Larry G. Spangler)
Soul Soldiers/Red White and Black (1970, John Cardos)
The Spoilers (1914, Colin Campbell; 1930, Edwin Carewe; 1942, Ray Enright; 1956, Jesse Hibbs)
Squaw's Love: An Indian Poem of Love in Pictures (1911, D.W. Griffith)
The Squaw Man (1914, 1918, 1931, all Cecil B. De Mille)
Stagecoach (1939, John Ford)
Star Wars (1977, George Lucas)
Stone of Silver Creek (1935, Nick Grinde)
Strange Lady in Town (1956, Mervyn LeRoy)
Strawberry Roan (1948, John English)
A Streetcar Named Desire (1951, Elia Kazan)
Sunrise (1927, F.W. Murnau)
Sunset (1988, Blake Edwards)
Support Your Local Sheriff (1968, Burt Kennedy)
Sutter's Gold (1936, James Cruze)
The Taking of Jim McLane (1915, William S. Hart)
Tall in the Saddle (1944, Edwin L. Marin)
The Tall Men (1955, Raoul Walsh)
The Tall T (1957, Budd Boetticher)
Tell Them Willie Boy is Here (1969, Abraham Polonsky)
Terminator 2: Judgement Day (1991, James Cameron)
Terror Trail (1933, Armand Schaeffer)
The Texans (1938, James Hogan)
Texas Across the River (1966, Michael Gordon)
They Died with their Boots On (1941, Raoul Walsh)
The Thief of Bagdad (1924, Raoul Walsh)
Three Amigos! (1986, John Landis)
Three Godfathers (1948, John Ford)
The Three Musketeers (1921, Fred Niblo)
Thunderhoof (1948, Phil Karlson)
A Time for Dying (1969, Budd Boetticher)
The Tin Star (1957, Anthony Mann)
To Hell and Back (1955, Jesse Hibbs)
The Toll of Fear (1913, Romaine Fielding)
Tomahawk (1951, George Sherman)
Tomb Raider (2001, Simon West)
Tombstone (1993, George Pan Cosmatos)
Tom Horn (1980, William Wiard)
Toy Story (1996, John Lasseter)

The Trail of the Lonesome Pine (1916, Cecil B. De Mille; 1936, Henry Hathaway)
The Treasure of the Sierra Madre (1948, John Huston)
The Treasure of Silver Lake/Der Schatz im Silbersee (1962, Harald Reinl)
Tribute to a Badman (1956, Robert Wise)
The Trooper of Troop K (1916, Lincoln Motion Picture Company)
True Grit (1969, Henry Hathaway)
The True Story of Jesse James/The James Gang (1957, Nicholas Ray)
Tumbleweeds (1925, King Baggot)
Tumbling Tumbleweeds (1935, Joseph Kane)
12 Angry Men (1957, Sidney Lumet)
Two Flags West (1950, Robert Wise)
Two Gun Lady (1956, Richard H. Bartlett)
Two Mules for Sister Sara (1970, Don Siegel)
Two Rode Together (1961, John Ford)
Ulzana's Raid (1972, Robert Aldrich)
Uncle Tom's Cabin (1903, Edwin S. Porter; 1910, J. Stuart Blackton; 1913, Sidney
    Olcott; also 1913, Otis Turner; 1914, William Robert Daly; 1918, J. Searle
    Dawley; 1927, Harry Pollard)
Unconquered (1947, Cecil B. De Mille)
The Unforgiven (1959, John Huston)
Unforgiven (1992, Clint Eastwood)
Union Pacific (1939, Cecil B. De Mille)
Valdez is Coming (1970, Edwin Sherin)
Vera Cruz (1954, Robert Aldrich)
Virginia City (1940, Michael Curtiz)
The Virginian (1914, Cecil B. De Mille; 1923, Tom Forman; 1929, Victor Fleming;
    1946, William Berke) (also TV series 1962–70; 2000, Bill Pullman for TV)
Viva Maria! (1965, Louis Malle)
Viva Zapata! (1952, Elia Kazan)
Waco (1966, R.G. Springsteen)
Wagonmaster (1950, John Ford)
Walk Like a Dragon (1960, James Clavell)
Warlock (1959, Edward Dmytryk)
War of the Plains (1912, Thomas H. Ince)
Waterhole 3 (1967, William Graham)
Way Down East (1920, D.W. Griffith)
The Way West (1967, Andrew V. McLaglen)
Welcome to Hard Times/Killer on a Horse (1966, Burt Kennedy)
Wells Fargo (1937, Frank Lloyd)
Western Blood (1918, Lynn F. Reynolds)
The Westerner (1940, William Wyler)
Western Justice (1907, Francis Boggs)
Western Union (1941, Fritz Lang)
Westward the Women (1952, William Wellman)
Westworld (1973, Michael Crichton)
When the Legends Die (1972, Stuart Millar)
Where the River Bends/Bend of the River (1952, Anthony Mann)
The White Buffalo (1977, J. Lee Thompson)
White Feather (1955, Robert Webb)

Wild and Woolly (1917, John Emerson)
The Wild Bunch (1969, Sam Peckinpah)
Wildfire (1915, Edwin Middleton)
Wild Rovers (1971, Blake Edwards)
Will Penny (1967, Tom Gries)
Winchester '73 (1950, Anthony Mann)
Windwalker (1980, Keith Merrill)
Winterhawk (1975, Charles B. Pierce)
Woman of the West/Una signora Dell'Ovest (1942 Carlo Koch with Lotte Reiniger)
The Wonderful Country (1959, Robert Parrish)
Wyatt Earp (1994, Lawrence Kasdan)
The Yacqui Cur (1913, D.W. Griffith)
Yellow Sky (1948, William Wellman)
Yojimbo (1961, Akira Kurosawa)
Young Guns (1988, Christopher Cain)
Young Guns II (1990, Geoff Murphy)

Television Titles (dates of short and long series of production)

Alias Smith and Jones (1971–3)
The Big Valley (1965–9)
Bonanza (1959–73)
Cheyenne (1955–63)
The Cisco Kid (1951–6)
Dr. Quinn, Medicine Woman (1993–8)
The Gene Autry Show (1950–6)
Gunsmoke (1955–75)
Have Gun, Will Travel (1957–63)
The High Chaparral (1967–71)
Kung Fu (1972–5)
Laramie (1959–63)
Little House on the Prairie (1974–82)
The Lone Ranger (1949–57)
Lonesome Dove (1989)
Maverick (1957–62)
The Mystic Warrior (1984, Richard T. Heffron)
Rawhide (1959–62)
The Rifleman (1958–63)
Roy Rogers Show (1952–7)
Star Trek (1966–69)
The Virginian (1962–70)
Wagon Train (1957–65)

INDEX

Illustration entries *italicised* in bold: